EVOLUTION OF INTERNATIONAL AVIATION

Evolution of International Aviation
Phoenix Rising

Third Edition

DAWNA L. RHOADES
Embry-Riddle Aeronautical University, USA

Routledge
Taylor & Francis Group

LONDON AND NEW YORK

First published 2014 by Ashgate Publishing

Published 2016 by Routledge
2 Park Square, Milton Park, Abingdon, Oxon OX14 4RN
711 Third Avenue, New York, NY 10017, USA

Routledge is an imprint of the Taylor & Francis Group, an informa business

British Library Cataloguing in Publication Data
A catalogue record for this book is available from the British Library

ISBN 9781472420169 (hbk)

The Library of Congress has cataloged the printed edition as follows:
Rhoades, Dawna L., 1958-
  Evolution of international aviation : phoenix rising / by Dawna L. Rhoades. -- Revised edition.
     pages cm
  Includes bibliographical references and index.
  ISBN 978-1-4724-2016-9 (hardback) 1. Aeronautics, Commercial--History.
2. Aeronautics, Commercial--Law and legislation--History. 3. Airlines--United States--History. 4. Airlines--Deregulation--United States. 5. Airlines--Finance--Case studies. 6. Strategic alliances (Business)--Case studies. I. Title.
  HE9774.R48 2014
  387.7--dc23
                                                                        2014018340

MIX
Paper from
responsible sources
FSC   FSC® C013985
www.fsc.org

Printed in the United Kingdom
by Henry Ling Limited

Reviews of
Evolution of International Aviation
Third Edition

'This book is an excellent review of international commercial aviation past, present and future, with Dr Rhoades' observations for future commercial space transportation to excite the spirit. From the humble beginnings of the International Civil Aviation Organization (ICAO) and its efforts to provide a unified international air traffic system, to the growth of today's Mega-alliances responding to market forces and national governments, to the search for an open skies concept that calls for the liberalization of rules and regulations, I welcome you aboard. Please sit back, relax and enjoy your journey.'
Captain V. Carl Thompson, Jr, Delta Air Lines (retired) and Auburn University,
USA

'An exceptional book providing a comprehensive overview and critique of the exciting world of international aviation past, current and future. It is particularly pleasing to see the inclusion of commercial space in a book on international aviation. The use of chapter learning objectives and full references at the end of each chapter facilitates self-managing learning and engagement.'
Siobhan Tiernan, Kemmy Business School, University of Limerick,
Ireland

'Anyone interested in the evolution of the air transport industry will benefit from reading this book, which discusses the challenges airlines face in their search for new markets in an increasingly global environment, and how airlines and aircraft manufacturers are working together to find solutions to help the air transport industry become more financially and environmentally sustainable.'
Wilfred S. Manuela Jr., Ateneo de Manila University,
Philippines

Reviews of the Second Edition

'An exceptional book giving a first-rate insight into a wide array of international aviation issues. The reader takes off with the Wrights and navigates through the aviation landscape, past and present, right into the uncertain future. Dr Rhoades writes in a radiant style that makes the book a pleasure to read for everyone interested in the aviation industry: airline executives to students alike.'
Prof. Sveinn Vidar Gudmundsson, Dir. CERMAS—European Centre for Aerospace and Air Transport Research, Toulouse Business School

Contents

PART III   FACING THE FUTURE (2008–)

List of Figures

List of Figures

List of Tables

Acknowledgements

No book is truly the work of a single individual even though the title page may not reflect the contributions of these other individuals; this is the role of the acknowledgement section. First, I want to thank my colleagues and students at Embry-Riddle Aeronautical University for their support during the writing of this work. They not only supported me during the frantic days of writing and editing, but inspired me to write a text that would help to make aviation accessible to all interested parties. Three graduate assistant in particular deserve special thanks for their help in the research and editing of this third edition—Izyan Ishak, Mina Benjouali, and Nicole Leong. They represent the best of Embry-Riddle and the future of the aviation industry.

Finally, I would like to thank my husband, John, and two children, Deanna and Ben. They inspire me to achieve great things as an example to them of what hard work and persistence can accomplish. Their understanding and support have also been greatly appreciated during this hectic time.

Preface to the Third Edition

The writing for the first edition of this book was completed a little over a year after the events of 9/11. There is little doubt that this single event has had deep and enduring effects on the aviation industry. It is also clear now from the recovery after 9/11 that some sectors and regions of the industry were better positioned to come back from these events than others. The reality is that the airline sector has struggled from its inception to make a long term, consistent profit. It seems a great irony that airlines cannot make the kind of profits necessary to attract investment in such a capital intensive business when the number of people traveling by air continues to rise. The second edition of the book came out in early 2008 before the scale and scope of the Global Financial Crisis (GFC) were truly known. This global crisis and the general economic struggles that have unfolded in its wake have also had a definite effect on the aviation/aerospace industry. When the GFC is combined with the appearance of $100 plus oil, the effect on the industry was even more pronounced. At this stage, there is no way to predict what, if any, key event might occur as this latest edition goes to print, but the history of the aviation/ aerospace industry suggests that there will be something. The event could be a new war or a new peace, an economic downturn or a new boom, new concerns over carbon and climate change or a new technology to dramatically reduce carbon. The only certainty is that there will be change and the aviation/aerospace industry will be right in the middle it.

The first edition of the book dealt mainly with airlines and air cargo. It explored ways in which international business in this industry differs from international business in other industries because of the intense involvement of government and the impact of the industry on the economy. The second edition added chapters on the manufacturers. After all, airlines are but one part of this industry. These manufacturers represent the largest exporters in their respective regions, generating plenty of jobs and new technology. They drive innovation, manufacturing, and related and supporting industries. Yet, when airlines struggle, manufacturers also struggle. They have some advantages over their airline customers in that they are truly global in their marketing, but this is small consolation to firms spending millions on research and counting every plane sold in a march to breakeven. The relationship between the airlines and the manufacturers is a fascinating one. Airlines push manufacturers to innovate, reduce operating costs, and improve operating characteristics. They play one manufacturer off against the other looking for deals. Manufacturers make far reaching decisions on modifying existing products or developing new designs while trying to decide if the market will justify the costs of research and development over a ten-year timeframe. They want early and firm commitment to aircraft that have yet to be built and might not be delivered for ten years.

This latest edition adds a new and exciting new sector to the mix—commercial space. In the US, new policies are attempting to create a viable private sector space industry that would serve the needs (and potential needs) of Low Earth Orbit (LEO). These needs include delivery of people and supplies to the International Space Station (ISS), low cost private satellite launch, space tourism, office/research space on a private space station, and private, extra planetary exploration. We are witnessing the beginnings of a new industry much as people watched the development of the airline industry after the first Wright Brothers flight. The possibilities and risks are great. It seemed only appropriate to add chapters in this edition that trace the beginning, current, and prospective future of this sector of the industry.

Six years is a relatively short time in the life of a redwood tree or a Galapagos tortoise, but it is an eternity in the volatile aviation/aerospace industry, hence, it was time to re-examine this book, updating the details and making new projections based on 'what we know now.' For the airline industry, there is some indication that the old pattern of responses to crisis are changing. For the air cargo operators, the question still remains 'will next year be the one in which things finally turn up?' For the manufacturers of commercial aircraft, the emergence of the Middle Eastern carriers and continued growth in developing nations like China and India have offset weakness elsewhere. While the number of competitors that manufacture large commercial aircraft (LCA) is very small—Boeing and Airbus at present, the match is fiercely fought and a complacent company can find itself in serious trouble or with a new rival. In fact, new competitors are emerging in Asia that could change the whole dynamic of the aviation manufacturing industry. Finally, the commercial space industry that is now in its infancy could not only change how we fly but where we fly. Space may no longer be the domain of wealthy nations and large corporations; there might be a place there for all of us.

In short, this new edition is a significant change, and I hope, improvement over the last two editions. It should help tie together developments in a number of areas of the aviation industry and provide a better overall understanding of the challenges and promises of the aviation/aerospace industry as it moves through the twenty-first century.

Dawna L. Rhoades

Chapter 1
Phoenix Rising

Learning Objectives

After reading this chapter, you should have a good understanding of:
- LO1: the CRAF program and its relationship to national defense.
- LO2: the link between aviation and economic growth.
- LO3: how national pride affects attitudes toward the airline industry.
- LO4: the cyclical nature of the aviation industry.

Key Terms, Concepts, and People

CRAF	EADS	"Carry the flag"
Industry lifecycle	Punctuated equilibrium	Discontinuous change

Of Phoenixes and Airlines

According to the most famous legend of the phoenix, the phoenix was a bird of brilliant red and gold plumage whose death in a fiery blaze gave rise to a new phoenix. Like the phoenix, the airline industry seems to have established it own cycle of destruction and renewal. From its very inception, the airline industry has been at the mercy of the business cycle, experiencing soaring profits in the upturn and rapidly falling into losses when the market turns down. The so-called new economy that combined technological innovation, globalization, and abundant venture capital began transforming the US and global economy around 1995. This new economy was predicted to end the business cycle or at least smooth it out so that the booms were not so high and the busts so low. Under this new era of prosperity, the U.S. economy grew at about 4.4 percent a year while unemployment dropped to near 4 percent. At the same time, productivity rose at an annual rate of 2.8 percent (Mandel, 2000). In short, growth, productivity, and employment seemed on an unstoppable path upward. The events of 9/11 and the Global Financial Crisis (GFC) have clearly shown us that the death of the business cycle was greatly exaggerated.

In any event, the boom times for airlines have always meant adding capacity through new aircraft acquisitions, opening new routes to unserved destinations, and negotiating bigger labor contracts (or contracts that gave back what was lost in the last downturn). The bust has always been a downward ride into declining profits, falling load factors, and destructive price wars. Unfortunately, even before the events of September 11, the US airline industry was facing the return of its most dreaded foe, the business cycle, and US airlines were expected to post a US$3 billion loss (ATA, 2002). While the rest of the airline world was not yet expecting losses of this magnitude, the US downturn was expected to have an effect on those carriers with a sizable percentage of traffic to North America (Sparaco and Wall, 2001). Post 9/11, the downturn became even steeper as many carriers struggled to avoid bankruptcy, a valiant struggle that failed for many of the major carriers in the US. The US airline industry would not return to profitability until 2006, just in time to watch the 2007 rise in oil prices (ATA, 2007). This was followed by the 2008 GFC and the peak of rising fuel prices (US$147 per barrel). According to the Air Transport Association (ATA), industry losses in 2008 were US$18.2 billion, twice the 2006 high of US$9 billion in profit. As the industry struggled back to profitability after posting a smaller loss of US$2.3 billion loss in 2009 on slumping cargo and passenger traffic, the global economy lost altitude again (Airlines for America, 2013). By comparison, US airline losses in the early 1990s were nearly US$10 billion while the losses for the industry in 2001 alone were US$7 billion (Foss, 2002; Rosen, 1995). In short, the industry continues to set new records for losses.

The airline industry is no stranger to bankruptcy. In the US, the first passenger on a regularly scheduled airline flew from Tampa Bay to St. Petersburg, Florida on January 1, 1914. The airline chalked up another first when it folded four months later after running into financial difficulty (Wells, 1994). In Europe, war and financial crisis in the 1930s and 1940s led to the nationalization of many of the continent's premier carriers as a means of insuring their survival (Graham, 1995; Sinha, 2001). Back in the US, aviation continued to expand in fits and starts aided by airmail contracts from the US Postal Service (USPS), however, since the deregulation of the US airline industry in 1978, the industry has experienced a financial crisis in the early years of each decade. In the first decade of the twenty-first century, the industry has managed to top even its own records for losses. To those outside the industry, this brief history raises many questions. Why can't the industry make money? Why does it expect (and often get) special treatment from governments? What, if anything, can be done to stop the cycle? What is the future of the airline industry and the related aviation/aerospace firms around it? These questions are the subject of this book. The first question to tackle is why the industry is considered "special."

A Special Case

The aviation industry has long been treated as a special case in international business, subject to different rules and held to different standards. In fact, international aviation has been "a serious problem in international relations, affecting the way governments view one another, the way individual citizens view their own and foreign countries, and in a variety of direct and indirect connections the security arrangements by which we live" (Lowenfeld, 1975). There are several reasons for the special status and serious problems associated with international aviation. Originally, the most compelling argument was national defense. Under programs such as the US Civil Reserve Air Fleet (CRAF) plan, civilian fleets could be used during times of military action to ferry troops and supplies. It was, therefore, vital to insure the existence and health of this civilian reserve. In the case of CRAF, the US government gets a reserve fleet for times of emergency without the cost of maintaining it and the airlines get paid a rate that during the first Middle East conflict, Desert Storm, was 1.75 times the seat mile or cargo mile rate (Kane, 1999). National defense has also been cited as the reason for insisting on home country ownership of these airlines and the aerospace manufacturers that supplied their airframes, engines, and other parts. The premise of the argument is the notion that home country nationals would or could be made to cooperate in the defense of their country. As we will see, the connection between civilian and military technology at the manufacturers level has always been close; the innovations in technology first deployed and tested on military aircraft were quickly applied to the commercial fleet. In a number of countries such as the US, funding for research and development for these "military" innovations came from the government and went to firms who also had sizeable civilian operations, a situation that has led foreign competitors to charge "unfair subsidy."

The second most cited reason for special treatment has been the economic impact of aviation. The Air Transport Action Group estimates that air transport supported 3.5 percent of global gross domestic product (GDP), provided 56.6 million jobs and having a global economic impact of US$2.2 trillion (Air Transport Action Group, 2012). Passenger traffic grew on average 6 percent per year during the decade of the 1980s and early 1990s driven by a number of factors: falling real costs of air travel, increasing economic activity, intensifying international trade, increasing disposable incomes, political stability, relaxation of travel restrictions, expanding ethnic ties, increasing leisure time, tourism promotion, air transport liberalization, and growth in emerging regions and countries. Historically, air traffic has grown at about twice the rate of GDP and during the period 1960–1990 80 percent of traffic growth could be explained by growth in GDP. Beginning in the 1990s, falling real prices (fares) played a greater role in traffic growth. As air travel grows, the direct (value of airline and on-airport activities) and indirect (value of off-airport activities of passengers and shippers) economic impact grows as well. In addition, there is an induced impact from the successive spending of recipients of these direct and indirect benefits. In short, the economic impact of the air transport industry makes its health a major concern of governments, businesses, and passengers around the world and keeps it from being seen as "just another industry." Unfortunately, this historic link between economic growth (GDP) and air transport has decoupled in the US and appears to be decoupling in the EU as well. It is not yet clear what this change represents. It is possible that the industry in the US and EU has finally reached the stage of maturity that has permanently decoupled this link. It is also possible that consumers have found other ways to spend their discretionary dollars. The phenomena (14 years old in the US) may be temporary or it may be time to acknowledge that there are limits to all phenomenon and nothing including aviation continues upward forever (Michaels, 2013). Still, there is no denying that air transport contributes in many ways to national and global economies.

The third reason for aviation's special status is the link that exists in the minds of many between aviation and national achievement and pride. International airlines "carry the flag" around the world. This reason should not be underestimated as a driver of individual and government perception. When the bankruptcy and subsequent grounding of the Swissair fleet forced the Swiss football team to fly the Russian carrier Aeroflot to a qualifying match in Moscow, one article reported this event as a "further humiliation for the Swiss flag carrier" (Hall, Grant, Done, and Cameron, 2001). The uproar that occurred in UK over the replacement of the Union Jack on the tail of many British Airways planes by the so-called ethnic tails intended to show British Airways as the airline of the world was motivated by similar nationalistic sentiment (BBC News, 1999). Likewise, the debate in Belgium over the bankruptcy of Sabena and the need for a national carrier to serve the interest of the people of Belgium has more to do with nationalistic pride than airline economics (BBC News, 1999; Sparaco, 2001). Most recently, the Italian efforts to save their national carrier, Alitalia, can be linked to the same national pride that has motivated so many other governments (*The Economist*, 2013). At the manufacturing level, nations have also mourned the loss of their aviation pioneers. One of the key arguments for the European formation of Airbus was the dominance of manufacturing by US firms. According to Aris (2004), the Airbus project was seen by the French as "*Un Grand Projet*: one of those brilliant combinations of technological skill and political will that serve to remind the French themselves— and everybody else—just what a great nation they are" (16). To the Germans, Airbus was the chance to rebuild an aerospace industry that had contributed many early innovations in aviation. In short, all things aviation have been linked to national pride in their technological achievement and visionary leadership. In the US, the announcement that the US Air Force had chosen Northrop Grumman and European partner EADS, parent of Airbus, for a refueling tanker deal worth US$35 billion was greeted with anger and calls for political investigation. In the US House of Representatives, Todd Tiahrt, whose district includes facilities of the losing bidder Boeing, has said that the US "should have an American tanker built by an American company with American workers" (Tessler, 2008: 2). In fact, this last example brings together all of the reasons why aviation is a special case— defense, economic impact, and national pride.

Changing Times

Even without the defense, economic, and national pride arguments, aviation/ aerospace is not likely to be seen as "just another industry." It is the stuff of dreams and has fired the imagination of much of the world's population. Alvin Toffler (1970) noted in his bestselling book *Future Shock* that in 6000 BC the fastest transportation available to mankind was the camel caravan that averaged 8 miles per hour (mph). By 1600 BC the chariot had raised this speed to approximately 20 mph. The first mail coach in England began operating in 1784 at an average of only 10 miles per hour and the first steam locomotive was capable of a mere 13 mph. In fact, it was not until the invention of an improved steam engine that mankind was able to reach a speed of 100 mph. It took almost 8,000 years to go from the 8 mph camel to the 100 mph train. However, in only 58 years, men in aircraft were exceeding the 400 mph line. Twenty years later that limit doubled. By the 1960s aircraft were approaching speeds of 4000 mph, and space capsules were circling the Earth at 18,000 mph. The newest pioneers are men like Elon Musk of SpaceX and Robert Bigelow of Bigelow Aerospace who are trying to shape the commercial space industry, giving us a private space station to visit and the means to get there.

The history of aviation/aerospace is filled with larger-than-life figures. These men and women were the entrepreneurs of Joseph Schumpeter who took on the thankless job of building and shaping an industry because "there is the dream and the will to found a private kingdom, usually, although not necessarily, also a dynasty ... Then there is the will to conquer: the impulse to fight, to prove oneself superior to others, to succeed for the sake, not of the fruits of success, but of success itself ... Finally, there is the joy of creating, of getting things done, or simply of exercising one's energy and imagination" (Schumpter, 1934: 93–94). After all, the Wright brothers started their business career as the owners of a bicycle shop before the dream of aviation led them in a different direction. Their innovation in heavier-than-air flight would start an industry and in many ways illustrate the promises, challenges, and pitfalls of aviation.

Whatever the challenges, there have always been individuals drawn to aviation. The stories of these individuals, the planes they flew, and the companies they founded still fascinate us today. While the level of innovation has slowed for the aviation industry, the manufacturers are continuing to face new challenges in design and performance. One of the greatest of these challenges will be increasing the fuel efficiency and improving the emissions profile of aircraft in a world of increasing oil prices and concerns about climate change. As the demand for air travel increases in developing nations, other challenges are facing the industry. There is a lack of capacity at many of the airports worldwide and crowding of the airspace in many countries demands new systems of traffic management and optimization such as the use of satellites for navigation. Expanding capacity requires long-term planning and sizeable investment from national and local government as well as private industry.

Sadly, despite the glories of the past, the worldwide airline industry has not fared well in recent years. It is now in the mature stages of its lifecycle, displaying all of the four basic characteristics of such an industry. First, growth slows or diminishes. Second, there are few new, key technologies that can provide an advantage to the first competitor to deploy it as was true in the days when newer, better, faster, and safer were changing with each new innovation. The few new technologies to be deployed by the airlines in recent years have provided little advantage because they were easily and quickly imitated. Third, the experience (or learning) curve no longer provides an advantage to one competitor over another. Finally, there are few new forms of differentiation and competition is largely based on price. The issue of price is critical because industries in this stage find that their profits are very sensitive to price, price advantages are short-lived, customers begin to expect lower prices, and customers shop for low price rather than value or benefits (Miller, 1998). Alfred Kahn, the Father of US airline deregulation, wrote about the possibility of destructive competition within an industry as a result of fixed and sunk costs that represent a high percentage of total cost and long sustained and recurrent periods of excess capacity (1988). He did not anticipate this occurring in the airline industry, but, in fact, it has come to pass.

Stephen M. Wolf, then Chairman of United Airlines, blamed the financial crisis of the early 1990s on three issues: overcapacity, international competition, and the lack of infrastructure. On the question of overcapacity, he said that in a truly free market overcapacity is temporary, but that liberal US bankruptcy laws allowed carriers "to operate literally for years without repaying their debt obligations; consequently, their capacity is retained in the system and the result is economic havoc for all" (Wolf, 1995: 19). Allowing carriers, any carrier, to continue to operate while receiving the benefits of bankruptcy protection not only fails to reduce overcapacity, but spreads the "bankruptcy virus" to other carriers who are disadvantaged by the competition from this protected carrier. Speaking at the end of the 1990s, Warren Buffet, Chairman of Berkshire Hathaway and "world famous as the greatest stock market investor of modern times," articulated an even dark vision of the airline industry (Bianco, 1999). He compared the internet industry to "two other transforming industries, auto and aviation" (Loomis and Buffet, 1999). According to Buffet, the early aviation industry was full of promise and home to many young, vibrant companies, most of whom are a distant memory. He cited some 129 airlines that had filed for bankruptcy between 1980 and 2000. The reason for these troubles, he said, was clear; the industry as a whole had not made money overall in the long run. Buffet brutally suggested that a farsighted and public-spirited individual would have done the world's investors a favor by shooting down the Wright Flyer in 1903. He said all of this before the losses after 9/11 and the GFC, losses greater than all the profits made by the industry since the first flight at Kitty Hawk (Gahan, 2002).

Like Joseph's Dream of Egypt, the aviation industry seems condemned to experience years of plenty followed by years of famine. Unlike the Egyptians, airlines have rarely saved in years of plenty to survive the coming famine. Instead, they have bought new planes, expanded route systems, and signed ever sweeter labor contracts. It was as though they were convinced that the airline that fattens up the most in the good times will simply outlast the others in bad times. In a truly free market, this strategy might work, but airlines do not operate in such a market.

The events of 9/11 and 2008 did not create this situation, but they made the situation worse for the airlines and those that supplied them. Just as many of the world's airlines had come through the dark post-9/11 days and returned to profitability, oil prices began to rise and fuel became the number one category of expense for many carriers. Unfortunately, fuel is an expense that airlines have very limited control over, other than hedging. Airlines that had hedged well as fuel began to rise such as Southwest and JetBlue managed to continue their profitability. As these hedges run out, however, there will be less room to maneuver. Then 2008 came along with US$147 per barrel oil and a financial crisis that spread around the world to make the first decade of the twenty-first century one that many in the aviation industry would like to forget. Of course, airlines do seem to have finally resisted the urge to add capacity in a quest for market share. Capacity control (and consolidation) in the US at least has allowed airlines to maintain some pricing power. In fact, the US industry removed 13 million seats from their capacity since the beginning of 2012. Load factors rose to 87 percent in June of 2013. Airlines have not only been able to hold the line on fares but discovered a new fare-and-fee strategy that allowed carriers to raise pre-tax profits 8 percent since 2009 (Saporito, 2013). With the latest mega-merger between American and US Airways, there are now three titans standing astride the US (Flottau, Ray, and Shannon, 2013).

As Buffet pointed out, air travel has transformed the way we live and do business. It is itself in the process of transforming; it is *becoming* something new. A debate has raged in the fields of paleontology, genetics and evolutionary biology over whether change in living organisms takes place in a gradual, step-by-step manner or in periods of rapid, major change followed by stasis. The latter theory is called punctuated equilibrium (Gould and Eldredge, 1977). This theory has been adapted and applied to the evolution of technology (Tushman and Anderson, 1986) and to the lifecycle and evolution of organizations and their industries (Hannan and Freeman, 1984). The idea of punctuated equilibrium or discontinuous change has caught on in so many areas because it "seems to fit" the observed evidence. In other words, investigators in all of these fields have been unable to trace a slow, clear development from one form to the next. Instead, they see periods of relative stability and little change interrupted by sudden, radical alterations in form. In the evolutionary sciences, these periods of sudden change are usually connected to mass extinctions of older, existing life forms. In the areas of technology and organizations, startling innovations have arisen that make the technology and knowhow that came before obsolete. Think of the impact of the telephone on the telegraph or the airplane on the long-distance train system. For organizations, these periods of rapid change have been hardest on the firms of the prior age, firms that developed, grew, and adapted to life in another time. This is the traditional stockbrokerage coping in the new world of the internet or the corner bookseller competing with Amazon.com. The question in the minds of organizational theorists is whether these old age firms can change quickly enough to survive in the new age. If not, they will become the dinosaurs of this new age, dying out to make room for the newer, faster, smaller mammals. The fossil records show that dinosaurs had reached their maximum size not long before the meteor that changed everything. It is possible that the airline industry has entered just such a period of discontinuous change.

Where Do We Go?

The introduction began with a twisted quote from Lewis Carroll's classic "The Jabberwocky." This passage begins "The time has come ... to talk of many things." Because the aviation industry is a special case for all the reasons stated earlier, it is important for the people of the world to be involved in the debate about the future of aviation. We are the tourists that fly to our long-awaited vacation, the businessmen that fly to important meetings, the shippers that send out goods around the world, the customers that buy grapes from Chile and wine from France, and the citizens that count on the airline industry and all the industries it helps support for a growing, healthy economy. The purpose of this book is twofold. First, the book explores the foundations of the industry (1903–1950), looking at the forces that shaped the international aviation industry in terms that can be understood by anyone interested in aviation. Starting with the first transborder crossing in a lighter-than-air balloon, it will trace the early technological innovations, the international conferences, and government interventions that set the early path of the industry up until World War II. Next, we will examine the opportunities that shaped the industry that entered the era of deregulation and liberalization (1951–2000). This era changed all the rules. Finally, we will explore the industry that emerged from the events of 9/11 only to face the GFC of 2008. 9/11 presented the industry with many choices: pulling back from the trend toward liberalization or embracing the liberalization trend, merging in search of profitability or fragmenting in search of economies, embracing a role in addressing climate change or fighting inclusion in the post-Kyoto regime and the EUs Emissions Trading System, building a twenty-first century airspace or muddling along with an aging World War II infrastructure, funding the next steps into space through governments or encouraging the type of entrepreneurial individuals that created the glories of the past. In fact, one of the major changes in this edition is the inclusion of two chapters on space and the future of this latest frontier.

Because this book is intended for both the interested amateur and the more serious student, references are provided in the text and at the end of each chapter to allow for more in-depth study. The book is NOT intended to be a definitive work on the aviation/aerospace industry; it would require a series of books to even attempt such a feat. The book does try to include most of the major sectors of the industry in order to give the reader an overall understanding of this complex industry. Perhaps the only major sector left out is the airport. It is obviously vital to the industry but airports vary widely within a country much less across nations and regions. The book does include discussions about the development of spaceports as their creation is vital to expanding and developing this latest section. Still, even within sectors such as the aerospace manufacturers, the book only touches on the major players. There is a vast group of aviation suppliers that range in size from Honeywell and GE to small mom-and-pop operations dealing with maintenance and repair of select avionics. Unless otherwise stated, the views expressed in this book are those of the author and do not represent those of the airline industry, any governmental organization or private institution associated with aviation.

The book has been organized into three parts. The first part will address the early development of the aviation system. Chapter 2 will explore the inventions and innovations in aviation technology that laid the foundation for commercial success. This period saw the start of heavier-than-air flight, the first use of the airplane in military action, and the foundations of passenger travel. The implications and possibilities of this new technology would come to hold greater sway in the minds of individuals and governments in the years ahead. Chapter 3 will explore the role of airmail and freight in shaping the industry. Chapter 4 will discuss early aviation conferences and the beginning of the struggle between the proponents of free markets and those favoring tight national control. Chapter 5 will examine the most famous international aviation meeting, the 1944 Chicago Conference. This conference resulted in the Chicago Convention which spells out the rights and obligations of states in international aviation, the creation of the international body responsible for establishing the rules and standards governing international aviation, and numerous technical drafts on recommended practices. Chapter 6 will examine in more detail the structure and role of the new International Civil Aviation Organization (ICAO) in developing the standards and practices of international aviation. If the world had not already learned at the Chicago Conference that aviation could not be divorced from its economic and political consequences, it came to learn these lessons over time in the operation of ICAO. In fact, any illusion that ICAO could deal with these technical problems on their own merit was quickly dispelled when accidental shoot downs of civil aircraft and a growing number of brutal hijackings and criminal attacks against civil aviation came to dominate the agenda of the ICAO council and its subordinate bodies (Sochor, 1991). This chapter will also address the development of another international organization, the International Air Transport Association (IATA), and its role in shaping the international aviation system through the setting of international fares.

Part II of the book explores the period between 1950 and 2000. Chapter 7 will examine the early efforts into outer space beginning with Sputnik and ending with the Apollo flight. The industry was growing up, maturing. Chapter 8 will return to the story of the manufacturers in an era in which air travel was becoming available to a growing number of consumers. Chapter 9 will look at another time of dramatic change for the airline industry, domestic deregulation. Domestic deregulation changed the rules of the game allowing competition based on price as well as market-based decisions on routes served and the level of service quality provided. It also freed up the industry for greater competition through the relaxation of rules for air carrier entry. This chapter will explore the link between domestic deregulation and efforts to liberalize international aviation markets. Chapter 10 will discuss the view from Europe and Asia. In Europe, aviation would become part of a greater effort to create an integrated free market system among the EU nations. While the Europeans disagreed with the pace and implementation of deregulation in the US market, they have taken the concept of aviation liberalization further than their US counterparts by opening up domestic markets to foreign competition. The vast geographical diversity of the Asian region makes sweeping generalizations; however, most of this region has witnessed substantial growth in air transportation as part of its overall economic growth. Chapter 11 examines the alliance movement whose initial impetus was overcoming the national restrictions on air transportation. In an environment of heavy international regulation, the alliance became the airline tool of choice for serving new markets and extending the global reach of your alliance. There have been and will continue to be obstacles to the use of the alliance. Airlines may also consider trading the weaknesses of alliances for ownership if given a choice. Chapter 12 will outline some of the remaining legal blocks to international aviation while Chapter 13 explores the question of airline and alliance quality in an increasingly competitive industry. Chapter 14 will look at the air cargo industry in the new era of the logistics revolution.

In the final part of the book, the future of international aviation will be examined in light of changes in the environment before and after 9/11. Chapter 15 explores the industry's search for profitability in the wake of 9/11 and the growing threat of continuing high fuel prices. Chapter 16 will examine the trend in market liberalization that began with the 1978 deregulation of US domestic markets and has continued in Europe and Asia. Will deregulation and liberalization bring more competition or more losses? Chapter 17 will address the uneven development of international aviation and the regions that have yet to benefit from the economic promises of aviation, particularly those in Africa. Chapter 18 looks at the aviation industry in an era of concern about climate change and carbon emissions. In Chapters 19 and 20, we revisit the manufacturing and air cargo industry to see where each of them is heading in the new century. Chapter 21 looks at the infrastructure that will support aviation as it moves forward, the technology, the costs, and the controversies. Chapter 22 explores the future of space exploration, particularly the exciting new efforts to foster a commercial space industry. Chapter 23 will summarize where we are and where we appear to be going. Finally, it should be noted throughout the book that all financial matters are expressed in US dollars unless otherwise note. Tables presenting traffic numbers and revenues follow the convention of excluding the last three zeros. Since the information is as current as the date that the book goes to print, it is certainly possible that information in the fast moving aviation industry will change thus the reader may assume that the information is current as of June 2014.

Imaging the Future

The airplane (spacecraft) and the industry that fostered them have captured the imagination of generations around the world. It is time to apply that imagination to creating a viable, stable environment for international aviation that delivers on the great promise of air travel to link the world together in peace and prosperity. It is time to regain the Star Trek desire to seek out new worlds. Thomas L. Friedman has said of his work that he hopes that it will evoke one of four reactions from his readers: I didn't know that, I never looked at it that way before, you said exactly what I feel, but I didn't know how to express it, or I hate you and everything you stand for (Friedman, 2002: xi). These reactions seem a worthy goal for any book that attempts to examine and explain complex issues. Even if the book evokes the last reaction at least it should foster a debate on the ideas. It is time to begin the debate. I believe that you will find it an exciting and challenging journey.

Questions

1. Discuss the role that aviation plays in economic development and why it is described as a cyclical industry.
2. What is a mature industry? Does the airline industry qualify?
3. What was Warren Buffet's point about profits in the airline industry?
4. What new developments are likely to shape the aviation industry?

References

Airlines for America (2010), "When America flies, it works," retrieved online January 2013 from http://www.airlines.org/Pages/A4A-Economic-Reports-of-the-U.S.-Airline-Industry.aspx.

Air Transport Action Group (2014), "Facts & figures," Available online from http://www.atag.org/facts-and-figures.html, retrieved January 14, 2013.

Air Transport Association (ATA) (2007), "Quarterly cost index: US passenger airlines," retrieved online January 16, 2013 from http://www.airlines.org/economics/finance/cost.

Air Transport Association (ATA) (2002), *State of the Airline Industry: A Report on Recent Trends for U.S. Air Carriers*, Air Transport Association, Washington, DC.

Aris, S. (2004), *Close to the Sun: How Airbus Challenged America's Domination of the Skies*, Agate Press, London.

BBC News (1999), "BA to fly flag again," BBC News Online Edition, June 6, www.bbc.co.uk.

Bianco, A. (1999), "The Warren Buffet you don't know: ace stockpicker, of course- and now, an empire-builder," *Business Week*, July 5, pp. 55–66.

Flottau, J., Ray, S. and Shannon, D. (2013), "Scale tale," *Aviation Week & Space Technology*, November 25, pp. 35–36.

Foss, B. (2002), "Airlines expect to lose $8 billion," Associated Press Wire Service, September 26.

Friedman, T.L. (2002), *The Lexus and the Olive Tree*, Farrar, Strauss & Giroux, New York.

Gahan, M. (2002), "Aviation's continuing crisis," BBC News Online, August 13.

Gould, S.J. and Eldredge, N. (1977), "Punctuated equilibria: the tempo and mode of evolution reconsidered," *Paleobiology*, vol 3, pp. 115–151.

Graham, B. (1995), *Geography and Air Transport*, John Wiley & Sons, New York.

Hall, W., Grant, J., Done, K. and Cameron, D. (2001), "Swissair grounding causes travel chaos," October 2.

Hannan, M.T. and Freeman, J. (1984), "Structural inertia and organizational change," *American Sociological Review*, vol. 49, pp. 149–164.

Kahn, A.P. (1988), *Economics of Regulation*, Wiley and Sons, New York.

Kane, R.M. (1999), *Air Transportation*, Kendall/Hunt Publishing Company, Dubuque, IA.

Loomis, C. and Buffet, W. (1999), "Mr Buffet on the stock market," *Fortune*, Special Issue, vol. 140 (10), pp. 212–220.

Lowenfeld, A. (1975), "A new take-off for international air transport," *Foreign Affairs*, vol. 54, p. 47.

Mandel, M.J. (2000), "The next downturn," *Business Week,* October 9, pp. 173–180.

Michaels, K. (2013), "The great stagnation," *Aviation Week & Space Technology*, October 14, p. 20.

Miller, A. (1998), *Strategic Management* (3rd ed.), Irwin-McGraw-Hill, Boston, MA.

Rosen, S.D. (1995), "Corporate Restructuring: A Labor Perspective" in Peter Cappelli (ed.), *Airline Labor Relations in the Global Era: The New Frontier*, ILR Press, Ithaca, New York, pp. 31–40.

Saporito, B. (2013), "Cabin pressure," *Time Magazine*, September 9, pp. 36–41.

Schumpeter, J.A. (1934) *The Theory of Economic Development*, Harvard University Press, Cambridge, MA.

Sinha, D. (2001), *Deregulation and Liberalization of the Airline Industry: Asia, Europe, North America, and Oceania*, Ashgate Publishing, Aldershot.

Sochor, E. (1991), *The Politics of International Aviation*, University of Iowa Press, Iowa City.

Sparaco, P. and Wall, R. (2001), "Europeans map airline survival," *Aviation Week & Space Technology,* September 24, pp. 35–36.

Sparaco, P. (2001), "The curtain falls on Sabena," *Aviation Week & Space Technology*, November 12, pp. 43–44.

Tessler, J. (2008), "Northrop, EADS win $35B Air Force deal," *The Associated Press*, retrieved online from http://abcnews.go.com/print?id=4367303.

The Economist (2013), "How not to rescue an airline," retrieved online January 16, 2013 from http://www.economist.com/news/europe/21588109-italian-government-pumping-even-more-cash-its-ailing-carrier-how-not-rescue?zid= 303&ah=27090cf03414b8c5065d64ed0dad813d.

Toffler, A. (1970), *Future Shock*, Bantam Books, New York.

Tushman, M.L. and Anderson, P. (1986) "Technological discontinuities and organizational environments," *Administrative Science Quarterly,* vol. 31, pp. 439–465.

Wells, A.T. (1994), *Air Transportation: A Management Perspective,* Wadsworth Publishing Company, Belmont, CA.

Wolf, S.M. (1995), "Where Do We Go from Here? A Management Perspective." in Peter Cappelli (ed.), *Airline Labor Relations in the Global Era: The New Frontier*, ILR Press, Ithaca, New York, pp. 18–22.

PART I
In the Beginning (1903–1950)

Chapter 2
Invention to Commercial Success

Learning Objectives

After reading this chapter, you should have a good understanding of:
- LO1: the difference between invention, innovation, and commercial success.
- LO2: why the DC-3 is considered one of the first commercially successful aircraft.
- LO3: the early history of aircraft design and aviation pioneers.
- LO4: how the airlines and the aircraft manufacturers established the close but often contentious relationship that continues today.

Key Terms, Concepts, and People

Invention	Innovation	Commercialization
The Wright brothers	Glenn Curtiss	Louis Bleriot
Donald Douglas	William Boeing	DC-3

Inventions, Innovations, and Commercializations

An idea is said to have been invented when it has been proven to work. It "becomes an 'innovation' only when it can be replicated reliably on a meaningful scale at practical costs. If the idea is sufficiently important, such as the telephone, the digital computer, or a commercial aircraft, it is called a 'basic innovation' and it creates a new industry or transforms an existing industry" (Senge, 1990). Senge, author of *The Fifth Discipline: The Art and Practice of the Learning Organization*, goes on to note that ideas move from invention to innovation by combining different technologies, often from isolated developments in diverse fields. Until these diverse components come together in the right combination the product is not truly able to achieve its potential as a successful commercial product (commercialization). Until it is able to prove itself safe and reliable it may capture the imagination of the daring, those first movers who are willing to try anything new and different, but it will not capture the market, the laggards who are not interested in thrills but in performance and cost. The first 50 years of heavier-than-air flight would lay the groundwork for the conquest of the laggards and a new commercial aviation industry.

First, of course, an idea needs pioneers and aviation had more than its share of larger-than-life characters. There are accounts dating back to the twelfth century BCE of people in China riding in balloons. The quintessential Renaissance Man himself, Leonardo Da Vinci, sketched images in the sixteenth century of craft he believed capable of supporting a man in flight. However, it was not until 1783 that history has its first confirmable account of a manned lighter-than-air flight. Jean-Francois Pilatre de Rozier and Francois d'Arlandes flew over Paris for 25 minutes while the residents of the city watched and wondered. However, simply floating with the wind was not enough; a way needed to be found to direct these lighter-than-air craft. Thus was born the dirigible and the name forever linked in the minds of many with these dirigibles is Count Ferdinand von Zeppelin whose airships were carrying passengers and mail on regularly scheduled trips by 1914. However, even without the tragic 1936 disaster of the Hindenburg in Lakehurst, New Jersey, it is doubtful that the dirigible could have held anything more than a minor place in aviation besides the new heavier-than-air craft that took to the sky in the first decade of the twentieth century (Carlson, 2002).

December 17, 1903 was the fateful day that Orville Wright became the first person to pilot a powered heavier-than-air craft. He remained aloft for 12 seconds and covered a distance of only 120 feet, but this single event would change the way people around the world viewed the sky; heavier-than-air flight had been invented. For the next 30 years, the new industry would struggle through a series of experiments in search of the right combination of component technologies to make it a viable, commercial product. At first much of the focus was on the development of military aircraft, then airmail/cargo aircraft, but more was needed for viable commercial passenger travel. Finally, the Douglas DC-3 would demonstrate the right combination of features to make passenger air travel safe, comfortable, and economical to operate. The DC-3 combined five key innovations—variable-pitch propellers, retractable landing gear, lightweight molded body construction, radial air-cooled engine, and wing flaps—to produce a plane that was aerodynamic and economical to operate (Senge, 1990). This chapter traces the beginning of this journey from invention to commercially viable product. The airplane will go from a barnstorming thrill to an essential tool of military operations to a transportation mode for the well-to-do, time-sensitive, risk-taker.

Visionaries

During the three years after their historic flight, the Wright brothers worked to improve the reliability, range, and maneuverability of their design, receiving US patent 821,393 in 1906 (Paradowski, 2002). By 1908, the Wright brothers were working under a contract with the US War Department to build aircraft for the Army (Tischauser, 2002). In 1909, the Wright Company was incorporated in Dayton, Ohio, and over the next several years, would pursue a lawsuit against another aviation pioneer, Glenn Curtiss, claiming that he violated their patent for ailerons, devices to control the roll of an aircraft during flight. In fact, the Wright technology involved wing-warping rather than the use of separate attachments to the wing that would achieve the same thing, however, in the early days of aviation these distinctions were lost to most people outside the industry.

Today, the Curtiss' White Wing is cited as the first US plane to take-off on wheels and use ailerons to control roll in turns, the point of contention with the Wrights. Another Curtiss aircraft, the June Bug, would set a new speed record in 1909 at the first great international air competition in Rheims, France and become the first flight filmed and witnessed by the press. Curtiss would go on to set a number of firsts including the first US licensed pilot, the first person to land an aircraft on the deck of a ship in 1910, and the designer of the first aircraft to cross the Atlantic. He founded the Curtiss Aeroplane and Motor Company before World War I and engaged both in aircraft design and flight training for the US Army and Navy. In addition to the legal battles over the invention of ailerons, Curtiss would side with Albert Zahn, Director of the Smithsonian Institute in Washington, DC, suggesting that Samuel Langley not the Wright Brothers actually invented the airplane. Even though the courts would eventually side with the Wrights on the question of ailerons granting some money to Orville, the surviving brother, and the Smithsonian would recognize the Wrights as first in flight, Orville would sell out all of their patents by 1915 and the company that they founded in 1909 would be bought by Glenn Curtiss in 1929 and become known as the Curtiss-Wright Corporation (Neimann, 2007; Tischauser, 2002).

Two other aviation pioneers would get their start before World War I, William Boeing and Donald W. Douglas. On July 15, 1916, Bill Boeing would incorporate the company founded the previous year, Pacific Aero Products. The company would begin by producing a seaplane copied from a Martin aircraft. They would also work on an aircraft later called the Model C that they hoped to sell to the US Navy (50 would be ordered with the start of World War I). This contract and one to manufacture the Curtiss HS-2L would occupy the company through the war (Serling, 1992). Meanwhile, Donald Douglas would go to work for the Glen L. Martin Co as a chief engineer where he would design the Martin MB-1 bomber, the first US-designed bomber to enter production (Boeing History, 2014).

On the other side of the Atlantic, other visionaries were hard at work. In 1909, Louis Bleriot became the first pilot to cross the English Channel in a craft he designed himself called the Bleriot XI. Two years later, this plane would go to war with the Italian forces in North Africa (Allaz, 2004). Another pioneer, Anthony Fokker, started his first aviation company at the age of 21 and built his first aircraft, called the Spin, in 1910. Both the Spin I and Spin II would crash. Spin III, however, would be sold to the German army. Fokker would go on to design the Tri-plane made famous by Manfred von Richthofen, the Red Baron, in World War I.

Airplane in War

The US government intervened in the lawsuit between the Wright brothers and Curtiss as the US entered World War I. The Curtiss Company would go on to become the largest US aircraft manufacturer in World War I, supplying over 10,000 aircraft to the war effort. The US Navy for whom Curtiss began building planes in 1911 would also use the Curtiss NC-4 to make the first transatlantic flight in 1919 (Marchman, 2002; Roseberry, 1991). The French and the English entered World War I with the English Channel crossing Bleriot XI. The English also deployed the BE.2 designed by Geoffey de Havilland prior to the war. These aircraft started the war classified as scouts and many would end the war with the same designation, however, Fokker would introduce his Eindecker series of monoplanes equipped with fixed, synchronized, forward firing machine guns during this war and they would become known on the Western Front as the "Fokker Scourge" (McDermott, 2002; Milstein, 2002) In addition to the famous Red Baron Tri-plane, the British took to the skies in an aircraft designed by Royal Aircraft called the Sopwith Camel, the favorite aircraft of Snoopy from the Charlie Brown cartoons. Other aircraft such as the DH-4 were used in battle as bombers or in support of advancing ground forces. Another important force in the world of aviation would find the wartime experience invaluable in staking its claim to the future—Rolls-Royce. Rolls-Royce came out of WWI ready to take its place as one of the foremost manufacturers of aircraft engines.

In short, the aircraft that emerged from World War I would be sleeker, faster, more powerful, and better armed. World War I saw the introduction of the low-wing aircraft, the all-metal body, and the thickened cantilever wing, however, most of the aircraft that entered the war would not emerge; the attrition rate on all sides would be very high. The mass production of aircraft needed to supply the war effort had supported many of the newly emerging aviation companies. With the end of the war, most of these companies had to find other means of support although the military was still the best game in town and the lucky few would continue to research and produce the newest weapon in the military arsenal (Allaz, 2004).

Back to Business

In the years immediately after WWI, the fledgling US aircraft manufacturers continued to focus on the military side of the market with some initial forays into aircraft designed for the growing airmail market. Both Boeing and Douglas introduced an airmail plane during 1925, the Model 40 and M-1 respectively. When Boeing replaced the old Liberty engines with the new Pratt & Whitney 425-horsepower air-cooled Wasp engine, the Model 40 not only became a reliable cargo craft but the addition of two passenger seats made it Boeing's first commercial passenger aircraft. This new engine made it superior to its competitors—the

Douglas M-2 and the Curtiss Carrier Pigeon—which continued to use the Liberty. Boeing bid for and won one of the early airmail routes and established its first subsidiary, Boeing Air Transport to handle the growing airmail business (Serling, 1992).

In 1927, Boeing purchased Pacific Air Transport (PAT) and introduced the Model 80 and 80A trimotors equipped with Pratt & Whitney Hornet engines and capable of carrying 18 passengers attended by a registered nurse who acted as a flight attendant. It should be noted that the engines of the 80A were enclosed in streamlined cowlings that improved their performance. In 1929, the Boeing/Pratt & Whitney relationship grew even closer when the two companies merged to form United Aircraft & Transport Corporation. The new company acquired several other aircraft companies including Stearman Aircraft, Northrop Aircraft, and Sikorsky. The new holding company purchased several airlines including Varney, Stout, and National Air Transport which it combined with PAT to form United Air Lines, Inc. While the company was consolidating, it was also working on its next major entry into the market—the B-247. This aircraft started the familiar Boeing numbering scheme. Given the company structure, it is not surprising that United Airlines took delivery of the first 60 B-247s, leaving the other carriers to look for their own answer to the fleet question (Johansen, 2002; Serling, 1992). The airmail scandal that resulted in the Air Mail Act of 1934 hit Boeing very hard. Airline executives who had participated in the illegal "division" of mail contracts with the US Post Office were prohibited from holding office in an airline and no airline that had participated could bid on an airmail contract. Further, aircraft and engine companies were prohibited from owning airlines. This scandal would break up the holding company of United Aircraft and Transport and destroy one of William Boeing's great dreams (Serling, 1992).

For the Boeing Company, the exclusive deal with United also proved to be a very bad move, but for the Douglas Aircraft Company it started a wonderful thing (Serling, 1992). Transcontinental & Western Air (TWA), anxious to replace its Fokker-10 trimotors after the fatal 1931 crash involving Knute Rockne, was looking for a plane. The first plane they considered was the B-247, but United Air Lines order pushed the TWA delivery date well into the future. After the TWA Technical Committee examined several other proposed aircraft it chose the Douglas Aircraft Company and the DC-1. The DC-1 introduced in 1933 would be the first of a series of aircraft destined to dominate the industry for many years (Rummel, 1991). The DC-2 released the following year was capable of carrying 14 passengers for 1,000 miles. With the introduction of the DC-2 even United would race to sell its 247s for less than half their original price (Serling, 1992). In 1935, the best known plane in the series, the DC-3, would be released. With 14 seats capable of folding into sleeping berths, the DC-3, first sold to American Airlines, would set a new standard in passenger travel. By the 1940s, approximately 90 percent of the passenger aircraft flying in the US would be either DC-2 or DC-3s (Clouatre, 2002).

Another legendary US manufacturer would be incorporated in the years between the wars—Lockheed Aircraft. Lockheed, founded by Allan Loughead and Jack Northrop, began work on a Northrop designed aircraft later called the Vega. Wiley Post used the Vega to set his around-the-world record of eight days, 16 hours in 1931. Lockheed was purchased in 1929 by Detroit Aircraft Company. Jack Northrop left to found Avion Corporation, later known as Northrop Corporation. Detroit Aircraft went into bankruptcy during the Great Depression and emerged after a buyout in 1932 as the Lockheed Aircraft Company. Lockheed went on to build the Electra in which Amelia Earhart would make her last flight (McCoy, 2002).

In Europe, Anthony Fokker incorporated his aircraft company in the Netherlands in 1919 and released the F.II, one of the first passenger transport aircraft in 1920. Although he became the main supplier of KLM, the Dutch airline, his passenger aircraft would fall out of favor when Douglas introduced his all-metal aircraft with retractable undercarriages (Millstein, 2002). In England, DeHavilland continued to focus on his single and two-seat bi-plane powered by the Gipsy engine. First came the Gipsy Moth, the Tiger Moth, the Hornet Moth, and then the Moth Minor, a low-wing, wooden monoplane. Dehavilland, like Fokker, would continue to produce cutting-edge aircraft for military and civil use through both wars and beyond.

A Strange, Yet Beautiful, Relationship

The aviation industry has always been imperfect by economic standards. First and foremost, it is characterized in both the manufacturing and the airline sides of the industry by small numbers. Perfect competition, according to Adam Smith, is possible when there are many buyers and many sellers. It is assumed that such a market will drive prices down toward costs. Even in the early days before crisis would fuel consolidation and market power would come to rival innovation, there were a limited number of buyers and suppliers. This has not meant that there has been no competition between manufacturers or within the airline and manufacturing sectors, but at times it has led to some very strange relationships, sometimes too close for comfort and at other times as antagonistic as a divorcing couple. Airlines would come to play one manufacturer off against another while at the same time cooperating closely on design and specifications. They would threaten to "go to the competitors" and then seek out special first delivery rights. For their side, the manufacturers will come to the airlines with concepts seeking orders for yet-to-be-built planes, promising first delivery for key orders, and, eventually, using political clout of all forms to make the sell. These patterns started early.

The story of the DC-1 illustrates this close but imperfect relationship. Frustrated with the progress of his Technical Committee, Jack Frye, the TWA CEO, wrote directly to the manufactures' saying the airline was interested in purchasing ten or more aircraft meeting an attached specifications and performance. He requested them to give notice of interest and approximate date of first delivery. His requirements: capacity for 12 or more passengers, 1,080 range at 150 mph and a one-engine-out ceiling of 10,000 feet. Three companies responded—Sikorsky, General Aviation, a subsidiary of General Motors who had purchased the troubled Fokker, and Douglas Aircraft. TWA proceeded with a series of visits, reviews, and expert analyses that would pit each aircraft maker against the other to improve performance, reduce costs, and speed up delivery dates (Rummel, 1991).

The Next War

The decade of the 1930s saw the beginning of a race in military aviation between the Great Powers of Europe. In Germany, Junkers, Domier, Messerschmitt, Focke-Wulf, and Heinkel emerged as leading aircraft manufacturers turning out a series of aircraft that would lead the Germany Luftwaffe into World War II. The Heinkel He-178 became the first turbojet aircraft to fly successfully in 1939 and began a new era of aerial warfare. Other notable achievements of these manufacturers include the Me-262 Komet which utilized a thrust rocket motor to travel at almost 600 mph and the Ju-287 which sported forward-swept wings over back-swept wings, the Messerschmitt P-1011 with a swept-wing design later used in the US on the F-14, and the Blitz, a twin-engine Arado 234B bomber capable of speeds of up to 461 mph (Graetzer, 2002)

In the UK, the defense industry tripled its employment between 1930 and 1936 even as the industry struggled to adapt its manufacturing methods to the mass production. Still, the Hawker Hurricane, Spitfire, and Lancaster bomber would prove the value in the coming war (McCoy, 2002). The Spitfire gained fame during the famous Battle for Britain. By the end of the war, the Spitfire version equipped with the Rolls-Royce Griffon engine would reach speeds of 460 mph (Wheeler, 2002)

In the US, Boeing had continued work despite the airmail controversy on two aircraft designs that would be critical to the war effort—the B-17 Flying Fortress and the B-29 Superfortress. Although these two aircraft represented only 17 percent of all US bombers, they were responsible for 46 percent of the ordinance dropped on Germany during the war. Further, the B-17 has been credited with shooting down 67 percent of the enemy fighter in the European theatre of operations. At the height of production, Boeing was producing 363 B-17s a month for the Army Air Corp (Johansen, 2002; Serling, 1992).

Table 2.1　　Aviation firsts

Date	Event
1903	First heavier-than-air flight Wilbur and Orville Wright
1906	First European flight Alberto Santos-Dumont
1908	First airplane fatality Lt. Thomas E. Selfridge
1909	First cross-channel flight Louis Bierot
	First international aviation competition Rheims, France
1910	First licensed woman pilot Baroness de la Roche
	First aviation conference Paris, France
1913	First multi-engine aircraft Igor Sikorsky
1914	First aerial combat
1917	First black combat pilot Eugene J. Bullard
1918	First regular US airmail
1919	First transatlantic flight Lt Cmdr Albert Read
1921	First naval vessel sunk by aircraft
1924	First round-the-world flight Maj. Frederick Marin
1927	First solo nonstop transatlantic flight Charles A. Lindbergh
1931	First nonstop transpacific flight Hugh Herndon and Clyde Pangborn
1932	First woman transatlantic flight Amelia Earhart
1933	First round-the-world solo Wiley Post
1937	First successful helicopter flight Hanna Reitsch
1939	First turbojet flight He-178
1947	First piloted supersonic flight Capt Charles E. Yeagar

Source: Information gathered from Infoplease. www.infoplease/ipa/A0004537.html

Seeing the Enemy

The airplane had grown far more deadly in the decade leading up to World War II, but another invention was to be the salvation of Britain during the early years of the war. Radar, an outgrowth of the radio experiments of the 1930s, sent radio waves out into the atmosphere and measured the time that elapsed before the signal reflected off of a solid object and returned to the receiver. The UK had begun deploying this new technology along their coast before the start of the war and its use during the early years of the war would help Britain beat back the waves of German bombers that would stream across the Channel. In addition to detecting incoming aircraft, the system could be used to direct intercepting aircraft to their target, help aircraft determine their height from the ground, and identify friendly and enemy aircraft with the use of small broadcasting beacons. The "enemy" would eventually deploy radar as well, but the invention of the microwave-cavity magnetron which generated a high-power radio wave and required a smaller antenna would continue to give the British the advantage during the war. Of course, this new technology had civilian applications and would become the backbone of the civil aviation systems that developed after the end of World War II In fact, the system currently in use today to track, identify, and direct aircraft is not very different from this early system, a fact that we will discuss in Chapter 20 as the industry searches for a twenty-first century solution.

Conquering the Civilian Market

During its first 50 years of life, the aviation industry witnessed a number of high-profile firsts (Table 2.1) and captured the imagination of a whole generation, but it had not yet conquered the traveling public, ordinary citizens who would pay to ride on a flight from point A to point B. The airplane had proven its value in war and was being mass produced on a large scale by the end of World War II. The basic elements of a successful and viable product had been invented and tested in the heat of war. Still, the airplane probably still looked in 1950 like the playground of the rich and the daring; it was not yet the transportation mode-of-choice for visiting grandma in Iowa or Ontario. The task of creating a commercial aviation industry that would attract this kind of a market would be left to the pioneers of the next 50 years who would make flying a commonplace occurrence, even a necessity (Chapter 7). First, the industry would conquer the cargo market, specifically airmail. Chapter 3 will discuss the development of this industry and how it came to shape the future of the US airline industry. The tale of how a few daring individuals would be thrown on top of the mail will have to wait, but it would come.

Questions

1. What is the difference between invention and innovation?
2. How is war "good" for the aviation industry?
3. What combination of innovations made the DC-3 a commercial success?
4. What legal battle divided the Wright Brothers and Glen Curtiss?
5. Discuss the early history of the Boeing Company.

References

Allaz, C. (2004), *The History of Air Cargo and Airmail from the 18th Century*, Christopher Foyle Publishing, Paris.

Boeing History (2013), retrieved online February 6, 2013 from http://www.boeing.com/boeing/history/narrative/n002boe.page.

Carlson, R.V. (2002), "Dirigibles" in Tracy Irons-Georges (ed.), *Encyclopedia of Flight*, Salem Press, Pasadena, CA, pp. 211–215.

Clouatre, D. (2002), "DC Plane Family" in Tracy Irons-Georges (ed.), *Encyclopedia of Flight*, Salem Press, Pasadena, CA, pp. 205–207.

Graetzer, D.G. (2002), "World War II" in Tracy Irons-Georges (ed.), *Encyclopedia of Flight*, Salem Press, Pasadena, CA, pp. 779–785.

Johansen, B.E. (2002), "Boeing" in Tracy Irons-Georges (ed.), *Encyclopedia of Flight*, Salem Press, Pasadena, CA, pp. 154–156.

Marchman, J.F. (2002), "Glenn H. Curtiss" in Tracy Irons-Georges (ed.), *Encyclopedia of Flight*, Salem Press, Pasadena, CA, pp. 203–204.

McCoy, M.G. (2002), "Lockheed Martin" in Tracy Irons-Georges (ed.), *Encyclopedia of Flight*, Salem Press, Pasadena, CA, pp. 420–423.

McDermott, D.P. (2002), "World War I," in Tracy Irons-Georges (ed.), *Encyclopedia of Flight*, Salem Press, Pasadena, CA, pp. 774–779.

Milstein, R.L. (2002), "Fokker Aircraft" in Tracy Irons-Georges (ed.), *Encyclopedia of Flight*, Salem Press, Pasadena, CA, pp. 275–278.

Niemann, G. (2007), *Big Brown: The Untold Story of UPS*, John Wiley & Sons, San Francisco, CA.

Paradowski, R.J. (2002), "Wright Flyer," in Tracy Irons-Georges (ed.), *Encyclopedia of Flight*, Salem Press, Pasadena, CA, pp. 786–788.

Roseberry, C.R. (1991), *Glenn Curtiss: Pioneer of Flight*, Syracuse University Press, Syracuse, NY.

Rummel, R.W. (1991), *Howard Hughes and TWA*, Smithsonian Institution Press, Washington.

Senge, P.M. (1990), *The Fifth Discipline: The Art & Practice of the Learning Organization*, Doubleday, New York.

Serling, R.J. (1992), *Legend and Legacy: The Story of Boeing and Its People*, St. Martin Press, New York.

Tischauser, L.V. (2002), "Wright Brothers," in Tracy Irons-Georges (ed.), *Encyclopedia of Flight*, Salem Press, Pasadena, CA, pp. 785–786.

Wheeler, H (2002), "Spitfire" in Tracy Irons-Georges (ed.), *Encyclopedia of Flight*, Salem Press, Pasadena, CA, pp. 625–626.

Chapter 3
The Other Source of Revenue

Learning Objectives

After reading this chapter, you should have a good understanding of:
- LO1: the beginnings of the air cargo industry.
- LO2: the role that aviation prizes had in fostering the development of aviation.
- LO3: the role of the Post Office in the US in shaping the aviation industry, including the scandal over airmail contract.
- LO4: the background that shaped UPS.

Key Terms, Concepts, and People

US Post Office	Kelly Act of 1925	CAM
William Folger Brown	Trunk route	Airmail Act of 1934
Deutsche Lufthansa	UPS	Charles Lindbergh

Following the Money

The first non-mail cargo flight took place on November 7, 1910 from Dayton to Columbus, Ohio. Commissioned by Max Morehouse to celebrate the annual autumn sale of his Home Dry Goods Store, the Wright Model B carried the 200 pounds of silk and ribbon 70 miles to successfully deliver its goods. While this delivery is a noteworthy first, it should probably be considered an even more successful marketing and publicity event (Allaz, 2004). In the beginning, airmail and air cargo were more novelty and show than serious business. In fact, 1911 marked the first airmail exhibition in which souvenir cards and stamps were flown around a local area in India and then sold to collectors. Other such events followed in the UK, France, Germany, and the US. In 1911, The Grahame-White Aviation Company carrier 130,000 cards and letters between London and Winsor Castle as part of the celebration for the coronation of George V (Glines, 1990).

While the idea of airmail and air cargo fired the imagination of aviators and some businessmen around the world, it was the William Randolph Hearst announcement of the creation of a US$50,000 prize to the first pilot who could fly coast to coast in the US within 30 days that set off efforts to prove this new technology. Calbraith P. Rodgers was one of the pilots determined to collect the prize. He eventually completed the coast to coast flight, crashing only 16 times. Unfortunately, it took him 55 days and he was unable to collect the Hearst prize (Glines, 1990). Others would follow, but it was not until the US government got involved that regularly scheduled, transcontinental airmail became a reality in the US. In Europe, sporadic efforts would be interrupted by World War I.

Officially Speaking

India not only holds the honor of having the first airmail exhibition but the first official airmail flight on February 18, 1911, however, like so many other efforts this first flight did not translate into a regular service (Allaz, 2004). In the US, the Post Office Department had asked for US$50,000 in 1911 to explore airmail delivery, but it was not until 1916 that funds were made available. By 1918, Congress was prepared to authorize US$100,000 for an experimental airmail route between Washington and New York. It was left up to Major Reuben H. Fleet of the Army Air Service to make this air service work despite the fact that there was 1) a shortage of pilots, 2) almost no pilots with cross-country flying experience, 3) no adequate maps, 4) few experienced mechanics, and 5) no planes modified to carry airmail. Still, with President Wilson set to attend the official take-off, Glen Curtiss was contacted and asked to modify his Curtiss JN6H to leave out the front seat and front controls and add a second gas tank. While this experiment had its share of mishaps and lost pilots, it was deemed a success and the US Post Office Department officially took over the service in August of 1918, buying their own planes and hiring their own pilots. According to official records, the Army Air Service delivered 193,021 pounds of mail completing 92 percent of their scheduled flights. They flew 128,255 route miles without a fatality. Ben Lipsner who had officially organized the experiment for the Army Air Service became the first Superintendent of the United States Aerial Mail Service. One of his first tasks upon assuming his position was to commission the design of the first aircraft specifically for airmail delivery. This plane, the Standard Aero-mail, was designed by the Standard Aircraft Company of Elizabeth, New Jersey. It was powered by a 150 horse power engine and had a load specification of 180 pounds. It could travel at speeds of 100 mph and climb to a height of 6,000 feet in 10 minutes. The next task was to begin transcontinental service with the first leg from New York to Cleveland followed over the next two years by New York-Chicago, Chicago–Omaha, Chicago–St. Louis, Chicago–Minneapolis, and Omaha–San Francisco. On July 1, 1924, regular transcontinental service was inaugurated. In 1923 and 1924, the Airmail Service received the Collier Trophy for "the greatest achievement in aviation in America" (Glines, 1990).

The US Post Office would gradually close down its Airmail Service with the passage of the Kelly Act of 1925 entitled "An Act to Encourage Commercial Aviation and to authorize the Postmaster General to Contract for the Mail Service." US Representative Clyde Kelly who sponsored the act believed that private operators not the government should assume the risks and reap the rewards of the airmail business. With this act, advertisements were placed in newspapers asking for bids on eight feeder airmail routes to be awarded by the Postmaster General. By 1926, 12 airmail contracts had been awarded. The last flight of the Post Office was conducted in 1927 (Kane, 1998). In order to qualify for these routes, individuals had to be US citizens backed by at least 75 percent US-controlled capital stock. Aircraft had to qualify for airworthiness certificates and pilots had to produce certificates of fitness (Glines, 1990)

Table 3.1 lists the route number and the company receiving the award. There are several items of note in this list. The first route to be put into operation was Ford Air Transport. This company was another venture by a man more associated with the automobile, Henry Ford. Ford Air Transport manufactured a plane designed by William B. Stout. This aircraft was an all-metal monoplane with internally stressed wings and a liberty engine. A later version, the Ford Trimotor, would go on to become one of the great classic airplanes of the period. Western Air Express which had the airmail route from Los Angeles to Salt Lake City would become one of the first carriers to try to boost revenues by carrying passengers. In 1927, Western received a grant from the Daniel Guggenheim Fund to purchase passenger aircraft. A slightly later effort to combine cargo and passengers was Transcontinental Air Transport (TAT). TAT planned to use train by night and air by day to offer luxury passenger service. The venture lost almost $3 million in the first year and a half. TAT would later merge with several other carriers to become Transcontinental & Western Air (TWA). Eventually, the name would become Trans World Airlines (Glines, 1990). It should be noted that the original list of Contract Airmail (CAM) awards includes carriers that would go on to form the nucleus of familiar US major and national carriers.

Table 3.1   The first contract airmail routes

Route Number	Company
CAM 1	Colonial Air Lines
CAM 2	Robertson Aircraft Corp
CAM 3	National Air Transport
CAM 4	Western Air Express
CAM 5	Varney Speed Lines
CAM 6 & 7	Ford Air Transport
CAM 8	Pacific Air Transport
CAM 9	Charles Dickenson
CAM 10	Florida Airways Corp
CAM 11	Clifford Ball
CAM 12	Western Air Express

Source: Kane, R.M, *Air Transportation*

National Air Transport and Pacific Air Transport would go on to combine with a later CAM awardee, Boeing Air Transport, to form United Airlines (Davies, 1998). Varney Speed Lines would go on to become Continental Airlines (Davies, 1984). Robertson Aircraft Corporation would become one of 80 carriers merged to form American Airlines (Bedwell and Wegg, 2000). All American Aviation who would receive a CAM in 1939 would go on to become US Airways (Jones and Jones, 1999). This consolidation would not occur by accident. As the TAT and Western experiments proved passengers could provide good additional revenue; airmail revenue was essential. In fact, these CAM routes would establish a basic pattern of air transportation in the US that continues to this day. Creating this pattern of trunk routes, large coast-to-coast operations flowing east-to-west, would be the "mission" of Walter Brown.

In 1929, Walter Folger Brown was appointed postmaster general. Brown would work diligently for the passage of the Air Mail Act of 1930, also known as the McNary-Watres Airmail Act, which gave the postmaster total control over the airmail bidding process. He believed that airline business model should be based on passenger revenue not excess airmail payments (Glines, 1990). According to Brown, the aviation industry suffered from four problems: "1) being unwilling to invest in new equipment, 2) operating obsolete aircraft, 3) demonstrating questionable safety performance from cost cutting, and 4) maintaining marginal operations with no growth" (Kane, 1998: 107). To remedy this situation, Brown eliminated the competitive bidding process for contract airmail routes in favor of a system that granted awards to large, well financed operators. Only these large operators were invited to attend the so-called spoils conferences that were held in Washington, D.C. to award contracts. In essence, the U.S. government through the postmaster forced small carriers to merge in order to obtain the lucrative airmail contracts (Glines, 1968). Brown envisioned an air map of the US with three transcontinental routes—a northern, a central, and a southern. These routes would be connected by shorter, regional north-south routes (Glines, 1990). A look at a map of the early airmail routes and stops will show that he succeeded to some extent, creating a long east–west trunk route with shorter north–south legs. This general structure would be the backbone for the airline networks that followed. Unfortunately, this heavy-handed "indirect" intervention did not set well with many stakeholders. Certainly, the carriers left out of the spoils conferences had ample reason to complain and they did (Airmail Pioneers, 2012).

By 1932, charges of graft and collision led US President Franklin Roosevelt to cancel all contracts and return responsibility for the airmail to the US Army. It was decided that the Army Air Corps would operate only 12 of the 26 civilian routes. Unfortunately, even this reduction was not enough for the Corps which had a limited number of pilots and even fewer with night flying or instrument experience. Their aircraft often did not have landing, navigation, or cockpit lights nor were they equipped with the new gyro instruments or radios. Given these deficiencies, it is not surprising that the Corps quickly ran into trouble. After a series of accidents, the airmail service was returned to private operators by June 1, 1934 (Glines,

1990). The Airmail Act of 1934, also known as the Black-McKellar Act provided for a return to the competitive bidding process of the past and prohibited awards to carriers involved in the supposed collusion. Three of these carriers, American Airways, Eastern Air Transport, and Transcontinental & Western Air changed their names respectively to American Airlines, Eastern Airlines, and Transcontinental & Western Air Inc. to avoid this restriction and continue in the airmail business. The administration of contracts would be divided between the Post Office, Interstate Commerce Commission (ICC), and the Department of Commerce. Beginning in 1938, rates would be set by the newly created Civil Aviation Bureau (CAB) (Kane, 1998).

Mail, Morale, and War

In Europe, the years just before World War I saw a number of efforts to start airmail service. In 1911, Henri Pequet transported 6,500 letters and postcards from Allahabad to Naini Junction in France while in Italy a similar shipment was made between Bologna and Venice. In 1912, both Germany and Japan celebrated their first official airmail flight, however, as World War I approached the balloons of Paris which had operated during the Prussian siege of the city between 1870–71 remained the only example of a regularly scheduled airmail service (Allaz, 2004). Europe would have to wait until the end of the war to achieve this milestone; however, military airmail was established between several areas of the continent during the war. For the most part, these services utilized military aircraft, but allowed some civilian correspondence.

As World War I wound down, aircraft had a new cargo and a new mission— humanitarian relief. In 1919, an airlift was established between Folkestone and Ghent to provide bedding, medicine, and food. In France, similar efforts were organized between Paris–Lille, Paris–Maubeuge-Valenciennes, Paris–Longwy, Paris–Mulhouse, Paris–Strasbourg, and Paris–Brussels. Most of these efforts were short-lived, but they did give a number of individuals and firms experience in airmail and air cargo. This experience combined with the flying experience of former soldiers would prove useful after the war when nations moved to re-establish their commercial aviation systems. As we will discuss in Chapter 4, Europe would move quickly in association with the Universal Postal Union (UPU) to integrate airmail into the postal system of Europe.

Like in the US, airmail would continue to receive priority in the air cargo business of Europe until after World War II, however, several airlines did attempt to expand into other forms of cargo By 1938, Deutsche Lufthansa was already the world's leading scheduled carrier for freight, a position that it continued to hold in 2008 according to the latest Air Cargo World survey. It would introduce the first long-haul transoceanic freight charter in 1939. According to Allaz (2004) a total of 57,000 tons of cargo were shipped by air in 1938. As is still true today, the most common items of shipment were highly perishable, urgent, and high value. These included newspapers, bank notes, perfumes, spare parts, and the occasional live animal. With the introduction of new aircraft designed with cargo operations in mind such as the Junkers W33 and the Ju52, the volume and size of cargo improved lowering the cost. By 1940 TACA (Transportes Aereos Centro-Americanos) was the world's leading all-freight company shipping 12,640 tons of goods throughout Central America. In other regions with poor or challenging surface transportation features, the idea of offering bulk, low rates for air shipment was considered and tried; however, the volumes of air freight would continue to be relatively minor in the period between the World War I and World War II.

A Brown Beginning

In 1899, 11-year-old Jim Casey went to work to help support his family. His first job was with the delivery department at Bon Marche, a Seattle department store. From here, he would go on to start several of his own businesses in the area including a messenger and telephone service. American Messenger Company was founded in 1907. It would later merge with the Motorcycle Delivery Company to become Merchants Parcel Delivery. This new company would handle outsource department store delivery with a small fleet of brown trucks. After World War I, the company would begin the process of expanding down the US west coast. They would purchase the Motor Parcel Company in Oakland, California and change the name again to United Parcel Service (UPS).

These early years would lay the foundation for many of the features that would later "define" UPS. The first, of course, was the color of their delivery vans, selected so that the original department store customers would not see them as a threat. Second, the early years established the pattern of learning the intimate details of an area and utilizing this knowledge to provide better, faster time-definite service. Third, each new merger, acquisition, or key hire would bring more people into the family that would become UPS. These employees would be seen as the backbone of their success. When the company expanded to Los Angeles, it would advertise their delivery men as the type "you yourself would hire" and they would become known for their neat appearance and prompt, courteous service.

Evert "Mac" McDabe, one of the UPS partners, was an early enthusiast of the airplane. Eventually, he would convince the others to form United Air Express in 1929. United Air Express contracted with three air companies to fly packages delivered by UPS to selected airports. At the same time, UPS was looking to expand its delivery business into the New York City area. The Curtiss Aeroplane Motor Company which had recently merged with Wright Aeronautical to form the Curtiss-Wright Corporation made an offer to UPS to buy the company for US$2 million and 600,000 shares in Curtiss Aeroplane. The UPS partners would remain with the company and were guaranteed management control for five years.

This deal seemed a perfect way to expand the business to the East Coast, but the financial collapse that followed the 1929 stock market crash ended the deal and UPS' first foray into the air service business (Neimann, 2007).

Conclusion

It has been noted that the first decade of aviation in the US was synonymous with airmail. In part, this was due to the drive of Otto Praeger who became the second Assistant Postmaster General in 1915 and Walter Folger Brown, Postmaster General beginning in 1929 who was determined to "create" the airline industry in the US. Even after the Post Office officially left the airmail delivery business to the private sector, its indirect influence was substantial and far reaching. While the accomplishments of the early airmail pilots were significant steps in establishing airmail and air cargo as viable modes of transportation, it was probably the 1927 flight by Charles A Lindbergh, himself an airmail pilot, that truly captured the imagination of the world and the attention of serious business investment. One month after the historic New York to Paris flight, there was a 20 percent increase in mail on contract mail routes (Glines, 1990).

Thirty-five years after the first air cargo flight, the world had not yet fully accepted the concept but had seen enough evidence of potential in air cargo to set the stage for the post-World War II industry that was to come. Like all things aviation, World War II would be a turning point. The technical innovations and individual and collective achievements that occur during this war will change the nature and shape the popular perception of the industry as it moves into the second half of the twentieth century. However, it would be the logistics revolution and the globalization movement of the latter part of the twentieth century that would make air cargo a force to be reckoned with in the aviation industry (Chapter 13). For now, the fantasy of the balloon would give way to the cold, hard calculation of governments and businessmen. These calculations are the subject of the next three chapters.

Questions

1. What role did the US Post Office play in air cargo?
2. Discuss the first airmail routes and trace these early companies through history.
3. What were the spoils conferences and how did this scandal affect the industry?
4. What role did air cargo play during and after World War II?
5. Discuss how the beginnings of UPS helped to shape its culture and future.

References

Airmail Pioneers (2012), "Map," retrieved online February 16, 2013 from http://www.airmailpioneers.org/.

Allaz, C. (2004), *The History of Air Cargo and Airmail from the 18th Century*, Christopher Foyle Publishing, Paris.

Bedwell, D. and Wegg, J. (2000), *Silverbird: The American Airlines Story*, Plymouth Press, Boston.

Davies, R.E.G. (1984), *Continental Airlines: The First Fifty Years*, Pioneer Publications, The Woodlands, TX.

Davies, R.E.G. (1998), *Airlines of the United States Since 1914*, Smithsonian Institution Press, Washington, DC.

Glines, C.V. (1968), *The Saga of the Airmail*, D. Van Nostrand, Princeton, NJ.

Glines, C.V. (1990), *Airmail: How it All Began*, TAB Aero, Blue Ridge Summit, PA.

Jones, G. and Jones, G.P. (1999), *U.S. Airways*, Ian Allan, Shepperton, England.

Kane, R.M. (1998), *Air Transportation* (13th ed.), Kendall/Hunt Publishing, Dubuque, IA.

Niemann, G. (2007), *Big Brown: The Untold Story of UPS*, John Wiley & Sons, San Francisco, CA.

Chapter 4

A Dangerous Idea?

Learning Objectives

After reading this chapter, you should have a good understanding of:
- LO1: the early developments in manned flight.
- LO2: the issues that divided the 1910 aviation conference.
- LO3: the regulations proposed in the 1919 convention.
- LO4: the domestic development of the aviation industry on both sides of the Atlantic between the world wars.

Key Terms, Concepts, and People

Paris Convention	Freedom of the skies	
UPU	Par Avion	British Airways
Air France	Rolls-Royce	Messerschmitt

Imagined Possibilities

On January 7, 1785, less than two years after the first recorded balloon flight, Jean-Pierre Blanchard and John Jeffries became the first individuals to cross above a national border when they flew their balloon across the English Channel to France. This event was not viewed at the time as an "invasion" but a triumph of mankind. While experimentation with lighter-than-air flight continued, the balloon did not inspire the same sense of fear that powered flight would in the early 20th century. Even the development of the dirigible, an elongated balloon with a system of propulsion and guidance did not change the general view of lighter-than-air flight. Still at the mercy of the winds, the balloon did not seem to pose the threat or hold the promise of heavier-than-air travel. It is true that the French used balloons in a military setting as early as 1793 when they provided reconnaissance during conflicts following the French Revolution. It is also true that the first recorded air-to-air combat occurred in 1870 between a French and a Prussian balloonist during the siege of Paris, but the balloons of war still did not raise the international concerns that their heavier-than-air cousins would provoke (Glines, 1968; Wirth and Young, 1980). The world's governments, however, would not wait for the aircraft to enter battle before acting. By 1910, they had already seen enough to know that the airplane was no passing fancy but a new technology with great promise and dangerous potential. New regulations were needed to insure the development of international aviation and to protect the interests of nations. This was the goal of the Paris Conference. This conference would not achieve the goals that its organizers had hoped, but it did make one thing abundantly clear; international aviation would not be divorced from politics and national interest (Sochor, 1991).

Let the Conferences Begin

The French government convened the first ever conference on aviation in 1910 to draft a convention on air navigation. The conference was attended by the representatives of 19 European countries. It quickly became apparent that there were conflicting opinions among the delegates present over the rights and privileges of flying. The French and German delegations favored a system of extensive freedom based on the Freedom of the Seas model of Hugo Grotius. The British insisted on complete state sovereignty and control over the airspace above a country's land borders. This fundamental disagreement prevented the conference from achieving its principle goal of establishing a broad framework for international aviation, however, the convention did identify many of the key terms, concepts, and technical provisions that would become standard in later conferences. In the absence of agreement over an international framework, the British became the first nation to declare its sovereignty over the airspace above their country in 1911. The British Aerial Navigation Act gave the Home Secretary full power to regulate the entry and activities of aircraft into its airspace. The other European nations quickly followed suit in the years prior to World War I (Sochor, 1991). The debate over freedom of the skies would resume at the 1913 Madrid Conference which would also fail to reach consensus (Allaz, 2004).

The Peace Conference at the end of World War I faced two key aviation issues. The first was the disposition of the military and civilian fleets of the defeated countries. The second issue was to complete the work begun in 1910. The meeting, known as the Convention Relating to the Regulation of Aerial Navigation, accepted the US position that permitted German civil aviation development within their national borders while eliminating all of the military aspects of aviation. The conference also produced the so-called Paris Convention of 1919. The first article of the Convention declared the complete and exclusive sovereignty of each nation over its airspace. It went on to call for 1) prescribed national registration of aircraft, 2) restricted movement of military aircraft, 3) prescribed rules of airworthiness, that is, certification that an aircraft is safe to fly through a range of operations, 4) regulation of pilots, and 5) establishment of police measures. A permanent commission was established in Paris to continue the study of international aviation legal issues, the International Commission on Air Navigation (ICAN) (Kane, 1998; Sochor, 1991). The Paris Convention was eventually ratified by 26 countries, the most notable exceptions being the US and Russia who both chose to distance themselves from international affairs after the end of World War I. The US did later sign the Commercial Aviation Convention, also known as the Havana Convention, in 1928. This convention resulted from the Sixth International Conference of the American States and differed from the Paris Convention in several key respects. The Havana Convention did not seek to establish a uniform international standard on aviation for aircraft or pilot regulation nor did it contain any provision for influencing future aviation development such as ICAN (Groenewedge, 1996).

Postal Agenda

The Universal Postal Union (UPU) was established in 1874 on the initiative of Heinrich von Stephan, the Director General of Post for Prussia (later Germany). The primary concern of the UPU was the free transit of international mail and Article I of the UPU considered all the countries under the treaty a single territory over which the UPU imposed fixed transit fees for sea and rail. In 1920, the UPU met in Madrid and began the process of incorporating air services into the Convention. This proceeded in three phases: recognition (1920–1927), integration (1927–1938), and full incorporation (1938–). Article 4b—Aerial Services was inserted into the Convention. It stated that:

> Aerial services established for the conveyance of correspondence between two or more countries are considered as analogous to the extraordinary services to which Article 4, section 6 refers. The conditions of conveyance are settled by mutual consent between the Administrations concerned. The transit charges applicable to each aerial service are, however, uniform for all Administrations which use the service…

As an extraordinary service, however, there was no uniform regulation common to all companies or air routes. A special conference called by the UPU at The Hague in 1927 would change this status including aerial conveyance under all the articles covering other modes of conveyance and establishing a basic and surcharge rate based on weight. It would also require that the classic blue label "Par Avion" be applied to the outside of the correspondence. Three further conferences were held prior to the outbreak of World War II—Brussels in 1929 and 1931 and Cairo in 1934. The unstated goal was to eliminate the surcharge. No official action was taken but a number of European postal administrators began to unofficially remove it beginning in the 1930s. The surcharge was officially removed in the Brussels Conference of 1938 (Allaz, 2004).

Domestic Developments

While the international aviation community remained divided on the general question of freedom versus sovereignty, the course of domestic aviation development diverged as well in the years leading up to World War II. Direct governmental intervention became the most frequent method of promoting the growth and development of domestic aviation. Governments either provided direct subsidies and/or assumed full or partial ownership of domestic air transport companies. British Airways and Air France are two classic examples of this strategy. A privately owned British Airways was formed in 1935 from the merger of several smaller British carriers. British Airways and Imperial Airways were merged and nationalized to form British Overseas Airways Corporation (BOAC) in 1939. BOAC and British European Airways (BEA) would be merged under the name British Airways in 1974 and remain under government ownership until 1987 (Marriott, 1998). Air France was founded in 1933 through the merger of five smaller French carriers and negotiated with the French government to become the country's national carrier. In 1948, the government assumed a 70 percent ownership stake in the newly reincorporated Air France. All four of the government-owned airlines of France were merged in 1990 into the Air France Group (Gross, 2002). By the mid-1950s, most of the carriers of Europe were wholly or partly owned by their respective governments (Graham, 1995). Although many of Asia's national carriers were formed after their European counterparts, the pattern of government ownership was widespread there as well (Sinha, 2001).

This direct intervention did not suit the philosophical and political tastes of US lawmakers and officials. The US government would influence the development of domestic aviation through indirect intervention. As noted in Chapter 3, the early development of US aviation was closely tied to airmail and it was largely at the urging of the US Post Office that experimentation with airmail delivery and route creation was begun. After the transition from government to private airmail delivery prompted by the Kelly Act of 1925, the Postmaster General would unofficially continue intervene in the private airlines that emerged to shape the aviation industry. While this intervention was later deemed illegal, it provided the financial support and strategic vision that shaped the industry that went to war in World War II.

By the beginning of World War II, the domestic aviation environment of the Americas and Europe was in place, although the strain of the Great Depression was putting pressure on these systems. Government ownership was the preferred method of domestic support and development in most of the world's nations while the US government intervened in equally significant, though indirect, ways to create a large, stable aviation system. A question occasionally arises from aviation-interested individuals from outside the US as to what factors account for the different, that is, indirect path taken toward the development of domestic aviation by the US government. There are probably a number of concrete economic and geographical explanations, but the more intuitive and less obvious answer may lie in the basic, shared attitude of many of the individuals that originally colonized and later immigrated to the US, namely a general distrust of organized government. This distrust grows in direct proportion to the distance that government is from the individual or individuals in question. It has been said in a number of slightly varying ways that citizens in the US tend to believe that their government was invented by geniuses to be run by idiots (Friedman, 2000). These sentiments are clearly and forcefully expressed by such economists as Hayak, Milton Friedman, and other individuals associated with the so-called Chicago School. Simply put, government intervention distorts the functioning of free market forces preventing the efficient allocation of resources and the establishment of natural prices (Friedman, 1980, 1982; Hayak, 1960, 1980, 1994; Yergin and Stanislaw, 2002). Clearly such an attitude does not predispose the average US citizen to favoring greater government involvement in their daily life. The federalization of airport screening in the wake of 9/11 probably reflects the confusion, shock, fear, and uncertainty created by those events far more than it represents a true belief that the government can perform this function better than private enterprise. It is likely that within a few years there will be increasing pressure to "privatize" that which was once "federalized" for just these reasons. Likewise, the US reluctance to privatize airports and air traffic control service like so much of the rest of the world would do so in the latter part of the twentieth century has more to do with entrenched political forces and powerful labor groups than it does with a belief in the efficiency and effectiveness of governments, although airports in the US tend to be run by local (city, county) governments who do meet the "closer-to-me" test of the US citizen and thus get a slightly higher level of trust.

Lessons of War

During the first half of the twentieth century, the world would experience two great wars. The airplane would play a role in both of these conflicts. Although the airplane first went to war in 1911 with the Italian forces in North Africa, its role was to provide reconnaissance. In World War I, it would assume an offensive role first as a bomber and later in aerial combat with mounted machine guns. The airplane that went into World War I was propelled by an engine capable of about 90 horse power and 75 mph. By the end of the war, Rolls-Royce and American Liberty engines were producing 360 and 400 horse power, speed had doubled, and innovations such as cantilever wings and all metal fuselages were in place (Allaz, 2004). While World War I evokes images of flying aces such as Manfred von Richthofen, commonly called the Red Baron, twisting and turning in an aerial ballet with his opponents, the war also saw the first large scale bombing of such cities as London. On June 13, 1917 alone, the Germans dropped 118 high-explosive bombs on the city of London. The airplane had clearly arrived as a weapon of war.

If World War I saw the airplane become more than an observer of the action, then World War II saw it become an integral, vital part of the grand strategy of nations and allies. The war itself began with the Blitzkrieg of Poland and later much of Europe. The aircraft made these lightening strikes possible and devastating. The desperate Battle of Britain demonstrated the important role of aircraft for both offensive and defensive purposes. The aircraft in fact took several major leaps forwarding design and performance during the war years. One of the most significant developments was the turbojet aircraft. Germany followed this innovation with the Messerschmitt (Me-262), which was capable of carrying 550-pound bombs installed on the aircraft's wing racks as well as 12 R4M rockets fitted under the wings. The Me-163 Komet was fitted a rocket motor that could propel it at almost 600 mph and climb vertically at 11,810 feet per minute. Other advances during the war included the use of rocket boosters for short takeoffs, pressurized cabins, four engine aircraft, forward-swept wings mounted over swept-back wings to establish stability at low speeds, and drag-resistant body designs (Badsey, 1990; Cooksley and Robertson, 1998).

Aircraft were not the only beneficiaries of the wartime push to innovation. The British development of radar discussed in Chapter 2 was critical to the defense of Britain and the Allies' ability to avoid detection during bombing raids over Germany. This innovation led to early efforts at reducing aircraft detectability, stealth technology, through the use of deflected radar beams and radar-absorbing materials. Work was also begun on the use of thinner, flatter, heat-resistant materials for aircraft construction. Finally, unmanned, armed aircraft and guided missiles would make their appearance toward the end of the war (Cooksley and Robertson, 1998).

In short, the aircraft came out of these two conflicts a more powerful and deadlier device. As has always been the case with aviation, however, the innovations developed for military application also can have important impacts on the civilian sector. By 1946, aircraft such as the Douglas DC-6 would be carrying 102 passengers at 20,000 feet in a pressurized cabin (Badrocke and Sunston, 1999). Commercial aviation was coming of age and prepared to launch the world on a path to globalization.

Coming Out with Different Agendas

As World War II was coming to an end, the Allied Powers would turn at least some of their attention back to the issue of creating an international aviation system. This interest would result in the Chicago Conference (Chapter 5), but the countries attending that conference had been changed by the years of war in ways that would echo through the halls in Chicago. It has been said that the US was the only country to emerge from World War II richer. In fact, the US gold reserves at the end of the war totaled US$20 billion, two-thirds of the world's total (Matloff, 1959). The US would be responsible for more than half of the total manufacturing production of the world and account for one-third of the production of all types of goods

(Ashworth, 1975). In the aviation area, the US production of aircraft had risen by 1945 to 49,761 per year, up from 5,856 in 1939. It would account for more aircraft per year than the combined manufacturing of Britain and the USSR (Overy, 1980).

For its part, the USSR had not only lost 20–25 million citizens between 1941 and 1945; it had lost a substantial portion of its infrastructure (Hosking, 1985). It is estimated that in the transportation sector alone the USSR "was hit by the destruction of 65,000 kilometers of railway track, loss of or damage to 15,800 locomotives, 428,000 goods wagons, 4,280 river boats, and half of all the railway bridges in the occupied territory" (Nove, 1969: 285). The losses to infrastructure were devastating in the nations of other Allied and Great Powers as well. In 1946, German national income and output was one-third of its 1938 level (Landes, 1969). Japanese real income had fallen to only 57 percent of its 1934–1936 levels and exports were only 8 percent of the 1934–1936 figures (Allen, 1981). Italy's gross national product had declined by 40 percent to its 1911 level (Ricossa, 1972). The Allied Powers, with the exception of the US, had not fared any better. By 1944, years of war and occupation had left France with a situation where "most of the waterways and harbors were blocked, most of the bridges destroyed, much of the railway system temporarily unusable" (Wright, 1968; 264). The French national income in 1945 was half of its 1938 level. In Great Britain, years of bombing had severely weakened the industrial base and damaged the overall civilian infrastructure. Exports had fallen to 31 percent of their 1938 figures with a resulting surge in the British trade deficit (Kennedy, 1981).

It is with this backdrop that the Allied and Neutral Powers would meet in Chicago to decide the shape of the post-war international aviation system. The fact that the meeting would take place even before the conclusion of the war was an indication of the importance this young industry had gained in the eyes of world governments and their citizens. While the industry itself was young, the arguments heard in Chicago were old. The aviation community had heard them before Chicago and would hear them again over the subsequent years. The successes and failures of Chicago would live on in the international aviation system of today.

Questions

1. Why was the sky not treated in the same way as the seas when it came to freedoms?
2. Why do you believe the UK favored strict regulation of international aviation?
3. How did the US and European approaches to the aviation industry differ in the 1930s?
4. Justify the US approach to domestic development between the wars.
5. How did the end of World War II affect the agendas going into the Chicago Conference?

References

Allaz, C. (2004), *The History of Air Cargo and Airmail from the 18ᵗʰ Century*, Christopher Foyle Publishing, Paris.

Allen, G.S. (1981), *A Short Economic History of Japan*, McMillan, New York.

Ashworth, W.A. (1975), *A Short History of the International Economy Since 1850*, Printise Hall Press, London.

Badrocke, M. and Sunston, B. (1999), *The Illustrated History of McDonnell Douglas Aircraft from Cloudster to Boeing*, Osprey, Oxford.

Badsey, S. (1990), *Modern Air Power: Fighters*, Gallery Books, New York.

Cooksley, M.K. and Robertson, B. (1998), *Air Warfare: The Encyclopedia of Twentieth Century Conflict*, Frank Cass, London.

Friedman, M. (1980), *Free to Choose*, Harcourt Brace Jovanovich, New York.

Friedman, M. (1982), *Capitalism and Freedom*, University of Chicago Press, Chicago.

Friedman, T.L. (2000), *The Lexus and the Olive Tree* (2nd ed.), Farrar, Straus & Giroux, New York.

Glines, C.V. (1968), *The Saga of the Airmail*, Van Nostrand, Princeton, NJ.

Graham, B. (1995), *Geography and Air Transport*, John Wiley and Sons, New York.

Groenewedge, A.D. (1996), *Compendium of International Civil Aviation*, International Aviation Development Corporation, Quebec.

Gross, P.M. (2002), "Air France" in Tracy Irons-Georges (ed.) *Encyclopedia of Flight*, Salem Press, Pasadena, CA, pp. 52–54.

Hayek, F.A. (1960), *The Constitution of Liberty*, University of Chicago Press, Chicago.

Hayek, F.A. (1980), *Individualism and Economic Order*, University of Chicago Press, Chicago.

Hayak, F.A. (1994), *Hayek on Hayek: An Autobiographical Dialogue*, University of Chicago Press, Chicago.

Hosking, G.A. (1985), *A History of the Soviet Union*, Fontana Press, London.

Kane, R.M. (1998), *Air Transportation* (13th ed.), Kendall/Hunt Publishing, Dubuque, IA.

Kennedy, P.M. (1981), *The Realities Behind Diplomacy*, Allen & Unwin, London.

Landes, D. (1969), *The Unbound Prometheus: Technological Change and Industrial Development in Western Europe from 1970 to the Present*, Cambridge University Press, Cambridge.

Marriott, L. (1998), *British Airways Book* (2nd ed.), Plymouth Publishing, Plymouth, MI.

Matloff, M. (1959), *Strategic Planning for Coalition Warfare, 1943–1944*, US Government Printing Office, Washington, DC.

Nove, A. (1969), *An Economic History of the USSR*, Penguin Group, Harmondsworth.

Overy, R.J. (1980), *The Air War, 1939–1945*, Potomac Books Inc., New York.

Ricossa, A. (1972), "Italy 1920-1970" in C. Cipolla (ed.), *The Fontuna Economic History of Europe*, Barnes & Noble, London.

Sinha, D. (2001), *Deregulation and Liberalization of the Airline Industry: Asia, Europe, North America, and Oceania*, Ashgate, Aldershot.

Sochor, E. (1991), *The Politics of International Aviation*, University of Iowa Press, Iowa City.

Wirth, D. and Young, J. (1980), *Ballooning: The Complete Guide to Riding the Winds*, Random House: New York.

Wright, G. (1968), *The Ordeal of Total War, 1939–1945*, Harper & Row, New York.

Yergin, D. and Stanislaw, J. (2002), *The Commanding Heights: The Battle for the World Economy*, Simon & Schuster, New York.

Chapter 5
Chicago—The Windy City

Learning Objectives

After reading this chapter, you should have a good understanding of:
- LO1: the four proposals considered at the Chicago Conference.
- LO2: the meaning of Open Skies as used by President Roosevelt and its implication for international aviation.
- LO3: the freedoms of the air – their application and limits.
- LO4: how the British All-Red Line ploy helped to bolster their position on international regulation.
- LO5: the economic and political interests that played out in Chicago among nations and airlines.

Key Terms, Concepts, and People

Dominion and Empire Conference	Chicago Conference	Technical freedoms
ICAO	All-Red Line	IATA
Committee I	Bilateral	Bermuda Agreement

Crosswinds

The wind can be a friend or a foe to the air traveler. A strong headwind can add time to your journey. A strong tailwind can help speed you along your way. Crosswinds, however, are unpredictable, often dangerous. At the very least they can make it very difficult to maintain your planned course and reach your planned destination. Chicago has long been called the Windy City and anyone who has ever looked out over the lakefront on a fall day can understand the nickname. It is perhaps fitting that Chicago was the chosen site for the most famous aviation conference in history. The events that happened and didn't happen at Chicago still echo in the events of today. To understand the forces that created the international aviation landscape of today, you must understand Chicago.

Even as US President Franklin D. Roosevelt and British Prime Minister Winston Churchill were meeting in Quebec to plan the cross-channel invasion of Normandy and turn the tide of war in Europe, the topic of a general meeting to discuss the future of air transportation came up as an issue. US politicians had already begun to explore the nature of a post-war aviation system. Henry

Wallace, the US Vice-president, proposed a global network of air routes and international airports under the envisioned United Nations (UN) while Clare Boothe Luce denounced this notion as "globaloney" in her maiden address to the US Congress. Edward Warner, the vice-chairman of the US CAB, envisioned air navigation agreements that would prevent the "return to the evil days when air transportation was regarded with caution and suspicion" (Sochor, 1990: 4). The British had also been considering the issue of aviation. At the 1943 Dominion and Empire Conference and a May 1944 meeting of the Dominion ministers there were discussions about creating some system of reciprocal rights. In a White Paper shortly after the 1944 meeting, the British proposed an international regulatory body with the power to decide on routes, frequencies, and fares. Clearly, the crosswinds would be blowing in Chicago.

Setting the Table

When the delegates arrived in Chicago on November 1, 1944, they found four proposals awaiting them on shaping the international environment. The opening message of President Roosevelt called on the delegates "not to dally with the thought of creating great blocs of closed air, thereby tracing in the sky the conditions of future war" (Sochor, 1990: 8). His call was for an open sky that could be exploited for the good of all mankind. Not surprisingly, the US proposal called for a system of complete market access without restrictions on routes, frequency, and fares. The British who rightly feared that the large, undamaged aviation infrastructure, commercial fleet, and manufacturing capacity of the US would dominate the war-ravaged systems of Europe saw the US proposal as self-interest masquerading as philosophical principle. The British plan reiterated their earlier White Paper calling for a tightly regulated system governed by an independent international regulatory body. The Canadian proposal attempted to offer a compromise between the US and British positions by creating a multilateral regulatory body that would allow for limited competition within the system. The last proposal, jointly sponsored by the Australians and New Zealanders, called for the international ownership and management of all international air service. Committee I of the Chicago Conference would clearly have its work cut out for it.

Meanwhile, the other three committees worked on the technical issues of the conference eventually completing work on the Interim Agreement on International Aviation, the Chicago Convention on International Civil Aviation, and the International Air Transport Agreement. The first treaty or convention established a temporary organization called the Provisional International Civil Aviation Organization to operate until the permanent organization created in the second document came into effect, the International Civil Aviation Organization (ICAO). The third convention is also known as the Five Freedoms Agreement (see Table 5.1, including the subsequently added sixth, seventh, and eighth freedoms). The first two freedoms are known as technical freedoms. The remaining freedoms deal with the commercial rights of aviation to pick up and discharge passengers and cargo to, from, and through foreign nations.

While the technical committees were concluding their work, Committee I was deadlocked. Despite several exchanges between Roosevelt and Churchill on the issues facing the Committee and a series of private meetings between the key players, there would be no compromise on the basic positions of either the US or the UK. The US might have the planes to fly, but without landing rights they had only half the resources needed for a viable international system of carriers. They needed landing rights and the UK had potential landing sites galore. In fact, as the conference was opening the British publicized a "plan" for creating an all-Commonwealth airline called the All-Red Line after the cartographic practice of showing Commonwealth nations in red. This All-Red Line would be given exclusive rights to land on Commonwealth territory. In a world in which the sun never set on the British flag, the All-Red Line was a reminder that the British did not come to the table empty-handed nor would they allow a system of international aviation to be put in place that created serious disadvantages for Britain and other small aviation nations.

Table 5.1   The freedoms of the air

Freedom	Description
First	The right to fly over the territory of a Contracting State without landing
Second	The right to land on the territory of a Contracting State for non-commercial purposes
Third	The right to transport passengers, cargo, and mail from the State of registration of the aircraft to another State and set them down there
Fourth	The right to take on board passengers, cargo, and mail in another Contracting State and to transport them to the State of registration of the aircraft
Fifth	The right to transport passengers, cargo, and mail between two other States as a continuation of, or as a preliminary to, the operation of the third or fourth freedoms
Sixth	The right to take on board passengers, cargo, and mail in one State and to transport them to a third State after a stopover in the aircraft's State of registration and vice versa
Seventh	The right to transport passengers, cargo, and mail between two other States on a service which does not touch the aircraft's country of registration
Eighth	The right to transport passengers, cargo, and mail within the territory of a State which is not the aircraft's State of registration (full cabotage)
Ninth	The right to interrupt a service

Just as it began to seem that nothing would be achieved in Committee I, the Netherlands broke the deadlock by suggesting that the British might join in an agreement on the first two freedoms of overflight and technical landing or stopover. The Netherlands then moved immediately to guarantee these rights as part of a multilateral agreement. The British agreed to this proposal which became the fourth treaty or convention to come out of the Chicago Conference. The International Air Services Transit Agreement would eventually be signed by all of the participants and go into effect on June 30, 1945. It is now recognized by over 100 nations. The International Air Transport Agreement which contained the remaining commercial freedoms would be signed by 19 of the participants, but nine, including the US, would subsequently denounce it. The remaining nations would not endorse it, primarily for its fifth freedom condition. One final document would come out of the Convention. This form, the Bilateral Agreement for the Exchange of Routes and Services, would be adopted as part of the Final Act and serve to move the international aviation community forward in the absence of a broader, multilateral agreement on commercial aviation rights. The gavel fell on December 7, 1944 ending the Chicago Conference and the governmental delegates went home with their treaties and the bilateral form to decide on the next steps in the process of creating an international aviation system.

Not all of the individuals present in Chicago, however, went home immediately. Airline executives who had attended the conference as delegates or advisors to their national governments had quickly realized the implications of a failure by the conference to reach a broad multilateral agreement on commercial rights and fares. Showing admirable restraint, they waited until December 6 to begin discussions on the formation of a trade association for international carriers. This new association would be their voice in the international system and they hoped to be able to fill the void left in the commercial aviation system by the events in Chicago. The newly formed IATA called its first meeting in Havana in April 1945.

A Bilateral World

Without a multilateral agreement, it was left to the national governments of the world to begin the process of negotiating bilateral air service agreements. In fact, the US had opened bilateral talks with the Dominions, Chinese, and Russians even before the conference began and quickly returned to this process after the conference, signing a bilateral agreement with Spain on December 2, 1944, Denmark and Sweden on December 16, 1944, Iceland on January 27, 1945, Canada on February 7, 1945, and Switzerland and Norway on July 13, 1945 (Kane, 1999). However, it was not until 1946 that the US and the UK were ready to sit down again and discuss the aviation issues that had not been resolved at Chicago. The agreement that emerged from these talks would be called the Bermuda Agreement and would, by agreement of both governments, become the model for all of the future agreements either side would negotiate. This form would henceforth replace the Chicago form as the world's standard Air Service Agreement.

The US agreed to accept the British position on fares and rates which allowed the airlines to mutually set these matters subject to prior approval by both governments. The UK agreed to allow airlines to unilaterally set their own capacity, that is, aircraft size and service frequency subject to subsequent review for unfair practices. Other key features of the agreement included designated (or named) routes and multiple carrier designation. In total, "the Agreement clearly favored the US which then accounted for about 60 percent of the world's passenger airline traffic and which had the largest and most efficient international airlines" (Toh, 1998: 61). This may reflect the fact that the British were also in negotiations with the US over a US$3.75 billion loan to rebuild its economy and thus had to negotiate from a position of some weakness (Sochor, 1990). As a concession to the British, the US did agree to allow the IATA to set international fares and cargo rates. They also decided to limit their pursuit of fifth freedom rights which are seen in aviation circles as placing a foreign carrier in too close a competition for domestic traffic with a state's national carriers (Toh, 1998). By 1947, over 100 bilaterals had been signed around the world and the fare-setting power of IATA accepted in subsequent aviation accords (Sochor, 1990).

The last bilateral between the US and UK illustrates the key points of bilaterals as well and the specific and restrictive nature of such air service agreements (Air Transport Association of America, 2001). Under the portion of the air service agreement (Table 5.2) entitled United Kingdom Routes: Atlantic combination air service is the following list:

Table 5.2   US–UK bilateral agreement

(A) UK Gateway Points	(B) Intermediate Points	(C) Points in US Territory
London, Manchester, Prestwisk/Glascow, Belfast. Any UK Point, excluding London.	Points in Luxembourg The Netherlands, and The Republic of Ireland. Points in Belgium, France and Germany	Atlanta, Boston, Charlotte, Chicago, Dallas/Ft Worth, Denver, Detroit, Houston, Las Vegas, Los Angeles, Miami, New Orleans, New York, Orlando, Phoenix Philadelphia, San Diego San Francisco, Seattle, Tampa, Washington/Baltimore. Up to two points to be selected and notified to the United States.

In addition to the Atlantic combination air service, lists are provided of named routes for Atlantic regional combination air service, Atlantic combination air service via Canada, Atlantic combination air service beyond Mexico City,

Atlantic combination air service beyond to South America, Atlantic combination service beyond to Japan, Atlantic combination service beyond to the Pacific, Atlantic combination service beyond to Australia, Pacific combination service, Pacific combination service via Tarawa, Bermuda combination service, Caribbean combination service, Caribbean combination air service, Atlantic all-cargo service, Atlantic all-cargo service beyond to South America, Atlantic all-cargo service beyond to Mexico, Pacific all-cargo services, Pacific all-cargo service via Tarawa, Bermuda all-cargo service, Caribbean all-cargo service, and Caribbean all-cargo air service.

Conversely, the principle of reciprocity demands that similar lists of named routes be included for US passenger and all-cargo service (Table 5.3). The following is the list of US Routes: Atlantic combination service.

Table 5.3   US-UK bilateral agreement

(A) US Gateway Points	(B) Intermediate Points	(C) Points in UK Territory	(D) Points Beyond
Anchorage, Atlanta, Boston, Charlotte, Chicago, Cincinnati, Dallas/Ft Worth, Detroit, Houston, Los Angeles, Miami, Minneapolis/St.Paul, Newark, New York, Philadelphia, Pittsburgh, Raleigh–Durham, San Francisco, Seattle, St. Louis, Washington/ Baltimore. Up to three points to be selected and notified to the United Kingdom.	Shannon	London Prestwick/ Glasgow. Any UK point exc.	Berlin, Frankfurt, Hamburg, Munich, Oslo, one point in Western Europe to be selected

These excerpts demonstrate the reciprocal exchange of named routes as well as the application of fifth freedom (beyond) rights between the US and the UK. By the old bilateral standards, the US–UK agreement was considered liberal in that it did not include capacity (aircraft size and route frequency) restrictions.

As an example of further restrictions, the US–Japanese bilateral distinguished between incumbent carriers which were provided for by the 1952 agreement (Northwest and United Airlines for the US and Japan Airlines and All Nippon Airways (ANA) for the Japanese) and non-incumbent carriers (Delta Air Lines, American Airlines, and Continental Airlines) in naming routes. It also included sections on restricted frequency routes. In this case, non-incumbent airlines are permitted to operate up to 42 additional aggregate weekly round-trip frequencies on the following city-pair markets: Tokyo–New York, Tokyo–Chicago, Tokyo–San Francisco, Tokyo–Los Angeles, Tokyo–Honolulu, Tokyo–Guam/Saipan, Osaka–Los Angeles, Osaka–Los Angeles, Osaka–Honolulu, Nagoya–Honolulu, and Fukuoka–Honolulu (Air Transport Association of America, 2001).

Looking Back

Looking back on the Chicago Conference, it is clear that no compromise could have bridged the gap between the basic US and British positions. In the tug-of-war between free markets and political reality, political reality was the victor. Ironically, the lever that had allowed the British to hold off the US push for Open Skies would not long survive the end of World War II. The British Empire would be replaced by a much looser Commonwealth of independent nations with the right to determine the disposition of their own landing rights. Unfortunately, the system created by the major aeronautical players to meet their needs would not give these newly emerging nations a great deal of clout in the international system even if it did recognize their sovereign rights to control their own airspace.

The US for all of its philosophical preaching on Open Skies was not willing to grant more open access to the US market as it proved later when it renounced the International Air Transport Agreement rather than grant foreign carriers greater fifth freedom rights through the US (Sochor, 1990). This was seen as an admission by the US that there could be no stable commercial aviation system without reciprocity between countries (De la Rochere, 1971). While the US was able to use its power and prestige following the war to sign a number of bilateral advantageous to the US carriers, it did so by giving up the right to allow the markets to determine price. The US would again be accused of abandoning philosophical principle in favor of commercial and political reality when it began to take up the cause of Open Skies again after airline deregulation (Chapter 5). Frederik Sorensen of the European Commission Air Transport Policy Unit has said that "[o]pen skies is an American term which, as we see it, is synonymous with a free for all system depending on the good behavior of air carriers and only partial opening of the market" (1998: 125).

Looking Ahead

Out of the ashes of the post-World War II world, the phoenix of international aviation took off. If it did not fly as high as some would have liked or take the paths its creators envisioned, it did at least fly. The winds blowing out of Chicago did not make its flight either smooth or steady, but it has remained aloft. The next decades would see less dramatic but no less significant progress in the world of international aviation. The two international organizations born in Chicago, ICAO and IATA, would build on the framework laid out there (Chapter 6) only to have many of the structures set in place challenged by deregulation of the US airline industry (Chapter 8) and liberalization in European and Asian markets (Chapter 9). The events of the past would come back to challenge the future and demand that the world community grapple with them again.

The preamble to the Convention on International Civil Aviation laid out the goals of the Chicago Convention as follows:

> WHEREAS the future development of international civil aviation can greatly help to create and preserve friendship and understanding among nations and peoples of the world, yet its abuse can become a threat to the general security; and
>
> WHEREAS it is desirable to avoid friction and to promote that cooperation between nations and peoples upon which peace of the world depends;
>
> THEREFORE, the undersigned governments having agreed on certain principles and arrangements in order that international civil aviation may be developed in a safe and orderly manner and that international air transport services may be established on the basis of equality of opportunity and operated soundly and economically (Reprinted in Sochor, 1990).

This vision of international aviation as a global force for peace was perhaps utopian, but air travel has certainly brought the world closer together in time and space. Unfortunately, the events of 9/11 temporarily replaced this unifying vision with a grimmer reality. This reality too is overstated. An airplane was merely the tool used to perpetrate the destruction of 9/11. Like any tool, it serves the wishes of its user; the terrorists used their tool to drive the world apart. Others continue to use it to bring the world together. While the vision of ICAO has proven elusive, the goals have also presented their own challenges. As we will see in the next chapter ICAO would work hard to create a safe, orderly, and economical air transportation system and, by-and-large, they will achieve this goal.

The difficulty lies in the basis for this system—equality of opportunity. Free markets guarantee all the right to participate. They do not guarantee that the opportunities are equal or that the outcomes are equitable. In fact, free markets are about access not success and neither of these commodities is equally distributed. In a free market the opportunities of large, wealthy nations are greater than small, poor nations. The chances of success are also greater for the large and wealthy. Equity is about fairness, impartiality, and justice. Free markets are about competition and winner-take-all. Governments intervene in the market to provide opportunity and equity. All governments intervene to some extent. The level of intervention or regulation has been a subject for debate in economic and policy circles since Adam Smith. The push for liberalization in the airline industry would raise these issues once again for policy makers and the people they represent.

Questions

1. Analyze and assess the interests of the US and the UK in Chicago.
2. What were the four proposals for international regulation discussed in Chicago?
3. Imagine a world in which the Australian–New Zealand proposal had come to pass. How would it look?
4. Outline the freedoms of the air including origin, destination, and any intermediate points.
5. Discuss the achievements of the Chicago Convention.
6. Identify the defining features of a bilateral air service agreement.

References

Air Transport Association of America (2001), "Air Service Rights in U.S. International Air Transport Agreements: A Compilation of Scheduled and Charter Service Rights Contained in U.S. Bilateral Aviation Agreements," Washington, D.C.

De la Rochere, J.D. (1971), *La Politique des Etats-Unis en matiere d'aviation civile*, Libraire de Droit et de Jurisprudence, Paris, pp. 30–36.

Kane, R.M. (1999), *Air Transportation* (13th ed.), Kendall/Hunt Publishing, Dubuque, IA.

Sochor, E. (1990), *The Politics of International Aviation*, University of Iowa Press, Iowa City, IA.

Sorensen, F. (1998), "Open Skies in Europe," in US Department of Transportation (ed.), *FAA Commercial Aviation Forecast Conference Proceedings: Overcoming Barriers to World Competition and Growth*, Office of Aviation Policy and Plans, Washington, DC, pp. 125–132.

Toh, R.S. (1998), "Toward an international open skies regime: dvances, impediments, and impacts," *Journal of Air Transportation World Wide*, vol. 3 (1), pp. 61–70.

Chapter 6

Shaping the World

Learning Objectives

After reading this chapter, you should have a good understanding of:
- LO1: the founding of ICAO and IATA.
- LO2: the structure and policy-making process at ICAO.
- LO3: how IATA contributed to the early success of international aviation.
- LO4: the issues and outcomes of IATA Traffic Conferences.
- LO5: the economic and political interests that drive these two international organizations.

Key Terms, Concepts, and People

ICAO	IATA	ICAO Council
Warsaw Convention	SARPs & PANS	Traffic Conferences
Bermuda Agreement	Annexes	

First Chicago then the World

The interim Agreement on International Civil Aviation established the framework for a Provisional International Civil Aviation Organization (PICAO), which functioned until 1947 when the required number of countries ratified the agreement to create a permanent organization. Over the coming years the International Civil Aviation Organization (ICAO) would work to develop the standards and practices followed by much of the world's aviation community. They would do so amidst the push and pull of the Cold War, the rapid development of aviation technology, and the limited funding often available to organizations associated with the UN. Like the UN, their actions could not be enforced on the world community, but could only be considered advisory. ICAO would thus struggle like the UN to achieve a consensus that would allow it to foster and develop the aviation system while balancing the needs of a diverse and fractious constituency.

The other organization born in Chicago, IATA, would receive recognition of its role at the 1946 bilateral talks between the US and UK. It would not suffer from the kind of tension that divided ICAO. Its members, international airlines, would set about the task of setting the fares, dividing the world's international routes, establishing the standards for interlining (transfer between carriers), and devising the methods of revenue sharing that would govern the international aviation system until these powers were slowly eroded by domestic air transport deregulation and international liberalization (Chapter 8). ICAO and IATA would work together on many issues related to safe air transport operation, standardization of documentation and procedures, and the development of legal agenda such as the Warsaw Convention on airline liability. Together these two organizations would shape the post-World War II international aviation system.

Setting the Standards

ICAO is composed of appointed representatives of all nations interested in international civil aviation (now totaling 188 Contracting States). ICAO is governed by a sovereign body, the Assembly, which meets at least once every three years. Each nation represented has one vote on key matters and majority rules. The governing body of ICAO is the Council. The Council is elected from the Assembly for a three-year term and is composed of 36 members elected from three categories of ICAO general members. The first category is states of chief importance to air transport. The second is states that make the largest contribution to the provision of air navigation facilities. The final category is composed of states designated to insure that all of the regions of the globe are represented. Table 6.1 provides a list of the nation's currently serving on the Council.

Table 6.1   ICAO Council Membership—2013

Argentina	Malaysia
Australia	Mexico
Bolivia	Nicaragua
Brazil	Nigeria
Burkina Faso	Norway
Cameroon	Poland
Canada	Portugal
Chile	Republic of Korea
China	Russian Federation
Dominican Republic	Saudi Arabia
Egypt	Singapore
France	South Africa
Germany	Spain
India	United Arab Emirates
Italy	United Kingdom
Japan	United Republic of Tanzania
Kenya	United States
Libya	Venezuela

These nations maintain a permanent presence at ICAO's headquarters in Montreal, Canada where they are responsible for the day-to-day operations of the organization. The Council adopts the Standards and Recommended Practices (SARPs) and approves the Procedures of Air Navigation Services (PANS) that are the heart of the work of ICAO. Assisting the Council are the Air Navigation Commission which is responsible for technical matters, the Air Transport Committee responsible for economic matters, the Committee on Joint Support of Air Navigation Services, and the Finance Committee. Proposals to amend or add new SARPs come from ICAO-sponsored international meetings, deliberative bodies within the organization itself, the Secretariat, the UN, or other interested international organizations. ICAO works closely with such organizations as the World Meteorological Organization, the International Telecommunications Union, the Universal Postal Union, the World Health Organization, the International Maritime Organization (all UN affiliated), the International Air Transport Association, the Airports Council International, the International Federation of Air Line Pilots, and the International Council of Aircraft Owner and Pilots Association (all non-governmental organizations).

Once an issue is brought to ICAO for consideration, it is referred to the Air Navigation Commission, which is composed of 15 persons who have "suitable qualifications and experience in the science and practice of aeronautics." These individuals are nominated by Contracting States and appointed by the Council. The Commission is assisted by the Air Navigation Bureau and panels and working groups nominated by Contracting States and appointed by the Commission. These individuals serve based on their personal expertise and not as representatives of any Contracting State. Once the Commission submits a SARP to the Council, a two-thirds vote of its members is required for adoption. If a majority of the Contracting States do not disapprove it, the SARP becomes effective on the established date. SARPs are considered binding, although States that cannot comply can file a "difference" that is published by ICAO in Supplements to Annexes. This process takes roughly five to seven years to reach completion which means that the work of ICAO progresses slowly. PANS are developed in a similar way, however, they are not binding and no difference needs to be filed. Table 6.2 lists the annexes and areas, which are covered by ICAO.

Other activities of ICAO include joint financing of navigation service on the high seas or in areas were no nation can be charged with the responsibility. Iceland and Greenland are examples of the latter. Considering that their own aircraft represent less than 3 percent of the trans-Atlantic traffic, the burden for navigational services is shared by other nations. The Legal Affairs Committee prepares drafts for key international conferences related to aviation such as the Geneva (1948) and Rome (1952) Conventions. ICAO's Technical Co-operation Programme works with the United Nations Development Programme (UNDP) on projects aimed at developing the aviation system of developing nations. The Trainair programme provides assistance to national and regional civil aviation training institutes. Finally, ICAO provides expert services such as site selection

Table 6.2   Annexes to the ICAO Convention

Annex	Subject
1	Personnel licensing
2	Rules of the air
3	Meteorological service
4	Aeronautical charts
5	Units of measurement to be used operations
6	Operation of aircraft
7	Aircraft nationality and registration
8	Airworthiness of aircraft
9	Facilitation
10	Aeronautical telecommunications
11	Air traffic service
12	Search and rescue
13	Aircraft accident investigation
14	Aerodromes
15	Aeronautical information service
16	Environmental protection
17	Security
18	Safe transport of dangerous goods

and design of airstrips and design of air traffic control systems. The magnitude of work of ICAO seems overwhelming, particularly in light of their limited funding. Much of their efforts depend on the support, both technical and monetary, that comes from the Contracting States (ICAO, 2002).

The key to understanding ICAO is in realizing that like the UN in general it has *no* independent enforcement power; it cannot make it members implement any of its standards. Its main bodies may act to support or condemn certain actions by members that relate to aviation, but this is an exercise in public relations and free expression. When or if a vote is taken on the issue of SARPs or PANS, it is the perfunctory end to months or years of consensus building at ICAO. If consensus is not initially achieved on certain issues, then all parties revise, rework, or reframe the issue until consensus is obtained. It is a painstaking process, but it has and is producing some very positive results. After years of debate, ICAO established in January 1999 the Universal Safety Oversight Program which "consists of regular, mandatory, systematic, and harmonized safety audits carried out by ICAO in all 187 countries ... it has proven effective in identifying and correcting safety deficiencies in areas of personnel licensing and airworthiness and operations of aircraft" (ICAO, 2002: 1). The program has been expanded to include air traffic service and airports. ICAO has been requested to help in the resolution of deficiencies through educational activities, funding and technical coordination, and the creation of a Quality Assistance Function. Given the politically sensitive nature of safety for governments and airlines, the Safety Oversight Program was a great victory for ICAO in their efforts to further advance the cause of international aviation. Most recently, ICAO has been directed by its Assembly to establish a Universal Security Oversight Audit Programme that would assess the implementation of ICAO security-related SARPs (ICAO, 2002).

Setting the Fares

Under the 1945 Articles of Association, the aims of IATA are:

> To promote safe, regular, and economical air transportation for the benefit of the peoples of the world, to foster air commerce, and to study the problems connected therewith;

> To provide means for collaboration among the air transport enterprise engaged directly or indirectly in international air transport service;

> To cooperate with the newly created International Civil Aviation Organization and other international organizations (IATA, 2002).

In the early years, IATA worked on such issues as the Multilateral Interline Traffic Agreements, Passenger and Cargo Services Conference Resolutions, and Passenger and Cargo Agency Agreements & Sales Agency Rules. The Interline Agreements involved insuring acceptance of other carrier's tickets and waybills. The Conference Resolutions prescribed standard formats and specifications for tickets and waybills. The Agency Agreements governed the relationships between IATA airlines and their accredited agents. A Clearing House was also established in 1947 to handle debt settlements between carriers largely arising from interlining.

It was the role of IATA's Traffic Conferences that would eventually come under intense scrutiny by a liberalizing world air transportation system. Under the Bermuda Agreement of 1946, IATA was delegated the role of establishing fares and rates subject to government approval. According to IATA, the goal of the system was to establish "coherent fares and rates patterns." Such a system would avoid "inconsistencies between tariffs affecting neighboring countries— and thereby avoiding traffic diversion" (IATA, 1996). In effect, there was a set fare for any given international route that any IATA member was expected to charge. If there continued to be an imbalance in the revenues earned by the designated carriers on such a route, then a revenue-sharing or pooling agreement could be worked out to equalize the revenues of both sides (Taneja, 1988). There were intermittent efforts in ICAO to question the tariff (fare) setting role of IATA, but during the last such effort ICAO concluded that "at present, there is no justification for ICAO to undertake specific studies and other economic work on the subject of airline tariffs" (Sochor, 1990: 17).

Following the events discussed in Chapter 8, IATA would be forced to reconsider its role in fare setting. It did so first by establishing a "two-tier" system. Under this system, the IATA Trade Association became responsible for technical, legal, financial, and traffic services. The Tariff Coordination became responsible for fares and rates. An airline could participate in the Trade Association without participating in the Tariff Coordination activities. Over time, IATA has placed increasing emphasis on the trade association activities and come to derive much of its funding from the educational and product marketing activities of the Association. For all intents and purposes, the new IATA does not engage in fare or rate setting but allows these activities to be the domain of the airlines themselves.

A New Day Dawning

IATA and ICAO would emerge from the Chicago Convention to shape the aviation system that would develop after World War II. This system would preside over an aviation era in which air travel would come to be seen as a safe and reliable mode of transportation, but it would not yet be seen as a transportation mode for the masses; achieving this goal would require fares to fall to levels that the "common man" could afford. This vision of air travel was the goal of deregulation. Markets and competition, not governments, would determine fares, destinations, and service levels (Chapter 8). First, the manufacturers and the airlines that they supplied would have to get back to the business of civil aviation and establish the industry that would be turned on its head in the late 1970s. Few people in the international aviation system would realize that the "end of an era" was coming, but the passage in the US of the Airline Deregulation Act of 1978 would be such a watershed. For the cozy system of routes and fares set up by IATA, it would mean radical change. For ICAO, this new era would mean more issues of safety and security would be added to their already full plate of issues.

Questions

1. How is ICAO structured and funded?
2. How are SARPs developed?
3. What role does ICAO play in developed and developing nations?
4. Has ICAO fulfilled the vision of its founders? Why or why not?
5. Who controls the bulk of the work and agenda at ICAO?
6. What was the effect of IATA's Traffic Conferences on fares and competition?
7. Assess the role of IATA in aviation. Whose interests does it serve?

References

International Air Transport Association (IATA) (1996), "Early days," electronic edition, retrieved online from www.iata.org.

International Air Transport Association (IATA) (2002), Early Days, electronic edition, retrieved online March 5, 2007 from http://www.iata.org/about/Pages/history_2.aspx.

International Civil Aviation Organization (ICAO) (2002), "Meeting caps most productive triennium in recent ICAO history," News Release, October 9, pp. 1–4.

Sochor, E. (1990), *The Politics of International Aviation*, University of Iowa Press, Iowa City, IA.

Taneja, N.K. (1988), *The International Airline Industry*, Lexington Books, Lexington, KY.

Toh, R.S. (1998), "Towards an international open skies regime: advances, impediments, and impacts," *Journal of Air Transportation World Wide*, vol. 3 (1), pp. 61–70.

PART II
The Industry Grows Up
(1950–2008)

Chapter 7
The View from Space

Learning Objectives

After reading this chapter, you should have a good understanding of:
- LO1: the early history of the US and USSR space programs.
- LO2: the history and extent of satellite activity, including early commercial launches.
- LO3: the unmanned exploration activity of various countries.
- LO4: the current space station activity.

Key terms, Concepts, and People

V2 rockets	Werner von Braun	
Yuri Gagarin	Neil Armstrong	Soyuz
Mercury	Apollo	Sputnik

Science Fiction

It is amazing to remember that Jules Verne published *From the Earth to the Moon* in 1865 while the US was still struggling to overcome the Civil War, but Verne was but the first of many authors in what would become known as the field of science fiction to imagine trips to the Moon, Mars, or other distant places in the dark of space. Even as aviators like as Jorge Chavez were striving to set new altitude records by flying over the Alps, a feat he accomplished on September 8, 1910 reaching a height of 1,647 meters, space was still the stuff of science fiction for much of the rest of the world (Gagliardi, 2009). Still, this did not stop a young man like Robert H. Goddard from experimenting with rockets and the fuel to propel them. On March 26, 1926 these experiments paid off and he is credited with the first launch of a liquid-fuel rocket. This event was not well known at the time and did not fire the imagination or the fears of the world as much as the 1957 launch of Sputnik. Weighing 183 lbs and only the size of a basketball, this little satellite "fired the shot" that started the Great Space Race (Bellis, 2013).

Racing for Space

Neil Armstrong would sum up the space race in his introduction to the 1994 book *Moon Shot: The Inside Story of America's Race to the Moon* by fellow astronauts Alan Sheppard and Deke Slayton as an effort to demonstrate ideological superiority through technological leadership. The effort, he noted, would consume enormous resources, enjoy great successes, suffer tragic failures, and end with the Cold War enemies joining forces to continue exploring space. While Armstrong saw the race ending with the Cold War, the truth is that Americans claimed victory in the race in 1969 when Armstrong set foot on the Moon and the human spaceflight program in the US has been largely adrift since achieving this goal (Coppinger, 2010). However, this is a question to explore later in the chapter. For now, it is enough to relive the excitement of the first steps into space.

If Sputnik was the public event that started the race, then the hidden beginning was in Germany at the end of World War II when wartime allies the US and the Union of Soviet Socialist Republics (USSR) were quietly appropriating scientists from the German V2 project (Boyne, 2007). The US was fortunate to accept the surrender of Dr Werner von Braun and 117 of his key V2 team near the Bavarian ski resort of Oberjoch in May of 1945; however, they would languish in Fort Bliss, Texas until 1950 when the US Army confirmed Soviet rocket activity. They were then moved to Huntsville, Alabama to begin work on the Redstone rocket, named after the arsenal there. Meanwhile in Central Asia at a site that would become the world's first spaceport (Baikonur Cosmodrome), the Russians were working hard on the R-7 (Shepard and Slayton, 1994). The initial goal was the development of Inter-Continental Ballistic Missiles (ICBM), a race the Russians won in 1957 with the launch of the R-7, a rocket four times more powerful than the Redstone. It was certainly powerful enough to launch Sputnik I and Sputnik 2 31 days later. The US response would be the Atlas rocket which would launch America's first satellite, Explorer I, in 1958 (Godwin, 2006).

For the sake of simplifying our journey, we will divide the discussion of space into the following sections: manned spaceflight, space stations, orbital satellites, and exploration. Each of these areas would witness great progress over the decades, but nothing would evoke the excitement of humanity as much as the thought of manned exploration.

Manned Spaceflight

Table 7.1 outlines the key events in the race for space with both its accomplishments and its tragedies, but the men who would be part of the race were already breaking speed and altitude records as military test pilots for the US and USSR. The manned space effort of the US would officially begin with the April 9, 1959 announcement of the selection of the first seven astronauts for the Mercury program—Malcolm Scott Carpenter, Leroy Gordon Cooper, John Herschel Glenn, Virgil Grissom, Walter M Schirra, Alan Shepard, and Deke Slayton. Their story was chronicled in the

Table 7.1   Key events in the race for space

Date	Event
March 26, 1926	Robert H Goddard launches the first liquid-fuel rocket
June 13, 1940	The first V-2 rocket launched from Peenemunde, Germany
October 4, 1957	The USSR launches the first manmade satellite named Sputnik
January 31, 1958	The US successfully launches its first satellite, Explorer I
August 27, 1958	The USSR launches Sputnik 3 with two dogs aboard
October 1, 1958	NASA is established to take over from NACA
May 28, 1959	The US launches monkeys Able and Baker into space
April 12, 1961	Russian Yuri Gagarin becomes the first man in space
May 5, 1961	Alan Sheppard Jr becomes first American in space
May 25, 1961	President John F. Kennedy calls for the US to put a man on the Moon
February 20, 1962	John Glenn becomes the first American to orbit the Earth
June 16, 1963	Russian Valentia Tereshkova becomes the first woman in space
March 18, 1965	Russian Aleksei Leonov performs the first spacewalk.
February 3, 1966	Russian probe Luna 9 becomes the first manmade object to land on the Moon
January 27, 1967	US–USSR sign a treaty banning nuclear weapons in space Apollo I cabin fire kills astronauts Grissom, White, and Chaffee
April 23, 1967	Cosmonaut Vladimir Komarov killed in Soyuz 1after failure during orbit led to crash landing
July 20 1969	Neil Armstrong and Buzz Aldrin make the first successful manned landing on the Moon
November 1969	Apollo 12 lands on the Moon
April 1970	Apollo 13 launches for the Moon but a liquid oxygen tank prevents landing
February 1971	Apollo 14 lands on the Moon
July 1971	Apollo 15 lands on the Moon
April 1972	Apollo 16 lands on the Moon
December 1972	Apollo 17 is the last manned spacecraft to land on the Moon

book (and movie) *The Right Stuff.* The book first appeared in 1979 with the movie appearing in 1983 (Wolfe, 2001). Of the seven, Alan Sheppard would be selected to become the first American in space (May 1961). He would be followed in July 1961 by Virgil Grissom. Of course, neither could claim to be the first man in space. That honor would go to the Russian Yuri Gagarin who would launch in April 1961. The Russians had scored another first in the Great Race. Two days after Gagarin's flight, US President John F. Kennedy would call together a group to discuss the US response. This response would be clear 20 days after Shepard's first flight when President Kennedy would tell Congress that the US was committed to landing a man on the Moon before the end of the decade (Shepard and Slayton, 1994). The finish line had now been set and the racers now had their sights set on a clear goal.

Of course, there was a long way to go from the first man in space to a landing on the Moon. For the US, the single-man Mercury program would give way to the Gemini program which launched its first two Americans, Virgil Grissom and John Young, into space in March 1965 in Gemini 3. While the Mercury program involved a largely automated craft, the Gemini was designed to maneuver in space and would be the testing ground for the spacewalk (Gemini 4 and 9) and docking between two orbital craft (Gemini 6–8).

For the US, the next step would now be the Apollo manned lunar landing program. The program began with tragedy as the crew of the Apollo I, Virgil Grissom, Edward H. White, and Roger B. Chaffee, would die in a command module fire on January 27, 1967. This is also the same day that the US and USSR signed a treaty banning nuclear weapons in space. In a 3,300-page report, the investigating committee cited deficiencies in design, engineering, manufacturing, and quality with examples of flaws in installation, wiring, welding, and soldering of joints that led to flammable coolant in the module. This coolant combined with a spark to kill the astronauts in 8 and a half seconds, destroying the module and dealing the US space effort its first major setback. It also prompted a massive effort of redesign and construction that would result in a new Apollo. In 1968, the backup crew for Apollo I would launch in Apollo 7. The US space effort was firmly back on track (Shepard and Slayton, 1994).

The Russians had been busy during the Mercury and Gemini program making more history with the 1963 launch of the first woman in space and the first man to walk in space in 1965. They had also landed the first spacecraft on the Moon. Sadly, 86 days after the Apollo I fire, they too experienced tragedy as Cosmonaut Vladimir Komarov crashed in Soyuz 1 after technical problems in orbit caused the spacecraft to lose stability. The Russians would experience further problems with their N-1 superbooster. In early 1969, the N-1 had a catastrophic failure on launch that would clear the way for the US to achieve its goal of landing a man on the Moon by the end of the decade. While there would be six more Apollo flights after Apollo 11 made the first manned landing on the Moon, it is the Apollo 11 flight that captured the imagination of Earth. With the exception of Apollo 13 whose malfunctions put in doubt the survival of its crew, none of the other Apollo missions is remembered, although five did land on the Moon in various locations. Apollo 18-20 was cancelled in the aftermath of the failed Apollo 13 mission amid growing complaints about the cost and risk of manned exploration. After the Apollo 17 landing in December 1972, there would be no new footprints on the Moon or any other heavenly body. Human exploration would now focus on a series of space stations. The unmanned activity in satellites and exploration would continue, but without the same fanfare that accompanied the Great (Manned) Race to Space.

Space Stations

While President Kennedy made the Moon the ultimate goal of the Great Space Race, it was certainly not the ultimate goal for many of those involved in the space effort in either the US or USSR; they had even more far reaching ambitions for mankind's space efforts, but as Neil Armstrong noted above, political ideology and military ambitions drove many of the supporters of space exploration. These backers would decide on the short- and long-term goals and the budget to achieve them. Still, as far back as the 1940s Werner von Braun and his German collaborators had envisioned a path into space that started with a space station, then bases on the Moon and Mars. For the engineers and early visionaries in the space movement, space held many goals. For them, the station was not a goal in itself but a means to reach many grander objectives; it was to be where great interplanetary spaceships were constructed and launched to avoid the technical problems of launch through the atmosphere. Not everyone would agree with the stepping stone approach to interplanetary exploration and colonization, but it would become the default, notional vision against which others would argue (Zubrin and Wagner, 1994). In the US, the National Aeronautics and Space Administration (NASA) had been considering and planning for an orbiting station since the early 1960s, however, the Apollo program with its goal of landing a man on the Moon had pushed the idea off the radar until NASA engineers proposed launching the third stage of the Saturn rocket (used for the Apollo program) as a first step space station. The idea had obvious appeal because of the relatively low cost since it involved existing technology. The program was named Skylab and it would consist of an orbital workshop, airlock, multiple docking adapter, and telescope mount (Belew and Stuhlinger, 1973). All components were launched over a period in 1973 and housed nine astronauts for 171 in 1973–1974. For NASA, Skylab was already a race against government funders. With the space race to the Moon won and the failure of Apollo 13 (1970), many critics of the cost of the space program were questioning what they saw as a waste of taxpayer money (Sheppard and Slaton, 1994). Skylab would keep the US manned space effort alive until a new goal (and budget) could be agreed upon in Washington. While its mission was officially over in 1973, Skylab stayed in orbit until 1979 when it disintegrated in the Earth's atmosphere.

While the US was developing SkyLab, the USSR launched Salyut-1 in 1971. Several versions of the first generation station were launched before a second generation of Soviet stations replaced them beginning in 1977. The third generation Soviet station was the Mir which first launched in 1986. Cosmonauts Titov and Maranov set a record for the longest stay in space when they returned to Earth after a year of Mir. The Mir Station continued in operation until January 2001 (Launius, 2003). Over this period, the Soviets would amass a great deal of experience in space from their space station platforms.

The International Space Station (ISS) is a cooperative program between various national space agencies with each country contributing and operating different modules on the ISS. The current members of the ISS program are the US (NASA), Europe (ESA), Russia (Russian Federal Space Agency), Canada (CSA), and Japan (JAXA). The ISS presented several challenges. The first was integrating hardware produced through different engineering approaches and built by different manufacturing processes (Stockman, Boyle, and Bacon, 2009). The second challenge was a legal one and was resolved with the Intergovernmental Agreement signed in January 1998. The agreement established each partner's rights and responsibilities in addition to guaranteeing that new inventions would be registered in the country of their discoverer. Modules launches were conducted with the Space Shuttle and Soyuz rocket then assembly occurred in space over the course of 125 flights (Stockman, Boyle, and Bacon, 2009). Table 7.2 outlines the contribution of each partner to the ISS. In addition to the many science experiments conducted on the ISS, the station has hosted the first space tourists who have traveled courtesy of the Russian Space Agency, Roscosmos.

Table 7.2   ISS equipment and components

Component	Country
Centrifuge	USA
Columbus Laboratory	Europe
Cupola Observational Module	Europe
Destiny Lab Module	USA
Hab Module	USA
Integrated Truss Assembly	USA
Joint Airlock	USA
Kibo Laboratory	Japan
Multi-purpose Logistics Module	Europe
Port Solar Panels	USA
Progress Resupply Vehicle	Russia
Science Power Platform Solar Panels	Russia
Space Robotics System	Canada
Soyuz Russian Capsule	Russia
Starboard Solar Panels	USA
Thermal Control System Radiators	USA
Zarya Control Module	Russia
Zvezda Service Module	Russia

Source: http://old.mfb-geo/lev0/News_old_e/news_old_e4.html

The Chinese have announced plans for their own space station, Tiangong (Palace of the Heavens), to be fully operational in the 2020–2022 timeframe. The first module was launched in September 2011. It is composed of a laboratory, resource module, and docking mechanism and will be powered by two solar arrays. In June 2012, three Chinese astronauts became the first to visit the station (David, 2011).

Space Shuttle

For the US, the era of the space station was also the era of the Space Shuttle. Born in a time of declining NASA budgets and questions on the direction of the US space program, the Space Shuttle was the first reusable spacecraft, designed to launch like a rocket and land like an aircraft (a glider actually). It was also designed to carry large payloads such as satellites and equipment needed for the ISS. In essence, the Shuttle would be the bus that flew people and material to the space station to prepare for the long-range exploration of space envisioned by the early pioneers. In an effort to gain funding for the project, NASA would design a shuttle to meet military as well as civilian needs. Originally estimated to cost US$10 billion to develop and US$2 billion annually to operate, NASA envisioned a launch rate of 30 flights per year, but military requirements raised the payload weight and design costs. Ultimately, compromises to get military support and Congressional budget approval meant "getting" a shuttle that was not what NASA wanted. Conflicting goals and constant budget wars would take its toll on the Shuttle. The true launch costs would be 20 times more than the original estimates, too high to attract large numbers of commercial customers. Further, the engines were not powerful enough to support the original projected payload weight. Turnaround times for this reusable space vehicle would be longer than anticipated. In short, the Shuttle would never even achieve 12 launches a year. It would never breakeven and there would be no profit with this bus line to the space station (Vaughan, 1996). The Shuttle would fly 135 missions between April 2, 1981 and July 21, 2011 from its home base at Kennedy Space Center in Florida before it retirement (NASA, 2013). It would give the world many thrilling takeoffs and landings as well as a number of major accomplishments, but it is perhaps the tragedies associated with it that will linger the longest in the memory of a generation. These tragedies would tarnish the image of NASA as Congressional investigations, mountains of official reports, and a series of books would explore how the agency and industry that "put a man on the Moon" could fail so badly. The official verdicts would argue that the Challenger and Columbia accidents were not simply the result of individual mistakes, although these did occur. Officially, it would be concluded that the accidents were "socially organized and systematically produced" by a dysfunctional organization (NASA) that had allowed the shifting winds of government funding and goal setting to distort their decision-making, risk-estimating, and organizational culture in ways that created the climate for these technological failures (Vaughan, 1996). Perhaps Robert Zubrin summed up the post-Moon landing US space effort best when he noted that "[t]here can be no progress without a goal. The American space program, began so brilliantly with Apollo ... has spent most of the subsequent ... years floundering without direction" (Zubrin and Wagner, 1994). He might have also added without adequate and stable budget as a further reason for floundering, but this is a topic that we will pick up again in Chapter 22.

Satellites

In 1945, a true science fiction writer, Arthur C. Clarke, proposed the concept of geostationary satellite communications. There are three types of orbits: geostationary (or geosynchronous), asynchronous, and polar. A geosynchronous satellite is always positioned over the same area of land. Asynchronous orbits pass overhead multiple times in a day. Polar orbits are designed for low altitude and are commonly used for mapping and photography. In order to place a satellite in a given orbit, a precise launch window must be calculated to consider escape velocity and the Earth's rotation around its own axis (Brown, 2000). Such issues will also affect the "ideal" location of a spaceport (Chapter 22).

The first commercial satellite launch in the US occurred in 1962 after President John F. Kennedy signed the Communications Satellite Act (1962). This satellite, Telstar 1, was privately funded by AT&T and Bell Telephone Laboratories (Findley, 1962). One of the missions for the Space Shuttle was satellite launch, however, after the Challenger accident, President Reagan stopped this activity opening the way for private launch providers (Fought, 1989).

According to LaFleur (2010), there were 6,854 satellites launched by 30 countries as of December 31, 2009 for a yearly average of 132. Of this total, Russia has launched 60.5 percent, the US 30 percent, and the rest of the world less than 10 percent. The most common type of satellite is used for forecasting and tracking weather. Communication satellites are another common type of satellite that makes possible satellite TV and radio as well as global phone coverage. Navigation systems such as the US Global Positioning System (GPS), the European Galileo, Russian GLONASS, Chinese Compass, and India Regional Navigational Satellite System also rely on satellites. The US system includes 31 Navstar satellites in six orbital planes to provide global coverage. A number of other satellites provide either search and rescue services (Emergency Locator Transmitters or ELTs) or they provide information of a military nature.

Finally, there is a large class of satellites used for scientific research. One of the most famous is the Hubble Space Telescope which was launched in 1990 from the US Space Shuttle. Other science satellites include the Compton Gamma Ray Observatory, the Chandra X-Ray Observatory, the Spitzer Space Telescope, and the James Webb Space Telescope (JWST). This last satellite is the planned replacement for the Hubble and is set to launch in 2018. Since it is estimated that over 9,000 scientific papers have been published based on the data from

Hubble alone, this class of satellite has been invaluable to the pursuit of scientific discovery (The Space Telescope Science Institute, 2013).

Building and launching satellites is an expensive proposition and was once the sole domain of large governments. It is estimated that the JWST will have a total cost of US$6.5 billion (JWST Independent Comprehensive Review Panel, 2010). Of course, not all satellites are this complex or expensive. Brown (2000) has estimated that the launching of a satellite costs between US$50 and US$400 million dollars. Thus, a growing number of private companies are launching their own satellites such as DirecTV and Dish Network. In addition, private companies such as SpaceX and Virgin Galactic are planning to enter the launch business. This, however, is a subject for Chapter 22.

Table 7.3   Highlights of unmanned space exploration

Mission (Country)	Launch Date	Purpose
Luna 1 (USSR)	January 2, 1959	Impact the Moon; Now orbiting the Sun
Luna 2 (USSR)	September 12, 1959	Impacted the Moon
Pioneer 5 (US)	March 11, 1960	Solar monitor
Mariner 2	August 27, 1962	Venus Flyby
Venera 7 (USSR)	August 17, 1970	Successfully landed on Venus
Mar 3 (USSR)	May 28, 1971	First successful landing on Mars
Pioneer 10	March 3, 1972	Jupiter flyby
Mariner 10	November 3, 1973	First aircraft to visit Mercury
Voyager 1 (US)	September 5, 1977	Flyby outer planets
Voyager 2 (US)	August 20, 1977	Flyby Jupiter and Saturn
Sakiqake (Japan)	January 7, 1985	Flyby Halley's Comet
Giotto (EU)	July 2, 1985	Flyby comets
Hubble Space Telescope	April 25, 1990	Exploration of deep space
Cassini and Huygen Probe	October 15, 1997	Saturn orbiter
New Horizon	January 19, 2006	Keiper Belt object
Mars Rover	November 26, 2011	Exploring Mars

Source: Windows to the Universe http://www.windows2universe.org/space_missions/unmanned_table.html

Exploration

The list of unmanned space exploration would stretch for several pages and include many failures. Excluding satellites intended for Earth orbit only, the first mission outside Earth orbit was Luna 1 launched by the USSR in 1959 and intended for impact with the lunar surface; it missed and ended up in solar orbit. Luna 2 became the first object to reach the lunar surface on September 12, 1959. Table 7.3 lists some of the successful highlights of unmanned exploration. Sadly, there have often been more misses than successes because the craft missed the target, failed to launch, or failed to land successfully. In fact, *Universe Today* (Cain, 2012) noted in 2008 that nearly two thirds of the mission to Mars failed in some way. While this is a very high failure rate, even for space exploration, it does show the risks involved in space exploration, manned and unmanned. Perhaps one of the most successful robotic missions to Mars has been the rover Opportunity which was launched in 2003 and continues to operate. It recently made one of its most amazing discoveries—a rock rich in clay materials with a water content that might have favored early life (less acidic than earlier discoveries). The more recently launched Curiosity rover has found similar formations (Morris, 2013). These types of missions have yield data that scientists around the world consider groundbreaking, but while the volume of information sent back to Earth would fill many library bookshelves, some have questioned to cost of such endeavors (Foust, 2012). It is certainly true that unmanned exploration has never captured the attention or imagination like the manned accomplishments of space. To a generation raised on Star Trek, the marvels of new special effects space adventures are poor compensation for the real thing—bases on the Moon and Mars, journeys beyond the solar system.

Conclusion

If Neil Armstrong took a small step for man and a giant leap for mankind when he stepped onto the Moon, then the space industry and the many supporters of space exploration have been waiting over three decades for the next great leap. Like Arthur C. Clarke, many space supporters were optimistic enough after the 1969 Moon landing to envision men on Mars by the 1990s (Clarke, 1993). Increasingly, many have begun to ask if not when. At the height of the Great Space Race (1966), the budget for NASA represented 4.41 percent of the Federal budget. This is 32 billion in 2007 dollars (Wikipedia, 2013). Given the War in Vietnam, the War on Poverty, and the social unrest of the Civil Rights movement, critics found it easy to argue that the money was better spent at home. The NASA budget for 2012 would be less than one-half of 1 percent of the US budget (Wikipedia, 2013).

As the US space program floundered and other countries stepped into space, the Soviet program would have its own identity crisis as the breakup of the USSR would see the greatest of their spaceport, Baikonur, become the property of a foreign government, Kazakhstan. Baikonur was the site of some of the USSR's greatest accomplishment in space—the first man and first women in space, all the manned Soviet missions, the first piece of the ISS, and so on. While Russia would continue to use the cosmodrome under an agreement with the government of Kazakhstan, they would plan for a true Russian port once again—Vostochny. This new cosmodrome is located near the Pacific Coast of Russia and is intended as the new home for Russian manned missions. As the price tag for this new home rises, some in Russia are calling this project a "dolgostroi" or Russian white elephant (Zak, 2013). Further, the announced plan to launch a manned mission to orbit the Moon was derided in the Russian media as "a 60 year old achievement" (Kramnik, 2013). In an announcement on the fifty-second anniversary of the Gagarin flight, Russian President Vladmir Putin called for an increase in the Roscosmos budget in order to catch up with NASA, preserve their achievements in manned spaceflight, and spur scientific discovery (Steadman, 2013). While it is easy to see why a resurgent Russia might want to re-run the Great Space Race or sponsor a new one with a new goal, it will likely take a new Sputnik moment to reawaken the US effort. In Chapter 22, we will look at the future of space for the old Space Race competitors and the rest of the world. Will mankind be reaching for the stars or simply staring at them from the back porch?

Questions

1. What role did German scientists play in the space programs of the US and USSR?
2. Discuss the milestones in the Race for the Moon.
3. What are the defining achievements of unmanned exploration?
4. Discuss the many aspects of satellite activity.
5. What role have the various space stations had in the activity of various countries?

References

Belew, L.F. and Stuhlinger, E (1973), *Skylab: A Guidebook EP-107*, US Government Printing Office, Washington, DC.

Bellis, M (2013), "First United States satellite and space launch vehicles," retrieved online June 4, 2013 from http://inventors.about.com.

Boyne, W.J. (2007), "Project Paperclip", retrieved online May 18, 2013 from http://www.airforcemag.com/MagazineArchive/Pages/2007/June%202007/0607paperclip.aspx, *Air Force Magazine*, Vol. 90 (6), Arlington, VA.

Brown, G. (2000), "How satellites work," retrieved online May 19, 2013 from How Stuff Works. http://science.howstuffworks.com/satellite.htm.

Cain, F. (2012), "Mars," Universe Today, retrieved online September 16, 2013 from http://www.universetoday.com/14701/mars/.

Clarke, A.C. (1993), "Forward" in Robert Zubrin and Richard Wagner, *The Case for Mars: The Plan to Settle the Red Planet and Why We Must*, Simon & Schuster, New York.

Coppinger, R. (2010), "Will Congress keep US space programme adrift," Hyperbola, retrieved online September 4, 2013 from http://www.flightglobal.com/blogs/hyperbola/2010/02/will_congress_keep_us_space_pr/.

David, L. (2011), "China's first space station: a new foothold in Earth orbit," Space.com, May 6, retrieved online September 4, 2013 from http://www.space.com/11592-china-space-station-tiangong-details.html.

Findley, R. (1962, May), "Telephone a star," *National Geographic*, pp. 638–651, retrieved online from http://www.beatriceco.com/bti/porticus/bell/pdf/nat_geo _telstar_ocr.pdf.

Foust, J. (2012), "House panel agrees on lack of NASA strategic direction, but disagrees on what it should be," retrieved online September 7, 2013 from http://www.spacepolitics.com/2012/12/13/house-panel-agrees-on-lack-of-nasa-strategic-direction-but-disagrees-on-what-it-should-be/.

Fought, B.E. (1989), *Legal Aspects of the Commercialization of Space Transportation Systems*, (Master's thesis, University of Berkley), retrieved online September 3, 2013 from http://www.law.berkeley.edu/journals/btlj/articles/vol3/fought.html.

Gagliardi, O. (2009), *The Feat of Jorge Chavez*, Emmitsburg, FAP.

Godwin, M. (2006), "The Cold War and the Early Space Race," retrieved online May 20, 2013 from http://www.history.ac.uk/ihr/Focus/cold/articles/godwin.html, Department of Science and Technology Studies, University College London, London.

JWST Independent Comprehensive Review Panel (2010), *James Webb Space Telescope Final Report*, NASA JPL.

Kramnik, I (2013), "Opinion: Roskosmos at a crossroads," retrieved June 14, 2013 from http://rbth.ru/articles/2012/03/16/roscosmos_takes_on_nasa_15096.html.

LaFleur, C. (2010), "Spacecraft stats and insights," The Space Review, retrieved online September 7, 2013 from http://www.thespacereview,com/article/1598/1.

Launius, R.D. (2003), *Space Stations—Base Camps to the Stars*, Smithsonian Institution, Washington, DC.

Morris, J. (2013), "Opportunity lives," *Aviation Week & Space Technology*, June 17, p. 34.

NASA (2013), "Space Shuttle," retrieved on June 13, 2013 from http://www.nasa.gov/mission_pages/shuttle/launch/index.html.

Sheppard, A. and Slayton, D. (1994), *Moon Shot: The Inside Story of America's Race to the Moon*, Turner Publishing, Atlanta, GA.

The Space Telescope Science Institute (2013), "HST publications statistics," retrieved online September 7, 2013 from http://archives.stsci.edu/hst/bibliography/pubstat.html.

Steadman, I. (2013). "Vladimir Putin announces big new budget for Russian space agency," retrieved online June 16, 2013 from http://www.wired.co.uk/news/archive/2013-04/12/russian-space-budget.

Stockman, B., Boyle, J.S. and Bacon, J. (2009), "International Space Station systems engineering case study," retrieved online September 3, 2013 from http://www.green-ebookshop.com/get_book.php?file=International-Space-Station-Systems-Engineering-Case-Study-d481411768.

Vaughan, D. (1996), *The Challenger Launch Decision: Risky Technology, Culture, and Deviance at NASA*, The University of Chicago Press, Chicago, IL.

Verne, J. (1865. Reprinted 2003), *From the Earth to the Moon*, BookSurge Classics, New York.

Wikipedia (2013), "ANSA annual budget," retrieved online June 13, 2013 from http://en.wikipedia.org/wiki/Budget_of_NASA#Annual_budget.2C_1958-2012.

Wolfe, T (2001), *The Right Stuff*, Bantam Books, New York.

Zak, A. (2013), "Vostochny (formerly Svobodny) Cosmodrome," retrieved online April 10, 2013 from http://www.russianspaceweb.com/svobodny.html.

Zubrin, R. and Wagner, R. (1994), *The Case for Mars: The Plan to Settle the Red Planet and Why We Must*, Simon & Schuster, New York.

Chapter 8
Taking Off

Learning Objectives

After reading this chapter, you should have a good understanding of:
- LO1: the beginnings of the "jet age."
- LO2: the factors driving aircraft size and speed.
- LO3: the early history of supersonic transport.
- LO4: the background for mergers, acquisition, and bankruptcy among the aircraft manufacturers.

Key Terms, Concepts, and People

Constellation	De Havilland Comet	
Pan Am	B-747	Eddie Rickenbacker
SST & Concorde	Henri Ziegler	Embraer & Bombardier
Airbus	Fly-by-wire	BoeingMcDonnell Merger

Back to Business

For obvious reasons, civil aviation in Europe was placed on hold during World War II. In the US, civil aviation continued on a somewhat limited basis, while the manufacturers thrived under government orders for military equipment. As the war approached a recognizable end, a number of manufacturers began to shift more focus back to the civilian market and anxiously waited to be released from government obligation. Within days of the events at Hiroshima and Nagasaki, others found their government contract cancelled and quickly had to shift gears back to a more civilian manufacturing position (Rummel, 1991). Most companies had prospered during the war, racing to keep up with demand. Many would struggle with the end of the war, converting aircraft built or partially built at contract cancellation to civilian use. Only part of the concern was the end of lucrative government contracts; the volume of war surplus aircraft also threatened to depress possible civilian orders (Rummel, 1991; Serling, 1992). Still, civil aviation was about to reap the benefits of all of that wartime innovation. The amazing feats of aerial combat and the list of aviation achievements had captured the imagination of the population. Now the industry needed to convince the general public that aviation was a safe, affordable, comfortable travel experience. The rise in passenger traffic indicates that they were successful; people around the world were getting ready to take to the skies. Airlines and the manufacturers would work closely together to create the planes that would attract new flyers, the kind that were not looking to push the envelope as first movers in a new and untried field but the more cautious followers. During the last half of the twentieth century, aviation would grow up.

First Out of the Gate

Lockheed and Douglas would be two of the first manufacturers released by the US government. Both would begin working on projects to bring the pressurized cabin to civil aviation. The DC series for Douglas and the Lockheed Constellations (popularly known as Connies) would compete with Convair (General Dynamics) to offer bigger and faster aircraft to the airlines. Two goals fuelled the competition—"fastest coast-to-coast" service and a transatlantic nonstop range (Rummel, 1991). Both companies would compete aggressively to sell their aircraft to the major carriers—United, American, TWA, and Pan Am. In this race, a few more feet in length (L1049) or more efficient engines and propellers (DC-7) were the selling points, although in some cases the delivery schedule became a make-or-break issue. The DC-6, first released in 1946, would feature a pressurized cabin and 102 passenger seating configuration. It would regularly be used in around-the-world flights by the major international airlines and become the first US Presidential aircraft (President Harry Truman). The next Douglas aircraft, the DC-7, would become the first aircraft to fly nonstop from New York to Los Angeles (Clouatre, 2002). Despite some early problems with the Constellation series, TWA and a number of other international airlines would make the aircraft a fondly remembered part of aviation history (McCoy, 2002; Rummel, 1991).

In 1950, the Farnborough Air Show would showcase the "wave of the future," the de Havilland Comet. The Comet, which had made its maiden flight the previous year, was set to enter commercial airline service in 1952 and become the first operational commercial jet transport. One of the people attending the air show would be Ron Allen, CEO of Boeing. Allen was convinced that Boeing could develop a better aircraft and would return to Seattle to get his engineers working. At the April 22, 1952 meeting of the Boeing Board, tentative approval would be given to proceed with the design and construction of a jet transport which would become the B-707. The plane would feature sweptback wings and engine pods. Seating for 100 passengers would compete well with the Comet's more limited 36 seat size. Development of the 707 would prove far more costly than the original Boeing estimate and the breakeven point far higher, but Pam Am agreed to be the launch customer. Meanwhile the rest of the industry appeared to be choosing the DC-8, the planned Douglas entry into the world of commercial jet transport. The DC-8 was only a "paper aircraft at this stage, that is, it was still in the very preliminary stages of design, but Douglas had a family of aircraft and a proven record of success. These factors gave them an edge and guaranteed that airlines would listen when they suggested that their aircraft would have greater range, power, and size than the Boeing aircraft for less money" (Serling, 1992).

On January 10, 1954, the industry was shaken when a BOAC Comet exploded in mid-air over the Mediterranean. A second Comet would disappear soon afterwards on a flight from Rome to Cairo. The cause of both crashes was explosive decompression of the fuselage caused by metal fatigue cracks, a result of the pressurization and depressurization of the cabin. This phenomenon was known from military jet aircraft. Fortunately, both Boeing and Douglas were aware of the problem and working on solutions. In fact, at the rollout of the B-707 prospective customers were shown a film entitled *Operation Guillotine*. The film showed the results of explosive decompression and the solutions that Boeing had implemented. These solutions included triple-strength windows rounded at the corners, thicker-gauged skin braced with metal stripping, and small stopper straps running the length of the fuselage. The result was that the cabin remained intact after being deliberately pierced by several blades. The Comet did convince Boeing that more pilot training would be needed to fly the faster, more unforgiving jet aircraft (Serling, 1992).

With the 1959 release of the DC-8 jet, the future of air transportation appeared clear to almost all. The DC-8 was equipped with four engines and capable of over 600 mph. An extended fuselage allowed for the seating of 260 passengers (Clouatre, 2002). Of course, not all airlines were convinced. Despite being impressed by the barrel roll of the Dash-80 (demonstration model for the B-707), Eddie Rickenbacker, former World War I flying ace and CEO of Eastern Air Line, preferred the propeller-driven craft which he viewed as safer and more reliable. This kept Eastern out of the jet era until the early 1960s when his successors began a buying spree to catch up that left the airline heavily in debt going into deregulation (Bernstein, 1999). While the new jets did prove to be fuel hogs, guzzling more fuel on takeoff than the *Spirit of St. Louis* consumed crossing the Atlantic, the new jet engines proved far safer and more reliable (Serling, 1992). In fact, the introduction of the jet engine would dramatically lower accident rates. These rates would experience a sharp decline in the 1950s and 1960s, primarily attributable to the widespread introduction of the jet engine and improvements in jet engine reliability (Barnett and Higgins, 1989). In their study, Oster and Zorn (1989) found an overall decline in accidents of 54 percent with a 71 percent reduction in accidents attributed to equipment failure.

Too Big to Fly?

Pan Am wanted a bigger plane and the B-707 could not be stretched any further. The answer was the B-747. In their letter of intent, Pan Am called for a 400-passenger aircraft with a range of 5,000 and a cruising altitude of 35,000 feet. The plane had to be able to takeoff in no more than 8,000 feet fully loaded and be capable of cargo nose loading. It seemed a very tall order for a company that did not even have a building large enough to construct such a plane. Nevertheless, three years after this letter, the first B-747 would be rolled out. Building the aircraft would strain Boeing to breaking point. The company laid off 5,000 people in a single week in 1970. By the end of that year, office staff had dropped from 24,000 to 9,000. Hourly workers declined from 45,000 to 15,000. This crisis inspired the famous billboard in Seattle asking "Will the last person leaving SEATTLE—turn out the light" (Serling, 1992). The first flight of the B-747 from New York to London would take place on January 22, 1970. Of course, anyone who has flown internationally in recent decades knows that the B-747 would become the symbol of international aviation. The B-747 would go through a number of variants over the years that would reflect extended range and capacity as well as special purpose, freighter. The latest is the -800 series. The B-747 would eventually prove to be one of the bestselling planes in history and the only plane in its "class" until the launch of the A-380.

Down But Not Out

The idea of supersonic commercial flight became part of the dream list of aeronautical engineers and their companies within a decade of the 1947 flight of the Bell X-1. Reaching a speed of 700 mph, Captain Charles "Chuck" Yeager officially achieved Mach 1.06, breaking the sound barrier. By 1953, the Douglas Skyrocket would break Mach 2, but Douglas would drop out of the US race for a commercial aircraft fairly early in the design competition in the US (Marchman, 2002). Boeing established its own small supersonic transport (SST) design team in 1957 and started building a supersonic wind tunnel three years later. In 1963, the Federal Aviation Administration (FAA) announced plans to invite US aerospace companies to submit plans for an SST (Lynn, 1998). Boeing's US competitors were Lockheed and North American. North American and its Curtiss Wright engine would eventually drop out of the race. In 1966, Boeing unveiled its US$11 million mockup to the media. Later that year, the FAA proclaimed the Boeing–cGE design the SST winner, but years of work would not result in an American SST; the US Senate would refuse to fund further development in 1971. Still, the dream would live on and be revived at Boeing briefly as the Sonic Cruiser before the decision was made to proceed with the plane that would become the B-777 (Serling, 1992).

Over in Europe, Sud Aviation unveiled a scale model of a medium-range SST named the Super Caravelle at the 1960 Paris Air Show. By 1962, the French and British had signed the Anglo–French Supersonic Aircraft Agreement to jointly develop an SST following a decision by the FAA and US companies not to consider a partnership with the British to design an aluminum SST. The Anglo–French alliance (with the later added Germans) would eventually result in the Concorde but the project was not without significant challenges. In addition to numerous technical challenges, the cost of the project continued to rise to well over ten times the original estimate, threatening to create a political backlash in each of the key countries. The French would ask Henri Ziegler, war hero, resistance fighter, head of Air France, and proponent of a very different concept in aerospace design, later called Airbus, to rescue the supersonic effort. The Concorde would make its maiden flight in March 1969, two months after the Soviet SST became the first SST into the air. The Soviet aircraft, the TU-144, would crash in 1973 at the Paris Air Show. Meanwhile, the Concorde would not make it into commercial service until 1976 with its maiden voyage from London to Bahrain. While TWA and Pan Am in the US had taken options to pursue the Concorde, both would eventually back out leaving British Airways and Air France as the only commercial operators. Despite safety concerns in the development stages, the Concorde would fly accident-free until the 2000 crash of AF 4590 on takeoff from Paris. Unfortunately the premium pricing for the very narrow-bodied Concorde and the high operating costs would never make the aircraft a money-winning proposition, sadly confirming the predictions of Henri Ziegler that the plane would not sell and amounted to little more than a remarkable technical achievement in aviation (Aris, 2002; Serling, 1992; Shuman, 2002).

Ziegler was particularly concerned that the Concorde would take away the European focus from the one project that he did believe had the potential to re-establish Europe in the commercial aviation industry—Airbus. Airbus would be headquartered in France, but the final product of its labor would come from the assembly of parts designed and manufactured all over Europe. Establishing common rules and standards would prove simple compared to the logistics involved in moving large aircraft parts from one end of Europe to another. Although many thought that the concept of a wide-body, 200-passenger, twin-engine airplane was madness, the Airbus A-300 would launch in 1972 and begin commercial service in 1974. By 1978, the A310, a shortened version of the A300 seating 218 passengers, had been launched. The Airbus family continued to grow with the A320, a single-aisle 130–170-passenger aircraft, the A321, a lengthened version of the A320 seating 180 to 200 passengers, the A330, a twin-engine 235-passenger aircraft, and the A340, an ultralong four-engine aircraft seating 295 passengers. Table 8.1 shows clearly the members of the Airbus family, basic seating number, release date of first aircraft, and total number of aircraft delivered. Several features distinguished the Airbus family from the start. First, the flight deck was standardized across models making training and operation simpler and less costly. Second, there was a two-person cockpit design, also a cost saver. Finally, the aircraft utilized the latest technology including the fly-by-wire controls which replaced the old mechanical systems with their cables attached to pulleys and later aided by hydraulics as the size of rudder and flaps increased with computer systems that would send electrical impulses to the moveable surfaces. Fly-by-wire had been used before in military aircraft and on the Concorde, but there was resistance to the new technology, particularly from pilot groups. Boeing would not take the plunge into fly-by-wire for another decade.

Table 8.1   Airbus family of aircraft

Aircraft	Seating	Released	Delivered	Backlog
A-300*	266–285	May 1969	561	0
A-310*	200–220	Jul 1978	255	0
A-320	107–220	Mar 1984	5,467	3,689
A-330	253–440	Jun 1987	951	295
A-340*	295–475	Jun 1987	377	0
A-350	250–375	Jul 2006	0	617
A-380	525–853	Dec 2000	99	163

*   No longer in production

Breaking the Mold

In the book *Twenty-first Century Jet: The Making and Marketing of the Boeing 777*, Chapter 1—"Why a New Plane?" – begins with a quote from Alan Mulally who eventually took over as general manager of the 777 team when Phil Condit was promoted to President of the Boeing Company (Sabbagh, 1996). His answer to the question was that airlines wanted an airplane bigger than the B-767 but smaller than the B-747. Boeing first tried several scenarios for stretching the 767 but the aerodynamics did not work well. In fact, the design was dubbed a Chipolata Sausage—very long and skinny—by unnamed representatives of a British airline. Design issues were not the only driver of a new plane; the 767 project was launched in 1978 and first delivered in 1982 and the technological advances since then seemed to argue for a new redesign rather than retrofit of an older one. The 777 would represent a number of firsts for Boeing including the first paperless design, the first fly-by-wire, first experiments in design–build teams (DBTs) and a new employee relationship, and first efforts to involve customers early in the process. In the early days of manufacturing, a plane was designed on paper and then a full-scale mockup was used to catch any "conflicts" in the design, that is, call button placed where an air duct was also planned. Computer-aided design (CAD) allowed the process to take place virtually. The 777 would use fly-by-wire like the Airbus aircraft on the market, but would rely on a backup system written separately to avoid the possibility of a "computer glitch" in the first software being recreated in the backup, a possible safety problem. Two new concepts would emerge with the 777—Working Together and DBTs. Working Together embodies the idea that the 777 team create an environment where everyone came together in "a shared thought, a shared vision, a shared appreciation, a shared understanding of what it is we're really going to try to accomplish together" (Sabbagh, 1996: 66). For a company with a history of tense labor relations, layoffs, and union strife, the concept was a departure. Equally novel for Boeing was the Japanese concept of

DBTs linked vertically and horizontally to each other by a common team member. The DBTs were to insure that communications did occur between the design teams so that "interferences" were reduced. The program eventually had 250 DBTs coordinating design. The final new element was the Boeing effort to involve customers early and often. In the past, "Boeing policy had been to dream up a new plane, design it, make it, and then sit around and hope that enough people would buy it" (Sabbagh, 1996: 27). The costs and uncertainties made this old approach too risky even for Boeing who had "bet the farm" on projects such as the 707 and the 747. The 777 would become everything that the designers hoped that it would be after some early issues with its twin-engine design. Since the aircraft range was intended to allow extended over water operations, there was some concern that the failure of one engine would create a safety hazard over water. This issue was resolved and the aircraft has proved to be remarkably successful, and safe (Sabbagh, 1996).

Table 8.2   Boeing family of aircraft

Aircraft	Seating	Released	Delivered	Backlog
B-707*	141	July 1954	1,010	0
B-717*	106	Oct 1995	155	0
B-727*	106–125	Nov 1962	1,831	0
B-737*	110–215	Jan 1967	3,113	0
B-737 N	110–220	Dec 1997	4,359	3,136
B-747	416–500	Sep 1968	1,458	67
B-757*	200	Jan 1978	1,049	0
B-767	224–409	Aug 1981	1,043	65
B-777	279–550	Apr 1994	1,079	363
B-787	210–300	Jun 2006	49	841

*   No longer in production

Let the Mergers Begin

As Boeing was struggling with the cost of bringing the B-747 to market, Donald Douglas was slipping further out of control at Douglas Aircraft, spending more and more time with his mistress, Peggy Tucker, who came to virtually control the company. By the middle of the 1960s, the company had amassed huge losses and was ripe for a takeover by McDonnell of St Louis, until then primarily a weapons manufacturer. Although the new McDonnell–Douglas would re-enter the commercial market with the DC-10, it would never achieve its former glory (Lynn, 1998). The main competitor for the DC-10 was the Lockheed L-1011

Tristar, Lockheed's first jetliner. Lockheed would sell 250 L-1011s, but the cost of developing the aircraft at the same time as the C-5, military cargo transport, would drive the company to the brink of bankruptcy, an event averted by a US government credit guarantee to lenders. The L-1011 would lose some US$2.5 billion by the time it was retired in 1981 (Newhouse, 2007). At McDonnell–Douglas, things were not much better. By the 1990s, employees of the Douglas unit would complain that the company pencils were designed so that when they were sharpened the Douglas disappeared. The DC-10 was in fact inferior to the L-1011 in a number of ways and would prove to be the last commercial aircraft produced by the company. It would increasingly rely on its military aircraft and weapons development for profit (McCoy, 2002; Newhouse, 2007).

It became clear to even those outside the industry that McDonnell–Douglas was struggling in 1992 when the company posted a 51 percent drop in earnings overall with a 62 percent drop for the Douglas unit. By 1996, Douglas Aircraft had only 40 new aircraft orders. Without a viable commercial business, the company had to commit to an all-out effort to win the Joint Strike Force (JSF) fighter project for the US combined forces aircraft of the future, estimated to be worth approximately US$300 billion in future sales. When McDonnell–Douglas was "deselected" by the Pentagon in 1996, there appeared to be little future for the company. Boeing would pay US$13.3 billion for this former competitor in 1997. This move was not widely popular within Boeing's Commercial Division who felt that the Douglas unit was even weaker than projected and that the two cultures would clash. Strategic reasons that favored the merger were that the combined company better balanced the commercial and military sides of the industry (Newhouse, 2007). Whether it will face the kind of long-term tension that arose from the inability of the McDonnell–Douglas merger to forge a common culture and identity remains to be seen.

Another commercial aviation pioneer was to disappear during this era—Fokker. The company began struggling in the 1970s and briefly explored a collaboration with McDonnell–Douglas in 1981. The company received a financial bailout from the Dutch government in 1987 as development costs for their new line of aircraft soared. One condition of the government was that they seek out new partners for the company. DASA, the parent company of Daimler-Benz, was that partner. Their decision to focus on core operations in 1996 forced Fokker into bankruptcy. Stork Aerospace took over the repair and maintenance business while various interests have continued to raise the prospects of a re-entry into the civil aviation market. Thus, a decade after Airbus entered the commercial airline industry, there were only four major players in the market with Boeing in the top spot. Lockheed and McDonnell–Douglas, as noted above, would continue to decline under the weight of their own mistakes. This would set the stage for the new kid-on-the-block, Airbus, to emerge as the dominant threat in the large commercial aircraft (LCA) market, but the major players would ignore a segment of the market that other companies would target, the small regional jet market.

Small is Beautiful?

In 1986, a Canadian company founded in 1942 to manufacturer tracked vehicles for transport over snow bought Canadair, a leading Canadian aircraft manufacturer. This company, Bombardier, purchased Short Brothers in 1989, de Havilland in 1992 (51 percent stake and remaining 49 percent in 1997), and LearJet in 1995. Aviation was part of a broader diversification into transportation that included bus, rail, and water vehicles as well as services such as FlexJet and SkyJet. Bombardier would develop a line of commercial vehicles ranging from the 30-seat Dash to the 145-seat C-130 (Table 8.3). A second entrant into this segment of the commercial industry was Embraer, a Brazilian company that began in the 1960s with general aviation and military aircraft. They too would go on to offer a line of commercial aircraft ranging from 30 to 122 seats. These aircraft are referred to in the industry as

Table 8.3   Regional jet families

Aircraft	Seating	Released	Delivered	Backlog
Bombardier				
Dash-8	37	1980	299	0
Q200	37	1980	105	0
Q300	50	Mar 1986	267	0
Q400	70–80	Jun 1996	416	44
CRJ 100/200	50	Mar 1989	935	0
CRJ700/705	70	Jan 1997	332	8
CRJ900	86	Jul 2000	259	15
CS100	110–125	*	0	66
CS300	130–160	*	0	72
Embraer				
EMB120	30	1985	352	0
ERJ135	37	1995	108	0
ERJ140	44	1995	74	0
ERJ145	50	1995	708	0
Embraer 170	70–80	Oct 2001	182	6
Embraer 175	78–88	2002	143	46
Embraer 190	98–114	2002	389	162
Embraer 195	108–124	2002	88	35

*   CSeries entry anticipated in 2013
Source: Various company websites

regional jets and have flourished on the wave of the strategic changes at the major carriers to move toward point-to-point service and/or a hubbing structure where these smaller aircraft are used to serve less dense routes that are channeled into the major carrier hubs where traffic is concentrated and placed on larger aircraft into the final destination. From a major carrier perspective, they can fill smaller aircraft and serve these markets more frequently. From an airport perspective, this has often resulted in more flights but little increase in overall passengers or revenue. This will become a bigger problem at heavily congested airports in the Northeast US. From a passenger perspective, it often meant more cramped seating and less overhead space. From the perspective of the LCA manufacturers, it represents a potential, but unrealized source of future competition.

Powering the Planes

Pratt & Whitney, the company that had been founded in 1925 and formed one leg of William Boeing's vision of a fully integrated air transport company, would continue to produce engines for both military and civilian use as part of the United Aircraft Corporation. The company would change its name in 1975 to United Technologies Corporation (UTC). UTC would eventually become a diversified company with business units such as Otis Elevator, Hamilton Sundstrand, Carrier Heating and Air Conditioning, Pratt & Whitney, and Sikorsky Helicopter. In 1996, Pratt & Whitney would form an alliance with another engine manufacturer, GE, to begin work on an engine that would power the world's largest commercial aircraft, the A-380. Table 8.4 provides an overview of the Pratt & Whitney commercial engine family (Pratt & Whitney website, 2008).

The company that first entered the "aviation business" in 1917 in response to a US government search for a way to boost engine power at high altitude would go on to produce the nation's first jet engine in 1942, the I-A. Further development would result two years later in the J33 which would power the US Air Corps' first operational jet fighter. Building on years of expertise in the military market, GE would move into the civilian market in 1971 with the CF6, a high bypass turbofan engine first installed on the DC-10. The same year GE began its partnership with Snecma, a French engine firm. The partnership was formalized in 1974 with the formation of CFM International, a 50/50 joint venture. CFM International would become one of the most successful aviation partnerships in history. Over the years, CFM engines would grab an increasing share of the short- to medium-range commercial aviation market and become the exclusive power plant for the long range A-340 (General Electric website, 2008).

Rolls-Royce, a company better known at the time for its cars, had entered the civilian market in the early 1950s with the Dart for the Vickers Viscount, the Avon for the Comet, and the Conway for the B-707. By 1966, the main British engine makers—de Havilland, Britol Siddeley, Blackburn, Napier Aero Engines—had merged into Rolls-Royce. Unfortunately, this was the same year that Lockheed

Table 8.4   Large commercial aircraft engines

Manufacturer	Engine	In-Service Date	Aircraft Example
Pratt & Whitney	JT8D	1964	B-737-100
	PW2000	1984	B-757
	PW4000	1987	B-747
	PW6000	2000	A-318
	V2500	2008	A-320 Family
	GP7200	2008	A-380
General Electric	CF34	1983	CRJ-100
	CF6	1971	A-300
	CFM56 (LEAP)	2016	A-320neo
	CT7	1984	Saab 340
	GE90	1995	B-777
	GEnx	2012	B-747-800
Rolls-Royce	RB211	1966	L-1011
	Trent 500	2002	A-340-500
	Trent 700	1995	A-330
	Trent 800	1996	B-777
	Trent 900	2012	A-380
	Trent 1000	2011	B-787
	Trent XWB	2014	A-350

Source: Company website

began work on its first jetliner, the L-1011 Tristar which would feature the Rolls-Royce RB211. The high cost of development would drive Lockheed to the brink of bankruptcy while costs and early problems with the engine would lead Rolls-Royce into state ownership in 1971. The car divisions would be separated in 1973 and Rolls-Royce would return to the private sector in 1987. In 1990, Rolls-Royce would form an aero engine joint venture with BMW, a venture they assumed full control of in 2000 (Rolls-Royce website, 2008).

Conclusion

As the twentieth century came to an end, there were only two manufacturers left standing in the LCA market—Airbus and Boeing—however, this would not reduce the competition. In fact, competition would intensify in the twenty-first century. The events of September 11 would naturally impact the manufacturing firms, but this time there would be a difference; the US domestic market no longer dominated the industry or the thinking of the aerospace manufacturers. The global airline industry would recover much more quickly than their US counterparts who would struggle to stay out or get out of bankruptcy. Meanwhile, the phenomenal growth in Asia would be reflected in their aviation industry as well. China and India would lead the region while airlines in the Middle East, notably Emirates and Qatar Air, would expand to position themselves as the link between Europe and Asia.

Even more noteworthy is that the twenty-first century would become the stage for a new battle between Airbus and Boeing, a battle of visions. These two companies would begin to diverge sharply in their strategic vision of the future of the aviation industry. Boeing would plan for a future where point-to-point traffic would become the growing and driving force behind air travel. Airbus would envision a future in which aircraft even larger than the B-747 would carry air travelers to the major international hubs. These visions would have a definite effect on the products each planned to release in the first decade of the new century and their fortunes would be measured by how the "market" appeared to be validating their vision.

Questions

1. What was the cause of the de Havilland Comet crashes and what was the solution to this problem?
2. Discuss the advantages and disadvantages of the jet engine and aircraft.
3. Discuss the founding of Airbus.
4. What events led to the merger of McDonald Douglas and Boeing?
5. Why did supersonic transport fail and what is the future of it in the airline industry?

References

Aris, S. (2002), *Close to the Sun: How Airbus Challenged America's Domination of the Skies*, Arum Press, London.
Barnett, A. and Higgins, M.K. (1989), "Airline safety: the last decade", *The Institute of Management Sciences*, vol. 35 (1), pp. 1–21.
Bernstein, A. (1999), *Grounded: Frank Lorenzo and the Destruction of Eastern Airlines*, Beard Books, Washington, DC.
Clouatre, D. (2002), "DC plane family" in Tracy Irons-Georges (ed.) *Encyclopedia of Flight*, Salem Press, Pasadena, CA, pp. 205–207.
Lynn, M. (1998), *Birds of Prey: Boeing Vs Airbus—A Battle for the Skies*, Four Walls Eight Windows, New York.

Marchman, J.F. (2002), "Supersonic aircraft" in Tracy Irons-Georges (ed.) *Encyclopedia of Flight,* Salem Press, Pasadena, CA, pp. 205–207.

McCoy, M.G. (2002), "Lockheed-Martin" in Tracy Irons-Georges (ed.) *Encyclopedia of Flight,* Salem Press, Pasadena, CA, pp. 420–423.

Newhouse, J. (2007), *Boeing versus Airbus: The Inside Story of the Greatest International Competition in Business*, Alfred A. Knopf, New York.

Oster, C.V. and Zorn, C.K. (1989), "Is it still safe to fly?" in Leon.N. Moses and Ian. Savage (eds), *Transportation Safety in an Age of Deregulation*, Oxford University Press, New York. pp. 129–52.

Rummel, R.W. (1991), *Howard Hughes and TWA*, Smithsonian Institution Press, Washington, DC.

Sabbagh, K. (1996), *Twenty-First Century Jet: The Making and Marketing of the Boeing 777*, Scribner, New York.

Serling, R.J. (1992), *Legend and Legacy: The Story of Boeing and its People*, St. Martin's Press, New York.

Shuman, R.B. (2002), "Concorde" in Tracy Irons-Georges (ed.) *Encyclopedia of Flight,* Salem Press, Pasadena, CA, pp. 420–423.

Websites

Airbus, http://www.airbus.com/

Boeing, http://www.boeing.com/boeing/

Bombardier, http://www.bombardier.com/

Embraer, http://www.embraer.com/en-US/Pages/Home.aspx

General Electric, http://www.geae.com/aboutgeae/history.html

Pratt & Whitney, http://www.utc.com/units/pw.htm

Rolls-Royce, http://www.rolls-royce.com

Chapter 9
A Brave New World

Learning Objectives

After reading this chapter, you should have a good understanding of:
- LO1: the US decision to pursue liberalization and the actions that were taken.
- LO2: the arguments for and against deregulation and liberalization.
- LO3: the history and progress of Open Skies.
- LO4: the basic elements of bilateral air service agreements.

Key Terms, Concepts, and People

Airline Deregulation Act	Bermuda II	Show cause
Encirclement	Open Skies	Anti-trust
Fifth freedom	Netherlands	

New Deal

In 1976, the British gave notice to the US government that it was terminating Bermuda I. According to the British, Bermuda I gave American carriers a disproportionate share of the traffic in large measure due to the liberal fifth freedom rights granted to US carriers. It had been 30 years since the events at Chicago and the signing of Bermuda I. The world was now a very different place. The Asian miracle saw, first Japan, then other Asian nations achieve double-digit levels of economic growth. Between 1950 and 1973, the Japanese GDP grew at a rate of 10.5 percent a year. By the 1970s, the Japanese were producing over half the world's tonnage of shipping and as much steel as their US counterparts (Kennedy, 1987). In Europe, most of the nations were back to their pre-war levels of output by 1950. Between the period 1950–1970, European GDP grew on average 5.5 percent a year while industrial product rose 7.1 percent (Landes, 1969). By contrast, the US economy had lost the relative advantages it possessed coming out of World War II. At the Bretton Woods conference in 1944, the world monetary system had been established pegging all major currencies to the US dollar. Unfortunately, US policies to finance both the war in Vietnam and domestic, social spending without increasing taxes had led the government to print more money, that is, increase the money supply. This in turn led to inflation and put pressure on the international monetary system. This system was abandoned in 1973 (Solomon, 1982). Rising inflation, declining shares of exports, and new foreign competition at home were taking their toll on the US economy.

For the British, the time appeared right to make a change. For their part, the US government fearing a complete breakdown of the commercial air traffic with the UK agreed to sign what became known as Bermuda II in 1977. This bilateral agreement virtually eliminated multiple carrier designations, established capacity limitations, and redressed the imbalance in fifth freedom rights. Bermuda II was seen as a major policy setback by the US government and a direct challenge to competitive markets.

Not Taking it Laying Down

To demonstrate its commitment to air transport liberalization, the US initiated three actions in 1978. The first action was to issue a statement entitled "Policy for the Conduct of International Air Transportation." This statement declared the US intention to "trade competitive opportunities, rather than restrictions" in order to expand competition and reduce prices (US Congress, 1978). This policy was a denunciation of Bermuda II and a clear challenge to the rest of the aviation community. Shortly afterwards, the US Civil Aeronautics Board (CAB) issued an order to IATA to "show cause" why they should not be considered an illegal cartel as prohibited by US anti-trust law. Since IATA membership was restricted to international carriers whose major tasks included setting fares and capacity, there was little argument of violation. This was also a warning to US carriers that their participation in the tariff and capacity setting activities of IATA would not be acceptable. Finally, in late 1978, the US became the first nation in the world to deregulate its air transport industry with the passage of the Airline Deregulation Act (Toh, 1998).

The purpose of the Airline Deregulation Act was "to encourage, develop, and attain an air transportation system which relies on competitive market forces to determine the quality, variety, and price of air services, and of other purposes." The Act phased out the CAB with its market control of entry/exit, pricing, and service levels. The proponents of deregulation argued that regulation forced competition based solely on service quality and thus created fares that in many cases were 50 percent higher than comparable intra-state (unregulated) fares. Studies had concluded that regulation also forced carriers to accept low, uneconomical load factors, raised labor costs, protected inefficient carriers, and prevented them from establishing economies of scale that would allow them to lower unit prices (Caves, 1962; Douglas and Miller, 1974; Jordon, 1970; Kahn, 1971). It should be noted that several studies found that the average cost per passenger did not fall as firm size increased which tended to indicate that airlines were not natural monopolies that should be subject to regulation (Eads, Nerlove, and Raduchel, 1969; Straszheim, 1969; White, 1969). On the other hand, larger aircraft and increasing density (increased frequency of flights, additional seats in existing flights) did appear to lower unit costs (Caves, Christensen, and Thetheway, 1984; Graham and Kaplan, 1982). Overall, deregulation was expected to improve service to the public, lower fares, allow carriers to achieve higher profits, and create a more competitive airline industry through the entry of new carriers as well as the freer regulatory environment afforded to existing competitors (Kane, 1998). These proponents have noted that there are more carriers flying today than in 1978 and that prices have fallen. Morrison and Winston (1997) have estimated that airfares fell 33 percent in real terms between 1976 and 1993. They attribute at least 20 percent of this decline to deregulation itself which increased competition and reduced costs at large and medium airports. A recent study of international carriers found that the major US carriers as a whole are most cost competitive than all but some of the lower wage Asian carriers (Oum and Yu, 1998).

While the impact of deregulation is still under debate, it is clear that following deregulation many US carriers were forced to undergo a painful process of restructuring that not all of them completed successfully. The financial crisis in the early 1980s hit all of the US carriers hard and led to industry consolidation and the creation of the hub-and-spoke system. In addition to the disappearance of such pre-deregulation carriers as Eastern Air Lines and Pan Am, more than 200 new entrant carriers have started and failed. By the early 1990s, another financial crisis had led the industry to develop complex holding structures, expand non-airline and/or discrete services, and race to create global seamless service through a network of strategic alliances (Rosen, 1995). Studies show that although there are more carriers flying, the top six carriers account for an increasingly large proportion of the total traffic. In 1985, the top six accounted for 62 percent of the domestic US traffic. By the early 1990s, these same six controlled 86 percent (Kim and Singal, 1993). Several studies have even suggested that real prices fell faster under regulation than they did in the post-deregulation period (Dempsey and Goetz, 1992; Dempsey and Gesell, 1997). In addition, it has been suggested that deregulation did not benefit all consumers in terms of the level of service or price. Small, outlying communities have in fact lost some portion of the service they enjoyed prior to deregulation and the fact that they may be linked to a single dominant hub may also increase their fares (Goetz and Dempsey, 1989; Jones, 1998). While there are no studies examining the pre- and post-deregulation levels of service quality among US carriers, there is a general consensus that it has declined significantly following deregulation and US carriers are conspicuously absent from surveys ranking the service quality of international carriers (Kahn, 1990; Dempsey and Goetz, 1992; Towers and Perrin, 1991; Zagat, 1992).

The benefits and costs of domestic regulation can and have been the subject of an entire book (or series of books) and are mentioned here only because freeing domestic markets added philosophical and economic pressure to the liberalization of international markets. The arguments briefly presented here are also intended to suggest some of the effects that might occur in a truly deregulated international market. Deregulation in the US market did appear to result in overall declines in fare prices and the appearance, at least temporarily, of new entrant carriers.

These pressures forced the industry to restructure to lower costs as noted above by Oum and Yu (1998). Whatever the successes or failures of deregulation in the long run, the US was now ready to push forward on the international scene with new initiatives designed to open international markets to greater competition and more market-based controls.

Encircling the World

In 1979, the US passed the International Air Transportation Competition Act which set out three goals for future US aviation policy. First, the US would push for multiple carrier designations, permissive route authority, and no operational restrictions on capacity and frequency. Second, air fares would be freed to respond to consumer demand. Finally, the US would work to eliminate discriminatory practices preventing US carriers from effectively competing in international markets. Some of the practices targeted for change included foreign computer reservation systems that favored other national carriers, government user fees at international airports that were excessive compared to domestic only airports (the contention being that national governments were using these fees to subsidize smaller, local airports), and policies that required exclusive contracts for ground handling and other services (Toh, 1998).

The US would now pursue its new Open Skies policy through the application of two levers. The first lever was laid out by the Director of the Bureau of Pricing and Domestic Aviation, and the CAB. The so-called Encirclement Strategy called for the US to bring pressure on smaller market countries to sign Open Skies agreements as a means of diverting traffic from larger aviation markets. The strategy was based on the assumption that Open Skies would lower fares between those countries involved in the bilateral agreement and cause passengers to change their traveling patterns in pursuit of lower fares. Two nations were primarily targeted for encirclement—Japan and the UK—because they represented the key entry ports for US travelers to Asia and Europe respectively (Levine, 1979). The US first targeted smaller market countries that generated very little third and fourth freedom traffic (to and from the US) since these countries stood to gain by simply getting greater access to US destinations. There could also be no question of exchanging domestic opportunities (cabotage) with these nations since they had little or no domestic markets to exchange for the sizable US domestic market.

The second lever to Open Skies came through the application of the US Department of Transportation's (DOT) policy on approving airline alliances. This policy based approval on either the coverage of the rights under existing bilateral or proven benefits to the US (Gellman Research Associates, 1994). In addition, the US DOT has granted immunity from anti-trust enforcement to alliances between carriers from Open Skies countries (see Chapter 11 for a further discussion). The arguments being that there were proven benefits to the US deriving from these agreements. Anti-trust immunity allows competitors to coordinate on issues of pricing, capacity, and scheduling. Thus, they are able to achieve greater levels of operational integration, cut costing, and improved quality through coordination (Oum and Park, 1997).

Table 9.1a   Open Skies agreements 1992–2001

Year	Month	Country	Year	Month	Country
2001	10	France	1997	7	Aruba
	9	Oman		2	Brunei
	5	Poland		10	Chile
	11	Sri Lanka		4	Costa Rica
				4	El Salvador
2000	11	Benin		4	Guatemala
	2	Burkina Faso		4	Honduras
	5	Gambia		6	Malaysia
	3	Ghana		12	Nether. Antilles
	10	Malta		5	New Zealand
	10	Morocco		5	Nicaragua
	2	Namibia		3	Panama
	8	Nigeria		12	Romania
	10	Rwanda		1	Singapore
	12	Senegal		3	Taiwan
	1	Slovak Republic			
	3	Turkey	1996	11	Jordan
				2	Germany
1999	8	Argentina			
	5	Bahrain	1995	6	Austria
	12	Dom Republic		3	Belgium
	4	Pakistan		12	Czech Republic
	12	Portugal		4	Denmark
	10	Qatar		3	Finland
	11	Tanzania		6	Iceland
	4	UAE		6	Luxembourg
				4	Norway
1998	11	Italy		4	Sweden
	4	S. Korea			
	5	Peru			
	2	Uzbekistan	1992	10	Netherlands

Opening Up

Table 9.1a lists the Open Skies agreements signed by the US prior to 2001 and the dates of their signing. Table 9.1b lists the Open Skies agreements since 2001. It is interesting to note the momentum that was building in the US efforts prior to September 11. In part, this momentum represented the liberalization focus of the Clinton presidency as well as the growing international movement toward liberalization. Following September 11, security issues dominated the aviation agenda. When aviation liberalization returned to the agenda, the issue that took center stage was the proposed multilateral agreement with the European Union (EU). This very complex and contentious agreement would take precedence over single country Open Skies.

Tables 9.1a and b also illustrate the advance of the Encirclement Strategy which dictated that the countries approached first were small market nations surrounding the target markets of Japan and the UK. Assuming that Open Skies did indeed divert traffic to Open Skies markets by lowering fares, then these nations would seek their own Open Skies to prevent traffic loss. To understand the difference Open Skies has made in the bilateral process, it is interesting to note that the length of the bilateral agreement discussed in Chapter 5 between the US–UK and US–Japan were 16 pages in length. The US–Netherlands agreement is one page (Table 9.2).

There is no mention of pricing, capacity, or frequency restrictions in these agreements. Clearly, Open Skies agreements have been helpful in saving the world's trees. One might ask whether they have achieved the goals set forth by US policy and whether the consumers of the world have benefited from these new bilateral agreements.

Conspicuously absent from the Open Skies list in Tables 9.1 are two countries—Japan and the UK. Understanding the reasons for their absence illustrates several key issues in international aviation. To those outside the industry it may be surprising to discover that not all the disagreement during the course of the bilateral negotiations between these countries took place between national governments; airlines on both sides of the debate disagreed among themselves and thus, did not present a unified voice to their respective governments. The 1952 agreement between the US and Japan had given broad rights to three carriers—United, Northwest, and Japan Airlines. The remaining US carriers and All Nippon Airways (ANA) received limited access in the 1980s due to a series of Memoranda of Understanding between Washington and Tokyo. Although Northwest, an incumbent carrier, supported Open Skies, United Airlines did not favor such an agreement, which would have allowed more US competition into the Japanese market. From a policy perspective, the non-incumbent US carriers would have received more access under a "not-quite-open-skies" agreement and felt that the US should not push for Open Skies if that push jeopardized an overall agreement (Goldman, 1997). Similar issues surfaced in the Open Skies negotiations between the US and UK. As part of their Oneworld alliance, American Airlines and British

Table 9.1b   Open Skies agreements 2002 to present

Year	Month	Country	Year	Month	Country
2012	6	Suriname[4]	2007	4	Latvia[1]
	6	Sierra		4	Lithuania[1]
	12	Seychelles		4	Slovenia[1]
	12	Yemen		4	Spain[1]
				4	United Kingdom[1]
2011	3	Brazil[3]		12	Georgia
	4	Saudi			
	7	Macedonia	2006	2	Cameroon
	11	St. Kitts		2	Cook Islands
	12	Montenegro		5	Chad
				8	Kuwait
2010	3	Zambia			
	4	Israel	2005	1	India
	5	Trinidad & Tobago		5	Paraguay
	6	Switzerland		5	Maldives
	7	Barbados[4]		5	Ethiopia
	10	Japan		9	Thailand
	11	Colombia		10	Mali
				11	Bosnia And Herzegovina
2008	2	Australia			
	3	Croatia[3]	2004	3	Madagascar
	5	Kenya		5	Gabon
	10	Laos		7	Indonesia
	11	Armenia		10	Uruguay
2007	2	Liberia	2003	9	Tonga
	3	Canada		9	Albania
	4	Bulgaria[1]			
	4	Cyprus[1]	2002	6	Uganda
	4	Estonia[1]		6	Cape Verde
	4	Greece[1]		7	Samoa
	4	Hungary[1]		10	Jamaica
	4	Ireland[1]			

[1] The US–EU Air Transport Agreement, signed April 30, 2007, was provisionally applied March 30, 2008, for all 27 European Union member states, and Amended by a Protocol, signed and provisionally applied June 24, 2010; [2] Comity and Reciprocity; [3] Agreement signed but not applied; [4] Date agreement reached, but not yet signed or applied; [5] Norway and Iceland joined the US–EU Air Transport Agreement as amended by the protocol on June 21, 2011.

Table 9.2   US–Netherlands Open Skies agreement

Netherlands
The Netherlands via intermediate points to a point or points in the US and beyond. The Netherlands Antilles via the intermediate points Santo Domingo, Port au Prince, Kingston, Montego Bay, Camaguey, and Havana, to Miami. The Netherlands Antilles to New York. The Netherlands Antilles to San Juan.

United States
The US via intermediate points to a point or points in the Netherlands and beyond. The US via intermediate points to Aruba, Curacao, St. Maarten and beyond (Air Transport Association of America).

Airways had asked the US government for anti-trust immunity which would only be granted in the presence of an Open Skies agreement. As Richard Branson, Chairman of Virgin Atlantic Airways has often noted, "they thought they had the British Department of Transport in their pocket, which unfortunately at the time was probably true. They also thought that the US DOT would be so eager to get rid of the Bermuda II disagreement, that it would be blind to the dire consequences such an alliance would hold for competition on the North Atlantic" (Branson, 1998: 100).

As this quote indicates, the competitors in both countries were generally more interested in simply gaining more access to US–UK markets than pursuing a broad Open Skies agreement. Carriers such as British Airways and American saw Open Skies initially as the only way to gain even more from the system. However, even these two carriers began to have doubts when they realized the price that the EU intended to extract for its approval. Access to Heathrow Airport in London, the number one destination airport for North Atlantic passengers, is tightly constrained. In order to free up landing slots for new entrant carriers, European officials have sought ways to encourage incumbent carriers to give up slots. It should be noted that unlike in the US, slots cannot be sold as an asset. In Europe, a carrier either uses a slot or loses it. The price of European approval was the surrender of 300 landing slots by British Airways and American (Phillips, 1999). British Airways "apparently decided the price for opening up Heathrow to new competition might not be offset by revenues gained from a full alliance with American" (Morrocco, 1998: 45).

If opening up Japan and the UK were the key goals of Open Skies, then the policy was a complete success. Although both markets are now part of Open Skies, the journey was far longer than anticipated and many other factors came to play bigger roles, however, the example of US–Japan and US–UK internal divisions illustrates the interplay that occurs in free market systems where competitors look to individual profit and advantage over mutual, assured benefits. According to Adam Smith, the father of market economics, individuals each acting in their own self-interest were supposed to result in a more perfect distribution of goods and determination of price. In the case of airlines, market operation is never separated from government intervention. In a broader sense, Open Skies has helped to spread a more liberal environment for international pricing and capacity. In 1984, the US signed a multilateral agreement with the European Civil Aviation Conference that created zones of reasonableness for each fare class allowing individual carriers latitude in setting prices. The US also pushed for the inclusion of language within bilateral agreements that disallowed fares only with the mutual disapproval of the two parties to the agreement. This new pricing freedom placed tremendous pressure on IATA members to find ways around the IATA set fares. Many IATA members resorted to illegal discounting of fares through extra commissions to travel agents (Toh, 1998). These "bucket shops" sold blocks of tickets at prices more competitive with US carriers, but without sales receipt documentation that would be evidence of violation. Over time the zones of reasonableness became so broad that for all intents and purposes, the market ruled in matters of pricing and IATA abandoned its role in fare setting.

Several studies by the US DOT have concluded that Open Skies bilateral agreements have been effective in lowering fares. In the 1999 report *International Aviation Developments: Global Deregulation Takes Off* (US DoT, 1999) the DOT reported that fares in Open Skies markets dropped 17.5 percent between 1996 and 1998 compared to only a 3.5 percent drop in non-Open Skies markets. Fares increased slightly in non-Open Skies gateway-to-gateway markets, but dropped 11.1 percent in Open Skies markets. In the 2000 report *International Aviation Developments: Transatlantic Deregulation—The Alliance Network Effect* (US DOT, 2000), the DOT concluded that average fares to Open Skies countries declined by 20 percent overall compared to 1996, and approached 25 percent in connecting markets beyond European gateways. Significantly, double-digit fare reductions have occurred even in gate-to-gate markets in Open Skies countries (US DOT, 2000: 3). This report goes on to suggest that the link between Open Skies and strategic alliances have created an "alliance network effect" that has further lowered prices. In fact, it concludes that "alliance-based networks are the principle driving force behind transatlantic price reductions and traffic gains" (US DOT, 2000: 5). In Chapter 16, we will discuss the benefits of the long-awaited EU–US Open Skies agreement.

The Next Step

The US deregulation of air transportation and the concomitant push for Open Skies would slowly erode the old system of international aviation set up in the post-World War II era. The liberalization and economic integration of Europe and Asia (Chapter 9) would further press the cause of liberalization. However, the fact remains that the system remained far from open. Branson (1998) has observed that the Virgin retail division in the US "has a rapidly growing chain of Megastores in this country (US), selling CDs, books, computer games, etc. We employ several thousand US staff and the increased competition our stores have brought clearly benefits the consumer. No one stands in our way when we want to invest ... What a difference from aviation, where if Virgin wanted to establish a US airline we would be restricted to a mere 25% of the voting shares, and thus prevented from exercising any form of control" (Branson, 1998: 101).

The events of 9/11 propelled the already slumping international airline industry to the brink of one of its greatest disasters, but in every crisis there is also the possibility of creating new futures. Some of these possible new futures will be the subject of later chapters. First, we will look at the progress of deregulation and liberalization in Europe and Asia (Chapter 10). Then, we will look at the way airlines attempted to create global seamless networks that extend their reach throughout the world before liberalization took hold (Chapter 11).

Questions

1. Discuss the "show cause" order the US filed against IATA.
2. Analyze the impact of domestic deregulation in the US.
3. What is encirclement and what were its goals?
4. How did the US define Open Skies? What is not included?
5. Did US policy succeed in opening markets?

References

Branson, R. (1998), "Luncheon Address," FAA Commercial Aviation Forecast Conference Proceedings: Overcoming Barriers to World Competition and Growth, March 12–13, pp. 99–102.

Caves, R. (1962), *Air Transport and its Regulators: An Industry Study*, Harvard University Press, Cambridge, MA.

Caves, R.E., Christensen, L.R. and Tretheway, M.W. (1984), "Economies of density versus economies of scale: why trunk and local service airline costs differ," *Rand Journal of Economics*, vol. 15 (1), pp. 471–489.

Dempsey, P. and Gesell, L. (1997), *Airline Management: Strategies for the 21st Century*, Coast Aire Publications, Chandler, AZ.Dempsey, P. and Goetz, A. (1992), *Airline Deregulation and Laissez Faire Mythology*, Praeger, Santa Barbara, CA.

Douglas, G.W. and Miller, J.C. (1974), *Economic Regulation of Domestic Air Transport: Theory and Policy*, The Brookings Institution, Washington, DC.

Eads, G., Nerlove, M. and Raduchel, W. (1969), "A long-run cost function for the local service airline industry: an experiment in non-linear estimation," *Review of Economics and Statistics*, vol. 51(3), pp. 258–270.

Gellman Research Associates (1994), "A Study of International Airline Codesharing," report submitted to Office of Aviation and International Economics, Office of the Secretary of Transportation, US Department of Transportation, Washington, DC.

Goetz, A.R. and Dempsey, P.S. (1989), "Airline deregulation ten years after: something foul in the air," *Journal of Air Law and Commerce*, vol. 54 (4), pp. 927–963.

Goldman, M. (1997), "Negotiating not-quite-open-skies," *The Journal of Commerce*, November 1, p. 4.

Graham, D.R. and Kaplan, D.P. (1982), "Airlines deregulation is working," *Regulation*, vol. 6, pp. 26–32.

Jones, J.R. (1998), "Twenty years of airline deregulation: the impact on outlying and small communities," *Journal of Transportation Management*, vol. 10 (1), pp. 33–43.

Jordan, W.A. (1970), *Airline Regulation in America: Effects and Imperfections*, Johns Hopkins University Press, Baltimore, MD.

Kahn, A.E. (1971), *The Economics of Regulation*, Wiley, New York.

Kahn, A.E. (1990), "Deregulation: looking backward and looking forward," *Yale Journal of Regulation*, vol. 7 (summer), pp. 325–354.

Kane, R.M. (1998), *Air Transportation* (13th ed.), Kendall/Hunt Publishing Company, Dubuque, IA.

Kennedy, P. (1987), *The Rise and Fall of the Great Powers*, Random House, New York.

Kim, E.H. and Singal, V. (1993), "Mergers and market power: evidence from the airline industry," *American Economic Review*, vol. 83 (3), pp. 549–569.

Landes, D. (1969), *The Unbound Prometheus: Technological Change and Industrial Development in Western Europe from 1970 to the Present*, Cambridge University Press, Cambridge.

Levine, M.E. (1979), "Civil aeronautics memo by Michael E. Levine," *Aviation Daily*, March 8, pp. 1–7.

Morrison, S.A. and Winston, C. (1997), "The fare skies: air transportation and middle America," *The Brookings Review*, vol. 15, pp. 42–45.

Morrocco, J.D. (1998), "Open Skies impasse shifts alliance plans," *Aviation Week & Space Technology*, November 9, pp. 45–46.

Oum, T.H. and Park, J. (1997), "Airline alliances: current status, policy issues, and future directions," *Journal of Air Transport Management*, vol. 3 (2), pp. 133–144.

Oum, T.H. and Yu, C. (1998), *Winning Airlines: Productivity and Cost Competitiveness of the World's Major Airlines*, Kluwer Academic Press, Boston, MA.

Phillips, E.H. (1999), "Oneworld late, but powerful," *Aviation Week and Space Technology*, August 23, pp. 63–64.

Rosen, S.D. (1995), "Corporate Restructuring: A labor perspective," in P. Cappelli (ed.), *Airline Labor Relations in the Global Era: The New Frontier*, ILR Press, Ithaca, NY, pp. 31–40.

Solomon, R. (1982), *The International Monetary System*, Harper & Row, New York.

Straszheim, M.R. (1969), *The International Airline Industry*, The Brookings Institution, Washington, DC.

Toh, R.S. (1998), "Towards an international Open Skies regime: advances, impediments, and impacts," *Journal of Air Transportation World Wide*, vol. 3 (1), pp.61–70.

Towers and Perrin (1991), *Competing in a New Market: Is Airline Management Prepared?*, Towers and Perrin, San Francisco, CA.

US Congress (1978), Hearings before the Subcommittee on Aviation of the Committee on Commerce, Science and Transportation, United States Senate, 95th Congress Second Session on S.3363, pp. 19–20.

US Department of Transportation (US DOT) (1999), *International Aviation Developments: Global Deregulation Takes Off*, Department of Transportation, Office of the Secretary, Washington, DC.

US Department of Transportation (US DOT) (2000), *International Aviation Developments: Transatlantic Deregulation—The Alliance Network Effect*, Department of Transportation, Office of the Secretary, Washington, DC.

White, L.J. (1979), "Economies of scale and the question of 'natural monopoly' in the airline industry," *Journal of Air Law and Commerce*, vol. 46 (4), pp. 545–573.

Zagat, W. (1992), *Zagat United States Travel Survey*, Zagat, New York.

Chapter 10
A Different View?

Learning Objectives

After reading this chapter, you should have a good understanding of:
- LO1: the differences in the European and Asian markets that influenced the approaches deregulation and liberalization.
- LO2: the EU approach to deregulation.
- LO3: the early results of deregulation.
- LO4: the remain barriers to open markets.

Key Terms, Concepts, and People

Big Bang	Common Transport Policy	Three packages
Charter operator	Two Airline Policy	LCC

Different Markets, Different Views

As the US struggled with its Big Bang deregulation and pressured the rest of the world to open up its markets, Europe and Asia proceeded to follow their own path to deregulation and liberalization. In Europe, the process of aviation liberalization would be a part of a much bigger effort to integrate the countries in the European Community into the EU and then deal with enlargement; aviation would be but one of the industries that would have to adjust to the changing times. In Asia, the story of liberalization and deregulation would be more mixed. In any event, international politics probably guaranteed that the rest of the world would not fall in line with the US position on deregulation. After all, the Cold War was still in effect in 1978 and independence needed to be demonstrated whatever side you took in that war. Still, some of the variations in attitudes and approaches had their roots in the fact that different regions and nations were faced with very different historic, geographic, and economic realities that inevitably shaped their approach to these issues.

The View from Europe

From a historical and geographic standpoint, Europe can be said to include all the nations west of the Russian Ural Mountains; however, this chapter will focus primarily on the nations of the EU (Table 10.1) with a brief look at the other nations that have asked to be considered for membership in the EU (Table 10.2). These nations represent a very diverse set of languages, cultures, histories, and geographies. As Table 10.1 shows, the landmass of the EU countries ranges from 316 square kilometers for Malta to 551,500 square kilometers for France. Likewise, the population of EU countries ranges from 411,277 for Malta to 81,147,265 for Germany. This diversity in size and population is reflected in the level of aviation infrastructure within these countries as well as the importance of aviation to domestic travel and commerce. The geographic location of nations also influences the ability of potential hub city airports to attract traffic. The countries requesting consideration for admission to the EU under enlargement plans also show considerable diversity in size and population as well ranging from Macedonia with an area of 25,713 square kilometers and 2,087,171 people to Turkey with an area of 783,562 square kilometers and 80,694,485 people.

There are a number of key differences between the air transport market in Europe and the US that have influenced the development of and approach to domestic deregulation and international liberalization. The Chicago Convention of 1944 led to the adoption of a one-airline policy in most of the nations of Europe. This airline, the de jure flag carrier, was seen as more of an instrument of state policy than a moneymaking enterprise (Graham, 1995). The typical European carrier was "to be completely or partially owned by the state, which would provide direct financial assistance to carriers (1) to compensate airlines for the imposition of a public service obligation; (2) to develop and operate domestic service; (3) to provide service to economically underdeveloped regions; (4) to encourage the acquisition and operation of specific airplanes; or (5) simply to cover an airline's operating losses" (Taneja, 1988: 59). This flag carrier would develop its national hub, usually at the nation's capital, and dominate that hub accounting for over 50 percent of the departures (Borestein, 1992). The network of airline routes would reflect national requirements and former colonial ties. As a whole, the old European air transport market was characterized by low productivity, high unit costs, and high fares. In contrast, the US domestic market was substantially larger than that of any single EU nation and benefited from a number of privately owned carriers throughout its history, although it too received government assistance in its early development from airmail rates (Graham, 1995; Sinha, 2001).

Another feature that distinguishes the European market from the US is the higher level of intermodal competition from automobiles and high-speed trains. The average length of a haul in Europe is 750 kilometers, half the US average length of a haul. This increases the competition from other modes of transportation

Table 10.1   Information on EU nations

Country	Area*	Population**	Airports (paved)
Austria	83,871	8,221,646	52 (24)
Belgium	30,528	10,444,268	41 (26)
Bulgaria	110,879	6,981,642	68 (57)
Croatia	56,594	4,475,611	69 (24)
Cyprus	9,251	1,155,403	15 (13)
Czech Rep.	78,867	10,609,762	128 (41)
Denmark	43,094	5,556,452	80 (28)
Estonia	45,228	1,266,375	18 (13)
Finland	338,145	5,266,114	148 (74)
France	551,500	65,951,611	464 (294)
Germany	357,022	81,147,265	539 (318)
Greece	131,957	10,772,967	77 (68)
Hungary	93,028	9,939,470	41 (20)
Ireland	70,273	4,775,982	40 (16)
Italy	301,340	61,482,297	129 (98)
Latvia	64,589	2,178,443	42 (18)
Lithuania	65,300	3,515,858	61 (22)
Luxembourg	2,586	514,862	2 (1)
Malta	316	411,277	1 (1)
Netherlands	41,543	16,805,037	29 (23)
Poland	312,685	38,383,809	126 (87)
Portugal	92,090	10,799,270	64 (43)
Romania	238,391	21,790,479	45 (26)
Slovakia	49,035	5,488,339	35 (21)
Slovenia	20,273	1,992,690	16 (7)
Spain	505,370	47,370,542	150 (99)
Sweden	450,295	9,647,386	231 (149)
UK	243,610	63,395,574	460 (271)

Source: CIA Factbook
* Square Km.
** Estimated July 2013 figures. Data on airports from 2013

Table 10.2   Information on selected EU enlargement countries

Country	Area*	Population**	Airports (paved)
Iceland	103,000	315,281	96 (7)
Macedonia	25,713	2,087,171	10 (8)
Montenegro	13,812	653,474	5 (5)
Serbia	77,474	7,243,007	26 (10)
Turkey	783,562	80,694,485	98 (91)

Source: CIA Factbook
* Square Km. **Estimated July 2013 figures. Data on airports from 2013

and has limited the ability of airlines to develop hub-and-spoke systems like their US counterparts. This in turn has limited consumer ability to achieve reduced fares by accepting indirect routing over direct flights to destination. With the exception of the northeastern corridor of the US, train service does not offer a viable substitute to air travel for US consumers (Graham, 1995; Sinha, 2001). With a cruising speed of 185 mph, the Trains a Grande Vitesse (TGV) in France has become a serious competitor for Air France. A market analysis by the French civil aviation authority found that only domestic routes not served by the TGV remain healthy for the air carrier. Similar concerns are arising in other European countries with high-speed train options (Sparaco, 2012a). European carriers have also faced competition from a well-developed air charter market. In the early 1990s, charter service in the US accounted for less than 2 percent of all passenger miles, but more than 25 percent of the passenger miles in Europe. These European charter passengers were predominantly leisure travelers, leaving scheduled carriers to serve business travel needs (Sinha, 2001). The rise of the low-cost carriers (LCCs) has also created new pressure on the legacy carriers. According to the European Low-Fare Airlines Association, their members carried over 200 million passengers in 2012 (Sparaco, 2012b). Finally, there was a significant difference in the product mix between US and European carriers as they deregulated. For US carriers, only 15.4 percent of the departures were international as late as 1990. In 1990, international departures represented 52.9 percent of the departures of European carriers (Sinha, 2001). In short, it was neither feasible nor probably possible to institute US-style deregulation in Europe.

The European way

When the European Economic Community, a predecessor of the current EU, was formed in 1957, it established a Common Transport Policy, but failed to include aviation in the original draft (Button, 1997). This oversight was corrected in a 1986 ruling by the European Court of Justice, which declared that air transport would henceforth be subject to the competition rules of the Treaty of Rome. The following year, the Council of Ministers adopted the so-called First Package which allowed multiple designation of carriers on country-to-country routes and high-volume city-to-city routes, fifth freedom rights on city-to-city routes up to 30 percent of capacity, automatic approval of discount fares up to 55 percent, and double approval of full fares. The Second Package, adopted in 1990, included a double-disapproval provision for full fares and an extension of fifth freedom rights on city-to-city routes up to 50 percent of capacity. Protection was also granted for routes designated as public service obligations. The Third, and final, Package was implemented in 1993 and ended on April 1, 1997. This package granted full access to all routes including cabotage, which went into effect on April 1. It removed all restrictions on fares subject to the right of the European Commission (EC) to intervene in matters of predatory pricing and seat (capacity) dumping. All distinctions were removed between charter and scheduled carriers and freedom was granted to start an airline provided it was (1) EU owned, (2) financially sound, and (3) in compliance with all safety requirements (Graham, 1997, 1995; Sinha, 2001).

Overall results

The early packages, combined with the more liberal bilateral agreements signed during the 1980s, does appear to have increased the frequency on some routes and reduced leisure fares, particularly where multiple carrier designation allowed new market entry (Button and Swann, 1989; Graham, 1995). A study of the air transport market between the UK and Ireland reported a 50 percent reduction in fares and a doubling in passenger numbers following deregulation (Barrett, 1999). Ironically, financial trouble at the Irish flag carrier Aer Lingus has seen "the other Irish carrier," Ryanair, attempt to buy it, a situation that would lead back to the near monopoly of yesteryear (Convery, 2012). Other early study results have been somewhat mixed. Morrell (1998) has found that the number of cross-border routes served increased by 11 percent between 1989 and 1992. This number rose to 25 percent between 1992 and 1995. The number of flights operated also increased during these periods by 14 and 18 percent respectively. The average frequency on all intra-EU routes increased from 13.9 departures per week in 1989 to 15.5 in 1992. Seat capacity did not increase between 1989 and 1992, but did go up after 1992 on routes that were served by three or more carriers. A 1995 study by the Civil Aviation Authority of Great Britain also found that consumers only gained from lower fares, better service, and better connecting flights when there were at least three competitors on a given route. In effect, actual, rather than threatened, entry was essential to realizing benefits from liberalization (Abbot and Thompson, 1989; Humphries, 1996). A study by the EC (1996) concluded that competition had little effect on routes run as a monopoly or duopoly. Unfortunately, approximately 94 percent of the intra-EU routes fell into this category.

The effect of liberalization on established EU legacy carriers has until recently been relatively limited. Carriers such as British Airways and KLM worked to improve their long-haul market and hub system more than their intra-EU system

(CAA, 1995). While one of the key features of the first two packages was the extension of fifth freedom rights, evidence indicates that few carriers exploited these rights (Graham, 1995). Some of the peripheral EU countries did initially attempt to exploit the intra-EU opportunities of cabotage, but many of these services were discontinued due to limited profitability (Morrell, 1998). Thus, there was generally little third carrier entry in many markets, certainly not by the traditional flag carriers. This has not been true for the LCCs. It is possible that Ryanair alone, now the seventh largest carrier in the world, has done more to reduce fares and increase passenger numbers than any other single factor associated with deregulation (Convery, 2012). Between 1992 and 1995, there was an EU net gain of six carriers (Morrell, 1998). The most successful of these carriers were Ireland's Ryanair and the UK's EasyJet. In 2001, these carriers continued to post significant profits compared to their traditional counterparts in the EU. In fact, it appears that 2001 was a turning point for the low-cost European entrants. Industry experts had expected LCCs to increase their share of intra-European passenger traffic from 7 percent in 2001 to over 14 percent by 2006 (Binggelli and Pompeo, 2002; R2A, 2002). It now appears that the number of seats offered by LCCs in Europe grew an average of 14 percent per year compared to 1 percent for legacy carriers over the same period. In some countries such as Spain, LCCs now account for over 50 percent of the market (Turner, 2013). As with US LCCs, the events of September 11 created new opportunities in Europe for this model of aviation business. The GFC of 2008 with its economy weakening effects has hit Europe particularly hard and continued the trend toward LCCs.

With liberalization, particularly the implementation of the Third Package, charter operators in the EU were presented with a number of options. They could now (1) enter scheduled service in a head-to-head competition with EU flag carriers; (2) enter scheduled service on leisure routes; or (3) stay in the core charter market and develop their long-haul operations. The evidence to date shows that option (1) was not very successful for these operators (Air Europe, Dan Air, Trans European). Some carriers did have limited success on certain routes (Maersk Air, Transwede, Transavia), but generally charter operators have not provided a serious challenge to the established carriers (Morrell, 1998). Wallace, Tiernan, Rhoades, and Linck (2008) found that despite a good deal of consolidation in the charter industry most of the charter companies have lost passengers since 2001 while the LCCs appear to be major winners.

Remaining obstacles

One of the most significant obstacles to progress in the EU is the continuing issue of airline subsidies. In 1993, six EU carriers—Air France, Olympic, Iberia, TAP-Air Portugal, Alitalia, and Aer Lingus—required government subsidies to remain in business (Graham, 1995). Then, the Belgium government stepped in to salvage something of its flag carrier, Sabena. These early subsidies were approved by the EC, although vigorously opposed by some members of the EU. Most recently, the eastern European carriers—LOT (Poland), Malev (Hungary), and AirBaltic (Latvia)—have been the subject of subsidies and debate. In early 2012, the EC ruled that Malev had to repay subsidies received from 2007 to 2010, forcing the carrier into bankruptcy (Clark and Jolly, 2012). The preference of governments for national carriers flies in the face of the objective to remove such barriers to free trade in the EU as a whole. It also keeps excess capacity in the European market in a way similar to the liberal bankruptcy laws of the US In both cases, artificial barriers prevent the market from adjusting quickly in market demand downturns and spread the problem to other carriers.

A somewhat related problem is the question of hubs. LLCs tend more often to fly point-to-point, so this is another legacy carrier problem. London Heathrow is a case in point. While it remains a major airport (and destination) in Europe, it does not truly operate under the traditional hub-and-spoke model since capacity constraints keep it from building the type of spoke traffic flows that are supposed to be the hallmark of "successful" hubs. Since hubs are an expensive operational feature, an unsuccessful hub becomes doubly disastrous. Restructuring at some hubs is attempting to reduce or eliminate the short-haul to short-haul operations in favor of short-haul to long-haul connections that are part of the traditional hub model. High fuel cost is the main issue as they make smaller aircraft less economical to fly and these have typically been the aircraft assigned to small feed markets (Flottau, 2013a and b).

The View from Asia

According to the ICAO regional classification, the Asia–Pacific is composed of 34 nations covering 16,000 kilometers. It extends from Afghanistan in the west to Tahiti in the east and from Mongolia in the north to New Zealand in the south. Asia–Pacific accounted for roughly 50 percent of the total world population and was responsible for 25 percent of the world's scheduled passenger traffic in 2001 (ICAO, 2012). ICAO has projected that the region could increase its share of traffic to 42 percent by 2020 (Sinha, 2001). This growth is obviously tied to the rapid economic development of the region and the rising level of income, both of which are closely linked to aviation activity.

Taneja (1988) attributed the early growth in Asian–Pacific aviation to a number of factors including high-growth export-oriented economies, productive and lower-cost airlines, and coordination and cooperation between airlines and their respective governments, all of which remain true today. According to ICAO (2012), the average annual growth in Asia from 2001 to 2011 was 6.4 percent with continued growth through 2014. While there is a great deal of variation in the general approaches of the countries in the Asia–Pacific region, they too have been on a path toward greater deregulation and liberalization even if the pace has been somewhat slower and more uneven than the North American and European markets.

Variations on a Theme

The Centre for Aviation (CAPA) divides Asia into three regions: (1) North Asia including China, Japan, and Korea; (2) South Asia including India; and (3) South Pacific, including Australia, New Zealand, and Singapore. These divisions will be used to explore the aviation environment in Asia (CAPA, 2013a; 2013b; 2013c).

North Asia—China. With a population of more than 1.3 billion and an area of 9,596,961 square kilometers (Table 10.3), China cannot be left out of any discussion on aviation. In 1988, China had only one state airline, CAAC which was a division of the Civil Aviation Administration of China. In 1998, the CAAC created six regional airlines—Air China, China Eastern, China Southern, China Northern, China Northwest, and China Southwest—which were expected to run as more or less independent carriers by 1995. In April 2001, the CAAC announced plans to merge nine airlines under its control into three larger groupings—China Southern Airlines Group, China Eastern Airlines Group, and Air China Group (Centre for Asian Business Cases, 2002). Air China, originally designated as the international division, took over China Southwest in 2002. Also in 2002, China Eastern took over China Northwest. In 2003, China Southern absorbed China Northern. The CAAC also announced plans to overhaul the domestic air route network, permit ticket discounting, encourage airport alliances, and raise air transport service fees (Centre for Asian Business Cases, 2002; *Aerospace Daily*, 2001). The CAAC is now attempting to rationalize the hub system for the three main carriers so that each would have only a single hub—Air China (Beijing), China Eastern (Shanghai), and China Southern (Guangzhou). All of these hubs are coastal with no clear central Chinese hub (Perrett, 2013). According to CAPA, Chinese carriers are not currently taking advantage of many sixth freedom rights and many are limited by their long-haul fleet. Chinese policy currently limits long-haul routes to a single carrier. Of the three carriers, China Southern is having the most difficulty in the long-haul market. The carrier is hoping to expand in the short-haul international market (CAPA, 2013a).

North Asia—Japan. As you will remember from Chapter 8, the US policy of encirclement in Asia was aimed at opening up the Japanese market, the key Asian market from North America at the time. The policy was less than successful. However, Japan has become a leading example of liberalization, recently signing Open Skies agreements with China, Taiwan, and Europe (CAPA, 2013a). Historically, Japanese policy was marked by a strict regulation of the aviation system after the so-called "aviation constitution" was adopted in 1972 dividing the market among the three Japanese carriers—Japan Air Lines (JAL), All Nippon Airways (ANA), and Japan Air Systems (JAS). JAL was to serve the main domestic trunk routes and the international market. ANA was assigned short-haul international charter flights and other domestic trunk routes. JAS was to serve primarily on local routes. Little or no competition was allowed between these carriers. In 1986, the Council for Transport Policy recommended the privatization of JAL, the introduction of greater domestic competition, including new entrant carriers, and the end of JAL's international monopoly. In 1996, a zone fare system was introduced allowing carriers to offer a discount up to 50 percent of the minimum fare, however, fares for all carriers operating on the same routes were to be the same. Although new entrants were allowed in the market, restrictive regulations and limited airport capacity hindered the development of more carriers for a number of years (Graham, 1995). In 2001, Sinha concluded that Japanese consumers have not yet fully benefited from the more liberal policies of the government, although there was some evidence that airlines had been able to lower their own costs. Internationally, JAL and ANA have suffered from higher input costs and lower efficiency than most of their US and European competitors and all but Thai Airways in Asia. According to Oum and Yu (1998), these carriers were 52.7 and 63.5 percent less cost competitive in 1993 than the benchmark US carrier American Airlines. Unfortunately, the airlines like the rest of the Japanese economy have been in crisis for over a decade. Passenger traffic has only grown in three years since 2002, the latest being 2012. No other major market in the world has experienced such sustained, weak growth. The international traffic for Japanese carriers in 2012 was only slightly better than 1999 levels. Domestic load factors have remained around 60 percent for the last two decades. Japan has recently encouraged LCC entry and 2012 saw three such carriers established— Peach, Jetstar, and AirAsia Japan (CAPA, 2013a). The AirAsia venture between AirAsia and ANA was very short-lived as the LCC and the traditional ANA could not mesh their differing philosophies. ANA established its own LCC, Vanilla Air in December 2013 (Schofield, 2014). It remains to be seen if Japanese consumers will benefit from this latest round of deregulation.

North Asia—Korea. South Korea has two major international carriers— Korean Airlines and Asiana. Both Korean Airlines and Asiana are privately owned. Beginning in 1992, the government ceased to set fares, although Korean domestic air travel has not seen significant drops in fares. The entry of Asiana in 1988 did begin to increase passenger enplanements but again had little or no effect on fares. In effect, the Korean government allowed a collusive duopoly to form following changes made in 1994 (Sinha, 2001). Korean Airlines and Asiana were hard hit by the Asian crisis, however, these problems were overshadowed in many ways by the decision of the US FAA to downgrade them from a Category 1 to a Category 2, meaning that they failed to meet the minimum international safety standards set by ICAO. As a result of this action, Asiana, the second largest carrier in South Korea lost its codesharing pact with American Airlines, costing it an estimated US$16 million. Korean Airlines had earlier lost its international alliance with the US carrier Delta Air Lines after a series of accidents in 1999. The Korean government temporarily banned it from international flights in 1999. Following joint efforts by the Korean government and the FAA, Category 1 status was renewed. Korean Airlines made a series of changes that allowed it to rejoin the SkyTeam alliance with Delta and Air France. Since the 1990s, both carriers appeared to make progress on the safety issues that had plagued them. In addition, Asiana was named the 2012 Best Overall Airline in the World by *Business Traveler*

Table 10.3   Information on selected Asia–Pacific nations

Country	Area*	Population**	Airports (paved)
Australia	7,741,220	22,262,501	480 (349)
China	9,596,961	1,349,585,838	507 (463)
Cook Islands	236	10,447	11 (1)
Fiji	18,274	896,758	28 (4)
India	3,287,263	1,220,800,359	346 (253)
Indonesia	1,904,569	251,160,124	673 (186)
Japan	377,915	127,253,075	175 (142)
Malaysia	329,847	29,628,392	114 (39)
New Zealand	267,710	4,365,113	123 (39)
Pakistan	796,095	193,238,868	151 (108)
Philippines	300,000	105,720,644	247 (89)
Singapore	697	5,460,302	9 (9)
Taiwan	35,980	23,299,716	37 (35)
Thailand	513,120	67,497,151	101 (63)
Timor-Leste	14,874	1,172,390	6 (2)
Vietnam	331,210	92,477,857	45 (38)

Source: CIA Factbook
**Square* Km. **Estimated July 2013 figures. Data for airports from 2013

magazine (Aratani, 2013). While the final report on the recent Asiana crash is not yet out, it is likely to renew scrutiny of the carriers.

South Asia. The South Asian region includes India, Pakistan, Bangladesh, Sri Lanka, and the small Himalayan states of Nepal and Bhutan. By far, India has had some of the most dynamic growth in the region. India is second only to China in population and since the 1991 crisis triggered by the collapse of the USSR, a major trading partner of India, it has been on a path toward economic liberalization. Until the early 1990s, the Indian government maintained a virtual monopoly on the airline industry with the market divided between Indian Airlines, which served the domestic market, and Air India, which provided international service and limited connecting flights. Under the Air Corporation Act of 1953, these two government-owned carriers were the only ones permitted to offer air service in India. The Open Skies policy introduced in 1990 allowed air taxi operations, charters, and new entrants to begin serving the domestic market. In 1993, Indian Airlines was allowed to begin international operations to the Gulf countries where many expatriate Indians worked. Indian Airlines continued to serve the bulk of the domestic markets, however, their share declined to only about 46 percent as of 2000 due to new carrier competition. During the mid-1990s, India witnessed the establishment of six private carriers intent on competing against state-controlled Air India and Indian Airlines. It seemed that Indian aviation was set to take off. Unfortunately, only one of these early private airlines, Jet Airways, survives. Four of these carriers amassed huge losses before ceasing operations while Air Deccan "survived" after a takeover by Kingfisher Airlines. Table 10.4 shows the seat capacity of Indian carriers as of May 2013. Most of these carriers would be classified as LCCs. In fact, since 2004 when LCCs represented only 1.3 percent of the market in India, this sector has grown to represent 67.5 percent in 2012. Non-Indian carriers flying in or to/from India include Air Arabia, Air Asia, Arkefly, and Tiger Airways (CAPA, 2013b). The primary international destination for Indian carriers continues to be the Middle East with South Asia second. Despite showing great promise, the Indian commercial aviation market remains only one-fifth of the Chinese market (*The Times of India*, 2012). In the wake of continuing financial troubles for its two historic carriers, the Indian government announced in 2007 that it had approved the merger of Air India and Indian Airlines under the Air India name (Air Transport Intelligence, 2008). This step has solved neither the financial nor the quality problems that plagued both carriers prior to the decision.

Table 10.4   Indian airlines' domestic seat capacity

Airline	Seats per week
IndiGo	516,420
Air India	442,646
Jet Airways	402, 610
Spicejet	386,973
GoAir	143,640
JetLite	109,732
Air India Express	72,198

Source: CAPA profiles

Many factors have been cited for the failure of early new entrants in India including overexpansion, high debt, and continued government control over routes served, aircraft imported, and feeder service requirements. In addition to these burdens, carriers were prohibited from exiting loss-making routes and required to purchase state-controlled aviation fuel at almost twice the world price. One of the most high-profile recent failures has been Kingfisher Airlines. Kingfisher Airlines was founded on May 7, 2005 by Vijay Mallya, an Indian tycoon best known for his beer, to celebrate the eighteenth birthday of his son. Mallya promised an "unparalleled in-flight experience"—personal flight entertainment systems, fine dining, and model-like attendants, but the growth of the LCC prompted Kingfisher to acquire troubled no-frills carrier AirDeccan several years later. This acquisition saddled the carrier with substantial debt that became unbearable as the GFC continued (Datta, 2012). Weighed down with debt, rising fuel costs, and price wars with its rivals, Kingfisher was unable to pay suppliers and pilots (50 of whom subsequently left for a rival carrier) and was forced to cancel flights and ground planes (Singhal, 2012; Sinha and Sinha, 2012). The carrier was grounded in October following unrest from a labor force seeking back wages (Menon, 2012). Supporters of Kingfisher and the airline industry have argued that government policies bear much of the blame for airline crises, citing continued restriction on bilateral traffic rights, above-global average taxes on aviation fuel, restrictions on foreign investment in domestic Indian airlines, infrastructure problems, and continued support for Air India (*The Times of India*, 2012). Those on the other side of the debate asked, "Will the heavens fall if Kingfisher Airlines shuts down?" and concluded that the failure was part of the creative destruction that is part of capitalism; there might be some structural unemployment as laid-off workers find jobs in other airlines or sectors, but Kingfisher's death would make way for a trimmer, more efficient carrier (Malik, 2012). The government change to allow greater foreign direct investment has yet to save Kingfisher, although it might benefit Jet Airways, the last of the early private carriers. Unfortunately, many of the same problems that plagued early start-up carriers continue to persist—high fuel costs, poor infrastructure, and so on (Menon, 2012)

South Pacific—Australia and New Zealand. The first act regulating aviation in Australia was the Navigation Act of 1920, but confusion over the role of state and Commonwealth governments in air transport regulation led to an amended Air Navigation Act in 1936. According to this act, the Commonwealth was authorized to control air transportation with other countries and within the two territories of Australia. It was left to the states to control intra-state air transportation, although this did not keep the Commonwealth government from attempting to regulate intra-state aviation.

One of the most significant aviation policies of the Australian government occurred in the 1950s when then Prime Minister Robert Menzies decided that it was essential to prevent a monopoly from developing in Australian domestic airline service. The Two Airline Policy became official in 1952 with the passage of the Civil Aviation Agreement Act. Henceforth, there would be two carriers in Australia. Trans-Australian Airlines (later Australian Airlines), the state-owned carrier, would operate alongside the privately owned Australian National Airways (later Ansett). The government guaranteed the loans of Australian National up to a specified limit and later loosened the requirement that all government employees fly Trans-Australian. International service would be the province of Qantas. In 1957, the government further declared that two and only two trunk carriers would exist in Australia and established a Rationalization Committee composed of a member of each airline and a coordinator nominated by the Transport Minister. The Airlines Equipment Act of 1958 authorized the government to restrict the size of each carrier's fleet. In 1961, two additional acts authorized the Rationalization Committee to establish timetables, frequencies, aircraft types, capacity, fares, freight levels, and overall load factors on groups of routes.

By 1981, criticism of the Two Airline Policy led to the Holcroft Inquiry which recommended a pricing policy based on cost that would be nationally consistent and allow discounted fares to be determined by the airlines. This same year, Trans-Australia Airlines was made a public company, although the government continued to maintain effective ownership. Other actions in 1981 created an Independent Air Fares Committee to review fares, approve discounts, and change fare formulas to consider cost and efficiency and strengthened the government's ability to control the capacity of regional and cargo carriers through licensing of aircraft imports (Sinha, 2001).

Overall, limited information suggests that while the Two Airline Policy did create a stable aviation system of high yield and profitable carriers with an excellent safety record, it was characterized by higher costs and lower productivity (Kirby, 1979; Sinha, 2001). The perception of Australian consumers was that it also resulted in higher fares than the deregulated market of the US. Under pressure, the Australian government decided in 1990 to deregulate its domestic market. In the first year of deregulation, the Australian market experienced a growth of 66 percent and average airfares dropped 41.3 percent, however, both of these numbers have fluctuated in the years since then in part due to the entry and failure of new carriers. Forsyth (1991) has argued that entry into the Australian market was destined to be difficult because of the advantages incumbent carriers possessed, particularly in terms of airport and terminal access. In a further effort to foster competition, the Australian government proposed a single trans-Tasman aviation market with New Zealand, granted Air New Zealand greater fifth freedom rights, and opened up the international market to other carriers (after allowing Qantas to purchase Australian). Two new carriers entered the Australian domestic market, Impulse Airlines and Virgin Blue (owned by Richard Branson of Virgin Airlines) which led to price wars on the main routes temporarily lowering fares to Australian consumers. In 2001, the Australian Competition and Consumer Commission approved the acquisition of Impulse Airlines by Qantas, which had also signaled its intent to improve fleet allocation, and costs to more effectively compete against the lower cost Virgin Blue (Cahners Publishing Company, 2000; M2 Communications Ltd., 2001a; M2 Communications Ltd., 2001b). Virgin Australia, as it is now called, has become the second largest carrier in Australia behind flag carrier Qantas Airways (Table 10.5), but they posted a loss for the 2012–2013 year citing carbon tax, booking system upgrade, and recent acquisitions (60 percent share in Tiger Australia and Skywest) as the cause. Given that Singapore Airlines, Air New Zealand, and Etihad Airways had recently invested in the carrier, this news was surprising to some (Kelly, 2013). Qantas, also facing financial troubles, further shook the global industry by announcing a partnership with Emirates Airlines that will shift its European hub to Dubai (Fickling, 2013). Both airlines are seeking a North Asia alliance partner to gain greater reach in this region. The battles between Qantas and Virgin Australia (that included acquisition of LCCs) have left Regional Express (Rex) the largest independent regional carrier in Australia (CAPA, 2013c).

Table 10.5   Top ten South Pacific carriers

Airline	Seats per week
Qantas Airways	758,452
Virgin Australia	523, 669
Jetstar Airways	371, 721
Air New Zealand	326, 019
Tiger Airways Australia	63, 720
Regional Express	44,846
Air Niugini	40,204
Air Pacific	30,157
Air Tahiti	20, 862
Airlines PNG	12, 138

Source: CAPA Country Profiles

Airline deregulation in New Zealand actually predates that of Australia, having begun in 1983 with the abolishment of domestic fare and entry controls. The flag carrier, Air New Zealand, was privatized in 1989 and Australian-based Ansett was invited to set up a subsidiary to serve the New Zealand domestic market. However, internationally, the market continued to be restricted, particularly between New Zealand and its neighbor, Australia. Beginning in 1992, there was some movement to provide greater flexibility in pricing, fares, and capacity in international service between the two countries. Like the Australian market, New Zealand has found it difficult to retain new entrant carriers. Kiwi Airlines started service in 1995 between Australia and New Zealand, but halted operations in 1996. After Ansett New Zealand and its parent company began to experience financial difficulty, Qantas considered making a financial investment in the New Zealand carrier. When this deal fell through, Qantas New Zealand was allowed to begin domestic service (Sinha, 2001). In an interesting twist on Australian–New Zealand aviation relations, Air New Zealand went on to purchase Ansett Australia in 2000 only to cut it loose on September 12 when it was placed in voluntary administration (bankruptcy). Following allegations that they had stripped Ansett of assets before its collapse, Air New Zealand agreed to pay the administrators of Ansett NZD180 million (M2 Communications, 2001a, 2002). Singapore Airlines had purchased 25 percent of Air New Zealand, but this share was reduced to 4.3 percent after the New Zealand government renationalized the carrier in October 2001 (BBC News, 2001). From 2002–2004, there were talks about a major alliance between Qantas and Air New Zealand that would have seen Qantas invest $550 million in Air New Zealand, assuming a 15 percent stake in the company. These were eventually abandoned and Qantas sold its remaining stake in ANZ in 2007 (Air

Transport Intelligence, 2008). In 2010, Air New Zealand purchased 19 percent of the shareholding of Virgin Australia as part of their trans-Tasman alliance. They have recently asked the Australian competition regulator to renew the alliance to help them compete against the Qantas–Emirates alliance (Freed, 2013). For its part, Qantas' New Zealand subsidiary, Jetconnect, has struggled, particularly on the Tasman route. The main domestic rival for ANZ is Jetstar, which has about a 30 percent share of the main trunk routes in New Zealand, that is, the routes between Auckland, Wellington, Christchurch, Dunedin, and Queenstown. After the withdrawal of Qantas from the Auckland–Los Angeles route, ANZ held a monopoly on the Pacific–North American market; however, Hawaiian Airlines has started a Honolulu–Auckland route. ANZ also serves Vancouver (CAPA, 2013c).

Resuming growth

Passenger traffic for all of Asia was flat for 2001, unlike world figures overall which posted a negative growth rate of 2.9 percent. While Asia was affected by the turmoil of the GFC, it continues to be one of the fastest-growing markets overall and for aviation. The Boeing market outlook for 2013–2032 projects Asian economies to grow at an annual rate of 4.5 percent over these 20 years and represent 28 percent of world GDP by 2032. Total air traffic is predicted to grow even faster at 6.3 percent a year (Boeing, 2013).

Looking Backward and Forward

Although both Asia and Europe were slower to liberalize and deregulate their aviation markets, they have both made great strides in developing their aviation systems and reducing fares while increasing services. While both areas have been affected by September 11 and the many crises that have plagued the world's airlines, many of their carriers have emerged far stronger than their US counterparts. Heading into the new century, the problems of infrastructure, competition, and costs will represent a major challenge to these regions.

Questions

1. Discuss the European approach to deregulation.
2. What role did charter airlines play in Europe?
3. What influenced the EU approach and has it been more successful than the US "Big Bang"?
4. Has deregulation led to more competition? Has it led to the creation of more carriers or more carrier entry at the route level? Have fares dropped?
5. Discuss the progress of deregulation in Asian countries.

References

Abbott, K. and Thompson, D. (1989), *Deregulating European Aviation: The Impact of Bilateral Liberalization*, Center for Business Strategy Working Paper Series no 73, London.

Aerospace Daily (2001), "CAAC readies for airport, carrier alliance," October 30, Aviation Week Group.

Air Transport Intelligence (2008), Air India news, retrieved online June 8, 2010 from www.rati.com.

Aratani, L. (2013), "Korean airlines have had a troubled past," *The Washington Post*, retrieved online August 6, 2013 from http://articles.washingtonpost.com/2013-07-06/local/40408386_1_asiana-pilot-south-korea-asiana-airlines-boeing.

Barrett, S.D. (1999), "Peripheral market entry, product differentiation, supplier rents, and sustainability in the deregulated European airline market—a case study," *Journal of Air Transport Management*, vol. 5 (1), pp. 21–30.

BBC News (2001), "Air New Zealand renationalized," BBC News wireservice, October 4.

Binggeli, U. and Pompeo, L. (2002), "Hyped hopes for Europe's low-cost airlines," *McKinsey Quarterly*, no. 4.

Boeing (2013), "Current market outlook 2013–2032," retrieved oonline January 6, 2014 from http://www.boeing.com/boeing/commercial/cmo/asia-pacific.page.

Borestein, S. (1992), "Prospects for Competitive Air Travel in Europe," in W.J. Adams (ed.), *Singular Europe: Economy and Policy of the European Community After 1992*, University of Michigan Press, Ann Arbor., pp. 126–142.

Button, K.J. (1997), "Developments in the European Union: Lessons for the Pacific Asia Region," in C. Findley, C.I. Sien, and K. Singh (eds), *Asia Pacific Air Transport: Challenges and Policy Reform*, Institute of Southeast Asian Studies, Singapore., pp. 170–180.

Button, K.J. and Swann, D. (1989), "European Community airlines—deregulation and its problems," *Journal of Common Market Studies*, vol. 37 (3), pp. 259–282.

Cahners Publishing Company (2000), "Virgin Blue launches service; second route to debut Sept. 7," Gale Group wireservice, September 4, retrieved online June 2, 2002 from www.findarticles.com.

Centre for Asian Business Cases (2002), *Preparing for China's Entry to the WTO: China's Airline Industry*, The University of Hong Kong School of Business, Hong Kong.

Centre for Aviation (CAPA) (2013a), *World Aviation Yearbook 2013—North Asia Pacific*, CAPA, available at centreforaviation.com.

Centre for Aviation (CAPA) (2013b), *World Aviation Yearbook 2013—South Asia*, CAPA, available at centreforaviation.com.

Centre for Aviation (CAPA) (2013c), *World Aviation Yearbook 2013—South Pacific*, CAPA, available at centreforaviation.com.

Civil Aviation Authority (CAA) (1995), *CAP 654 The Single Aviation Market: Progress So Far*, Civil Aviation Authority, London.

CIA Factbook (2013), retrieved online January 2, 2014 from www.odci.gov/cia/publications/factbook.

Clark, N. and Jolly, D. (2012), "Hungarian national airline halts flights," *The New York Times*, retrieved online August 1, 2013 from http://www.nytimes.com/2012/02/04/business/global/hungarian-national-airline-halts-flights.html?_r=0.

Convery, F. (2012), "Airline competition in Ireland – back to monopoly ," retrieved online August 1, 2013 from http://www.publicpolicy.ie/airline-competition-in-ireland-back-to-monopoly/.

Datta, K. (2012), "He predicted KF turbulence before takeoff," *The Economic Times*, February 20, pp. 1–6.

European Commission (EC) (1996), *Impact of the Third Package of Air Transport Liberalization Measures COM 96*, European Commission, Brussels.

Fickling, D. (2013), "Outsider CEO remakes Qantas allying with ex-nemesis Emirates, Bloomberg," retrieved online August 5, 2013 from http://www.bloomberg.com/news/2013-07-14/outsider-ceo-remakes-qantas-tying-up-with-ex-nemesis-emirates.html.

Flottau, J. (2013a), "Evolving paradigm," *Aviation Week & Space Technology*, July 8, pp. 36–39.

Flottau, J. (2013b), "Stabilizing at best," *Aviation Week & Space Technology*, July 8, pp. 38–39.

Forsyth, P. (1991), "The Regulation and Deregulation of Australia's Domestic Airline Industry," in K.J. Button (ed.) *Airline Deregulation: International Experiences*, David Fulton, London, pp. 48–84.

Freed, J. (2013), "Air NZ and Virgin want more time," *Business Day*, retrieved online August 5, 2013 from http://www.stuff.co.nz/business/industries/8994563/Air-NZ-and-Virgin-want-more-time.

Graham, B. (1995), *Geography and Air Transport*, John Wiley and Sons, New York.

Graham, B. (1997), "Air transport liberalization in the European Union: an assessment," *Regional Studies*, vol. 31(1), pp. 87–104.

Humphries, B. (1996), "The UK Civil Aviation Authority and European air services liberalization," *Journal of Transport Economics and Policy*, vol (2). 3, pp. 213–220.

International Civil Aviation Organization (ICAO) (2012), "Robust traffic growth expected until 2014," International Civil Aviation Authority, retrieved online August 1, 2013 from http://www.icao.int/Newsroom/Pages/robust-traffic-growth-expected-until-2014.aspx.

Kelly, R. (2013), "Virgin Australia warns of steep net loss," *The Wall Street Journal*, retrieved online August 5, 2013 from http://online.wsj.com/article/SB10001424127887323514404578649032614620240.html.

Kirby (1979), "An economic assessment of Australia's Two Airline Policy," *Australian Journal of Management*, vol. 5, pp. 105–111.

Malik, A. (2012), "Not at taxpayer's expense: by hinting at a bailout for Kingfisher, the government is making a mockery of market forces," *The Times of India*, February 29, p. 16.

Menon, J. (2012), "Last gasps? India's Kingfisher Airlines looks to Etihad Airways for salvation," *Aviation Week & Space Technology*, December 17, p. 38.

M2 Communications Ltd. (2001a), "Air New Zealand denies stripping Ansett assets," Gale Group wireservice, November 13, retrieved online February 10, 2003 from www.findarticles.com.

M2 Communications Ltd. (2001b), "Virgin Blue may be able to Open Review into Qantas' Takeover of Impulse Airline," Gale Group wireservice, September 7, retrieved online February 10, 2003 from www.findarticles.com.

M2 Communications Ltd. (2002), "Air New Zealand increases flights in Asia after Ansett collapse," Gale Group wireservice, retrieved online February 10, 2003 from www.findarticles.com.

Morrell, P. (1998), "Air transport liberalization in Europe: the progress so far," *Journal of Air Transportation World Wide*, vol. 3 (1), pp. 42–60.

Oum, T.H. and Yu, C. (1998), *Winning Airlines: Productivity and Cost Competitiveness of the World's Major Airlines*, Kluwer Academic Publishers, Boston, MA.

Perrett, B. (2013), "Hub envy," *Aviation Week & Space Technology*, July 8, p. 42.

R2A (2002), Unisys R2A Scorecard: Airline Industry Cost Measurement, Unisys Corporation, Blue Bell, Pennsylvania.Singhal, M. (2012), "Kingfisher likely to lose prime slots to rivals," *The Economic Times*, February 23, p. 5.

Sinha, D. (2001), *Deregulation and Liberalization of the Airline Industry: Asia, Europe, North America, and Oceania*, Ashgate, Aldershot.

Sinha, M.V. and Sinha, S. (2012), "Kingfisher left high and dry as 50 pilots quit in a week," *The Times of India*, February 23, p. 26.

Sparaco, P. (2012a), "Trains reign supreme," *Aviation Week & Space Technology*, September 3, p. 22.

Sparaco, P. (2012b), "Worst-case scenario," *Aviation Week & Space Technology*, November 26, p. 16.

Taneja, N.K. (1988), *The International Airline Industry: Trends, Issues and Challenges*, Lexington Books, Lexington, MA.

The Times of India (2012), "Turbulent flight: improving viability of airlines should be top priority for government," *The Times of India*, February 22, p. 12.

Turner, A. (2013), "Europe low cost carrier growth outstrips legacy airline rivals," retrieved online August 2 from http://www.airtrafficmanagement.net/2013/05/europe-lcc-growth-outstrips-legacy-rivals/.

Wallace, M., Tiernan, S., Rhoades, D.L. and Linck, T. (2008), "European tour operators and low cost carriers: strategic options in a changing marketplace," *Journal of Air Transportation*, 12 (3), pp. 39–58.

Chapter 11

The Defining Deal of the Next Century?

Learning Objectives

After reading this chapter, you should have a good understanding of:
- LO1: the definition of strategic alliance.
- LO2: the reasons for and growth of alliances in the international airline industry.
- LO3: the alliance types commonly found in airlines and their definition.
- LO4: the reasons for alliance failure.
- LO5: the meaning of mega-alliance, its shape and challenges.

Key Terms, Concepts, and People

Alliance	GM model	Joint venture
Mega-alliances	Airline alliance types	Instability
Resource commitment	Complexity	Multipoint Competition

A New Model?

While the US circled key markets trying to open the skies (Chapter 9) and the Europeans attempted to integrate the economies of 15 different countries, the airlines looked for ways to provide global service in a bilateral world. Part of the push for global networks is based on studies that indicate that consumers choose an airline based on schedule first rather than price and prefer to fly with an airline serving a large number of cities (Tretheway and Oum, 1992). Consumers also prefer a nonstop or single carrier connecting service to a non-interline connecting service. Interlining, which refers to the situation whereby a consumer changes from one carrier to another, carries certain penalties for the consumer such as aircraft and terminal changes, baggage transfers (and added risk of baggage loss), and so on. Carriers with an interlining agreement are expected to provide for more seamless service with joint ticketing and baggage transfers (Dempsey, 2001). If bilateral agreements prevented carriers from achieving nonstop or single carrier connecting service, then carriers needed to find ways to imitate this service to attract consumers. The strategic alliance seemed to offer an answer.

Less than a decade ago, conventional wisdom suggested that the primary business decision corporations had to deal with was to "make or buy." In other words, do we engage in arms-length contractual relationships to obtain important resources or do we internally develop and/or purchase the resources to carry out our strategic plan. The arms-length contractual choice created so-called transaction costs, costs of buying and selling. These costs include the time and financial resources involved in selecting partners, negotiating the deal, and monitoring the relationship to insure contract compliance. These costs could be substantial depending on the number of suppliers to be considered, the reputation of suppliers, and the information available on actual supplier costs. These costs multiplied exponentially for corporations with many suppliers. Not surprisingly, firms also felt at the mercy of suppliers when it came to guaranteeing deliveries and quality. These costs and the lack of control led many to adopt the "GM model." The "GM model" was a vertically integrated company that sought to do it all, making its own spark plugs, radiators, lights, ball bearings, and so on. Ownership eliminated transaction cost uncertainty and provided greater control of the operational aspects of the relationship. This obsession with "owning" in the US led to the merger mania of the 1980s and the takeover mania of the 1990s. During the three busiest years of the 1990s (1998–2000), merger deals totaled almost 44 trillion, which was more than the preceding 30 years combined (Henry, 2002). Greater economic integration in Europe has also led to an increase in owning, often fueled by economic crises that create deals out of stressed companies in many industries. However, evidence has indicated that this obsession may be waning in many industries and regions. A *Business Week* study indicates one reason why the trend is declining. According to their study, 61 percent of the "buyers" actually destroyed shareholder wealth by picking bad acquisitions and paying too much for them (Henry, 2002).

In 1999, *Business Week* declared that "the defining deal for the next decade and beyond may well be the alliance, the joint venture, the partnership" (Sparks, 1999: 106). This article argued that alliances provided more flexibility, speed, informality, and economy than traditional business arrangements. These qualities seemed to make them ideal in rapidly changing business environments. Industries cited as embracing the alliance movement include media, entertainment, financial services, pharmaceuticals, biotech, high tech, and airlines. However, a large body of evidence has accumulated on the instability in alliances across industries. As we will see, this instability can be attributed to a number of factors including poor selection, governance (control), and failure to meet expectations, largely in the area of financial return. There are signs that the alliance landscape merely shifted competition to a higher level of abstraction as alliance groups compete on price, choice, and brand. Within the airline industry, the primary focus of alliances has become the mega-alliance and even this form has come under pressure as merger, acquisition, and unaligned carriers have challenged their trajectories. Still, they have come to dominate 55 percent of the seats flown around the world. Even so, it is possible that liberalization of markets and ownership rules could cause some to rethink the "make-or-buy" decision once again in light of the instability and complexity in alliances as well as the failure of the alliance model to provide the kind of economic and legal incentives that lead to deeper cooperation between members (Flottau and Buyck, 2013).

Defining the Terms and Conditions

A strategic alliance can be defined as a "relatively enduring interfirm cooperative arrangement, involving flows and linkages that utilize resources and/or governance structures from autonomous organizations, for the joint accomplishment of individual goals" (Parke, 1991: 581). In other words, a strategic alliance is an agreement between two independent firms to share resources in a jointly governed project that helps each individual firm achieve specific, not necessarily shared, goals. While the old business model equated control with ownership, control in alliance arrangements is gained through one of three means. The first means of control is through active participation in the management of the enterprise or operation. The second means of exercising control is through withholding or threatening to withhold some resource or capability vital to the success of the overall operation and/or desired by the other partner. The final means of control is through legal or de facto prohibitions on the actions of alliance partners. Areas where firms might seek control include daily operations, quality of products or services, physical assets, brand name, tacit knowledge of procedures and processes, and codified knowledge such as computer reservation systems (Contractor and Kundu, 1998).

The international joint venture (IJV) used to be the preferred mode of conducting international business but a joint venture is a legally separate entity with a mission and administration separate from that of its parents. The alliance, on the other hand, can be formed and dissolved quickly, and "entail(s) little if any paperwork–maybe only a handshake" (Sparks, 1999: 134). According to Jurgen Weber, CEO of Lufthansa Airlines, Star Alliance started with a two and a half-page contract and its members "will cooperate forever as long as we like it" (Feldman, 1998: 27). This sounds very similar to a comment made by Leo Mullin, CEO of Delta Air Lines. Mullin declared that Delta was "extraordinarily committed to the Atlantic Excellence Alliance" (Flint, 1999: 33). Delta was so committed in fact that less than a year later, they announced the termination of its involvement and new partnership with Air France (Hill, 1999).

One issue that appears repeatedly in the popular accounts of airline alliances is the level of time and coordination required by many alliance arrangements. There are several issues involved. First, alliances often involve information sharing and/or the "outsourcing" of some activities to alliance partners. This requires trust. As Jurgen Weber, CEO of Lufthansa, has noted, a key issue in many alliances is trust and the willingness to sell the other's seats as forcefully as your own (Feldman, 1998). According to past research, trust is a function of three factors: ability, benevolence, and integrity. Trust develops when the trustor believes that the trustee has the ability to do what they promise, the desire to do good for the trustor, and the value set that is consistent with that of the trustor (Cook and Wall, 1980; McFall, 1987; Sitkin and Roth, 1993). Mayer, Davis, and Schoorman (1995) have suggested that the perceived integrity of a partner is more important early in the relationship when other information is not available. Benevolence develops in a relationship over time. In fact, the outcome of prior trusting behavior will influence a partner's perception of the ability, benevolence, and integrity of other parties in a relationship. A second key factor is differences in corporate culture and philosophy. Atlantic Excellence members found that different philosophies on service quality, pricing, and other important operational issues created problems. Strong personalities and size differences between members also contributed to the perception and resolution of problems (Feldman, 1998). A third factor affecting coordination is the number of partners involved. As noted above, the more parties involved in a negotiating situation, the more potential there is for disagreement and gamesmanship. A fourth factor is the compatibility of partner systems. The final factor relates to the very real limitations placed on international airlines by laws restricting foreign ownership and limiting the scope of allowed activities. Initial results from the earlier mentioned survey of international airlines confirm these problems in alliance governance. The most frequently cited problem with alliance partners was incompatible systems, policies, or procedures.

Table 11.1   Alliance summary 1994–2000

	1994	1995	1996	1997	1998	1999	2000
Number of alliances	280	324	389	363	502	513	579
With equity stakes	58	58	62	54	56	53	-
Without equity	222	266	327	309	446	460	-
New alliances	21	34	26	56	84	79	72
Number of airlines	136	153	159	177	196	204	220

Source: Airline Business June 1994–June 2000. Reporting of equity change in 2000

The result of these limitations is that airline alliances are most often coordinated or managed by a committee; agreement is achieved by arriving at the lowest common denominator or minimally acceptable standard to all members (Feldman, 1998). Star Alliance has struggled with governance arrangements. They reduced the number of coordinating committees several years ago from 25 to 15, and established a policy group to oversee the activities of these committees (Feldman, 1998; Nelms, 1999). Star was the first mega-alliance to take steps to create a more formal structure of governance for its alliance.

Alliances in the Airline Industry

According to Oum and Yu (1998), the first international alliance of the modern era was between Air Florida and British Island in 1986. It was not until the mid-1990s, however, that alliances in the airline industry began to soar. Table 11.1 summarizes the alliance activity documented by *Airline Business* over the seven years prior to 2001. September 11 was a watershed for the industry in many ways, certainly it temporarily halted new alliance activity in the industry and we have not seen a return to the 1990s. There are several striking trends in the 1990s numbers. First, the total number of alliances rose almost 45 percent from 1994 to 1999 (see Figure 11.1). Second, the majority of alliances did not involve equity stakes and those that do are declining. Third, between one-fourth and one-sixth of the reported total yearly alliances were newly created. Finally, the number of airlines participating in some form of alliance was steadily increasing.

The term "strategic alliance" covers a multitude of different forms or types of arrangements in the airline industry, possibly more than in any other industry. To understand the airline alliance, it is necessary to understand that alliance activities can range from a simple, single-route codeshare or bundle of codeshares all the way to the so-called "mega-alliances" created by international groups of competing airlines such as Star, Oneworld, and SkyTeam. Table 11.2 lists the most common types of alliance activities and a basic definition of each.

Not only is there a wide range of alliance activities or type of arrangements possible but there are also a large number of type combinations that can be created between any two or more carriers. The mega-alliance (discussed later) combines many of these types; however, not all types are equally likely to occur. Several studies have reported that the most common types of alliances involve codesharing, blockspace/franchising/feeding agreements, joint marketing, and joint service agreements (Table 11.3). Least common are alliances involving the sharing and/or adoption of information technology (IT) systems, including computer reservation systems. This is probably not surprising given the proprietary nature of such information in the airline industry (Rhoades and Waguespack, 2000; Zwart, 1999).

An airline's choice of alliance partner and alliance type is a function of its objectives, which are believed to center around four strategic drivers. The first and traditionally most popular driver has been the need to gain entry into international markets restricted by bilateral agreements. Alliances allow foreign carriers to serve international destinations without obtaining the right through country-negotiated bilateral agreements, a political process that many carriers have found difficult to influence. The second driver is the desire to build a global, seamless network that allows consumers to reduce travel costs, take advantage of expanded frequent flyer programs, and obtain better services. The third driver of alliance formation is cost reduction. Cost reduction can be achieved in several ways. Alliances can be used to enter and develop a new market without an actual presence in that market. In this case, the entering carrier may rely on its alliance partner to provide the aircraft, ground handling, maintenance, customer service personnel, and other services in the

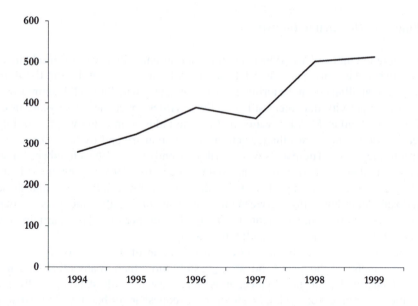

Figure 11.1   Number of alliances, 1994–1999

Table 11.2   Definition of airline alliances

Alliance Type	Definition
Codeshare	One carrier offers service under another carrier's flight designator
Blockspace	One carrier allocates to another seats to sell on its flight
Revenue sharing	Two or more carrier share revenues generated by joint activity
Wet lease	One carrier rents the aircraft/personnel of another
Franchising	One carrier "rents" the brand name of another for the purpose of offering flight service but supplies its own aircraft/staff
Computer Reservation System	One carrier shares and/or adopts the reservation system of another
Insurance/parts Pooling	Two or more carriers agree to joint purchase
Joint service	Two carriers offer combined flight service
Management Contract	One carrier contracts with another carrier to manage some aspect of its operation
Baggage handling Maintenance	One carrier contracts with another to provide services/personnel/facilities at specified sites
Joint marketing	Two or more carriers combine efforts to market joint services/activities
Equity swap/ Governance	Two or more carriers swap stock and/or create joint governance structures

new market. Carriers may also seek to reduce costs through arrangements creating joint activities such as marketing, maintenance, insurance, parts pooling, and so on. These joint activities not only reduce redundancy but also may create cost savings through economy of scale effects. A fourth driver can be the desire to maintain market presence in an area whose traffic pattern and growth make it unprofitable to serve alone (Merrill, Lynch, Pierce, Fenner & Smith, Inc., 1998; Oum and Yu, 1998). For many airlines, their alliance activity is driven by more than one objective and clearly, carriers may have a different set of objectives for each market or region that they serve. This diversity of objectives can make the scope and depth of interaction important issues in negotiating and governing an alliance.

Unstable Creations

Unfortunately, strategic alliances have also been defined as arrangements "characterized by inherent instability arising from uncertainty regarding a partner's future behavior and the absence of a higher authority to ensure compliance" (Parke, 1993: 794). Doorley (1993) found that 60 percent of the alliances he examined had a survival rate of only four years. Less than 20 percent survived for ten years. An Anderson Consulting survey found that 61 percent of corporate partnerships were either outright failures or performing below expectations (Sparks, 1999). Michael Porter of Harvard University believes that we should not be surprised by these numbers since he sees alliances as transitional rather than stable arrangements that rarely result in sustainable competitive advantage (Porter, 1990). Hamel (1991) has even suggested that many alliances are simply a race to learn in which the winner will eventually establish dominance in the partnership or dissolve it before its partner can catch up.

Whichever means of control partners select, the fact remains that most interfirm alliances involve attempts by competitors to cooperate in some aspect of their operation. It has been suggested that such firms have an "inalienable de facto right to pursue their own interests" (Buckley and Casson, 1988: 34). This perception, however, may make it inevitable that problems will arise as partners seek to control the alliance to their benefit. Another reason for instability in alliance arrangements may be the failure of partners to clearly define objectives and establish means of measuring performance. A surprising 49 percent of alliances in the *Business Week* survey did not have formal performance guidelines (Sparks, 1999).

The first step in understanding the issue of stability is achieving a consensus on the meaning of our terms. From an alliance point-of-view, failure occurs when one or all parties fail to achieve their objectives. Obviously, it is possible for one member to achieve their goals when other parties do not. This type of failure can occur either because of a problem in the objective-setting process or because of deliberate action on the part of one member. A more ominous reason for failure is the possibility that one or more partners enter an alliance seeking to gain competitive advantage (Buckley and Casson, 1988; Hamel, 1991). Given

Table 11.3   Alliances by type

Alliance Type	Description	Percentage of Total
Type I	Codeshare	29%
Type II	Blockspace	15%
Type III	CRS/Accting/IT	2%
Type IV	Pooling	6%
Type V	Joint Service	13%
Type VI	Commercial Agreements	3%
Type VII	Facilities/Ground Handling	9%
Type VIII	Marketing	16%
Type IX	Equity	7%

Source: Zwart, 1999, 'Duration and Stability of Strategic Alliances in the Airline Industry'

this definition, a terminating alliance is only unsuccessful if it is "unplanned and premature from the perspective of either or both partners" (Inkpen and Beamish, 1997: 182). Duration simply refers to the length of time between the initiation of an alliance and its termination.

Researchers have defined instability in terms of changes in equity and/ or governance control, termination, and duration (Franko, 1971; Killing, 1983; Kogut, 1988). From a theoretical perspective, instability should be separated from duration and termination. If a stable relationship is defined as one in which there have been no major changes in the relationship design to either increase or decrease the linkages between firms, then an alliance could terminate without experiencing instability. Actions which would indicate instability include changes in strategic direction, renegotiation of contracts or agreements, and reconfiguration of ownership and/or management structure (Yan, 1998). It would not include alliance termination. A stable alliance may terminate when the strategic goals of partners have been met or when the strategic needs of partners change. By the same token, an unstable alliance will not necessarily end in termination. Instability may arise because partners are adjusting their expectations or objectives. It may indicate that partners have decided to commit themselves to even higher levels of interaction or to a longer-term strategy to disengage from or de-emphasize the relationship.

Lasting relationships

Given the high failure rates already cited, it is reasonable to ask what factors contribute to longevity. Bleeke and Ernst (1995) have categorized alliances based on three factors—market strength of partners, motivation of alliance partners, and alliance outcome—to create six classes or types of alliances. These six types are (1) collisions between competitors; (2) alliances of the weak; (3) disguised sales;

(4) bootstrap alliances; (5) evolutions to a sale; and (6) complementary equals. According to their typology, an alliance between a weak firm and a strong firm can be either a disguised sale, that is, it will result in the weaker firm failing to gain strength and being acquired (and, hence, the alliance terminated) by the stronger firm or a bootstrap alliance in which the weaker firm increases its strength and dissolves the alliance. In their typology, only one type of alliance will survive longer than the median age of seven, complementary equals. This alliance involves two firms with truly complementary skills, assets, and/or resources. Unfortunately, many alliances are entered in the belief that partner complementarity exists. It is usually only in the process of implementing the alliance that partners discover incompatibility. The other weakness of the Bleeke and Ernst (1995) typology is that it is post hoc; it classifies alliances after the outcome of the alliance is known. It does not predict which alliances will succeed nor does it lay out conditions for success.

Park and Cho (1997) examined the market strength of codesharing partners and its effect on market share performance, presumably a goal of such alliances. They found that the most successful alliances occurred between partners of equal size. They also reported that the performance effects were greater in growing markets with few competitors and flexible market share changes. Here, at least, we have two factors that might be useful in selecting partners and/or predicting alliance outcome.

Khanna, Gulati, and Nohria (1998) offer us another way. They focus not on the strengths of alliance partners but on the nature of the benefits arising from alliance activity. They suggest that alliances create two types of benefits—common and private. Common benefits "accrue to each partner in an alliance from the collective application of the learning both firms go through as a consequence of being part of the alliance" (195). By contrast, private benefits can accrue to a firm that can pick up partner skills and apply them to areas unrelated to alliance activity. In the case of an alliance with purely common benefits, "all firms must finish learning in order for any of them to derive the common benefits" (197). Thus, such an alliance may be expected to last longer and result, even if terminated, in a successful alliance from the viewpoint of all parties. The alliance with purely private benefits is indeed a race to see which partner can finish learning first. That partner will then have no further incentive to incur alliance costs and will terminate the relationship. In reality, most alliances are a combination of both types of benefits. It is the ratio of private to common benefits that will affect a firm's decision to stay in or quit an alliance. All things being equal, the greater the scope of the alliance relative to the total market scope of the partners, the greater the common benefits and the lower the private benefits. In this regard, the mega-alliances with their increased alliance scope relative to firm scope should create more common benefits and last longer than their narrow alliance scope competitors. In connection with learning in alliance arrangements, Simonin (1999) has suggested that the more ambiguous and tacit the information to be transferred, the longer the process will take. In other words, it should be more difficult for Singapore Airlines to transfer the rich, experience-laden knowledge that has made it an industry leader in service quality than to train alliance partners in line maintenance procedures.

A number of studies have examined the role of resource commitment to alliance duration. Resource commitment involves dedicating assets to a particular use in such a way that their redeployment to other uses would result in some level of cost to the firm. By limiting strategic flexibility and acting as a barrier to exit, the willingness to commit resources lessens the perception of opportunistic behavior on the part of other alliance members (Parkhe, 1993). The more non-recoverable, alliance-specific the investment, the greater the potential effect on alliance duration.

Resource commitment can also have a positive effect on alliance stability and performance (Freeman, 1987; Heide and Johns, 1988; Smith and Aldrich, 1991). Resource commitment affects stability for much the same reason as it increases duration, namely that it creates incentives to stay in the relationship rather than quit. Its effect on performance is due to the link between resource commitment, firm control, and involvement in operations. The higher the level of commitment by the firm, the more likely it is to exercise control in the alliance and seek involvement in decision making (Anderson and Gatignon, 1986; Root 1987). On the other hand, high levels of commitment are often associated with more alliance complexity. The more complex the relationship, the greater the "fundamental problem of cooperation" (Ouchi, 1980: 130). Alliances that involve greater coordination and integration of resources require a level of trust and interaction that is generally foreign to competitive firms. The more highly concentrated the industry, the more unstable the relationship may be, particularly when the scope of the venture involved marketing and after-sales service (Kogut, 1988). The need for higher levels of coordination and integration is also likely to increase problems relating to incompatible systems, procedures, training, and organizational/national cultures.

According to Yan (1998), four forces act to destabilize alliance arrangements: unexpected changes in the environment, undesirable alliance performance, obsolescing bargain effects, and interpartner competitive learning. Clearly, changing environmental conditions and poor performance can cause partners to re-evaluate/restructure their relationship. The obsolescing bargain occurs when the foreign partners' relative bargaining power erodes over time as it invests increasing, unrecoverable resources in a local economy. Finally, the race to learn can lead to various strategic maneuvering in an alliance. Yan (1998) also cites four factors that can increase alliance stability: the political and legal environment at founding, the initial resource mix, the initial balance of bargaining power, and the interpartner, pre-venture relationship. As we have discussed earlier in this book, the airline industry is currently facing a series of challenges to the existing political and legal structure that has governed the industry since the end of World War II. When this challenge is added to alliance-specific differences in resource mix, balance of power, and pre-venture relationships, the results can be volatile.

Scott (1992) has noted that the forms organizations establish at founding are likely to persist over their lifespan. This is called structural inertia. The initial form may reflect the task environment (Stinchcombe, 1965), the characteristics of executives (Mintzberg and Waters, 1982) or top management team, (Eisenhardt and Schoonhoven, 1990) or institutional factors such as laws, organizational, or national culture (Meyer and Scott, 1983). The initial resources and bargaining power partners bring into an alliance can also create stability as can a pre-alliance relationship of trust and respect. The stability of the alliance depends on the delicate balance between these eight forces.

A balancing act

In a 1997 article in the *Journal of Air Transportation Management*, Rhoades and Lush proposed an alliance typology that involved another delicate balancing act. Their typology was based on the premise that airline alliances could be classified according to two dimensions: commitment of resources and complexity of arrangement. In general, the typology predicted that the level of resource commitment should increase both the duration and stability of alliances while the complexity of the alliance arrangement should decrease both duration and stability. These predictions are consistent with theory and research in other industries. The difficulty lies in assessing the interaction effects of these two dimensions on duration and stability. For example, what is likely to happen to an alliance that involves a low level of resource commitment to a complex task requiring partners to integrate different systems, cultures or tasks. Rhoades and Lush (1997) attempted to address this difficulty by assigning each of the activities defined above in Table 11.2 based on the level of resource commitment and complexity. Figure 11.2 outlines a refined version of the typology used in a test of the model. Type I alliances involve low levels of resource commitment and complexity. The relatively simple nature of the activity should make them more stable and lasting. However, these types of codesharing arrangements are normally driven by the desire for market access and/or market presence in a restricted or undeveloped market. The lasting nature of Type I alliances could change if liberalization continues and carriers can enter markets freely in their own right. On the other hand, the financial crisis in the wake of 9/11 has seen cost-cutting carriers withdraw from increasingly marginal routes in favor of alliance partners.

Diagonally across from Type I alliances is Type IX. These alliances involve multiple activities, complex integration efforts, extensive resource commitment, shared decision making, and often, equity investment. High resource commitment makes the exit cost of these alliance types high. On the other hand, the complex nature of the tasks to be coordinated and integrated will make these alliances unstable as well. On balance, resource commitment should provide Type IX partners with greater incentives to work through complexity. Type III alliances involve low complexity, and high resource commitment should make these alliances some of the most durable. On the diagonal from Type III are Type VIII alliances that tend to involve low levels of resource commitment and high complexity. These types of arrangements should experience some of the highest failure rates. An increasing focus on quality may make the potentially undesirable outcomes of some of these complex and important activities too great to bear. Of course, it is possible that the cost savings benefits of these arrangements and/or airport specific restrictions on facilities or eligible ground handling firms will override the destabilizing effects of complexity.

This typology was tested for its duration predictions using data from the *Airline Business* surveys. Gudmundsson and Rhoades (2001) found that alliances in general were at greater risk of termination in year 2. The rate of termination decreased from years 3 to 6. Four types of alliance arrangements demonstrated a lower risk of termination, Type IV-pooling, Type VIII-marketing, Type II-blockspace, and Type I-codesharing. Type V (joint service) and Type VII (ground/ facilities) showed a significant relationship with higher risk of early termination. Type IX (equity) alliances were also associated with high risk of termination. The remaining two types of alliances, Type III (CRS/IT) and Type VI (commercial agreements) contained too few cases to test. While this study did not provide unqualified support for the typology, it does demonstrate that different alliance activities are at greater risk for termination.

The Gudmundsson and Rhoades (2001) study also found that the more extensive the alliance, that is, the more types of activities involved, the lower the risk of termination. Since each additional alliance activity adds incrementally to the level of resource commitment, this finding is supportive of the general proposition that resource commitment increases duration. The attempt by mega-alliances to increase the breadth and scope of partner activity also supports the contention of Khanna, Gulati, and Nohria (1998) that the higher the level of common benefits to private, the more likely the alliance is to survive. In the case of the mega-alliances, resource commitment appears to outweigh complexity as a factor in alliance duration. In the case of Type IX equity alliances, the troubles of shared governance and organizational control created instability in a number of alliances, notably KLM-Northwest, and Northwest and Continental. However, the control benefits of ownership might create the incentive to remain in a relationship and work through instability.

To date, there has been no test of the stability predictions of the typology. As Rhoades and Lush (1997) noted in their original article, "instability in and of itself is not necessarily a 'bad thing'." It can be an indication that the parties in the alliance are committed to establishing a successful partnership" (113). On the other hand, too much instability should have a negative effect on an alliance's ability to function and produce profitable returns. Testing the stability predictions would require a careful year-by-year survey of changes (major and minor) within alliances. A related area of study would be to examine the possibility of sequencing as it relates to alliance stability and duration. For example, are alliances that begin their relationship with relatively simple, low-resource activities and then move to more complex arrangements more successful than those who jump right into equity and/or other complex activities?

Strategic Actions

As noted earlier, airlines that serve a large number of destinations tend to be preferred by consumers because such an airline can minimize their travel time and offer a higher quality of service (Tretheway and Oum, 1992). Responding

	-	COMPLEXITY	+	
+	**Type III (IT)** Accounting services CRS links Data processing Freight IT IT Development	**Type VI (Management)** Commercial agreements Commercial support mgmt Management Contract MOU Spares mgmt cooperation Strategic Partnership	**Type IX (Equity)** Equity	**+**
R E S O U R C E S	**Type II (Block-Space)** Block seat agreements Block space agreements Feeding agreement Franchise agreement Revenue sharing Wet Lease	**Type V (Joint-Service)** Cargo cooperation Freight handling Joint cargo terminal Joint flight Joint freighter flight Joint route development Joint venture Schedule coordination Shared routes	**Type VIII (Marketing)** Coop on Sales Gen sales agency Joint Mkt Joint FFP Joint advertising Mkting agreement Mkting alliance Reservations	D U R A T I O N
-	**Type I (Code-Share)** Cargo code-share Code sharing	**Type IV (Pooling)** Fuel purchasing Financial access arrangements Joint insurance purchase Freight return pool Joint purchase Pool agreement Revenue Pooling Space swap	**Type VII (Ground Facilities)** Slot-sharing Maintenance Catering JV Joint check-in Ground handling Shared Terminal Shared lounge Through check-in	**-**
	+	DURATION	-	

Figure 11.2   Alliance activity by type

to this preference, carriers sought to develop extensive domestic, continental, and international service networks. In the US, following deregulation, carriers consolidated and created hub-and-spoke networks to achieve continental coverage. Achieving international coverage, however, proved more difficult. American Airlines initially attempted to apply the domestic model of network coverage to foreign markets by creating foreign spokes to their US hubs. They encountered two problems: legal barriers created by the bilateral system and high financial costs. We have already discussed many of the legal barriers to establishing an efficient foreign network (Chapter 9). In regard to the financial costs, Oum, Taylor, and Zhang (1993) have estimated that the potential revenues of a "successful" global network would be more than US$30 billion. This is at least twice the revenue level of the largest existing mega-carriers. They argued that a single carrier simply could not marshal the financial resources to establish such a network. Whether a single carrier could administer such a network is a matter we will address later.

Given these problems and the legal restrictions on international mergers and acquisitions, strategic alliances became the method of choice in global network construction. They allowed individual carriers to compensate for strategic weaknesses in their operations or route structure. The savings in cost and time over internal development could be substantial. In fact, outsourcing to alliance partners was the easiest way to control costs but there were additional problems with this approach. First, it was difficult to restart an activity once it is discontinued. So, if the alliance fell apart or the quality of the work did not meet standards, bringing that activity back in-house would be expensive. Second, such cost savings required more airline integration than many carriers were currently willing to accept (Feldman, 1999).

Research on competitive behavior suggests that it is driven by both the ability to compete and the motivation to engage in competition (Chen, 1996). Global networks give alliances the ability to compete in numerous markets. The motivation to compete (or not to compete) is based on other considerations including expected retaliation by competitors. Research at the firm level indicates that multi-market contact "gives a firm the option to respond to an attack by a rival not only in the challenged market, but also in other markets in which both compete" (Gimeno, 1999: 102). In the US, major airlines seek to maintain some presence in all their competitors' markets. Those that are successful "are able to simultaneously: (a) enjoy lower intensity of price competition from their rivals, (b) display less intense competitive behavior of their own, and (c) maintain a higher equilibrium market share" (Gimeno, 1999: 122). Retaliation in an attacker's hub has been shown to be a powerful and effective response to attacks on one's own hub (Nomani, 1990a). Assuming that competition eventually moves from the airline to the alliance level, then multipoint alliance contact will gain increasing importance. This also assumes that a liberalizing global aviation system allows for the development of such a framework. Merrill Lynch (1999) has examined the market presence of the mega-alliances in 30 world markets. Of these 30 markets, 15 have an alliance with 50 percent or more market share. This indicates the basic framework of a multipoint system that, given regulatory freedom, would allow one alliance group to respond to an attack in their dominant market by acting in the attacker's market.

The Mega-Alliance

The frenzy of alliance activity was largely extinguished by 9/11 as airlines struggled for survival. The action shifted to the mega-alliance, although mergers and acquisitions of airlines from different groups have created some turmoil. Table 11.4 shows the current mega-alliance structure. Oneworld continues to lag behind the other two alliances in size as well as the integration of alliance members. What this table does not indicate is the level of within-group joint venture activity in the alliances fostered in part by the fact that some carriers have been legally freer to integrate their cooperation (Flottau and Buyck, 2013).

Oum and Park (1997) envisioned the following future for airline alliances. First, global alliances would consist of a two-tier system of super-hub anchor carriers on each continent and junior spoke carriers feeding the continental super-hubs. Star Alliance has even created third-tier members and all the mega-alliances have worked in the last decade to fill gaps in their network. Many of the smaller carriers have had to work very hard to get benefits from the mega-alliances and balance this with the sometimes substantial costs (Buyck, 2013). Second, the number of major global alliances, constrained by the limited number of major continental carriers, would be no more than five or so. Finally, carriers left out of the "system" would be forced to become niche players. Some of these predictions have come to pass with the formation of three major mega-alliances (Star, Oneworld, and SkyTeam) and the announcement of secondary and tertiary carriers (Merrill Lynch, 1999). Consolidation in the North American and European airline industry has shifted some alliance partnerships, and some alliance members have remained on the periphery of their mega-alliance unable or unwilling to deepen ties but it remains to be seen whether non-alliance status will consign carriers to niche status. This has certainly not been true of the Middle Eastern carriers to date. Since many of the niche players are LCCs, a growing segment of the airline industry, it is not clear what happens if the alliance and LCC model begin to collide more directly in international markets.

Table 11.4   Mega-alliance size and coverage

Global Alliance members	Oneworld	SkyTeam	Star Alliance
Americas	2	3	6
Europe	5	7	11
Middle East and Africa	1	3	3
Asia-Pacific	5	5	7
Total	12	18	27
Countries Served	155	187	194
Fleet	2,473	2,734	4,570

Source: Flottau and Buyck, Group Dynamics, *Aviation Week & Space Technology*, April 29, 2013

Internationally, competition has tended to shift to the alliance level. Research also points to other behavioral possibilities in alliance strategic action. At the firm level, organizational size has been positively associated with economies of scale, experience, brand name recognition, and market power (Hambrick, MacMillan, and Day, 1982; Kelly and Amburgey, 1991). Small firms tend to be more flexible, faster, innovative, and risk seeking. Such firms initiate more competitive moves and implement them quicker than their larger rivals (Chen and Hambrick, 1995; Fiegenbaum and Karnani, 1991; Hitt, Hoskisson, and Harrison, 1991; Katz, 1970).

Large firms initiate fewer actions, tend to be slower to implement agreed upon actions, and are less likely to change core features (Chen and Hambrick, 1995; Kelly and Amburgey, 1991). However, as Chen and Hambrick (1995) found, they respond quickly to perceived attack. This rapid response to attack may indicate a greater need to protect their reputation (Fombrun and Shanley, 1990), to signal to stakeholders (Pfeffer, 1982) and competitors (Axelrod, 1984) that they are not passive, and to deter further attack (Chen and MacMillan, 1992).

As we have noted earlier, the size of an organization or alliance necessary to establish a successful global network is tremendous (Oum, Taylor, and Zhang, 1993). There are signs that administering these networks are time consuming, frustrating, and cumbersome. Further, it is not always clear that alliances truly deliver the seamless service that was supposed to be one of their benefits, a challenge that alliances are trying to address to insure the survival of the model (Buyck and Flottau, 2013).

Strange Bedfellows

While international airlines appear committed to the idea of an alliance world, there are many problems facing alliances as they try to provide the seamless service that their founders promised, and the profits that they hoped to achieve. If the negotiating and governance process looks complex, then imagine the complexity of day-to-day activity. Michael E. Levine, the Executive VP–Marketing for Northwest Airlines has said that "the hardest thing in working on an alliance is to coordinate the activities of people who have different instincts and a different language, and maybe worship slightly different travel gods, to get them to work together in a culture that allows them to respect each other's habits and convictions, and yet work productively together in an environment in which you can't specify everything in advance" (Levine, 1993: 69). Resolving these human issues as well as the legal issues surrounding alliances is one of the chief challenges of the alliance movement and one of the causes of instability in alliance arrangements.

Questions

1. Discuss the reasons for the use of strategic alliances in international aviation.
2. Discuss the alliance types common in airlines and how they are combined in the complex mega-alliances.
3. Discuss stability and failure in strategic alliances.
4. How can firms foster greater stability in alliances?
5. Would airlines choose ownership or alliance if regulations permitted them?

References

Anderson, E. and Gatignon, H. (1986), "Modes of entry: a transaction cost analysis and propositions," *Journal of International Business Studies*, vol. 17 (September), pp. 1–26.

Axelrod, R. (1984), *The Evolution of Cooperation*, Basic Books, New York.

Bleeke, J. and Ernst, D. (1995), "Is your strategic alliance a sale?" *Harvard Business Review*, vol. 73, pp. 97–105.

Buckley, P. and Casson, M. (1988), "A Theory of Cooperation in International Business," in F.J. Contractor and Peter Lorange (eds), *Cooperative Strategies in International Business*, D.C. Heath & Company, Lexington, MA.

Buyck, C. (2013), "Filling in the blanks," *Aviation Week & Space Technology*, April 29, pp. 41–43.

Buyck, C. and Flottau, J. (2013), "From scale to service," *Aviation Week & Space Technology*, April 29, pp. 42–43.

Chen, M.J. (1996), "Competitor analysis and inter-firm rivalry: toward a theoretical integration," *Academy of Management Review*, vol. 1 (1), pp. 100–134.

Chen, M.J. and Hambrick, D.C. (1995), "Speed, stealth, and selective attack: how small firms differ from large firms in competitive behavior," *Academy of Management Journal*, vol. 38 (4), pp. 453–482.

Chen, M.J. and MacMillan, I.C. (1992), "Nonresponse and delayed response to competitive moves: the roles of competitor dependence and action irreversibility," *Academy of Management Journal*, vol. 35 (4), pp. 359–370.

Contractor, F.J. and Kundu, S.K. (1998), "Modal choice in a world of alliances: analyzing organizational forms in the international hotel sector," *Journal of International Business Studies*, vol. 29 (2), pp. 325–358.

Contractor, F.J. and P. Lorange (eds), *Cooperative Strategies in International Business*, Lexington Books, Lexington, MA, pp. 31–54.

Cook, J. and Wall, T. (1980), "New work attitude measures trust, organizational commitment and personal need fulfillment," *Journal of Occupational Psychology*, vol. 53 (1), pp. 39–52.

Dempsey, P.S. (2001), "Carving the World into Fiefdoms: The Anticompetitive Future of International Aviation" Working Paper.

Doorley III, T.L. (1993), "Teaming up for success," *Business Quarterly*, vol. 57 (summer), pp. 99–103.

Eisenhardt, K. and Schoonhoven, C.B. (1990), "Organizational growth: linking founding team strategy, environment, and growth among semiconductor ventures, 1978–1988," *Administrative Science Quarterly*, vol. 35 (4), pp. 504–529.

Feldman, J. (1998), "Making alliances work," *Air Transport World*, June, pp. 27–35.

Feldman, J.M. (1999), "Disappearing act." *Air Transport World*, February, pp. 25–30.

Fiegenbaum, A. and Karnani, A. (1991), "Output flexibility—a competitive advantage for small firms," *Strategic Management Journal*, vol. 12 (2), pp. 101–124.

Flint, P. (1999), "Alliance paradox," *Air Transport World*, April, pp. 33–36.

Flottau, J. and Buyck, C (2013), "Group dynamics," *Aviation Week & Space Technology*, April 29, pp. 39–41.

Fombrun, C. and Shanley, M. (1990), "What's in a name? Reputation building and corporate strategy," *Academy of Management Journal*, vol. 33(1), pp. 233–258.

Franko, L. (1971), *Joint Venture Survival in Multinational Companies*, Praeger, New York.

Freeman, R.E. (1987), "Review of the economic institutions of capitalism, by O.W. Williamson," *Academy of Management Review*, vol. 12 (3), pp. 385–387.

Gimeno, J. (1999), "Reciprocal threats in multimarket rivalry: staking out spheres of influence in the U.S. airline industry," *Strategic Management Journal*, vol. 20 (2), pp. 101–128.

Gudmunssson, S.V. and Rhoades, D.L. (2001), "Airline alliance survival: analysis, strategy, and duration," *Transport Policy*, vol. 8 (3), pp. 209–219.

Hambrick, D.C., MacMillan, I.C. and Day, D.L. (1982), "Strategic attributes and performance in the BCG Matrix—a PIMS-based analysis of industrial product businesses," *Academy of Management Journal*, vol. 25 (4), pp. 510–531.

Hamel, G. (1991), "Competition for competence and inter-partner learning within international strategic alliances," *Strategic Management Journal*, vol. 12 (1), pp. 83–104.

Heide, J.B. and Johns, G. (1988), "The role of dependence balancing in safeguarding transaction-specific assets in conventional channels," *Journal of Marketing*, vol. 52 (1), pp. 20–35.

Henry, D. (2002), "Mergers: why most big deals don't pay off," *Business Week*, October 14, pp. 60–70.

Hill, L. (1999), "Global challenger," *Air Transport World*, December, pp. 52–54.

Hitt, M.A., Hoskisson, R.E. and Harrison, J.S. (1991), "Strategic competitiveness in the 1990s challenges and opportunities for U.S. executives," *Academy of Management Executive*, vol. 5 (1), pp. 7–22.

Inkpen, A.C. and Beamish, P.W. (1997), "Knowledge, bargaining power, and the instability of international joint ventures," *Academy of Management Review*, vol. 22 (1), pp. 177–202.

Katz, R.L. (1970), *Cases and Concepts in Corporate Strategy*, Prentice-Hall, Englewood Cliffs, NJ.

Kelly, D. and Amburgey, T.L. (1991), "Organizational inertia and momentum: a dynamic model of strategic change," *Academy of Management Journal*, vol. 34 (4), pp. 591–612.

Khanna, T., Gulati, R. and Nohria, N. (1998), "The dynamics of learning alliances: competition, cooperation, and relative scope," *Strategic Management Journal*, vol. 19 (3), pp. 193–210.

Killing, J.P. (1983), *Strategies for Joint Venture Success*, Praeger, New York.

Kogut, B. (1988), "Joint ventures: theoretical and empirical perspectives," *Strategic Management Journal*, vol. 9 (4), pp. 319–332.

Levine, M.E. (1993), "Interview," *Air Transport World*, January, pp. 69–70.

Mayer, R.C., Davis, J.H. and Schoorman, F.D. (1995), "An integrative model of organizational trust," *Academy of Management Review*, vol. 20 (3) pp. 709–734.

McFall, L. (1987), "Integrity," *Ethics*, vol. 98 (1), pp. 5–20.

Merrill Lynch, Pierce, Fenner & Smith Inc. (1998), *Global Airline Alliances: Why Alliances Really Matter from an Investment Perspective*, Merrill Lynch, Pierce, Fenner & Smith Inc., New York.

Merrill Lynch, Pierce, Fenner & Smith (1999), *Global Airline Alliances: Global Alliance Brands Create Value*, Merrill Lynch, New York.Meyer, J.W. and Scott, W.R. (1983), *Organizational Environments: Ritual and Rationality*, Sage, Beverly Hills, CA.

Mintzberg, H. and Waters, J.A. (1982), "Tracking strategy in an entrepreneurial firm," *Academy of Management Journal*, vol. 25 (3), pp. 465–499.

Nelms, D.W. (1999), "Getting their acts together," *Air Transport World*, April, pp. 27–36.

Nomani, A.Q. (1990), "Fare warning: how airlines trade price plans," *Wall Street Journal*, October 9, pp. B1–B10.

Ouchi, W.G. (1980), "Markets, bureaucracies, and clans," *Administrative Science Quarterly*, vol. 25 (1), pp. 129–142.

Oum, T.H. and Park, J.H. (1997), "Airline alliances: current status, policy issues, and future directions," *Journal of Air Transport Management*, vol. 3 (3), pp. 133–144.

Oum, T.H., Taylor, A.J. and Zhang, A. (1993), "Strategic airline policy in the globalizing airline network," *Transportation Journal*, vol. 32 (1), pp. 14–30.

Oum, T.H. and Yu, C. (1998), *Winning Airlines: Productivity and Cost Competitiveness of the World's Major Airlines*, Kluwer Academic Publishers, Boston, MA.

Park, N.K. and Cho, D. (1997), "The effect of strategic alliance on performance," *Journal of Air Transport Management*, vol. 3 (2), pp. 155–164.

Parkhe, A. (1991), "Interfirm diversity, organizational learning, and longevity in global strategic alliances," *Journal of International Business Studies*, vol. 22 (4), pp. 579–601.

Parkhe, A. (1993), "Strategic alliance structuring: a game theoretic and transaction cost examination of interfirm cooperation," *The Academy of Management Journal*, vol. 36 (4), pp. 794–829.

Pfeffer, J. (1982), *Organizations and Organizational Theory*, Pitman, Boston, MA.

Porter, M.E. (1990), *The Competitive Advantage of Nations*, Free Press, New York.

Reuters (2000), "KLM, MAS in quite intensive Wings Talks," March 15.

Rhoades, D.L. and Lush, H. (1997), "A typology of strategic alliances in the airline industry: propositions for stability and duration," *Journal of Air Transport Management*, vol. 3 (3), pp. 109–114.

Rhoades, D.L. and Waguespack, B., Jr. (2000), "Divorce Airline Style," Working paper, Embry-Riddle Aeronautical University.

Root, F.R. (1987), *Entry Strategies for International Markets*, Lexington Books, Lexington, MA.

Scott, W.R. (1992), *Organizations: Rational, Natural, and Open Systems* (3rd ed.), Prentice-Hall: Englewood Cliffs, NJ.

Simonin, B.L. (1999), "Ambiguity and the process of knowledge transfer in strategic alliances," *Strategic Management Journal*, vol. 20 (4), pp. 595–624.

Sitkin, S.B. and Roth, N.L. (1993), "Explaining the limited effectiveness of legalistic "remedies" for trust/distrust," *Organizational Science*, vol. 4 (4), pp. 367–392.

Smith, A. and Aldrich, H.E. (1991), "The role of trust in the transaction cost economics framework." Paper presented at the annual meeting of the Academy of Management, Miami.

Sparks, D. (1999), "Partners," *Business Week*, October 25, pp. 106–112.

Stinchcombe, A.L. (1965), "Organizations and Social Structures" in James G. March (ed.), *Handbook of Organizations*, Rand McNally, Chicago, IL, pp. 142–162.

Tretheway, M.W. and Oum, T.H. (1992), *Airline Economics: Foundation for Strategy and Policy*, The Centre for Transportation Studies, University of British Columbia.

Yan, A. (1998), "Structural stability and reconfiguration of international joint ventures," *Journal of International Business Studies*, vol. 29 (4), pp. 773–796.

Zwart, M.L. (1999), "Duration and Stability of Strategic Alliances in the Airline Industry," Dissertation at Maastricht University.

Chapter 12
The Slippery Legal Slope

Learning Objectives

After reading this chapter, you should have a good understanding of:
- LO1: the early developments in aviation liability.
- LO2: the background of anti-trust and competitive policy.
- LO3: the different approaches to anti-trust/competitive policy around the world.
- LO4: the issues involving competition between airlines and between the large aircraft manufacturers.

Key Terms, Concepts, and People

FCPA	Warsaw Convention	Montreal Convention
Anti-trust	Sherman Act	Fair competition
EU Court of Justice	JETRO	Predatory behavior

Legally Speaking

One of the first issues that any student of international relations must deal with is the fact that there is no nice body of "law" for most things international. In this sense, the student of international aviation is better positioned to accept this reality because that student has already grappled with the bilateral system of treaties that governed (and still governs) airline affairs between nations. In international law, treaties (bilateral and multilateral) are negotiated and signed (or not signed) by the parties involved in the negotiation and they set out how the system in question works, what the rules are, and who (or how) disputes are resolved. As discussed in Chapters 5 and 6, aviation law still rests firmly on the Chicago Convention and ICAO. Just as a reminder of what this means, let's go back to Chapter 6 for the following quote:

> The key to understanding ICAO is in realizing that like the UN in general it has *no* independent enforcement power; it cannot make it members implement any of its standards. Its main bodies may act to support or condemn certain actions by members that relate to aviation, but this is an exercise in public relations

and free expression. When or if a vote is taken on the issue of SARPs or PANS, it is the perfunctory end to months or years of consensus building at ICAO. If consensus is not initially achieved on certain issues, then all parties revise, rework, or reframe the issue until consensus is obtained. It is a painstaking process, but it has and is producing some very positive results (page number required here).

In short, if a nation or a firm from a given nation violates the international rules set down by treaty, there may be little recourse for the aggrieved party except international mediation and dispute resolution by a body that both parties recognize (Abeyratne, 2002).

Within any given country's boundaries, the rules and laws of that nation, however they came into existence, are in force. In only rare occasions can a firm from one country operating in another country avoid complying with that country's laws. While one country may attempt to extend its laws beyond its borders (extraterritoriality), such attempts are widely frowned upon by the rest of the world. A case in point is the 1977 Foreign Corrupt Practices Act (FCPA) which prohibited US companies from making illegal payments to foreign government officials with the purpose of influencing their decisions in matters of business. Many saw this act as an attempt by the US to impose our standards on the rest of the world and objected. This example also illustrates the problem with "international law." In 1997 the Organization for Economic Co-operation and Development Convention on Bribery was signed by 36 of the nations that had addressed these issues. Any nation not signing the treaty is not obligated to abide by it and even nations that did sign it can renounce it, should they choose to do so. Aviation has recently experienced its own version of the FCPA as the EU sought to apply the Emission Trading System (ETS) to international carriers (Labrousse, DeVore, and Hayes, 2013). So while it is possible to discuss the question of aviation or aerospace law in an international context, we will either be talking about "domestic laws" relating to (or applied to) aviation or international treaties relating to aviation/ aerospace. Whole texts have been written and courses have been taught on these subjects. The goal of this chapter is simply to introduce some of the broad legal areas affecting aviation, aerospace, and strategic alliances—liability issues, noise, and non-carbon pollution issues, and economic issues, particularly anti-trust or competition policy.

A Bumpy Ride

It is not surprising that one of the first issues to concern the aviation industry was liability in event of a crash. The Warsaw Convention of 1929 was the first to address this matter in an attempt to protect the newly forming airlines from the possibility that a single crash would put them out of business. The Warsaw Convention, article 17 states that a carrier is liable for "damage sustained in the event of the death or wounding of a passenger, if the accident which caused the damage so sustained took place on board the aircraft or in the course of any of the operations of embarking or disembarking." Over the years, legal experts have debated the meaning of "accident" and wounding, whether passengers are duly notified of the opportunity to pursue liability insurance (and/or have the opportunity to do so), the meaning of willful misconduct and negligence, and the limits to liability. More recent issues are the liability in case of pulmonary embolism, lack of medical equipment on board aircraft, and contaminated cabins and the spread of disease such as SARS (see Abeyratne, 2002 for more discussion). The Warsaw Convention set a damage limit of US$8,300 per person. The Chicago Convention avoided this issue deferring to the agreement in Warsaw. Warsaw, however, did not settle the matter. Developing countries complained that the limit was too high and, over time, developed countries have considered the limit too low. The Hague Protocol of 1955 sought to examine the issue again. This was followed by the Montreal Agreement (1966), the Montreal Convention (1971), and a second Montreal Convention in 1999. The limit for liability was progressively raised, but the latest limit under the treaty is the equivalent of US$168,372 unless the carrier can prove that neither it nor its agents had been negligent or committed a wrongful act or omission. This does not preclude victims from filing a lawsuit against any and all defendants. It also does not preclude airlines from carrying liability insurance for more than the amount in the Convention (Abeyratne, 2002; Pender, 2013). The events of September 11 obviously raised the issue of airline liability (and insurance) again as we will discuss in Chapter 15.

Environmental Impacts

Like any other industry, aviation is subject to the rules and regulations in place to "protect" the environment and the health and wellbeing of the citizens within that environment. The set of rules that applies depends on the location not the nationality of the firm involved. When American Airlines is in London, it is the rules of the UK and the broader EC that apply. The ICAO's inventory of aviation environmental problems range from site-specific issues of noise and flora and fauna impacts in airport construction to acid rain and carbon pollution. The latter has taken on new meaning with the concern about climate change and will be discussed separately in Chapter 18. For now, we will examine the question of aircraft noise. This issue took on new meaning with the advent of the jet age. ICAO created the Committee on Aircraft Noise (CAN) to deal with this issue and the national regulatory bodies governing aviation in respective countries have extensive rules and procedures for addressing noise that attempt to establish acceptable decibel levels, hours of operation, distances involved, remediation efforts, and so on (Aris, 2002; Michaels, 2008b). A good deal of effort has been expended to determine what level of noise is harmful, physically and mentally. Daley (2010) provides an extensive discussion of aircraft noise in his book *Air*

Transport and the Environment including discussion of noise measurement, impacts, and methods of reducing it.

The Politics of Anti-trust

Perhaps no area of the "law" has bedeviled the aviation industry more than anti-trust (competitive policy as it is commonly called in Europe and Asia). Once you understand the concepts involved, it is not hard to see why. Anti-trust is that body of principles and statutes whereby governments seek to promote forms of competition that benefit society and consumers. In many cases, this means restraining the use of market power (ability to control prices, supplies, distribution channels, and so on) by firms within an industry or preventing mergers or acquisitions that would create excessive market power. In an industry in which many segments (airline, manufacturing, engines, avionics, air cargo, alliances) may have only a few players or a few players with most of the market share, anti-trust questions arise frequently. While all countries have some statutes addressing the behavior of firms within their domestic markets, the background and philosophy of countries regarding business itself, the role of government, and the limits of free enterprise differ. We will examine the background and philosophy of anti-trust law and its application to aviation in the US, Europe, and Asia. We will attempt to chart the future direction of anti-trust enforcement and discuss critical issues impacting airline alliances.

In the years following the American Civil War (1861–1865), the US witnessed a renewed westward expansion fueled by the growth of the US railroad industry. As the economy became more integrated, there was an effort by a number of smaller companies to combine their businesses to increase market power. The most notorious effort involved Standard Oil, led by John D. Rockefeller. The Standard Oil "trust" was a device to gain market power by requiring participants to transfer stock from their company to a trustee in exchange for trust certificates. This trustee was then empowered to fix prices, control output, and allocate markets to other trust members. A series of scandals fueled the public perception that "trusts" were designed to drive smaller competitors out of business through the use of predatory tactics. Public outcry led the US Congress to pass a series of acts designed to curb activities that sought to restrain trade or establish excessive market power. Anti-"trust" legislation was born.

United States

The first US legislation dealing with anti-trust was the Sherman Act (1890) which was concerned with "horizontal restraints," that is, agreements between rival firms in the same market or industry that sought to fix prices, restrain output, divide markets, exclude other competitors, or erect barriers that impeded free markets. In 1914, the Clayton Act (amended by the Robinson–Patman Act of 1936 and the

Cellar–Kefauver Act of 1950) attempted to correct publicly perceived flaws in the Sherman Act by clearly prescribing actions that were deemed "anti-competitive." These actions include price discrimination, exclusionary practices such as exclusive dealing contracts and tying arrangements (tie-in sales agreements), and mergers that may have the effect of reducing competition.[1] The Civil Aviation Act of 1938 applied anti-trust specifically to airlines. Section 408 of the Civil Aviation Act, later recreated in virtually unchanged form in the Federal Aviation Act of 1958 and amended by the Airline Deregulation Act of 1978, made it unlawful for (1) two or more carriers to merge; (2) any carrier to control a substantial portion of the properties of another; or (3) any carrier to acquire control of another carrier. Section 414 provided the CAB with the authority to grant limited immunity (exemption) from anti-trust enforcement if it deemed the action to be "in the public interest." With the termination of the CAB in 1985, the Assistant Secretary for Policy and International Affairs in the DOT was given anti-trust responsibility. Anti-trust issues for other segments of the industry tend to fall under the Department of Justice (DOJ) and the Federal Trade Commission (FTC), although other departments may be consulted.

Domestic airline issues
Table 12.1 lists the merger/acquisition and bankruptcy activity in the US among national and major carriers since deregulation. The rationale for some of the mergers was the "failing company doctrine," however, Robert Pitofsky, formerly with the FTC, told the Commerce, Science, and Transportation Committee of the US Senate that some of these mergers were clearly "anti-competitive." He specifically cited the TWA–Ozark merger in his testimony (The Impact, 1999). Alfred Kahn, the father of US deregulation, agreed and has commented that, "I said we should deregulate the airline industry. I didn't say we should abolish the anti-trust laws" (Reno, 2000). The general attitude of the US Republican party which was in power during much of the 1980s was to view most business-related legislation as an interference in the workings of the free market (Clarkson, Miller, Jentz, and Cross, 1992). This view was supported by the so-called Chicago School of anti-trust whose members argued that while monopoly pricing hurt consumers, it had little effect on overall economic growth and productivity (Mandel, France, and Carney, 2000). However, these political and economic arguments do not entirely account for the level of consolidation permitted during the 1980s. In an

---

1   Federal anti-trust laws are enforced by the Department of Justice (DOJ) and the Federal Trade Commission (FTC). Violations of the Sherman Act fall under the jurisdiction of the DOJ and can be prosecuted as either a criminal or civil case. The Department can ask companies to divest certain holdings or dissolve a partnership. The FTC has the responsibility to enforce the Clayton Act through civil proceedings. In addition, private parties may sue for damages as a result of violation of the Sherman and Clayton Acts. Private parties may also seek an injunction to prevent anti-trust violations. It should be noted that European law does not include possible criminal prosecution.

Table 12.1   US airline history since deregulation

Carrier Name	Status
AirTran	Merged with Southwest in 2011
Aloha	Ceased operations 2008
Alaska	Continuing
America West	Merged with US Airways in 2005
American	Bankruptcy in 2011; Merged with US Airways
Braniff	Bankruptcy 1994
Continental	Merged with United in 2010
Delta	Continuing
Eastern	Bankruptcy 1991; Ceased operations
Flying Tigers	Acquired by FedEx 1988
Hawaiian Airlines	Continuing
Northwest	Merged with Delta
Pan American	Bankruptcy 1991; Ceased operations
Piedmont	Acquired by USAir
Republic	Acquired by Northwest 1986
Southwest Air Lines	Continuing
Trans World Airways	Assets acquired by American 2001
United Airlines	Continuing
US Airways	Merged with American 2014
Western	Acquired Delta 1986

effort to ensure competition, the FAA and the DOT became caught in their own trap. When they allowed United Airlines to acquire the Pacific routes of the failing Pan Am, they created a carrier whose large domestic base and extensive, profitable international route system placed domestic rivals with smaller geographic reach at a major disadvantage. So when Northwest petitioned the Department to purchase Republic, citing the need to expand their geographic reach in order to counter the United threat, the DOT agreed and so it went as other carriers pressed similar arguments.[2] In effect, the FAA created, somewhat reluctantly, a domestic market dominated by six or seven major carriers each possessing an extensive continental network by the mid-1990s (Oum and Park, 1997; Gesell, 1993).

The airline crises following 9/11 and the GFC have provided a backdrop for even further consolidation as the FAA and DOT continued to fall down the

---

2   I am indebted to Paul V. Mifsud, Vice President, Government & Legal Affairs, US, for KLM Royal Dutch Airlines for his willingness to share his insight and experience.

rabbit hole trying to catch up to themselves and create a "balanced" group of competitors. This time neither US political party seemed to see a merger that they did not like until US Airways and bankrupt American Airlines proposed to take the number of major carriers down to three. In August 2013, the DOJ filed an anti-trust suit to block this proposed merger citing reduced competition on over 1,000 connecting markets. Both carriers vowed to fight the DOJ claiming that it not only fails to support its arguments that the merger is anti-competitive, but that it holds this merger to a different standard than the Delta–Northwest, United–Continental, or Southwest–AirTran mergers. Of course, past history offers little guide to the future of airline consolidation. American Airlines was permitted to go ahead with its acquisition of Reno Air based on the rationale that American had a very weak position in the California/West Coast market where Reno Airlines was relatively strong, thus, competition was not likely to be harmed. When the DOJ filed suit against Northwest Airlines over plans to acquire a controlling stake in Continental, the acquisition was stopped but it did allow the two carriers to implement a number of their planned marketing activities (Carey and McCartney, 2000). UAL Corp, parent company of United Airlines, once announced its own proposed US$11.6 billion deal to purchase US Airways with great fanfare, but ended its planned merger after consumer groups, fellow airlines, and local governments complained about the scope and nature of the acquisition which would have created an airline with a combined market share of over 30 percent, making it twice as large as its nearest US competitor at the time (Hatch, 2000; Zellner, Carney, and Arndt, 2000). In the ever larger mergers of America West and US Airways, Southwest and AirTran, United and Continental, and Delta and Northwest, the DOJ focused primarily on competition on nonstop service (Flottau, 2013). Unfortunately, on another level these mergers created situations such as the one at Baltimore–Washington International where following the Southwest–AirTran merger a single carrier controlled 72 percent of the flights (Rohrer, 2013). In its defense, the DOJ is arguing that the dynamics of a three airline oligopoly are much different that a four airline oligopoly, but this may only be a matter of where you stand (which airport you fly out of or which routes you fly most). As a consumer, the large market effects may matter less to you than the market share of the airlines at your local airport. This is what determines your fare, level of options, and possibly the quality of service (Flottau and Shannon, 2013). According to Mazzeo (2003), flight delays are more frequent and longer in duration when only one airline provides direct service or dominates the market share of the airport in question.

It should be noted that a study conducted by Lehn and Kole on 18 airline mergers from 1979–1991 found that most resulted in negative long-run stock returns for the acquiring airline, including the US Air/Piedmont merger (Lehn, 2000). Short-run stock performance indicates that the market had a positive perception of AirTran and a negative one of Southwest following the merger announcement. Presumably, the market is concerned that Southwest will be able to further reduce costs (Manuela and Rhoades, 2013). Short-run stock reaction to announcement of the other mergers was mixed, however, reaction to the completion of these mergers was positive (Manuela and Rhoades, 2014). It is not yet clear how the market will view these mergers as they begin the often painful process of merging operations. Still, American and US Airways argue that having allowed prior mega-mergers, the DOJ should permit this latest one so that they will be in a position to compete and drive down prices. Delta and United have expressed official approval for the merger as it would help with continued capacity discipline and pricing power (Flottau and Shannon, 2013). If this latest merger did meet the expectations of Delta and United, then it might be "good for the industry," but it remains to be seen if it will be good for shareholders or consumers in the long run.

The existence of these large, overlapping network competitors explains in part the failure of US carriers to form the type of joint activity alliances common in Europe. Two cases explain the historic US government's view that such joint activities are on balance anti-competitive. The first case, *In Re Passenger Computer Reservation System Anti-trust Litigation CCH 21 AVI 17, 732*, was brought against US carriers' use of computer reservation systems in booking and marketing. It was charged that these systems, created by individual carriers, restricted competition by (1) displaying flight information in a biased manner; (2) imposing discriminatory fees on competing carriers; (3) using the data to identify travel agents who could be persuaded to divert business to the carrier owning the Computerized Reservation System (CRS); and (4) delaying the entry of competitor data. Since the development of computer reservation systems is expensive and beyond the reach of many carriers, such practices were considered an unfair use of market power and proprietary technology. In addition, the courts upheld the decision of the CAB in *Republic Airlines vs CAB 756 f.2d 1304 (1985)* to prohibit an exclusivity provision of joint operating agreements between carriers (Gesell, 1993).

Since deregulation took effect in the US over 200 airlines have started up and failed, a number that is increasing by the week as we will discuss in later chapters (Rosen, 1995). Start-ups have also contended that major carriers unfairly use their market power advantages, specifically the ability to control price and capacity, to force them out of profitable markets. This is commonly called predatory behavior. Unfortunately for regional carriers, the record of anti-trust cases in the US courts, particularly those involving charges of predatory behavior, has been very poor. In *Brookes Group Ltd v Brown & Williamson Tobacco Corp* (1993), the US Supreme Court ruled that aggressive cost-cutting (even selling below costs) benefited consumers. Of the 37 cases to reach the Supreme Court since this decision not one has prevailed (Carney and Zellner, 2000). The record for other cases of predatory behavior is equally poor (Walker, 1999). There was a renewed effort by the DOJ under the administration of President Clinton to enforce legislation relating to predatory behavior. As part of this new commitment, the DOT issued the "Proposed Statement on Enforcement Policy on Unfair Exclusionary Conduct by Airlines." The statement outlined the following situations when the DOT was likely to act on predatory practice complaints: (1) a major airline adds seats and discounts fares reducing "local revenue;" (2) a major airline carries more passengers at the new low fare than the new entrant has capacity, reducing the major's "local revenue;" or (3) a major airline carries more at the new low fare than the new entrant carries reducing the major's local revenue. This issue had a number of implications for domestic alliances. First, many regional US carriers decided to avoid direct competition by entering into franchise agreements with major carriers acting as a feeder service to their hubs. Second, regional carriers themselves had begun to consolidate either through merger or alliance (AvStat, 1998). Most recently, successful regionals have avoided competition by pursuing an ultra-low-cost strategy like Spirit Airline and Allegiant (Saporito, 2013).

International airline issues

As discussed in Chapter 9, the deregulation of the US airline industry was accompanied by a renewed effort to liberalize international markets and anti-trust legislation had an important role to play in the US strategy, first as a means to attack the fare-setting power of IATA and then to encourage the spread of Open Skies bilateral agreements through the promise of anti-trust immunity for alliance partners from Open Skies countries. The first of the "approved" alliances was Northwest and KLM. Four of the approved alliances are no longer in effect due to the failure (merger) of one or more of the carriers involved in the immunized alliance—American with Canadian International Airlines; Delta with Swiss Air, Sabena, and Austrian Airlines (formerly the Qualifyer group); Swissair with American; and Northwest and KLM (PRNewswire, 2000; OIG, 1999). The new EU–US Open Skies (EurActiv, 2008) increased the pool of immunized alliances with American Airline–British Airways finally achieving immunized status.

The DOT released a report in 1999 on the benefits of Open Skies.[3] According to this report, fares in Open Skies markets dropped 17.5 percent between 1996 and 1998. Non-Open Skies markets experienced only a drop of 3.5 percent (DOT, 1999). Thus, the US rationale for waiving anti-trust provisions in approved alliances between Open Skies market partners is that the pro-competitive benefits to consumers of Open Skies outweighs the possible anti-competitive harm. A recent look at the effect of the EU–US Open Skies, a much anticipated agreement, is less positive, but may be more a reflection of the 2008 GFC and continuing weakness in the EU since traffic growth on the North Atlantic for 2009 declined 6.2 percent and has remained relatively flat. This report noted that immunized alliances now control 83 percent of the market across the North Atlantic (CAPA, 2013b).

Domestic issues in other sectors

Chapter 13 picks up the story of air cargo and notes that UPS struggled state by state with the ICC for the right to compete against the US Post Office in the

---

3   It should be noted that allowing cabotage in the US would require changes in US laws and would have to be approved by the US Congress. There is also some question as to whether the EC can negotiate a multilateral agreement with the US.

delivery of parcels. UPS pointed to the fact that the United States Postal Service (USPS) was subsidized, paid no taxes, did not show a profit, and was often the subject of hearings and public outcry over mismanagement and incompetence. Their legal arguments centered the value of competition, the lower rates of UPS, and the "benefits to consumers." They were ultimately successful in their struggles but not without years of effort (Neimann, 2007). Obviously, when an entity is owned by the government, whether it is an airline or a postal system, there are incentives to protect it that create conflicts with the stated obligation of that government to protect competition for the benefit of consumers. In the case of the USPS, actions by the US Congress since 2006 have actually gone against this prevailing notion of government protection and appear determined to destroy the USPS by placing added conditions and restrictions on this entity without giving them any of the freedom a private entity would have to pursue innovate strategic options (Hicks, 2013).

As noted in the introduction to this book, aviation is often seen as a special case. One of the reasons for this is national defense. Therefore, it is not surprising that there are a number of "activities" that may be exempted from the application of competition rules including any activity approved by the US president on the grounds of national defense (Defense Production Act), activity involving research consortium to develop new computer technology (National Cooperative Research Act) or any activity of a regulated industry that is approved by the regulatory agency in that area (Clarkson, Miller, Jentz, and Cross, 1992). Further, there are "special" circumstances that have led the US government for national security reasons to approve mergers or acquisitions deemed to affect national security. The approval of the Boeing/McDonnell–Douglas merger and the Lockheed–Martin Marietta merger are two relatively recent examples of aerospace firms (with military as well as civilian activities) that the US government felt merited exception.

International issues in other sectors
"Fair Competition," of course, has been the stated reason behind the ongoing battles between Boeing and Airbus. Boeing has claimed that the initial launch aid provided to Airbus represents an "illegal subsidy." In 1992, the US and EU had agreed that governments could provide money for no more that 33 percent of the development costs of a new aircraft. These development costs would be viewed as loans repayable if the plane was actually built, the first 25 percent at government rates and the remainder at commercial rates. Airbus has charged that the aid Boeing receives from the US military amounts to a sizeable "indirect subsidy." Neither side has ever been able to put a specific figure to the amounts of aid, but this has not stopped them from battling over the issue. The US would again revisit this issue at the urging of Boeing in 2004, after Airbus had surpassed Boeing in orders. Both sides eventually filed a complaint with the World Trade Organization. As Airbus went to EU governments for new launch aid, Boeing howled. As Boeing outsourced development costs to the Japanese heavies (supported by their government), Airbus cried foul. In 2008, the US Pentagon announced that it

would award a military refueling tanker contract to a group of firms that included the parent company of Airbus, EADS. Boeing "fought" this award, marshaling political pressure with presentations of job losses and gains in various political districts. One Washington State Congressman even worked to change the lifecycle cost calculations in the award process to assist in changing the cost dynamics of the bidding process (Giegerich, 2011). The battle continues.

The US engine manufacturers have also lodged complaints about subsidies against UK competitor, Rolls-Royce, who is reported to have received almost 450 million pounds from the UK government who also holds a "golden share" in the company. Pratt and Whitney have noted that the CFM56 was partly funded by the French government in support of GE partner Snecma. The V2500, designed for the A-380, by Rolls-Royce and Pratt is another example of development aid in action. Once again, all sides of the debate can charge "indirect subsidy" because of the engine manufacturers' relationships with their respective government and defense spending (Newhouse, 2007).

Europe

While each individual European nation has its own legislation relating to competitive activity, we will address the development of anti-trust or competitive policy as it is called in Europe from the perspective of European integration.[4] European competition policy is one of the most extensive in the world and is generally stronger than the individual policies of member nations. It is also highly centralized. The period 1981–1991 represented a significant strengthening of these policies. One case in point is the Merger Regulation of 1989. This was used to block a proposed merger of ATR and De Havilland in 1991 and was an early sign that the EU was prepared to take a harder line of mergers than their US counterparts (Warlouzet, 2010). Although a Common Transport Policy was one of the stated goals of the European Community, the Council of Ministers, under their authority to issue block exemptions, chose to exempt transportation from the enforcement of competition rules. In 1986 the Court of Justice ruled in the *Nouvelles Frontieres* case that the air transport sector was subject to the general rules of the EEC Treaty. In that same year, the Commission began proceedings against ten Community airlines for violation of various competition rules. The "First Package," adopted December 14, 1987, officially included an implementing regulation giving the Commission the authority to investigate alleged violations of the competition rules and fine violators.

---

4   Anti-trust legislation was first contained in Articles 4 and 65–67 of the European Coal and Steel Community treaty. It is incorporated in Articles 85–86, 90, and 92–94 of the Treaty of European Union. The European Commission (Directorate–General IV) is responsible for implementing competitiveness policy.

Domestic airline issues

The Commission's policy toward airline mergers has been shaped in large part by what they perceive as failures in US policy. According to European aviation experts, "the experience of deregulation combined with the lack of anti-trust enforcement, destroyed many of the benefits of that deregulation' in the United States" (Soames, 1990: 82). Mario Monti, a former ECs anti-trust commissioner, led a concerted effort to crackdown on industries that attempted to set prices or divide markets. While there is a general feeling that cross-border ownership would benefit the EU system by reducing the tendency to favor "local" firms and allow for more economies of scale, the Commission has also been very cautious in approving mergers and acquisitions. The Commission's policy was questioned several years ago when Air France/UTA were allowed to merge, however, a series of Commission rulings, including one involving AirTours' planned takeover of First Choice, appeared to indicate that the Commission is prepared to take a tougher stance in aviation/aerospace mergers/acquisitions (Soames, 1990; Taverna, 1999). The EU has continued to reject proposals to merge between Ryanair and Aer Lingus on the grounds that the merger would create a monopoly at Ireland's Dublin Airport. Ryanair CEO, Michael O'Leary, has complained that the decision is at odds with the decision to allow Air France and KLM to merge even though these two carriers would control about 60 percent of the aircraft movements at Charles-DeGaule Airport and Schiphol Airport respectively (Media Limited, 2007). The EU also blocked the merger of Olympic and Aegean Airlines (Giannino, 2012). Similarly, a previously suggested merger between British Airways/KLM raised questions over the fact that any merger would place a single airline in control of two of Europe's most important airports—Heathrow and Schiphol. The stated reason for ending the British Airways/KLM talks was "intractable commercial and regulatory issues," but clearly there were serious concerns over EC approval, The US was also concerned because The Netherlands was an Open Skies country while the UK still had not signed such as agreement (Field, 2000). In the case of Air France–KLM, the Commission obliged the parties to agree to an unlimited period of slot divestment as a condition for approval. Further, slots surrendered initially would not be available for return to the parties even if the new entrant misused or underused it (Giannino, 2013).

   While European officials have taken a hard line on the issue of mergers and acquisitions as a means of opening slots to new entrants, they were relatively quick to approve the American–US Airways merger with the provision that actions be taken to increase competition on the London–Philadelphia route (Business Spectator, 2013). The EU has also tended to have a more favorable view of cooperative agreements between carriers involving fleet rationalization and network efficiencies. While EC competition rules do not explicitly consider "the public interest," they have often held that these types of agreements "contribute to the promotion of economic progress and to the interests of consumers" (AEA, 1999). Some of the allowed practices include consultation on and coordination of tariffs, joint operations, interline agreements, route planning, coordination of schedules, and linked frequent flyer programs. Perhaps signaling its limits, the EC recently conducted a raid on the offices of Scandinavian Airlines and Maersk Air to determine whether Maersk Air stopped operating between Stockholm and Copenhagen "in concert with SAS" following their recent cooperation pact (Dow Jones Newswire, 2000). US officials, on the other hand, have tended to view almost all actions relating to route planning, schedule coordination, and joint operations as violations of anti-trust law.

In an address at the twenty-third Annual FAA Commercial Aviation Forecast Conference, Frederik Sorenson, Head of the Air Transport Policy Unit Directorate General of Transport, EC, addressed the issue of competitive behavior by stating that the EU did not agree with the US "free for all system depending on the good behavior of air carriers" (Sorensen, 1998: 125). The Commission has acted in several cases of alleged predatory behavior ruling in favor of plaintive airlines (easyJet–KLM, easyJet–British Airway's Go). British Airway's Go successfully lodged a complaint with the EC charging that Deutsche Lufthansa AG was selling tickets below cost (*The Independent*, 2000). Given sufficient protection, many of these carriers may opt to remain independent, niche players rather than franchising feeders for the major airlines. The rapid growth of Ryanair, however, may give this carrier the market power to dampen the growth and development of the low-cost competition that the EU hoped to see from its deregulation and Single Sky program.

At present, one of the most vexing problems for the EU is government intervention to support airlines in Eastern Europe. Hungary's Malev Airlines in one of the most egregious examples. In 2011, the Hungarian government made three contributions to the struggling carrier and the carrier has been ordered to repay them following an investigation (Flottau and Wall, 2011).

International airline issues
While the US chose to tie alliance approval to Open Skies, European officials have tied alliance approval to domestic market development. A key issue in alliance approvals has been the willingness of potential partners to relinquish slots at congested European airports (United–Lufthansa and British Airways–American Airlines, for example). These slots were deemed necessary to the development of viable start-up competitors. Under the European Merger Control Regulation (EMCR), the Commission defines relevant markets on an origin and destination basis, considering slot and route dominance. The new generation slot remedies imposed on any merger seem to be solving this EU problem. The rejection of Ryanair–Aer Lingus and Olympic–Aegean was based on concerns over route dominance (Giannino, 2013). The EC argued for a multilateral approach to traffic rights negotiations on the basis of the one market concept and launched a case against eight member states arguing that the bilateral agreements that they signed with the US violated the EU external competence. The 2002 ruling by the European Court of Justice gave the EC the go ahead to "demand" multilateral talks with the US (EurActiv, 2008). This effort finally resulted in the 2008 EU–US

Open Skies agreement. In 1991, the EU and the US had agreed to notify and give weight to the competition policies of the other party in instances where their own enterprises were concerned. Most of the notifications involved proposed mergers. Unfortunately, the principle of positive comity has often merely served to highlight the differences between EU–US policy on competition policy. In particular, US authorities explicitly consider "the public interest" when assessing the benefits of proposed action (AEA, 1999). Given that one part of the new multilateral agreement signed between the US and EU calls for regulatory convergence, it is not clear what criteria will be used for alliance approval in the future (The CalTrade Report, 2007). It is not clear whether the divergence of opinion on American–US Airways reflects different overall approaches to competition analysis or the basic realities of different domestic markets.

Domestic issues in other sectors
In aerospace, the EU did block the proposed GE/Honeywell merger, claiming that the merger would reduce competition. GE and Honeywell had offered to unload some assets in the avionics area, but the EC asked that GE either spin-off its aircraft leasing unit or sell shares (CNNMoney.com, 2001; CNN.com, 2001). In 1999, the EU rejected another aerospace merger between Honeywell and AlliedSignal on concerns over undue dominance in avionics. Complaints had been lodged several years earlier when the EC had approved French subsidies to Sextant and Smith Industries to build a flight management system for Airbus, a move that some saw as an attempt to reduce Airbus reliance on Honeywell (CNNMoney.com, 1999). It is not clear what the ruling of the EC would have been over the proposed British Aerospace (BAE) Systems and European Aeronautic Defense and Space Company (EADS) merger since disagreements between the three governments involved—UK, France, and Germany—over ownership and industrial structure led to a collapse in the merger talks, but the merger would have created a military/aerospace company to rival Boeing (Scott and Clark, 2012).

International issues in other sectors
It is not surprising given the battles between Airbus and Boeing that the EC waded into the debate about the Boeing–McDonnell merger, eventually approving the merger after Boeing agreed to give up an exclusive sales agreement with American, Delta, and Continental (Newhouse, 2007). The EC did agree to the merger between Travelport and Worldspan. Travelport was the second-largest Global Distribution System (GDS) in the EU while Worldspan, a subsidiary of the online travel provider Orbitz, ranked fourth in GDS systems. Amadeus and Sabre were the other main players. The EU has stated that although the merged entity would have a very high market share in some of its member states, it did not feel that it would be able to increase prices due to high competition with other providers (Michaels, 2008a).

Asia

There is no single legal framework for Asia, but most of its countries do have some kind of legislation dealing with monopoly and competition. The difficulty lies in understanding the degree to which these regulations are applied and/or enforced. In Japan, the Anti-Monopoly Act is intended "to eliminate excessive concentrations of business power and to encourage fair and free competition" (Jetro, 1999). It prohibits holding companies and places restrictions on share holding, interlocking directorates, mergers, and acquisitions. The Fair Trade Commission is responsible for enforcing the anti-monopoly guidelines. The Korean Fair Trade Commission is also charged with promulgating guidelines and enforcing policies of their Monopoly Regulation and Fair Trade Act. Like its Japanese counterpart, the Monopoly Regulation and Fair Trade Act is intended to prohibit excessive concentration, abuse of market power, and unfair business practices. To the outside observer, the Japanese Keiretsus and the Korean Chaebols, forms of tightly linked industrial groupings, appear to violate much of this legislation. Critics have often complained that the legislation is primarily directed at limiting foreign access to domestic markets (Gibney, 1985; Prestowitz, 1988). The financial crisis in Asia put a great deal of pressure on these structures. In Korea, this crisis prompted some consideration of dismantling or weakening the chaebol structure to improve efficiency and transparency within their market.

Domestic airline issues

Efforts were underway in a number of Asian countries to deregulate aspects of their air transport sectors before the Asian crisis of the late 1990s. The events of 9/11 and the GFC were not as severe in Asia as in other parts of the globe. As noted in Chapter 10, two countries are taking significant actions to further liberalize their domestic aviation markets—India and Japan. The Indian government allowed private entry into the airline industry in mid-1990s. Only one of the private carriers started at that time survives today. Four of the carriers founded in the last decade have also posted massive losses, including the once highly touted Kingfisher Airlines. The debate over possible intervention by the State Bank of India in favor of Kingfisher created a great deal of soul-searching in the ninth-largest aviation market in the world over questions of market versus intervention. It has also prompted the government to open the market to more foreign investment (Choudhury, 2012). The Japanese government changed its policy in 1995 to make discounted fares easier and in 1996 created a zone-fare system. On December 5, 1996, the Japanese Ministry of Trade announced an end to the supply–demand balance clauses that had effectively blocked new entry. A 1999 study of the changes, however, did not find a significant shift in market share or reduction in airfares (Yamauchi, 1999). Load factors for domestic routes have remained around 60 percent for the last two decades prompting the government to encourage new LCC entry. In 2012, three such carriers were established—Peach, Jetstar, and AirAsia Japan (CAPA, 2013a).

International airline alliances

As with aviation policy as a whole, there is no consistent "Asian" strategy toward international alliances. Market access through codesharing has been the dominant form of alliance arrangement. The economic crisis that started in Thailand and spread throughout Asia affected all of the region's air carriers. Hardest hit were Thai Airlines, Philippines Airlines, Korean Airlines, Malaysian Airlines, and Garuda from Indonesia. High operating and financing costs combined with outbound and inbound traffic decreases to place severe stress on these and other Asian carriers (Li, 1999). There were talks of regional consolidation, but little action took place until the 9/11, SARS, and Bird Flu crises added further pressure to some of the Asia carriers. Many of these talks (and actions) included Singapore Airlines which emerged as one of the strongest of the Asian carriers and has continued an aggressive campaign to improve its already impressive quality and position itself well in the mega-alliance world. Following the GFC, Asia has continued to be one of the strongest aviation regions of the world

Stumbling along

It should be clear from the above discussions that the line between politics and legal matters is very fine and frequently shifting in the aviation/aerospace industry. The industry is a highly visible, important employer with close ties to national security and defense; this places any matter affecting its profitability squarely into the political arena. In the all important area of competition, the EU has been most consistent, maintaining a relatively hard line on mergers/acquisitions, predatory behavior, and slot allocation. The approval of Air France–KLM certainly indicates that the EC is interested in selected cross-border merger activity. As noted above, the Commission has indicated on a number of occasions that it would like to see more consolidation in the relatively fragmented airline and aerospace industry, but this has not prevented them from denying several mergers for competition reasons (Sparaco, 1999). At present, the question of national government intervention on behalf of flag carriers continues to be hotly debated.

As for predatory behavior, the EU provided start-up carriers greater protection than is typically afforded them in the US market. This protection could help insure that deregulation increases competition at the route level within Europe, however, the start-up darling of Europe, Ryanair, has faced increasing charges that it has begun to practice the kind of market power tactics once used against it to compete against legacy and other start-ups (Creaton, 2005). The pool of start-ups in Europe has remained relatively small and many of the major European carriers did not feel the need to aggressively engage them. The events of 9/11 hit the major European carriers hard and regional European and LCC carriers began increasing their market share (Binggeli and Pompeo, 2002). The expansion of Ryanair alone has changed the dynamics of air travel in the EU. While a report in the late 1990s by the British Civil Aviation Authority found that no more than 7 percent of intra-European city pairs are served by three or more competitors, the expansion of easyJet and Ryanair have probably made air travel in the EU more accessible and price competitive than many US markets (Sparaco, 1998).

The US, under the Clinton Administration, moved toward stronger enforcement of its anti-trust provisions than previous Republican administrations. The Clinton Federal Trade Commission and the DOJ jointly issued anti-trust guidelines for collaboration among competitors which outlined those agreements that would be considered per se illegal from those that would be analyzed under the rule of reason to determine their effect on competition. According to these guidelines, any agreement addressing pricing or capacity was to be deemed per se illegal. All other agreements would be analyzed according to the rule of reason policy. The agencies would first define "relevant markets," then calculate "market shares" and concentrations to assess possible market power increases stemming from the agreement. If this raised concerns about anti-competitive harm, they would then assess the degree of independent decision making by partners to the agreement to determine the potential degree of collusion. They would then be interested in the ability and incentives of partners to compete independently. According to the guidelines, the agencies would focus on six factors: (1) the degree of exclusivity in the agreement; (2) the extent of independent asset control; (3) the nature and extent of inter-partner financial interest; (4) the control of competitive decision making; (5) the degree of information sharing; and (6) the duration of the partnership. These guidelines were largely a consolidation and elaboration on existing law. A somewhat more problematic issue concerned weighing anti-competitive harm against collaborative efficiencies and whether these efficiencies are considered pro- or anti-competitive (Federal Trade Commission, 1999). Previous US administrations had tended to accept the argument that pro-competitive benefits outweigh potential harm and this has been the view of the US government since the Clinton Administration. It remains to be seen if the recent DOJ action on the merger of American and US Airways represents a change in direction, a ploy to force further concessions, or a pause in consolidation. In the area of predatory behavior, the US government after Clinton has had very little to say on these matter. The Obama Administration has not changed this policy, leaving smaller carriers to plot their own path to success or ruin.

Questions

1. Discuss the following: The Warsaw Convention of 1929, The Hague Protocol of 1955, and the Montreal Conventions of 1971 and 1999.
2. What is anti-trust policy and what is the history of enforcement in the US?
3. What are predatory behaviors? Is it a problem in the airline industry and what can be done about it?

4. How does the EU policy to anti-trust or competitive policy differ from the US?
5. What is the purpose of these types of policies and have they been effective in protecting competition?

References

Abeyratne, R.I.R. (2002), *Frontiers of Aerospace Law*, Ashgate Publishing, Aldershot.

Aris, S. (2002), *Close to the Sun: How Airbus Challenged America's Domination of the Skies*, Arum Press, London.

Association of European Airlines (AEA) (1999), *Towards a Transatlantic Common Aviation Area*, Association of European Airlines, Brussels.

AvStat Associates Inc. (1998), "Summary of passenger service by state," AvStat Associates.

The Independent (2002), "BA's Go accuses Lufthansa of unfair competition, paper says," February 29, p. 17.

Binggeli, U. and Pompeo, L. (2002), "Hypes hopes for Europe's low cost airlines," *The McKinsey Quarterly*, No. 4.

Business Spectator (2013), "EU approves giant airline merger," retrieved online September 8, 2013 from http://www.businessspectator.com.au/news/2013/8/6/aviation/eu-approves-giant-airline-merger.

Carey, S. (2000), 'Travel Agents Ask the U.S. to Act Against Web-Site Plan', *The Wall Street Journal*, February 18.

Carey, S. and McCartney, S. (2000), "Antitrust trial pressures Northwest Airlines to cede controlling stake in Continental," *Wall Street Journal*, November 7, B10.

Carney, D. and Zellner, W. (2000), "Caveat predator?" *Business Week*, May 22, pp. 116–118.

Centre for Aviation (CAPA) (2013a), *World Aviation Yearbook 2013—North Asia Pacific*, CAPA, available at centreforaviation.com.

Centre for Aviation (CAPA) (2013b), "The North Atlantic: the state of the market five years on from EU-US open skies," retrieved online January 3, 2014 from http://centreforaviation.com/analysis/download/100315.

Choudhury, G. (2012), "SBI decides on 1,650-crone relief package for Kingfisher," *Hindustan Times*, February 22, p. 1.

Clarkson, K.W., Miller, R.R., Jentz, G.A. and Cross, F.B. (1992), *West's Business Law: Text, Cases, Legal and regulatory Environment* (5th ed.), West Publishing Company, New York.

CNN (2001), "EU kills GE-Honeywell," July 3, retrieved online June 6, 2002 from http://cnn.europe.business.com/pt/cpt?dropdown=Y&action=cpt%exp.

CNNMoney (1999), "EC probes avionics merger," August 30, retrieved online March 3, 2000 from http://cnnmoney.com/pt/cpt?action=cpt&title=EC+probes+AlliedSinanl.

CNNMoney (2001), "GE pessimistic on merger," June 14. Retrieved online June 6, 2002 from http://cnnmoney.com/pt/cpt?action=cpt&title=GE%2C+Honeyw ell.

Creaton, S. (2005), *Ryanair: How a Small Irish Airline Conquered Europe*, Arum, London.

Daley, B. (2010), *Air Transport and the Environment*, Ashgate Publishing, Farnham.

Department of Transportation (DOT) (1999), *International Aviation Developments: Global Deregulation Takes Off*, DOT, Washington, DC.

Dow Jones Newswire (2000), "EU raids Maersk, SAS In connection with cooperation pact," June 21.

EurActiv (2008), "EU-US 'Open Skies' agreement," retrieved online March 16, 2011 from http://www.euractiv.com/en/transport.

Federal Trade Commission (1999), retrieved online June 6, 2000 from www.ftc. gov/opa/1999/9910/jointven.html.

Field, P. (2000), "BA, KLM ground merger plan. Airlines faced opposition from government which feared massive layoffs," *USA Today*, September 22, 1B.

Flottau, J. (2013), "Court of contingency," *Aviation Week & Space Technology*, September 16, p. 37.

Flottau, J. and Shannon, D. (2013), "Connecting flight," *Aviation Week & Space Technology*, August 19, pp. 24–27.

Flottau, J. and Wall, R. (2011), "Weighed down," *Aviation Week & Space Technology*, October 17, pp. 24–25.

Gesell, L.E. (1993), *Aviation and the Law* (2nd ed.), Coast Aire Publications, Chandler, AZ.

Giannino, M. (2013), "The European Commission appraisal of airline mergers: the rise of a new generation of slot remedies," retrieved online March 7, 2014 from http://aerlinesmagazine.files.wordpress.com/2012/03/52_giannino_eu_ slot_remedies.pdf.

Giegerich, S. (2011), "Bumpy road to Boeing tanker contract," *St. Louis Post-Dispatch*, retrieved online March 3, 2012 from http://www.stltoday.com/ business/local/bumpy-road-to-boeing-tanker-contract/article_4b7e1993-c4f4-508a-89ee-1baf9e13ecd7.html.

Gibney, F. (1985), *The Fragile Super-Power*, New American Library, New York.

Hamm, S., Greene, J. and Reinhardt, A. (2002), "What's a rival to do now?," Aviation Week & Space Technology, November 18, pp. 44–46.

Hatch, M. (2000), "Minnesota Attorney General letter to the DOJ re US-UA," Aviation Week & Space Technology, June 5, p. 10.

Hicks, J. (2013), "Postal service financials improve, but big losses continue," The *Washington Post*, retrieved online March 16, 2014 from http://articles. washingtonpost.com/2013-08-11/politics/41299747_1_u-s-postal-service-comprehensive-postal-reform-legislation-postmaster-general-patrick-donahoe.

The Independent (2000), "BAs GO accuses Lufthansa of unfair competition," February 28, p. 17.

JETRO (1999), www.jetro.go.jp.

Labrousse, F., DeVore, J.S. and Hayes, J.M. (2013), "European Union: aviation and the EU ETS—what's next?" Jones Day, retrieved online from http://www.mondaq.com/unitedstates/x/223598/Aviation/Aviation+and+the+EU+ETS+Whats+Next.

Lehn, K.M. (2000), "Why airline mergers are a disaster—Soaring labor costs may ground airline mergers," *Aviation Week & Space Technology*, May 25.

Li, M.Z.F. (1999), "Asia-Pacific Airlines amidst the Asian Economic Crisis," Presented at the Air Transportation Research Group Conference, Hong Kong, June 1999.

Mandel, M.J., France, M. and Carney, D. (2000), "The great antitrust debate," *Aviation Week & Space Technology*, June 26, pp. 40–42.

Manuela Jr., W.S. and Rhoades, D.L. (2013), "Southwest's acquisition of AirTran: An analysis of short-term stock performance," *World Review of Intermodal Transportation Research*, vol. 4 (4), pp. 227–246.

Manuela Jr., W.S. and Rhoades, D.L. (2014), "Merger activity and short-run financial performance in the US airline industry," *Transportation Journal*, vol. 53 (3).

Mazzeo, M.J. (2003), "Competition and service quality in the US airline industry," *Review of Industrial Organization*, vol. 22 (3), pp. 275–296.

Media Limited (2007), "EU steps in on Irish airline merger," June 27, retrieved online April 14, 2012 from http://www.airport-technology.com/news/news1701.html.

Michaels, J. (2008a), "Travelport completes acquisition of Worldspan," *Aviation Daily*, retrieved online January 8, 2012from http://aviationow.com/pt/cpt?action=cpt&title=Aviation+Week%3A.

Michaels, D. (2008b), "Heathrow makeover to heat up airline wars," *The Wall Street Journal Online*, March 6.

Newhouse, J. (2007), *Boeing versus Airbus: The Inside Story of the Greatest International Competition in Business*, Alfred A. Knopf, New York.

Niemann, G. (2007), *Big Brown: The Untold Story of UPS*, John Wiley & Sons, San Francisco, CA.

Office of Inspector General (OIG) (1999), "Aviation safety under international code share agreements," 30 September AV-1999-138.

Pender, K. (2013), "Who will pay, collect claims arising from Asiana crash," SFGate, retrieved online from http://blog.sfgate.com/pender/2013/07/08/who-will-pay-collect-claims-arising-from-asiana-crash/.

Prestowitz, C.V. (1988), *Trading Places: How We Are Giving Our Future to Japan and How to Reclaim it*, Basic Books, Inc, New York.

PRNewswire (2000), "Northwest Airlines and Malaysia Airlines receive antitrust immunity; approval represents first immunized alliance between a US and Asian carrier," November 21.

Oum, T.H. and Park, J. (1997), "Airline alliances: current status, policy issues, and future directions," *Journal of Air Transport Management*, vol. 3 (1), pp. 133–144.

Reno, R. (2000), "In several ways, United/US Airways merger might not fly," *Star Tribune*, June 1.

Rohrer, K. (2013), "Where was DoJ in Southwest-AirTran merger?" *The Baltimore Sun*, retrieved online January 16, 2014 from http://www.baltimoresun.com/news/opinion/readersrespond/bs-ed-merger-letter-20130815,0,5846611.

Rosen, S.D. (1995), "Corporate Restructuring: A Labor Perspective." in P. Cappelli (ed). *Airline Labor Relations in the Global Era: The New Frontier*, ILR Press, Ithaca, NY., pp. 31–41

Saporito, B. (2013), "Cabin pressure," *Time*, September 9, pp. 36–41.

Scott, M. and Clark, N. (2012), "BAE and EADS merger talks disintegrate," *The New York Times*, retrieved online May 6, 2013 from http://dealbook.nytimes.com/2012/10/10/eads-and-bae-systems-abandon-merger-talks/?_r=0.

Soames, T. (1990), "Joint Ventures and Cooperation Agreements in the Air Transport Sector," in P.D. Dagtoglou and T Soames (eds), *Airline Mergers and Cooperation in the European Community*, Kluwer Law and Taxation Publishers, Boston, MA.

Sorensen, F. (1998), "Open Skies in Europe," in *FAA Commercial Aviation Forecast Conference Proceedings*, US Department of Transportation, Washington, DC, pp. 125–131.

Sparaco, P. (1998), "European deregulation still lacks substance," *Aviation Week & Space Technology*, November 9, pp. 53–57.

Sparaco, P. (1999), "EC pushes quick aviation accord with US," *Aviation Week & Space Technology*, November 29, pp. 40–41.

Taverna, M.A. (1999), "European rulings signal tougher antitrust stance," *Aviation Week & Space Technology*, October 4, pp. 42–43.

The Cal Trade Report (2007), "US, EU pact opens Transatlantic market," 17 July, retrieved online May 23, 2008 from http://www.caltradereport.com/eWebpages/front-page-1178627781.

"The impact of recent alliances, international agreements, DOT actions, and pending legislation on air fares, air service, and competition in the airline industry" (1999) 10x Cong., 2 Sess.

Walker, K. (1999), "American Justice," *Airline Business*, July, pp. 66–67.

Warlouzet, L. (2010), "The rise of European competition policy, 1950–1991: A cross-disciplinary survey of a contested policy sphere," EUI Working Papers RSCAS 2010/80, retrieved online September 16, 2013 from http://cadmus.eui.eu/bitstream/handle/1814/14694/RSCAS_2010_80.pdf.

Yamauchi, H. (1999), "Air Transport Policy in Japan: Policy Change and Market Competition." Paper presented at the Air Transportation Research Group Conference, Hong Kong, April 1999.

Zellner, W., Carney, D. and Arndt, M. (2000), "How many airlines will stay aloft," *Business Week*, June 19.

Chapter 13
The Quality Question

Learning Objectives

After reading this chapter, you should have a good understanding of:
- LO1: the many definitions of quality and the selection of metrics to measure it.
- LO2: the metric and sources of quality data for the airline industry.
- LO3: the measurement of quality across alliances.
- LO4: ways to approach quality improvements.

Key Terms, Concepts, and People

Word-of-mouth	(WOM)	Quality	Loyalty
Repurchase	Satisfaction	J.D. Powers	
ATCR	AQR	SDI	

Know It When You See It

Quality is a very elusive term. Consumers know (or think they know) it when they see it and firms have spent billions trying to get them to articulate their preferences or to convince them that what they get is what they want. A researcher will tell you that you cannot measure something until you define it. Unfortunately, the very act of defining and measuring a concept can change the concept itself, marketing's own "Uncertainty Principle." The term "quality" has been defined as excellence, value, conformance to specification, and so on. The most commonly used definition comes to us from the total quality movement. It defines quality as "meeting and/ or exceeding customer expectations." To comply with this definition of quality, companies must first know who their customers are and then continually strive to understand and meet their expectations (continuous improvement). While this sounds simple on paper, many companies find it difficult to put into practice. For airlines, revenue management systems that divided customers by their preferences on booking time, price, class, and so on and frequent flyer surveys of services provided to these customers have often been considered sufficient to comply with this quality definition. However, the growing movement to "brand" airline and alliance service is focusing new attention on issues of quality. This movement is fueled by the belief that "a very real risk exists that the flight will be reduced to a commodity status, and that the individual choice of airlines will be factored out of the buying process" (Fraser, 1996: 61). In short, consumer choice would be driven almost solely by price, a factor that drives down profits and forces airlines to continually strive for new cost-cutting measures whose revenue benefits would be transferred almost immediately to customers in lower prices. While this might sound great for customers, an airline that cannot make money cannot stay in business very long. The airline answer to the price/quality dilemma, as we discussed in Chapter 11, is to create products and services that send images and messages to the consumer that reassure them about quality, convenience, comfort, and so on. In short, the very name must separate one airline (one alliance) from another in terms of key consumer expectations whether they are "global reach," "superior service," or "value for the money."

Measuring a Concept

For individual carriers, consumers have three basic sources of information on quality—personal experience (or word-of-mouth), third-party surveys, or secondary reports. Personal experience or the so-called word-of-mouth (WOM) information that comes to us from friends and strangers alike is clearly a powerful force. For many companies this source calls to mind the old adage that a satisfied customer tells five other people about their experience while a dissatisfied customer tells at least ten. In the age of social media, this WOM phenomenon can be magnified greatly. Thus, a positive (or negative) experience by one customer can suddenly "go viral" and have effects unheard of ten years ago. For most firms in the so-called service industries, satisfying customers is the first step toward creating loyal customers who repurchase your product. Taking this concept one step further, marketing gurus such as Fred Reichheld (2006) have suggested that "The Ultimate Question" is "Would you recommend us to a friend?" Reichheld believes that the best measure of a firm's success is the size of their net promoter score (promoters less detractors). Reichheld's promoters are the truly loyal customers. Loyal customers repurchase your products or services and recommend them to others.

Loyalty, repurchase, and satisfaction are among the most significant concepts in marketing research and the key to superior performance. Loyalty, repurchase, and satisfaction play an important role for understanding consumer behavior. The academic literature provides a number of research findings on relations between loyalty, repurchase, and satisfaction. However, Szymanski and Henard (2001) report that, despite numerous studies, the research findings are conflicting. Loyalty is a multidimensional construct, which is defined and viewed differently by researchers. Despite the large number of studies published in the area of satisfaction and loyalty, Oliver (1999) stated that loyalty–satisfaction relations are not well defined. The general assumption is that loyal consumers are satisfied, however, some research has indicated that satisfaction itself is an unreliable predictor of loyalty. While many researchers consider loyalty and repurchase as highly related concepts, and often use those two terms interchangeably, other researchers have identified differences. High repurchase rates do not necessarily indicate loyalty; low repurchase rates do not always indicate disloyalty. Bloemer and Kasper (1995) have suggested that the actual re-buying of a product or service is all that matters, not the customer's degree of commitment. In contrast, loyalty takes into account the actual behavior's antecedents, including the psychological state of a consumer's mind. Many researchers, including Jacoby and Chestnut (1978), distinguish between the psychological aspect of loyalty and the behavioral aspect of loyalty, which is identified with repurchase.

While personal experience and WOM clearly influence opinions about quality—real or perceived—surveys are one of the most popular sources for information about products and services. Publicly available surveys involving airlines are typically conducted by such organizations as J.D. Powers, Zagats, or Conde Nast utilizing information from frequent flyers to rank or award airlines on quality performance. The 1997 J.D. Powers' survey found that there are ten factors that drive consumer satisfaction with airline quality: on-time performance, airport check-in, schedule/flight accommodations, seating comfort, gate location, aircraft interior, flight attendants, food service, post-flight services, and frequent flyer programs. Specifics in the pre-flight categories include availability of flight when desired, helpfulness of reservations agents, ability to get seat preference, ability to get priority boarding, and frequent flyer qualification levels. In-flight issues judged important by consumers include effective communication on flight delays/cancellations, carry-on luggage space, seating comfort, and helpfulness of flight attendants. In the area of airport activities, consumers want such things as speedy baggage delivery, good connecting flight information, short check-in times, and good airport lounges (Glab, 1997). While surveys are a source of valuable information to consumers, they have several weaknesses from a research perspective. First, it is difficult to compare the surveys from different organizations because the factors included vary between them. Second, the cross-sectional nature (that is, the respondents in 1996 are not the same as in 1998) and changing factors across years for the same organizations limit the ability to evaluate trends in the data. Finally, these surveys do not generally provide an overall ranking of all the airlines included but a category-by-category ranking of the top performers.

The final source of information on airline quality is reported secondary data. This information is gathered either routinely by airlines or is mandated by the regulatory authority in that country (region). This information may or may not be publicly available. If publicly available, it may be provided by the regulatory agency upon request, periodically published, or posted to a publicly accessible website. To illustrate the type, use, and limitation of such data, we will use the US example. The US DOT has published the Air Travel Consumer Report (ATCR) monthly since 1987. The ATCR contains data on areas of service quality of interest to consumers, but has changed somewhat over time as issues such as flight cancellation and animal handling in transport have become more important and problems of smoking on aircraft have declined in importance and occurrence. The data is provided in raw form with no effort made to adjust the data for the size of airline operations. Such adjustment is important for evaluating the performance between airlines and is usually based on either departures, miles, or hours flown. Two groups of US researchers have used the data in the ATCR to explore issues of airline service quality. In 1991, the Aviation Institute at the University of Nebraska published its first Airline Quality Rating (AQR) report on the ten major US carriers. The weighted AQR has been revised since its inception to disaggregate service, safety, and financial indicators. The second group of researchers began reporting on airline service in 1998 with the Service Disquality Index (SDI), although they went back to the first publication of the ATCR in 1987 to begin their analysis of service quality (Rhoades, Waguespack, and Treudt, 1998; Rhoades and Waguespack, 2008). Service and safety quality were separated from inception to construct two different rankings of airline performance which could be compared for each carrier and the industry overall (Rhoades and Waguespack, 1999, 2004). Further, Rhoades and Waguespack (2000a) examined the service and safety quality of US national and regional carriers whose performance could be compared to the traditional legacy (major) carriers. Comparisons were also made between legacy and LCCs (Rhoades and Waguespack, 2001, 2005). In their most recent work, Rhoades and Waguespack (2014) reported on 25 years of US airline service quality. During these years the airline industry has seen the recession of the early 1990s, the dot-com bubble (1999–2000), 9/11, the GFC (2008), and several oils spikes with the US$147 a barrel oil of 2008 being the worst.

One of the advantages of the consistent application of secondary data is that it allows for trend analysis. For example, it is possible to say (based on the work of Rhoades and Waguespack) that the industry average service quality for the major carriers improved from 1987 to 1993 and remained relatively stable at around 40 service problems per departure for 1994–1997 before it began to climb in 1998 reaching 47 service problems per departure in 2000. Service quality improved after 2001, but slowly began to climb to an industry high of 72 service problems per departure in 2007. Following the GFC, quality began to improve to a rate of 43 service problems per departure in 2012. This same analysis can apply at the firm level to analyze how a given firm has changed over time where it is often easy to identify airlines in financial and/or labor trouble or those in the midst of merger reorganization. Secondary data is also easy and cheap to obtain. As with anything else, there are also disadvantages as well. First, this secondary data does not specifically ask about many of the areas identified as important by the survey research—food service, legroom, aircraft interior. The primary focus of the measures in the secondary data is basic service—on-time performance, delays, baggage delivery. Critics have suggested that amenities are important to flyers and are not considered in the secondary data. A final criticism has to do with the issue of perception.

Perception Versus Reality

The dictionary defines perception as the "recognition and interpretation of sensory stimuli based chiefly on memory" (The American Heritage College Dictionary, 2000: 1014). Since individuals vary in terms of memory, sensory acuity, and cognitive ability, it is clearly possible that no two individuals will perceive a situation or event the same way. Parasuraman, Zeithaml and Berry (1985) have argued that service quality is the difference or gap between customer expectations of performance and customer perceptions of that performance. They used this starting point to develop the SERVQUAL instrument. In the SERVQUAL instrument, quality is defined or operationalized in the form of five dimensions; tangibles, reliability, responsiveness, assurance, and empathy (Parasuraman, Zeithaml and Berry, 1988). Cronin and Taylor (1992) have taken the argument one step further to suggest that all that matters is perception of performance; perception equals service quality. Only a few of studies have attempted to integrate a scale such as SERVQUAL or SERVPERF into the airline service research literature. One such study utilized the SERVQUAL scale adopted for an airline situation in 1994 (Sultan and Simpson, 2000) and found the SERVQUAL factor of reliability (one example: excellent airlines will provide their services at the time they promise to do so) was the most important dimension among air passengers. However, there has been no longitudinal perceptual study on airline service quality published in the academic realm. This lack of follow-up study or an update of the work done is common in much of marketing research, not just airline service quality research. A further issue that deserves study is the relationship between perception and "reality." In other words, how does customer perception compare to some sets of "objective" measures of performance. One of the first attempts to address this question is Tiernan, Rhoades, and Waguespack (2008). They compared survey data asking for the respondents to identify the percentage of certain service failures—lost baggage, delayed flights, cancelled flights, and so on—to the available secondary data for the US and EU. They found that the perception of airline quality was for the most part far worse than the secondary metrics of performance would suggest. Even when secondary service metrics were reaching over 99 percent, respondents reported perceptions of increasingly poor service. This phenomenon is also clear from a recent National Public Radio article (Memmott, 2013) discussing the 2013 AQR (AQR at http://www.airlinequalityrating.com) report. The article noted that the AQR was showing an all-time high in airline service quality at the same time that customer complaints had soared 22 percent. While the level of actual complaints to the DOT is low compared to total enplanements (15,335 out of 51,618,136 enplanements for 2012), the industry is still troubled by a perception that it does not provide quality or create customer satisfaction. The annual American Customer Satisfaction Index (ASCI) for 2006 ranked the airline industry below the US Internal Revenue Service in customer satisfaction (ASCI, 2006; Yu, 2007).

And the Winner is...

The "reality" of airline service quality is that it is highest when the industry is experiencing economic difficulty (recession, high fuel prices, and so on). During these times of crisis, airlines and customers retrench. Fewer planes fly thus reducing congestion in the airspace and on airport tarmacs. Less congestion means more on-time flights and less delay in takeoff. Fewer passengers also means fewer bags to lose or mishandle. While some quality woes can be traced to the very public meltdown of carriers such as JetBlue Airways where bad weather and lean operations resulted in the stranding of over 5,000 passengers during the Valentine's Day holiday and projected costs to JetBlue of US$14 million in refunds and overtime, many other quality problems are chronic and long standing (Sloan and Ehrenfeld, 2007). United Airlines has suffered through several extended periods of low quality, often finishing last among major US carriers in operational quality (Rhoades and Waguespack, 2014). In the US, several cases of tarmac stranding (passengers stuck in planes on the airport tarmac either waiting to takeoff or waiting to arrive at the gate for disembarking) have raised new threats of government intervention that appears to be expanding beyond stranding to issues of ancilliary fees and airline disclosure (Rhoades and Waguespack, 2014; Waguespack and Curtis, 2013).

Achieving Airline Quality

Airlines are organized by function—flight operations, engineering and maintenance, marketing, and services. Under marketing, which composes approximately 50 percent of the workforce, there are units concerned with reservations and ticketing, cabin service, ground service, food service, and so on (Wells, 1994). The consumer view, however, is not segmented into functions. Consumers experience airline service as a series of processes. The order fulfillment process begins with check-in and proceeds to final destination and baggage retrieval (Ekdahl, Gustafsson, and Edvardsson, 1999). When a problem arises during the travel experience, consumers are not interested in fixing the blame on a particular function and they certainly do not wish to stand around while the airline attempts to do so. Consumers want the issue resolved to their satisfaction as quickly as possible by their first contact point. They do not wish to be shuffled from department to department or supervisor to supervisor looking for resolution. One of the greatest drawbacks to a functional structure is that consumers often "feel they are forced into a system characterized by contradictions, redundant or insufficient information, misguided authority, and confusion" (Ekdahl, Gustafsson, and Edvardsson, 1999). In other words, the traditional functional structure often finds it difficult to provide a seamless service. Many companies claim that "quality is everyone's business," but they fail to realize that quality must also be "someone's responsibility."

There are basically two ways to approach the process quality issue. The most obvious way is to restructure the organization on a process basis—order fulfillment, new product development, customer acquisition, and so on. In a process-structured organization, coordination within the process eliminates the "cracks" through which customers often fall. This coordination is usually achieved through the establishment of cross-functional teams that include at least one member from each functional areas involved in that process. All elements of the process become the responsibility of the process leader and his team. Their job is to (1) insure that all elements of the process are addressed; and (2) act as liaison to the functional departments, providing input from and guidance to the process. According to Scandinavian Airlines (SAS), three principles should govern the design of the process: (1) give passengers control; (2) make the process transparent; and (3) empower the staff (Ekdahl, Gustafsson, and Edvardsson, 1999). A related option would be to institute a matrix structure that would in fact overlay the functional structure with a process structure. This type of organizational restructuring was popular in the 1980s but met with resistance from employees who in effect now had two bosses—the function leader and the process leader.

There are many personal and organizational barriers to process restructuring. At the personal level, teamwork requires good interpersonal skills and demands more emphasis on cross-functional skill development. Since many companies tie some portion of an individual's compensation to team results, individuals may also feel a loss of control in this important area of organizational life. If team results are not compensated in any way, then firms run the risk that team activities will not receive the necessary level of individual attention. Organizationally, team make-up and training are critical. Firms must decide on functional skill requirements for membership, number of representatives from each function, level of functional representatives (customer service manager, vice-president of customer relations, and so on), leadership of groups, and so on. These decisions can become very politicized. Functional conflicts over resource allocation and differing goals or objectives require the establishment of some process or procedure for conflict resolution. There are clearly costs associated with such a massive change in structure. There is also likely to be resistance from within the organization.

Quality Function Deployment (QFD) is one way to retain a functional structure while "systematically deploying operations and functions that make up the quality into step-by-step detail" (Akao, 1999). QFD requires companies to identify consumer desires, translate them into specific components, establish standards and procedures for delivery, and follow-up on delivery. For example, consumers want reliability in a number of company-provided areas. One such area is food service. They expect food to be consistent in quality, to taste and look good, to provide a good portion, and to be hot or cold (depending on the type of food). Companies must translate these desires into specific parameters (that is, temperature of food, size of portions, and so on), then establish and enforce standards on the "function" charged with delivering the item. Finally, there must be feedback and improvement

(Barlow, 1999). While there is elaborate software to support the implementation of QFD, it is still a complex process that has yet to be fully embraced outside Japan (See Akao (1990) for a fuller discussion of QFD).

A Case Study in Quality—Baggage Handling

To illustrate some of the issues and problems encountered in airline service quality, an exploration into baggage handling is in order. According to SITA's (2013) ninth annual Baggage Report, baggage mishandling rates have dropped worldwide to 8.83 per 1,000 passengers. This is a 44.5 percent improvement from the prior year. Delayed baggage, the primary cause of mishandling, also dropped 2.4 percent from the prior year. The SITA report outlined the primary causes of baggage delay as follows: transfer mishandling, failure to load (17 percent), ticketing error/bag switch/security/other (13 percent), loading error (7 percent), airport/customs/ weather/space–weight restriction (7 percent), and tagging error (4 percent). Of course, these are global figures and will not necessarily reflect the exact numbers for any given airline or airport. The distinction is important for several reasons. First, airlines may have very different policies, procedures, and training related to this area. Second, the baggage handling system at one airport can be very different from another airport in speed, configuration, and so on. Third, airlines may vary by location, that is airport, the nature of the baggage handling staff—airline employee, alliance partner employee, or third-party outsource handlers. The SITA report outlines several different approaches that airports and airlines have taken to address baggage handling. On the airport side, the report notes that Iberia Airlines in Spain are trying to identify passenger baggage that requires priority handling (short connections and so on) so that it can be diverted to higher speed belts. At Helsinki Airport, a transfer monitoring tool notifies staff of delayed flights so that special procedures can be implemented to insure that connecting bags make their next flight. On the airline side, airlines are investing in technology for self-printed bag tags, assisted self-baggage drop, software for bad tracking including Radio Frequency Identification Device (RFID) tagging, smart phone apps for tracking, and portable scanning devices. Many of these efforts will allow airports and airlines to gain an even better understanding of the processes resulting in loss and delay. Understanding the process and measuring and tracking the historical outcomes are the keys to quality improvement in any area.

Alliance Quality—Scale and Scope

To date, there have been few attempts to evaluate the quality of alliances, but many of the same issues cited for individual carrier quality would apply such as whether the data comes from surveys or secondary sources. Unfortunately, there is no single entity that collects the type of secondary data available in the US and EU for individual carriers. Thus, it is not possible to take data from all of the global members of an alliance, combine them, and compare across alliances. Tiernan, Rhoades, and Waguespack (2008) reported three areas of comparison available across the airline alliance groupings for US and EU carriers only based on reported data from both the US DOT and the EU Association European Airlines (AEA). Their findings indicate very few statistically significant differences across the main alliance groupings and the three indicators of service quality examined; on-time arrivals, baggage reports, and flight cancellations. While there are some yearly differences between each of the alliance groupings it is the overall similarity which is of note.

There have been at least two other attempts to use secondary data to access alliance quality, mostly in terms of scale and scope (Chapter 11). Chapter 11 also outlined four basic reasons that carriers form alliances: (1) to gain market access; (2) to build global seamless networks; (3) to reduce costs; and (4) to maintain market presence. From a consumer perspective, airline cost reduction is only important if it allows the carrier or alliance to reduce consumer costs and/or improve other aspects of airline service valued by consumers. Reasons 1 and 4 relate to the scope and/or depth of the alliances' coverage and the area of schedule/flight accommodation identified above for customer satisfaction with an individual carrier. From an alliance perspective, the more destinations they serve and the more frequently they serve them should be a quality issue for consumers.

This issue of alliance coverage proved to be a key factor in the Merrill Lynch (1999) report on alliances. Merrill Lynch rated the mega-alliances in terms of geographical network, market size, network density, financial strength, and regulatory freedom. This study drew a distinction between geographic scope (number of destinations/departures) and network density (utilization of network or extent of duplication). In this regard, an alliance such as Wings (KLM–NW) outscored the other mega-alliances on network density but ranked lowest on geographic scope. From an alliance point-of-view, less duplication in the network lowers fears of anti-competitive outcomes and means more overall extension of geographic scope. From a consumer point-of-view, greater density means more frequency to desired destinations. Thus, the ideal alliance configuration would involve partners having extensive depth within their geographic scope but little network duplication of alliance partner networks. This has not been an easy combination to create. One of the major stumbling blocks to the proposed British Airways–American Airlines alliance (part of Oneworld) was the extent of network overlap and the fear that such overlap would encourage the alliance partners to "rationalize" their networks (that is, divide markets between partners in such a way that only one partner would effectively serve a particular route). Of course, the failure of the British to sign an Open Skies agreement with the US was another key factor in the US refusal to grant anti-trust immunity. With the 2008 multilateral Open Skies with the EU, this objection disappeared on the US side even if the overlap did not.

Anderson Consulting identified three integration platforms in strategic alliances based on the level of control (degree of carrier control over resources) and degree of global coverage (Ott, 1999). According to Anderson, bilateral strings are essentially based on a series of international codeshares between partners. These alliances string together a moderate number of international destinations. Andersen Consulting classified US Airways, Japan Airlines, and America West as string airlines. The Regional Cluster is the second type of integration platform. As the name implies, the backbone of this platform is several regional airlines. The geographic coverage is approximately equivalent to the bilateral string, but the level of control is greater. Swissair and the Qualifier alliance were examples of this type of platform. The final integration platform is the global skeleton which has greater coverage than the other two and slightly lower levels of control than the Regional Cluster. Based on their analysis, the four mega-alliances that existed at the time of their study were roughly equivalent in terms of global coverage while the ranking on control was as follows: Wings, Star, SkyTeam, and Oneworld. The informally named Wings alliance of KLM–Northwest was officially abandoned with the KLM–Air France merger and both are now part of SkyTeam now. Thus, there are officially now only three global alliances—Oneworld, SkyTeam, and Star. In any event, Andersen Consulting had envisioned all three platforms moving toward the Global Network with its maximum global coverage and balance between alliance control and member independence. According to Andersen, there were a number of areas of alliance development. The first area was route overlap or increasing "unduplicated route miles/kilometers." Several studies have shown that complementary (non-overlapping) alliance networks increase overall demand and passenger volumes (Park and Cho, 1997; US GAO, 1995) while parallel alliances decrease demand (Park and Cho, 1997). The problem for airlines and regulators lies with addressing pre-existing alliance overlap. Airlines clearly have some incentives to reduce overlap, especially if the overlap results in decreased demand and/or lower fares. The degree of intra-alliance competition could also damage efforts to build a cooperative alliance arrangement. Regulators are concerned with the degree of competition/cooperation and any action that decreases capacity and increase fares. The second area of development involved "filling the gaps" in overall global coverage and in specific destination departure levels. Given the stated consumer preference for airlines with wide coverage and increased connections, the goal of a superior global alliance is to serve more destinations more frequently than their competitors. All of the four old mega-alliance groups looked to fill major gaps in Asia, the Middle East, and Africa during the 1990s (Flint, 1999; Merrill Lynch, 1999; Taverna, 1999). Gap filling continued with the three mega-alliances. Oneworld stills trails the other two alliances in total number of members as well as membership by region (Flottau and Buyck, 2013). In many ways, the alliance is still essentially a string-configured alliance that has yet to fill its gaps and place more meat into its structure. In line with the notion of a superior global alliance is the third key area of alliance branding. In addition to the sort of advertising employed by the Star alliance, alliances sought other areas of alliance integration and standardization such as joint facilities, alliance terminal grouping, harmonized (merged) distribution networks including CRS systems, and joint internet booking sites, and common service standards such as seat pitch and reclining angle. The goal is to demonstrate that an alliance can do more than just extend networks; it needs to ease travel and deliver consistent services across the globe (Buyck, 2013). Cost reduction through such actions as facility sharing and maintenance and other ground personnel utilization is a fourth area for further development while a fifth area of development has been the creation of the secondary and tertiary tiers of national/regional carriers whose job it will be to increase feed to alliance hubs. From an alliance perspective, the more developed and exclusive these arrangements the better they will be able to extract benefits (Berardino and Frankel, 1998). However, such exclusivity raises anti-competitive fears in many countries as we have already discussed in the chapter on anti-trust law.

Coordinating Quality

While the Merrill Lynch Index does not provide a comprehensive overview of alliance quality, it is an important first step in the process of understanding alliance quality. From a consumer quality perspective, a more difficult area to address is the issue of "global, seamless service." "Global" is a function of geographic reach, but "seamless" suggests a great deal more. What does it mean to provide seamless service? How do independent airlines provide such service? This area continues to bedevil alliances. In fact, it has been suggested that seamless travel is often little more than a marketing gimmick. It is true that alliances can offer coordinated schedules, shared lounges, frequent flyer redemption, and coordinated baggage tracing, but there are still inconsistencies in product quality, communication, and service. Offering seamless quality service may be the key to revitalizing the alliance movement in the wake of recent shake-ups such as the Qantas departure from Oneworld (Buyck, 2013). To explore what it takes to get to seamless travel, let us start at the airline level.

As difficult as process quality can be for individual airlines, it is potentially nothing compared to the prospect of integrating the process across multiple carriers. As Deming and others have pointed out, no two processes are identical. Each process will invariably produce a certain amount of random variation (flaws or problems related to the nature of the system(s) in place). Special variations (flaws or problems related to a change in the system such as change in training procedures, receipt of a batch of faulty parts, and so on) also occur from time to time. Management must understand their process well enough to distinguish between random and special variation. Management must act to identify the source of special variation and remove its cause. Random variation, on the other hand, can only be reduced by changing the process itself.

When attempting to integrate the processes of two or more carriers, there are two primary areas of concern. First, are the processes compatible? A simple case from early integrations efforts is the airline boarding pass. All carriers issue them and most require that they be run through an electronic device before boarding. However, if the size of these boarding passes differs between carriers such that the boarding pass issued by one carrier will not pass through the system of the other (and customers are required to check-in again at the second airline for a new pass), then some of the seamlessness of the process is lost. The same question applies for many other standards and procedures such as upgrade requirements, carry-on specifics, seating assignments, boarding procedures, and so on. To the extent that these differences create snags in the seamless fabric of air travel for consumers, they will detract from perceived quality and can result in loss of business to higher quality alliances. We will discuss strategies for avoiding these snags later.

The second area of concern is potentially more serious and more difficult to resolve. It relates to differences in the quality level (or random variation) of alliance partners. Consumers who book a flight on one airline but find at least one leg of their journey flown by a carrier of lesser quality can develop a negative perception of the alliance as a whole. Obviously, the greater the difference in quality levels the more severe the problem becomes. In a truly seamless alliance, consumers should perceive no difference in quality levels. The most worrisome difficulty lies in equalizing the quality level of alliance partners. Again, there are no studies examining the overall quality levels of alliance partners or the effects of quality equalization, but a recent study suggests one possible scenario. Research on quality levels at major US carriers indicates that over the last ten years quality levels have begun to converge and now show little variation across the major US carriers (Rhoades and Waguespack, 2000b). In statistical research, the term "regressing to the mean" refers to the tendency for extremes at both ends of a particular phenomena to move over time toward the mean for that population. In the case of quality levels between alliance partners, there might be a similar tendency for quality levels to converge toward a mean. At the lower end, alliance partners' quality will tend to rise. On the other hand, the alliance quality leaders could see declines in their quality toward the alliance mean. Singapore Airlines would likely find this prospect disturbing.

Of course, this is not the only possible scenario. However, an alliance seeking to brand itself as one of high quality must be aware of the fact that upward equalization of quality standards will not just happen. Higher quality standards will not just "rub-off" on alliance partners. This is where "cross-alliance" teams become important in insuring the quality of lateral/cross-airline processes. In the early years of their alliance, United and Luftansa found it difficult to agree on something as seemingly simple as the joint purchase of airsick bags (Feldman, 1998). Imagine the potential for disagreement on an issue such as the operation of a key hub or yield management integration. At the very least, alliances are finding that coordination takes time and effort. Jurgen Weber, former Luftansa CEO, had estimated that alliances consumed approximately one-third of his time (Feldman, 1998).

Improving Alliance Quality

There are two important steps in achieving and insuring overall alliance quality. The first factor is conducting pre- and post-alliance audits of safety and service issues. These audits would establish a baseline quality level for each partner. Assuming that each alliance partner understands the needs and expectations of its customers, the next step is to reach some consensus among alliance partners on the level of desired quality and the priority of service quality goals. Finally, a plan must be created that outlines the goals, objectives, and tactics to be used by each carrier to achieve the necessary changes. The second step is to create a process that "shows one face to the customer." Alliances, like individual firms, are finding that it is essential "to make it easy for the customer to access resources, products, and services across the horizontal spectrum" (Ashkenas, Ulrich, Jick, and Kerr, 1995: 128). When customers can enter into the company or alliance through multiple doors (or portals as they are sometimes called), there are several problems that can arise that have the potential to adversely affect process quality. Without careful coordination, customers may find that the point-of-entry changes the final destination. For example, if alliance members are not familiar with the products and services offered by their partners, then a customer accessing the alliance through one partner may receive different scheduling, information, and service than another customer accessing the "system" from a different partner. A related problem occurs when the parts of the system are not aware of the actions of each other and fail (or are unable) to take these differences into consideration when assisting customers.

In their book, *The Boundaryless Organization: Breaking the Chains of Organizational Structure*, Ashkenas, Ulrich, Jick, and Kerr (1995) outline five warning signs of dysfunctional horizontal boundaries: "(1) slow, sequential cycle times, (2) protected turf, (3) suboptimization of organizational goals, (4) the enemy-within syndrome, and (5) customers doing their own integration" (115). Slow, sequential cycle times occur whenever multiple divisions, departments, units, and so on must be consulted one by one to create new products or respond to customers demands. Whenever protecting one's own resources or power interfere with customer service, quality suffers. The same thing is true when members of a process come into decision-making situations with different, often, conflicting goals such as cost reduction versus higher service level or higher yield versus higher load factor. One of the most damaging problems related to horizontal boundaries occurs when members of a process come to see each other as enemies. Ashkenas, Ulrich, Jick, and Kerr (1994) give an example of an airline where baggage handling at a particular airport was the responsibility of two separate teams. One team handled check-in and ticketing while the other was responsible for loading, transferring, and off-loading. Teams were reluctant to help each other, to accept advice from "them," and frequently argued over which team was responsible for baggage handling errors. Finally, horizontal boundaries can also create problems if it forces customers to do their own integration of products and services. In the airline industry, there are customers who would prefer to customize their own bundle of products and services in order to accommodate special needs in terms of price, scheduling, and destination. On the other hand, there are customer groups that want a one-stop shopping experience. They do not want to be handed from one airline to another because an airline cannot book to a codeshare partner directly or to be told that seats cannot be assigned through to final destination, and so on.

Several problems can arise on the way to upward equalization of quality. First, the traditional customers of alliance partners may not have similar expectations. After over 20 years of deregulation, the expectations of many US travelers in seating comfort, food, and so on have declined below the expectations of many European and Asian travelers. This difference in expectations may make agreeing on a level of service more difficult. This is further complicated by airline cost, pricing structure, and available resources for quality improvements. Alliance partners may find it necessary to establish inter-alliance programs for training, cost sharing, and other quality improvements. Another stumbling block to success is the need to share more information between partners on service offerings, prices, and amenities. In short, partners may be called upon to share the revenue management information that has traditionally been treated as proprietary or share facilities that certain partners have spent years developing. Such attempts can create three problems for alliance members. The first problem is a legal one; without anti-trust immunity, this level of sharing would be deemed illegal in most regions of the world. The second problem relates to the technological difficulties of systems integration. The sheer size and cost of integrating information systems can be very daunting to alliance members. Finally, alliance members must perceive a benefit to such information sharing that is greater than the risk of "giving up" the potentially valuable information on customers and operations. Alliances will need to find ways to track the costs and benefits of joint alliance activities and to maximize joint benefits (Beradino and Frankel, 1998).

Conclusion

Although it may seem to customers that airlines sometimes forget that they are a service industry, international competition and the pursuit of profit in a tough industry are forcing airlines to pay more attention to issues of quality, customer satisfaction, and customer loyalty. At the carrier and the alliance level, airlines are trying to distinguish themselves from their competitors. At the carrier level, attention to basics is essential but branding requires memorable amenities. At the alliance level, seamless service requires intensive coordination to achieve high quality, consistent service. To satisfy the desire for global coverage, alliances are taking two basic approaches—weave and throw a wider web or throw a finer web over a smaller area. While avoiding the legal stumbling block of anti-trust has been difficult for many alliance partners, it has not been as visible a failure to consumers as the hurtle of achieving seamless service. In large part, the alliance movement is about breaking down the barriers that separate companies from their suppliers, their customers, and, in many cases, their competitors. It is about creating linkages and networks. Alliances are "about spinning a web to catch more customers" (Sparks, 1999: 106).

Questions:

1. Give four definitions of quality and four metrics to measure it.
2. Discuss some of the studies examining airline quality. What are their strengths and weaknesses?
3. How can alliances provide "global, seamless service?"
4. Is there a link between service and safety quality?
5. What are the impediments to alliance service quality?

References

Air Travel Consumer Reports (1987–2012), "US Department of Transportation," retrieved online March 17, 2013 from http://www.dot.gov/airconsumer/air-travel-consumer-reports.

Airline Quality Rating (AQR) (2013), retrieved online April 6, 2014 from http://www.airlinequalityrating.com/; http://docs.lib.purdue.edu/aqrr/23/.

Akao, Y. (1990), *Introduction to Quality Function Deployment*, JUSE Press Tokyo, Japan.

Akao, Y. (1999), "ISO 900 and 14000 Systems Supported by QFD," in S.K.M. Ho (ed.), *Proceedings of the Fourth International Conference on ISO 900 and TQM*, pp. 325–331.American Customer Satisfaction Index (ASCI) (2006), "Quality suffers in energy utilities, airline industries" in *Quality Progress*, vol. 39 (7), p. 21.

Ashkensas, R., Ulrich, D., Jick, T. and Kerr, S. (1995), *The Boundaryless Organization: Breaking the Chains of Organizational Structure*, Josey-Bass, San Francisco, CA.

Barlow, G.L. (1999), "QFD within the Service Sector—A Case Study on how the House of Quality was used within Service Operations," in S.K.M. Ho (ed.), *Proceedings of the Fourth International Conference on ISO 900 and TQM*, pp. 332–340.

Berardino, F. and Frankel, C. (1998), "Keeping score," *Airline Business*, September, pp. 82–87.

Bloemer, J. and Kasper, H. (1995). "The complex relationship between consumer satisfaction and brand loyalty," *Journal of Economic Psychology*, vol. 16 (2), pp. 311–329.

Buyck, C. (2013), "From scale to service: alliances improve customer services in a move to keep the model relevant," *Aviation Week and Space Technology*, April, 29, pp. 42–44.

Cronin, J.J. and Taylor, S.A. (1992), "Measuring service quality: a reexamination and extension," *Journal of Marketing*, vol. 56 (3), pp. 55–68.

Ekdahl, F., Gustafsson, A. and Edvardsson, B. (1999), "Customer-oriented service development at SAS," *Managing Service Quality*, vol. 9 (6), pp. 403–410.

Feldman, J.M. (1998), "Making alliances work," *Air Transport World*, June, pp. 27–35.

Flint, P. (1999), "Alliance paradox," *Air Transport World*, April, pp. 33–36.

Flottau, J. and Buyck, C. (2013), "Group dynamics: once de regueur for legacy airlines, alliance membership is an evolving model," *Aviation Week & Space Technology*, April 29, pp. 39–41.

Fraser, D. (1996), "A personal approach," *Airline Business*, March, pp. 58–61.

Glab, J. (1997), "The people's choice," *Frequent Flyer*, June, pp. 24–28.

Jacoby, J. and Chestnut, R.W. (1978), *Brand Loyalty: Measurement and Management*, Willey & Sons, New York.

Memmott, M. (2013), "Complaints soar, but airlines' quality rating stays high," National Public Radio, retrieved online August 8, 2013 from http://www.npr.org/blogs/thetwo-way/2013/04/08/176566213/complaints-soar-but-airlines-quality-ratings-stays-high.

Merrill Lynch, Pierce, Fenner & Smith (1999), *Global Airline Alliances: Global Alliance Brands,* Merrill Lynch, Pierce, Fenner & Smith Inc., New York.

Oliver, R.I. (1999), "Cognitive, affective, and attribute bases of the satisfaction," *Journal of Consumer Research*, vol. 20 (3), pp. 451–466.

Ott, J. (1999), "Alliances spawn a web of global networks," *Airline Business*, August 23, pp. 52–53.

Parasuraman, A., Zeithaml, V.A. and Berry, LL. (1985), "A conceptual model of service quality and its implications for future research," *Journal of Marketing*, vol. 49 (4), pp. 41–50.

Parasuraman, A., Zeithaml, V.A. and Berry, LL. (1988), "SERVQUAL: a multiple-item scale for measuring customer perceptions of service quality," *Journal of Retailing*, vol. 64 (1), pp. 12–40.

Park, N.K. and Cho, D. (1997), "The effect of strategic alliance on performance," *Journal of Air Transport Management*, vol. 3 (3), pp. 155–164.

Reichheld, F.F. (1996). *The Loyalty Effect: The Hidden Force behind Growth, Profits, and Lasting Value.* Harvard Business School Press, Boston, MA.

Rhoades, D.L. and Waguespack, B. (1999), "Better safe than service? The relationship between service and safety quality in the US airline industry," *Managing Service Quality*, vol. 9 (6), pp. 396–400.

Rhoades, D.L. and Waguespack, B. (2000a), "Judging a book by its cover: the relationship between service and safety quality in US national and regional airlines," *Journal of Air Transport Management*, vol. 6 (2), pp. 87–94

Rhoades, D.L. and Waguespack, B. (2000b), "Service quality in the US airline industry: variations in performance within and between firms," *Journal of Air Transportation World Wide*, vol. 5 (1), pp. 60–77.

Rhoades, D.L. and Waguespack, B. (2001), "Airline Quality: Present Challenges, Future Strategies" in G.F. Butler and M.R. Keller, M.R. (eds), *Handbook of Airline Strategy: Public Policy, Regulatory Issues, Challenges and Solutions*, McGraw-Hill, New York, pp. 469–480.

Rhoades, D.L. and Waguespack, B. (2005), "Strategic imperatives and the pursuit of quality in the US airline industry," *Managing Service Quality*, vol. 15 (4), pp. 344–356.

Rhoades, D.L. and Waguespack, B. (2008), "Twenty years of service quality performance in the US airline industry," *Managing Service Quality*, vol. 18 (1), pp. 20–34.

Rhoades, D.L. and Waguespack, B. (2014),"Twenty five years of measuring airline service quality or why is airline service quality only good when times are bad," *Research in Transportation Business and Management*, vol. 4 (1), pp. 68–81.

SITA (2013), *2013 Air Transport Industry Insights: The Baggage Report*, STAT and Air Transport World.

Sloan, A. and Ehrenfeld, T. (2007), "Lessons from Jetblue's meltdown," *Newsweek MSNBC*, retrieved online July 8, 2012 from www.msnbc.cim/id/17313450/site/newsweek.

Sparks, D. (1999), "Partners," *Business Week*, October 25, pp. 106–112.

Sultan, F. and Simpson, Jr., M.C. (2000), "International service variants: airline passenger expectations and perceptions of service quality," *Journal of Services Marketing*, vol. 14 (3), pp. 188–216.

Szymanski, D.M., and Henard, D.H. (2001), "Customer satisfaction: a meta-analysis of the empirical evidence," *Journal of the Academy of Marketing Science*, vol. 29 (1), pp. 16–35.

Taverna, M.A. (1999), "Star alliance approaches next phase of collaboration," *Airline Business*, August 23, pp. 58–60.

The American Heritage College Dictionary (2000), (3rd ed.) Houghton Mifflin Company, Boston, MA.

Tiernan, S., Rhoades, D.L. and Waguespack, B. (2008), "Airline service quality: an exploratory analysis of consumer perceptions and reported operational performance in the US and EU," *Managing Service Quality*. Vol. 18 (3), pp. 212–224.

US General Accounting Office (US GAO) (1995), "Airline alliances product benefits, but effect on competition is uncertain," *GAO/RCED-95*, April.

Waguespack, B. and Curtis, T. (2013), "Ancilliary revenue and price fairness: An exploratory study pre- and post-flight," presented at the 2013 Air Transport Research Scoiety, 27–29 June, Bergamo, Italy.

Wells, A.T. (1994), *Air Transportation: A Management Perspective*, Wadsworth Publishing Company, Belmont, CA.

Yu, R. (2007), "Flight delays worst in 13 years," *USA Today* online edition, retrieved online January 6, 2008 from www.usatoday.com/travel/flights/2007-06-04-airline-delays_N.htm.

Chapter 14
The Need for Speed

Learning Objectives

After reading this chapter, you should have a good understanding of:
- LO1: the aircraft needs of cargo operators.
- LO2: the elements of the logistics revolution.
- LO3: the development of the integrated cargo carriers.
- LO4: the role of belly cargo and freight forwarders.

Key Terms, Concepts, and People

Berlin Airlift	Perfect cargo plane	Logistics revolution
Containerization	Air–Cargo Deregulation Act	Malcolm McLean
Federal Express	Belly cargo	
Hazmat		

Freight Comes of Age

If airmail was the driving force in aviation development in its first decade of life, then the decade of the 1940s and World War II were the time when other types of freight began to become a more prominent element in the air cargo story and to capture the interest of the aviation community. In 1938, freight accounted for only about 17 revenue ton kilometers (RTKs) of the total 53 RTKs of air activity. By 1951, freight RTKs had risen to 870, far outstripping the 230 RTKs for airmail in that year (Allaz, 2004). Military forces around the world would come to recognize the value of air freight in support of distant troops and far-flung activities. They would also begin to demand and order aircraft that could deliver these troops and supplies. The Berlin Airlift would prove its strategic geopolitical value as the British and Americans would be airlifting over 4,740 tons of cargo a day to Berlin within five months of the start of the blockade (Allaz, 2004).

Beginning in the 1970s, deregulation of domestic industries and liberalization of the rules of international trade began to spread throughout the world. Market forces would now trump the tight rules and standards that once protected firms and employees in their national markets. Firms would begin to look outside for lower-cost labor and the lower-cost manufacturing that came with them. The concepts of outsourcing and just-in-time inventory would capture the imagination of the business community. These new concepts, however, created new dispersed supply chains that demanded a new system of logistics to support them. As computing power rose and IT costs fell, the technology was ready for tracking and optimizing. The decline in transportation costs that came with deregulation, and later, with falling oil prices made it faster and cheaper to ship from distant locations. Further, consumers came to crave customized products delivered door-to-door. Faster, cheaper, and better was the new consumer mantra. This meant that businesses had to find ways to meet these new demands or risk falling victim to a host of new competitors.

These trends continued to pick up speed as the twentieth century approached its end. They also fostered tremendous growth in air cargo operations and operators. Airlines would offer cargo-only flights and order so-called combi-aircraft, half passenger and half cargo, to provide greater cargo capacity and additional revenue. New scheduled and charter cargo operators would come into the market offering to ship everything from letter-sized packages to massive oil drilling equipment (Nelms, 2007). If the jet would make air cargo the transportation choice for speed, then FedEx would make overnight shipping a new business mindset. FedEx and UPS would lead the way for integrated shipping, that is, door-to-door delivery using multiple modes of transportation. However, before the commercial explosion of air cargo could take place, the industry needed a plane suitable for its purposes. Once it had such an aircraft, it could begin to take advantage of the new rules and the changing nature of business.

The Perfect Plane

From a cargo perspective, the perfect cargo plane would have a fuselage that was rectangular rather than cylindrical. The floor would be sturdy and low-lying to accommodate heavy freight with a maximum of vertical capacity. Large doors would be located at the sides and front (preferably) to make loading easy and quick. Using both would reduce loading time. The aircraft would be designed so that different types of cargo could be partitioned and anchored (Allaz, 2004). While cargo had and would continue to be flown in aircraft not specifically designed for cargo, there would often be a cost not only in terms of converting passenger aircraft to cargo use (reinforcing floors, adding, anchors, and so on) but in terms of productivity. As in passenger service, cargo operators have to be concerned with load factors. Because operators have little control over the prices they charge, costs are critical and an aircraft that has a low capacity either due to shape or weight constraints represents a problem. Aircraft that require high levels of labor or expensive equipment to load create added costs.

Between 1960 and 1962, freight capacity doubled, both in terms of belly cargo, that is, cargo carried in the belly of passenger aircraft, and cargo aircraft. Several factors account for this increase in capacity. First, the new jet aircraft coming on the market had a larger cargo capacity than previous aircraft. Second, as airlines switched to jet aircraft, there was a growing number of used, propeller aircraft on the market and available for use by cargo operators. The first jet aircraft went into service in 1958 under the Pan Am colors, but others would quickly follow (Allaz, 2004). According to Allaz (2004), the Canadair CL-44D was the first modern jet cargo aircraft. It featured a swing tail, unit load devices, and a maximum payload of 28,000 kg. Packages were loaded onto pallets fitted with retention nets or into containers. The famous Flying Tigers would be the first to take the CL-44D into service in 1961. With the arrival of the B-707-320C and the DC-8F, costs would significantly decline while speed and capacity would dramatically improve.

Of course, the aircraft that would become most closely associated with air cargo would be the B-747. The letter of intent signed with launch customer Pan Am specified a 400-passenger airline with a range of 5,000 miles, cruise altitude of 35,000 feet, and cargo nose loading. The latter requirement is telling; Juan Trippe, CEO of Pan Am, saw the B-747 primarily as a freighter that could also carry passengers. Of course, the B-747 would become one of the most popular passenger aircraft in the world and a symbol of international aviation, but this was certainly not clear when the project began (Serling, 1992). In fact, the story of the 747 is a fascinating one. Production problems, redesigns, a launch in 1970 just as the economy began to slow, and the coming oil crisis would put the Boeing Company almost into bankruptcy. The plane would not approach breakeven sales until 1978 (Lynn, 1998; Newhouse, 2007). Still, there is no doubt that it set new standards that few others could begin to meet. In the cargo area, the wide-bodied 747 could hold two standard pallets side-by-side on the main deck with nine additional positions in the lower hold for either pallets or containers. Overall, the 747 was capable of carrying 90 tonnes of cargo as compared to 30 tonnes for the 707 and 70–74 for the DC-10 (Allaz, 2004).

Play it Forward

Air freight had come a long way in the years just after the end of World War II, but in some ways it had changed very little from that early 1910 flight (Chapter 3) that carried the 200 pounds of silk and ribbon to Max Morehouse for his Home Dry Goods Store. In fact, a number of things were still true. First, small mom-and-pops still made up a large portion of the air cargo operators. Like the early airlines themselves, cargo operators started flying small piston-powered aircraft from one point to the next on an unscheduled, as-needed basis. They were private firms and many continue to be privately rather than publicly held companies making it difficult to assess their overall profitability. Second, the firms were essentially a specialized form of forwarder, that is, a carrier that transported freight by air under published freight tariffs. Shippers were responsible for seeing that the freight reached the operator and for arranging pick-up when it arrived at its destination. In some cases, shippers could add a step in the process and use a separate consolidator, someone who took their shipment and consolidated it with those of other shippers to form a "larger" shipment eligible for lower rates. Third, airlines would continue to see freight revenue as supplemental income. In the US, freight would continue to be a very small portion of the overall revenue. In Asia, freight tonnage would grow apace with the emerging economies of the region as the size and the scope of the shipments increased. As the volume increased and shippers began to ship to more markets around the world, pressure increased for industry consolidation. Both of these changes were driven in part by the logistics revolution that was sweeping the world.

Logistics Revolution

Logistics is defined as "the process of planning, implementing, and controlling the efficient, effective flow and storage of raw materials, in-process inventories, finished goods, services, and relevant information from point of origin to the point of consumption" (Boske, 1998). In the capitalist system, the goal is to match supply to demand, but the system has often proven itself prone to overproduction. Producers are then forced to carry excess inventory or find some ways to increase sales—discounts, advertising, credit extension, and so on. If the ideal is to carry only the inventory you need and produce only what consumers want, then the producers need accurate, readily available data to make their decisions. Point-of-sales (POS) data provides this type of information. Firms like Wal-Mart began to use computers and scanning equipment to collect this information. This helped Wal-Mart to insure that shelves were stocked with the goods consumers were demanding. As they linked the system to their vendors, vendors were able to see in near real time what was and was not selling which allowed them to adjust production accordingly, including controlling their own inventories. The ubiquitous bar codes are giving way in many areas to RFID. These devices collect and store (in many cases) lots of information that can be read and analyzed to improve the system. Unfortunately for the producers, there is a snake in the grass; this new system has shifted power to the retailers like Wal-Mart. As the Wal-Marts of the world got bigger so did their requirements and demands—lower prices, more frequent deliveries, chargebacks (fines for failing to meet specifications like misplacing a bar code). For the consumers, the new fast, flexible production system and the close tracking of stock meant shelves with "what I want when I want it" (Bonacich and Wilson, 2007, Castells, 1996; Fishman, 2006; Kumar, 1996).

All of these advances would still not have been enough to create the logistics revolution; it needed two more ingredients—changing regulatory environments and falling transportation costs. Thomas L. Friedman, the popular press advocate of globalization and author of the bestselling books *The Lexus and the Olive Tree* (1999) and *The World is Flat* (2005) has argued that success in the global economy demands that nations put on a golden straitjacket. This straitjacket is made from government and extra-governmental policies that promote: (1) an expanding private sector; (2) low inflation and price stability; (3) shrinking government bureaucracy; (4) balanced governmental budgets; (5) low tariffs and the elimination of import quotas; (6) no restriction on foreign investment, and currency conversion and mobility; (7) privatization of state-owned enterprises; (8) deregulation of markets and industries; (9) no domestic sector protection; (10) increasing exports; and (11) labor mobility. Taken together these policies laid the foundation for a global system in which production could take place wherever conditions favored it (cost of labor, environmental regulation, available resources, and so on), be shipped to wherever consumers demanded it, and be serviced (repair, 24/7 help lines) wherever it was most profitable for the company. Beyond the borders of individual nations, the global trading system advanced from the old Bretton Wood institutions of the World Bank and the International Monetary Fund to the General Agreement on Tariffs and Trade (GATT) to the World Trade Organization (WTO). Global trading blocks would also emerge such as the EU, North American Free Trade Agreement (NAFTA), and MERCOSUR, the Latin American trade area. The goal of these blocks was to reduce or remove the impediments to trade and the flow of goods, services, and people between the member nations.

Transportation was one of the areas that witnessed a wave of deregulation beginning in the US in the late 1970s and early 1980s with the Air–Cargo Deregulation Act of 1977, the Airline Deregulation Act of 1978, the Motor Carrier Act (that is, trucking) in 1980, the Staggers Rail Act in 1980, the Shipping Act in 1984, and the Freight Forwarder Deregulation Act in 1986. As noted in earlier chapters, transportation is considered in most countries to be an area of vital national interest and safety so there are still a great many areas of regulation remaining, however, the focus of transportation deregulation was to allow market forces to determine to a much greater extent issues of pricing, capacity, networks, and service quality. In many nations, deregulation also opened up greater opportunities for intermodal transportation. Intermodal transportation refers to the "process of transporting passengers and freight by means of a system of interconnected networks, involving more than one transportation mode, in which all the component parts in the systems process are seamlessly linked and efficiently coordinated" (Boske, 1998). The technical innovations that helped make the supply chain of Wal-Mart successful—computers, scanning, RFID, and so on— were utilized in intermodal transport systems to ensure that goods flowed with minimal delay through the system. Logistics leaders could use this technology to optimize their system based on specific needs—lowest cost, time-to-delivery.

There was one final piece of the puzzle that made the transportation and logistics revolution, the container. On April 26, 1956, the *Ideal X*, a converted tanker, became the first ship to have an aluminum truck body lifted onto the deck. The concept was the brainchild of Malcolm McLean, a trucker whose US firm had risen to become one of the ten largest in the nation. He had observed that lots of trucks traveled between the seaports of the Gulf and the East Coast and figured that if he could find a way to reduce the time spent loading and unloading cargo that he could gain an advantage on his competitors. Soon the aluminum container, now standardized to 8x8x20, would be decoupled from the wheels and stacked onto specially designed vessels. Huge port cranes would load and unload containers from larger and larger vessels. These containers would be lifted from the deck of the ship directly onto trailer trucks or railcars. Containerization made shipping cheap; the most expensive part of the process was shifting cargo from sea to land and the occasional need for drayage (transporting freight by truck, usually to link one mode of transport to another because it cannot be done directly on the dock). Containerization thrives on volume and the reduction in cost and time of shifting cargo has meant that a doubling of the distance cargo is shipped results in only about an 18 percent increase in shipping costs (Levinson, 2006).

Air cargo is often the choice for "high value goods, perishable and emergency shipments, but also electronic equipment, apparel, shoes, printed material, [and] chemicals" (Muller, 1995: 73). It has benefited somewhat less than other modes from containerization because of the size of the standard container. While a B-747 air freighter could be loaded through the nose with an 8x8x40 container, it would only have inches to spare on the door. There is also the question of container-to-fuselage fit; the typical rectangular box container leaves wasted space in the curve. There are specially designed air-surface 8x8x20 containers as well as containers for the lower decks on the B-747. A great deal of air cargo still travels on pallets (either 88inx125in or 96inx125in). There are also so-called pallet wings that attempt to utilize the full contour of the lower decks (Muller, 1995). One type of high-value good that gained increasing popularity in the cargo world was the document and small package shipment. As the pace of global business increased, so too did the need and desire of global firms to stay connected.

Expressing it

In 1971, Frederick W. Smith founded Federal Express, based on a concept first developed in his Yale dissertation. The dissertation was not a big success, but the company which began operations in 1973 became the industry leader in the express mail industry. By the end of the twentieth century, FedEx revenues exceeded US$22 billion and its fleet of 600 aircraft and 200,000 employees would be delivering packages around the world (Birla, 2005). Unlike competitor UPS, FedEx would start in the air and then move onto the ground. It would do this first through agreements with trucking and logistics companies such as RPS, Inc., Viking, Roberts, and Caliber Logistics. RPS, Inc. specialized in ground delivery of small packages. Viking used the less-than-truckload model to ship one and two-day packages. Roberts specialized in surface-expedited shipping. Caliber Logistics joined the FedEx family in the late 1990s with its specialized contract logistics services (FedEx website; *Aviation Week & Space Technology*, 2007).

The FedEx model would be based on five key principles: hub-and-spoke operations, weight and size limitations on shipments, integrated door-to-door service, guaranteed time-definite delivery, and end-to-end traceability. Table 14.1

traces the growth of FedEx from 2006 to 2012. As the table illustrates, FedEx experienced a steady increase in revenues, fleet, employees, and the volume of shipping. Over the coming decades in 1971, the weight limits would go higher while the time-definite options and the delivery area would increase. By 2006, the FedEx hub in Memphis would be the busiest in the world, shipping almost 3.6 million tonnes a year (*Air Cargo World*, 2005).

Table 14.1   FedEx growth 2006–2012

	2006	**2007**	**2008**	**2009**	**2010**	**2011**	**2012**
Revenues	32,294	35,214	37,953	35,497	34,734	39,304	42,680
Express Package #	3,287	3,399	3,536	3,376	3,479	3,607	3,975
Fleet	671	669	677	654	667	688	660
Employees	221,677	241,903	254,142	247,908	245,109	255,573	290,000

Source: FedEx website, www.fedex.com, Annual Reports
Revenue numbers in 000s

Brown is Back

The company whose first venture into air cargo ended with the 1929 stock market crash would not get back into the air for almost 60 years. When it did finally re-enter the air transport business in 1982 with new service from its hub in Louisville, Kentucky, it would do so under a very different set of circumstances than competitor FedEx. For one thing, UPS had acquired common carrier status with its early purchase of the Russell Peck Company in California. As a common carrier, it was regulated by the ICC as well as various state commissions. By US law, common carriers were required to serve any shipper, carry any package regardless of size, and deliver to any destination in its region. It also could not commingle wholesale and retail packages. The ICC was the first regulatory agency in US history and expanded from its early mandate to protect against railroad malpractice to all areas of surface shipping. In effect, the ICC defined the rights of shippers and customers, engaging in rate making, regulation, and labor dispute resolution. UPS would fight the ICC for the right to expand its ground services and network one city and one state at a time. While the ICC could become involved in labor disputes involving interstate transport, UPS was unionized relatively early in its history on a local and regional level; the UPS–Teamsters National Master Agreement was not signed until 1979. Its labor relationships were largely positive until the 1997 strike that lasted two weeks and cost the company US$750 million.

The FAA would grant UPS authorization to operate its own aircraft in 1988 and over the next year, UPS would become the fastest-growing airline in FAA history, adding 110 aircraft by the end of 1989. These new employees would challenge some of the long-held ideas of the "Brown" culture with its notion of working your way up the ladder from part time to full time, driver-to-top manager, but Big Brown would adjust (Neimann, 2007). By 1985, UPS Next Day Air was available in the lower 48 states. The Louisville hub, located on 550 acres at the Louisville International Airport, would become known as Worldport. The UPS facility would grow to 4 million square feet and explode with activity between 11 p.m. and 4 a.m. with over 5,000 employees engaged in sorting, routing, scanning, and loading/ unloading. Like competitor FedEx, package tracking and time-definite options would become an essential element to long-term success. As the first decade of the twenty-first century drew to a close, UPS would also see sustained growth (Table 14.2).

Table 14.2   UPS growth 2006–2012

	2006	2007	2008	2009	2010	2011	2012
Revenues	47,547	49,692	51,486	45,297	49,545	53,105	54,127
Express Package#	1,267	2,177	2,344	3,800	3,940	2,905	4,100
Fleet	607	579	571	510	527	523	530
Employees	428,000	425,300	426,000	408,000	400,600	398,300	397,600

Source: Company website, www.ups.com
Revenue numbers in 000s

Going Postal

A review of the UPS history reveals that its early beginnings were marked by an intense rivalry not with FedEx but the USPS. All countries have some form of a postal service that is involved, by definition, in the delivery of parcels and small packages. To illustrate the involvement of these postal units in air cargo, a brief look at two companies will have to suffice. The first Postmaster of the US was Benjamin Franklin, appointed in 1775. The Postal Reorganization Act of 1970 changed the status of the Postal Service to that of an independent unit of the Executive Branch of the US government with a Board of Governors appointed by the President of the US. Since it started as a unit of the US government, it had an obligation to serve all citizens wherever they were located. Further, it was not expected to make a profit on its operations. The German postal system officially began in 1490. In 1924 Deutsche Reichspost was founded as an independent agency. In 1995, the Posts and Telecommunications Act would reorganize the postal system into stock companies with the federal government holding all the initial shares but with private investment allowed. Deutsche Post would acquire Danzas Holding, a Swiss logistics company, in 1999 and go on to become the largest Initial Public Offering (IPO) in Germany in 2000 laying the groundwork for even greater changes in the coming century (www.dpwe.de). As we will see in Chapter 20, the fates of these two early systems begin to diverge in the twenty-first century with the USPS struggling to survive in an era of global cargo competitors and the internet. It will also have to fight the lawmaking body of the US, the US Congress, to be allowed the freedom to respond to markets and competition. Deutsche Post, on the other hand, would throw off the shackles of a 500-year history to embrace change and globalization (see company websites).

How the Airlines Do It

In airlines, cargo began its life in the belly of the aircraft, the so-called belly cargo. The airline was simply one more air freight forwarder looking to fill space. For some carriers, cargo became a great deal more than additional revenue. A study on the productivity and cost competitiveness of world airlines found that while passenger revenue accounted for almost 90 percent of the revenue of most US major carriers, a number of international carriers derived between 20 and 40 percent of their revenue from cargo operations (Oum and Yu, 1998). Among the world's top international cargo carriers, three airlines have consistently appeared at or near the top—Korean Air, Lufthansa, and Singapore Airlines (*Air Cargo World*, 2005). After a rocky start, Korean Air Lines (KAL) was privatized in 1969 and began transpacific cargo service to the US in 1971. KAL would continue to expand its cargo and passenger operations until a series of accidents in the 1990s would threaten their alliance membership and their future (Jeziorski, 1999). Fortunately, KAL would resolve these problems by the end of the decade and begin to post the kind of double-digit cargo growth that would propel them to the top of the cargo airline list in the early part of the new century (*Air Cargo World*, 2005). Lufthansa began operation in 1926 and carried over 258 tonnes of cargo in the first year of its operation. By 1966, they had converted a passenger B-707 to become their first dedicated freighter and would become the first airline to operate the B-747 Freighter in 1972. In 1977, Lufthansa created a cargo division, German Cargo Services (GCS), with a dedicated fleet of B-707-220F. A dedicated cargo center was completed at Frankfurt Main in 1982. Several events during the 1990s are indicative of the Lufthansa interest in cargo operations: (1) acquisition of an equity stake in DHL; (2) agreement with Deutsche Post for same day service; (3) launch of Lufthansa Cargo as a wholly owned subsidiary; and (4) founding membership in the first cargo airline alliance WOW with SAS and Singapore Airlines (Lufthansa Cargo website; WOW website). Singapore Airlines was formed after the Singaporean and Malaysian governments decided to separate their joint airline in 1972. By 1978, Singapore was operating cargo service from Singapore to San Francisco. The Singapore cargo division was formed in 1992 using both dedicated and belly cargo options (Chan, 2000).

Catering to Cargo

Given the growth in air cargo operations during the last half of the twentieth century, it is not surprising that airports would begin to seek this business out either in an effort to grow their overall revenue or to compensate for declining passenger traffic. Because cargo shippers often prefer night flights, airports could serve passengers during the day and cargo shippers during the usual nighttime lulls. While it is not surprising that the hub airport for the integrators (UPS, FedEx, DHL, and so on) or the major cargo-carrying airlines post sizeable numbers of freight tonnage, a number of other airports are attempting to attract cargo activity. In 2006, the 15 fastest-growing freight airports in Europe did not include the traditional big name hubs; the top three were Leipzig/Halle, Oporto, and Leige. The growth of these smaller airports is attributed to lower costs and improved service at these airports. It is not simply a matter of courting carriers and freight forwarders. Airports like Schiphol in Amsterdam are trying to draw businesses with interests in import/export near the airport itself (Conway, 2007). Of course, to attract cargo, the airport needs the necessary facilities—warehouse space, special services and facilities (refrigeration, Hazmat, customs), cargo handling equipment, and intermodal connections (the closer the better as drayage (short trucking) is one of the most expensive parts of the transportation equation (Muller, 1995). Given the explosive growth of the Asian export-oriented economies and the apparently insatiable appetite of the Western world for these cheap products, airports around the world are ready to play in the cargo game.

Flying High

The second half of the twentieth century would witness explosive growth in the air cargo world as the logistics revolution and globalization pushed firms to seek out better, faster, and cheaper means of shipping. However, the new century would challenge air cargo as it has not been challenged since the early days of aviation. There would be rising fuel costs, new security rules, a prolonged slump in the global economy, and growing competition to battle, but for a few halcyon decades at the close of the twentieth century, cargo would ride high, reveling in rates of growth that exceed passenger growth in many cases and utilizing the new form of IT and systems to track and manage rising volumes of goods.

Questions

1. Discuss the logistics revolution.
2. Define freight forwarder and integrated cargo carrier.
3. Outline the development of the US integrated carriers.

4. Discuss the airport infrastructure needs of cargo operators.
5. What role does belly cargo play in the air cargo industry?

References

Air Cargo World (2005), "The world's top 50 cargo airlines," September, pp. 22–28.

Allaz, C. (2004), *The History of Air Cargo and Airmail from the 18th Century*, Christopher Foyle Publishing, Paris.

Aviation Week & Space Technology (2007), "Evolution of the air cargo industry: road map," *Aviation Week & Space Technology*, 7 May, pp. 47–54.

Birla, M. (2005), *FedEx Delivers: How the World's Leading Shipping Company Keeps Innovating and Outperforming the Competition*, John Wiley & Sons, New York.

Boske, L.B. (1998), *Multimodal/Intermodal Transportation in the United States, Western Europe, and Latin America: Governmental Policies, Plans, and Programs*, Lyndon B. Johnson Schools of Public Affairs, University of Texas, Austin, TX.

Castells, M. (1996), *The Rise of the Network Society*, Blackwell, Oxford.

Chan, D. (2000), "The story of Singapore Airlines and the Singapore Girl," *Journal of Management Development*, vol. 19 (6), pp. 456–473.

Conway, P. (2007), "Driven to the edge" *Air Cargo World*, October, pp. 21–27.

Fishman, C. (2006), *The Wal-Mart Effect: How the World's Most Powerful Company Really Works—And How it's Transforming the America Economy*, Penguin, New York.

Friedman, T.L. (1999), *The Lexus and the Olive Tree*, Farrar, Straus, Giroux, New York.

Friedman, T.L. (2005), *The World is Flat: A Brief History of the Twenty-First Century*, Farrar, Straus, Giroux, New York.

Jeziorski, A. (1999), "Humbled Korean Air stages management upheaval," *Flight International*, 28 April.

Kumar, N. (1996), "The Power of Trust in Manufacturer-Retailer Relationships," in *Harvard Business Review on Managing the Value Chain*, Harvard Business Press, Boston, MA, pp. 91–126.

Levinson, M. (2006), *The Box: How the Shipping Container Made the World Smaller and the World Economy Bigger*, Princeton University Press, Princeton, NJ.

Lynn, M. (1998), *Birds of Prey: Boeing versus Airbus-The Battle for the Skies*, Four Walls Eight Windows, New York.

Muller, G. (1995), *Intermodal Freight Transportation* (3rd edition), Eno Transportation Foundation, Lansdowne, VA.Nelms, (2007), "Oversized ambition," *Air Cargo World*, April, pp. 16–20.

Newhouse, J. (2007), *Boeing versus Airbus: The Inside Story of the Greatest Competition in Business*, Alfred A. Knopf, New York.

Niemann, G. (2007), *Big Brown: The Untold Story of UPS*, John Wiley & Sons, San Francisco, CA.

Oum, T.H. and Yu, C. (1998), *Winning Airlines: Productivity and Cost Competitiveness of the World's Major Airlines*, Kluwer Academic Publishers, Boston, MA.

Serling, R.J. (1992), *Legend and Legacy: The Story of Boeing and Its People*, St. Martin Press, New York

Websites

Deutsche Post World Net, http://www.dpwe.de
Lufthansa Cargo, http://www.lhcargo.com
WOW alliance, http://www.WOWtheworld.com

PART III
Facing the Future (2008–)

Chapter 15
Searching for Profits

Learning Objectives

After reading this chapter, you should have a good understanding of:
- LO1: the history of financial instability in the airline industry and the usual responses to crisis.
- LO2: the key drivers of cost in airlines.
- LO3: the changing labor patterns in airlines.
- LO4: the range of new responses to crisis.

Key Terms, Concepts, and People

Economies of scale	Economies of scope	Diseconomies
Distribution system	SABRE	GDS

Old Dogs

There is a saying that you can't teach old dogs new tricks. Deregulation certainly seemed to prove this point for the traditional, full service airlines. Following the Airline Deregulation Act discussed in Chapter 9, the industry has experienced a major "financial crisis" in every decade. It is true that these crises have been associated with the business cycle which airlines themselves cannot control, however, the airlines did not follow the wisdom of saving in good times, making matters worse. The industry has been notorious for its "boom-or-bust" existence. An old airline joke notes that the best way to become a millionaire in the airline industry is to start with a billion. Jokes aside, there were already indications prior to 9/11 of the usual recession related slowdown in the airline industry, which is a canary in the economic coal mine. If the trigger was unique, then the industry responses were strikingly familiar because the basic issues remained the same: increasingly price sensitive consumers, overexpansion in the boom leading to overcapacity in the bust, high costs, contentious labor, and competition from low-cost and foreign carriers (Arndt and Woellert, 2001; Costa, Harned, and Lunquist, 2002; Derchin, 1995; Wolf, 1995). Table 15.1 shows the long, hard fight in the US and around the globe to return to profitability after 9/11.

Table 15.1   US and global profits 2000–2006

	2000	2001	2002	2003	2004	2005	2006
US							
Operating	7.0	(10.3)	(8.6)	(2.1)	(1.5)	0.4	7.5
Net	2.5	(8.3)	(11.3)	(3.6)	(9.1)	(10.0)	3.1
Global							
Operating	10.7	(11.8)	(4.8)	(1.4)	3.3	4.4	15.0
Net	1.2	(4.7)	0.0	(3.9)	4.9	4.0	(0.5)

Source: US figures from Airlines for America, www.airlines.org
Global figures from IATA www.iata.org/economics

In response to earlier crises, the industry created the hub-and-spoke system as a means of funneling and managing traffic, developed complex holding structures to manage debt, renegotiated labor contracts to manage wages and benefits, retired fleets and cut marginal routes to reduce capacity, merged and consolidated as weaker players faltered and stronger ones strived to position themselves for the next boom, and looked for marginal ways to reduce costs. With the next boom, the dominant logic of the industry reverted to expand and spend (Rosen, 1995). In the wake of 9/11, the industry did a better job of avoiding the "temptation of capacity," even though new aircraft orders soared for 2005 and 2006 (IATA, 2007). Then the 2008 GFC and record fuel prices became the latest shock to the industry. For now, it appears that old dogs can learn new tricks, if they are forced to run with the young dogs long enough and the LCCs have been running a hard race across the globe. In fact, it now appears that it is no longer possible for an airline to muddle through unless they can count on government support and this is becoming ever more scarce. Successful airlines live on the extremes. They either become high touch–high service like Emirates or low cost like Ryanair and Spirit (Saporito, 2013) As Table 15.2 shows, the US industry has been much quicker to react and more disciplined in it approach to expansion through the newest crisis.

This chapter will explore the historic struggle of the industry to remain profitable, including what has changed in the latest version of Airline Crisis 4.0. We will explore fundamental issues such as organizational scale (size) and scope, looking at the latest consolidation. We will examine the battle between the traditional carriers and the LCCs. Finally, we will look at three key areas of the airline industry—fuel, distribution, and labor—to understand the developments and trends driving airlines to get these costs under control.

Table 15.2   US and global profits 2006–2012

	2006	2007	2008	2009	2010	2011	2012
US							
Operating	7.5	7.7	(3.3)	2.4	8.9	15.7	UA
Net	3.1	16.5	6.3	(2.9)	2.7	0.39	0.152
Global							
Operating	15.0	19.9	(1.1)	1.9	28.9	14.1	14.8
Net	(0.5)	12.9	(16.8)	(11.0)	(5.6)	4.9	7.4

Source: US figures from Airlines for America, www.airlines.org
Global figures from IATA www.iata.org/economics

Too Big to Fail

The GFC led to a debate on the whole topic of too big to fail. For the most part, the discussion centered on banks, but after 9/11, United had argued for government assistance claiming that an airline can be too big to fail as well. The first question to answer in the case of airlines is does size really matter? If so, is it the scale of the operations or the scope? Is size important for some factors of production but not others? What exactly does an airline produce? Is there such a thing as too big or do airlines need to get big enough to finally make a sustainable profit? Where does an airline add value and how can this value be enhanced and captured?

In the latest round of consolidation, airlines have argued that consolidation is good for the industry and for consumers. Airlines benefit because it helps them maintain pricing power through a greater ability to control capacity. In defense of the American–US Airways merger, proponents suggest that the combination will create a competitor capable of providing truly "competitive" prices and service to consumers forced to rely on United and Delta for their international travel (Flottau and Shannon, 2013). Size or economies of scale was one of the primary arguments presented in the debate over deregulation of the US airline industry. Economies of scale occur when average costs decline as the production of a good or service goes up. These economies can derive from several sources: technological, managerial, financial, marketing, commercial, and research and development (R&D). Technological economies may result when a larger firm is able to employ more expensive machinery and use it more intensively. Managerial economies arise when a firm is able to divide tasks and employ specialists. Financial economies result when a firm is able to borrow money at lower rates (primarily because size is usually associated with greater assets, age, credit record, and so on). Marketing economies occur when firms are able to spread the high cost of advertising across a larger level of output. Commercial economies are gained from buying supplies in bulk and receiving larger discounts. R&D economies may appear when developing new or better products if basic research can give rise to multiple applications (Biz/ed, 2002). From this breakdown, it is obvious that a firm, industry, or strategic group within an industry may enjoy economies in one area and not in another. Technologically, the new generation of aircraft tended to be more economical and efficient, however, the hub-and-spoke system employed by the major carriers limited the utilization of aircraft that sat and waited for banks of smaller airplanes to feed passengers into the system. These small aircraft (50 seat) were not economical for larger carriers to operate since higher wage scales made them less productive. High fuel prices are now making them uneconomical for even regional carriers thus placing new pressure on the hub concept (Flottau, 2013). It has certainly been hard to argue that the major US carriers enjoyed financial economies over their smaller competitors given their low stock prices, high leverage, and negative growth. While major carriers may continue to enjoy economies in marketing, commercial, and R&D development, the level of this advantage is probably declining as technology, market fragmentation, and other factors come into play in the airline industry.

Since economies of scale are concerned with unit costs, it is important to define the unit of production in airlines. In other words, what does an airline produce? Does it produce a seat, a trip from point A to point B (called a leg), or an end-to-end experience, that is, many consumers connect from A to B to C as the final destination? The answer to this question may well matter since not all seats or trips are equal. The proverbial widget factory of business lore mass produces a product that is assumed to be the same—widgets. Economies of scale exist if the unit cost of the 10,000th widget are lower than the 1,000th. In the case of an airline, the seat on an aircraft from Atlanta to Boston is not necessarily the same as a seat from Atlanta to Denver or Atlanta to Dubai nor are the costs involved in producing these seats the same since they involve different lengths, flight crews, landing fees, aircraft types, passenger facilities charges, and so on. Sophisticated systems can be employed to analyze costs by route, but this unit of analysis problem greatly complicates the economies argument for carriers. In part, this focus on unit costs is driven by the traditional approach to accounting which basically adds direct material costs, direct labor costs, and overhead (rent, utilities, insurance, and so on) then divides by the unit of output to determine per unit costs. Activity-based costing looks at costs from an activity standpoint. Business activities includes "all of the processes that a company uses in order to conduct its business: order processing, procurement, engineering, production set-up, quality inspection, warehousing and material movement." Under this approach, firms would determine the activities it performs and analyze them to determine the cost drivers within that activity. Costs to products are assigned based on how often they require inputs from that particular activity. The benefits of activity costing are found in the detailed cost information it provides and the focus on cost drivers within activities.

The notion of increasing scale leads to the question of whether a carrier can be too big. With size comes complexity—vertically, horizontally, and geographically. Large firms have more layers of management separating the top where "decisions" get made from the bottom where "decisions" and the actual work of the organization get carried out. These layers often mean that actions are delayed and communications are poor, leading to misdiagnosis of problems or misapplication of solutions. Horizontal complexity occurs when firms become increasingly divided into ever finer units of specialized individuals who lose touch with the work (and importance) of other units as well as the overall goals of the organization. Geographic complexity occurs when firms spread across time zones and cultures, making collaboration difficult and product and managerial decisions culture-specific. A further complexity, external boundaries, is becoming more common as firms outsource functions and blur the lines between the firm and its external environment. In fact, each of these areas creates its own boundary within the firm. In many large (old) firms, these boundaries are clear and impermeable; what is inside stays inside and what is out cannot get in! Such organizations are slow to act, rigid in response, and poor in adaptation. Size becomes a disadvantage if the firm lives in a rapidly changing environment with younger, faster competitors (Ashkenas, Ulrich, Jick, and Kerr, 1995; Galbraith, 1995). Of course, one of the advantages of merger activity is that, in theory, firms can reduce redundancies, increase productivity, and spread costs. Larger firms can be said to have market power that could translate into a greater ability to control costs, capacity, or distribution. At the market level, the debate over the latest US merger—American and US Airways—was a matter of answering two questions. First, does a three-firm oligopoly act differently than a four-firm oligopoly? The key issue is whether the remaining three carriers would tacitly collude to maintain equilibrium, that is, do they accept a gentlemanly division of the market that allows them to maintain pricing power and profits or are there incentives to compete over routes and market share in a way that either lowers prices or improves service (factors important to consumers)? As the global industry lurches forward, creating ever larger airlines with each new wave of consolidation, it is not yet clear what the answer is to the question of too big. Until fares begin to rise to a point that provokes consumer calls for change, governments are not likely to answer the question of how big is too big.

Economies of scope differ from those of scale in that they are not derived from increases in volume, but occur as the result of circumstances that allow firms to achieve synergy in production, product development, and distribution. Economies of scope can occur in production when firms are able to lower the cost of producing one product by producing other, that is, an airline flying both passengers and cargo. Economies of scope in product development arise when common knowledge or equipment is used to produce more than one product, that is, laser technology can be used in many applications from surgery to metal cutting, an aircraft used for passengers during the day and cargo at night, a computer revenue management system used to manage airline seats, hotel room, rental cars, and so on. This last example is a classic one, that is, an infrastructure system capable of distributing one type of product used to distribute others. An airline distribution system can also be viewed as a scope generator. The hub can be seen as a very large airport operation or "a factory to combine itineraries" (Flottau, 2013). If consumers prefer more options to less, then an airline that can produce more combinations of services and routes would hold an advantage.

Of course, if size does create diseconomies of scale or scope, firms have several options in downsizing: retrenchment, downscaling, or downscoping (DeWitt, 1998). Retrenchment attempts to maintain scope and often even increases output by centralizing certain firm functions, changing supplier relationships, and realigning managerial functions. For example, firms may re-engineer processes to improve productivity or eliminate redundant facilities (Hammer and Champy, 1993). Downscaling operations entail the permanent reduction of human and physical resources to bring supply in line with demand (Harrigan, 1983, 1985; Mahoney, 1992). Downscoping involves efforts to actually shrink the boundaries of the firm by effecting permanent cuts in human and physical resources as well as simplifying the organization's structure by reducing vertical, horizontal, or product diversity (DeWitt, 1993). The path a firm takes to downsizing is a function of many factors, but one factor is clearly the barriers to exit and mobility. Exit barriers create an impediment to the removal of excess resources (Caves and Porter, 1976) while mobility barriers affect the ability of firms to move between segments in an industry (Caves and Porter, 1977). Firms make certain industry-specific investments that may make exit difficult or very costly. For example, labor contracts may lock a firm into maintaining certain levels of operation. Fleet acquisitions may mean that cutbacks will lead to underutilization in the short run, raising costs, and fleet sales may take time and not generate enough in certain market conditions to recoup costs. Cutting spokes out of the hub-and-spoke "factory" can multiply in a network to eliminate a number of possible city pairs. Likewise, a high-cost labor force with rigid work rules may prohibit a firm from shifting to a lower-cost segment of the industry. The task ahead for airlines is figuring out how economies and value-adding activities can be used to shape a profitable airline. As noted in the introduction to this chapter, it may now require them to decide on which of the two extremes to adopt—high touch or low cost (Saporito, 2013).

What's Your Strategy?

The US Transportation Department defines a LCC as one that is "recognized" as operating with a lower infrastructure and aircraft operating costs. This definition, however, is sadly lacking in details and hides a growing diversity in strategic approaches to "recognition."

Diversity

The original low-cost model was pioneered by Southwest Airlines in the US. This model had several key features: point-to-point service, secondary airport use, no-frills service, single fleet type, outsourced maintenance, and a host of employee-related/organizational culture features (employee ownership, teamwork, cross-training, and so on). This model has been the subject of several books including *Nuts: Southwest Airlines' Crazy Recipe for Business and Personal Success* (Freiberg and Freiberg, 1996). Following US deregulation, a number of new airlines attempted to implement this model with limited success. In the four decades since Southwest, a host of variations on the LCC model have appeared. Ryanair in Europe adopted the operational details (even taking the cost-cutting no frills to new heights by removing the window shade, charging for carry-ons, requiring online booking, and so on), but did not adopt the cultural elements that Southwest believes adds to employee productivity (Sparaco, 2011). Likewise, US carrier Spirit has been growing at 20 percent a year since adopting the LCC model in which everything is an extra charge to a low base fare (Saporito, 2013). As we will see later, this fare-and-fee approach is even being adopted by the traditional carriers. Carriers such as JetBlue in the US, EasyJet in the EU, and, of course, the Persian Gulf carriers (Emirates, Qatar Airways, and Etihad) have gone in the opposite direction in terms of frills, seeking to attract more business class passengers through the selected offering of additional services (Flottau, 2013; Sparaco, 2012).

The current question mark in airline strategy is whether a hybrid strategy that combines traditional and low cost is a viable option. After 9/11, LCCs were the only airlines expanding, but even the anointed kings of the LCC model—Southwest Airlines and Ryanair—have slowed their growth. In some countries, the LCCs have even gained a majority of the traffic (Flottau, 2011). More LCC competition and higher fuel prices changed the dynamics in many markets. A number of LCCs have tried to adopt a hybrid strategy to appeal to higher yield passengers, but the results to date seem to suggest that the operating margins for pure LCCs are better than the hybrids such as Virgin Australia, Air Berlin, or Gol (Airline Leader, 2013). If the traditional carriers had a hard time thinking like an LCC, then it is possible that the LCCs are finding it difficult to think (and act) more high touch. There is no question that adding frills will increase costs; the question is whether the added costs (of service) raise more revenues. It may be too early to declare the hybrid dead, but it is clear that it is struggling.

As for the LCC model, the decade following 9/11 was a very good one in the US. Southwest, JetBlue, AirTran, and other LCCs increased the size of their fleet, growing their share of passenger traffic from 15.7 percent in 2000 to 25.7 percent in 2009 (Nelson and Francolla, 2008; Reuters, 2010). While the LCC market share in the US has remained relatively flat since 2009, airlines like Spirit continue to see new opportunities to grow in selected markets (Saporito, 2013). The decade was even better for the European LCCs, led by Ryanair and EasyJet. In 2011, low-cost/low-fare carriers reported an increase of 9.5 percent in passenger traffic over the prior year. Although Ryanair's traffic growth slowed to a weak 5 percent for the 12-month period ending May 2012, its rival EasyJet posted an 8.9 percent increase (Sparaco, 2012). York Aviation estimated in 2011 that the LCC share of EU traffic was 38 percent and forecast it to expand 72 percent by the end of the decade (Sparaco, 2011). Whether an EU economic slowdown will accelerate the LCC growth or cause it to level off is not yet clear. Ryanair has issued its first profit warning in a decade and suggested that growth will slow, but it is too early to declare LCC expansion over in the EU (Thomas, 2013). For their part, Europe's largest traditional carriers are continuing efforts to reduce their own costs, including efforts to create their own low-cost units or shift short-haul flying to affiliated small carriers (Flottau, 2012). The prolonged recession in the EU could benefit the LCCs or act as a drag on the entire sector. Time will tell.

Searching for Profits

Don Carty, then CEO of American Airlines, told a Congressional panel after September 11 that American's main objective was to achieve permanent structural cost reductions (Fiorino, 2002). He singled out three factors for special attention— fuel, distribution, and labor (Zellner, 2002). The bankruptcy of American in 2011 illustrates the importance of these factors and the difficulties in reducing costs in these areas. Still, these factors deserve a closer look in order to identify the issues and possibilities for savings.

Fuel

At the time of Carty's testimony to Congress, fuel prices represented roughly 10–15 percent of airlines' costs. According to Airlines for America (A4A), the US industry trade group, fuel in 2013 represented 28 percent of the operating costs, surpassing labor which represented 23 percent (A4A, 2013). Even before oil passed the US$100 barrel mark, airlines were looking to save money. There are several obvious things that airlines can do to reduce or stabilize fuel costs. First, newer, more fuel-efficient aircraft reduce fuel costs as well as overall maintenance costs. Many of the aircraft "retired" after 9/11 and the GFC fell into the less efficient category. Unfortunately, financially troubled airlines often find fleet renewal difficult. Second, airlines can seek to hedge fuel costs, although this is not guaranteed to save costs since it depends on the financial and forecasting skill of the airline. Southwest Airlines has been one of the US carriers that has benefited from substantial fuel hedging, but even it has not always guessed right (*USA Today*, 2007). Hedging is difficult if there is no clear sense of the future trend in fuel. The question for many airlines is will fuel prices fall and how far? Will they rise further making it important to lock in current prices now? Given the very thin margins, "guessing right" by even a few dollars could make a big difference. Third, there are a number of operational measures that can be employed. The first edition of IATAs "Guidance Material on Best Practices for Fuel and Environmental Management" was issued in 2004. The manual goes through detailed information for weight management, pre-flight planning, engine start-up and taxing, reduced thrust takeoff, and so on. Fourth, many US airlines are simply shrinking their operations, particularly their regional jet operations which may be flying at a loss because of the generally higher operating costs of smaller aircraft. At Delta regional subsidiary Comair, the number of 50-seat aircraft has been reduced from 69 to 16 and these small planes are restricted to routes of 750 miles or less (Compart, 2010; Reuters, 2008). Overall, US airlines cut 13 million seats from inventory over the last year, raising the industry load factor to 87.1 percent (Saporito, 2013). In a piece of out-of-the-box thinking not common in the industry, Delta Air Lines even purchased its own oil refinery in 2012 to help them control fuel costs. Still, it is not clear that they will be rewarded for this innovation. The refinery, operated by Delta subsidiary Monroe Energy LLC, made a profit in the third quarter of 2013 after posting losses in the previous two quarters (Reuters, 2013). Even if Delta is able to get the refinery to a sustainable profit, this does not appear to be a strategy that most other carriers can or would adopt in the battle to reduce fuel costs.

Distribution

Distribution systems are areas over which carriers have greater control than fuel costs and IATA members are hoping to be able to exert even more control in the future. Unlike fuel costs, however, the issues are more complex. In its formative years, air transport growth and profit were driven by airmail revenues. As passenger traffic increased in importance, airlines needed a process to track seat sales on flights. Without such a system, two problems can occur. First, an airline may sell more tickets than it has available seats on a given flight. This overbooking leads to disgruntled passengers who will have to be placated in some way (free tickets, discounts, frequent flyer mile, upgrades, and so on) or potentially lost to another airline. Placating costs money, however, the second problem also costs money, namely not selling all available seats. Airlines need to return cancelled seats as quickly as possible to the available pool or risk losing the opportunity to maximize revenue. Airline seats, like cabbage, are perishable goods, meaning that at some point in time they become unusable and unsellable; once a flight takes off, the seat has perished.

The saga of airline distribution systems is a fascinating one and illustrates some of the potential issues facing airlines today. One of the earliest systems for tracking reservations was the Request and Reply system that required customers to contact ticket agents at the point of departure and wait for a reply confirming seat availability. The explosion in traffic following World War II, however, made this centralized point of departure system unwieldy. Agents in reservations offices soon used availability display boards to scan for seat openings and alternative flights. At the Chicago office of American Airlines, an observer would have been confronted by a wall covered with a large cross-hatched board filled with cryptic notes. Men and women sitting in row upon row of desks would continually check this board, compare it to thick reference books all the while talking on the telephone to potential customers and filling out cards. Clerks and messengers scurried around between the desks with cards and sheets of paper as the chatter of teletypes and card-sorting equipment filled the air (McKenney, Copeland, and Mason, 1967). American Airlines would replace this scene of mayhem with a machine called the Reservisor System which used a matrix of relays in which the columns represented dates and rows represented flights. Shorting plugs were inserted in the matrix to indicate a sellout. The system permitted fewer agents to book more flights, but maintenance of the system proved expensive. The next innovation introduced into the system was a magnetic drum computer memory to store data. By 1956, the Reserwriter, a computer that read punch cards of passenger data, converted them to tape, and telexed the data was in operation. However, even with these improvements, an estimated 8 percent of all transactions were incorrect and the process required 12 people, 15 steps, and three hours. To remedy these problems, American worked with IBM to produce the SABRE system. The Computerized Reservation System (CRS) was born (McKenney, Copeland, and Mason, 1967).

The CRS (now also called Global Distribution Systems or GDSs) was originally intended for use by travel agents and large corporate clients. By 1990, 93 percent of travel agencies were plugged into one of the major CRS/GDS systems (Bartimo, 1990). Not all carriers had their own CRS system and eventually began to accept the services of other carriers with CRS systems, however, since the CRS was initially developed by specific airlines, the systems that they each developed tended to favor their own flights. CRS systems also required a specialized knowledge of codes and procedures which made it profitable for many agencies to develop interfacing software that allowed them to use the system more efficiently and perform operations that their own customers wanted such as searching for best price (McKenney, Copeland, and Mason, 1967; Davidow and Malone, 1992). The relationship between airlines and travel agents began to change in the mid-1990s as airlines began their next major assault on distribution costs. This time the focus was on reducing the travel agents' commissions on domestic and international ticket sales which had been as high as 10 percent for domestic and 15 percent for international sales. By 1997, the number of agencies in the US had declined for the first time and the industry began to witness a wave of consolidation (Cook, Goff, Yale, and Wolverton, 1999). Most of the CRS/GDS systems have been spun-off from the airlines that gave them birth. The largest of these GDSs was SABRE, formerly a part of American Airlines. Travelport is the result of the merger of Galileo, Worldspan, and Appolo. The last major player in the GDS world is Amadeus which was formed by Air France, Lufthansa, SAS, and Iberia as an alternative to the US-controlled GDSs. It is the largest system in Europe (Michels, 2007).

Carty had estimated that American alone paid over US$400 in CRS/GDS charges in 2001 (Fiorino, 2002). This fact alone gave airlines an incentive to use the internet as a way to further cut distribution costs by selling directly to consumers. E-business became a new airline strategy. Orbitz was founded in 1999 by United, Delta, Continental, Northwest, and American as an online travel agent providing direct booking with the participating airlines. Other sites included Expedia, Priceline, Travelocity, Kayak, and so on. In short, there is a host online in addition to those directly linked to the airlines themselves (Methner and Rospenda, 2001). The internet has allowed carriers to reduce the fees to travel agents as well as to computer reservation systems which have now by-and-large been spun-off by the carriers into separate operating companies, but traffic on the internet itself did not grow as quickly as expected, slowing the dream of eliminating major costs by shifting a significant portion of customers to a system whereby they booked their own flight over the internet, printed out their own boarding pass and baggage tags, and deposited their own bags at a designated airport conveyor belt which has not yet arrived (Rosenbush, Crockett, Haddad, and Ewing, 2002). While many LCC airlines continue to pursue a self-help strategy for customers, this does not serve the high-touch strategy well.

In many ways, the internet has proved to be a double-edged sword for the airlines, at least for the major carriers. Using published fares, new software, and the internet superhighway; airline customers can quickly and cheaply search and compare pricing to get the lowest fare. In testimony before the US Congress on the American Airlines bankruptcy, Daniel Kasper, internet-based search and distribution channels have increased price transparency and led to a long-term, fundamental decline in airline prices. The ability to rapidly shop for the lowest fares has "commoditized airline travel" (Kasper, 2012). Thus, it seems that reducing distribution costs in any significant way will require more radical solutions. This will require several things, including extensive investment in new equipment and software. The truth of the matter is that the distribution systems of many large carriers are still heavily mainframe-based, using PCs as dumb terminals whose sole function is inputting data into archaic programs that use archaic protocols. The industry that represents "high tech" to many outsiders is in fact using old hardware and bad software to link to the high-tech internet.

The solution of IATA member airlines is what they are calling the New Distribution Capability (NDC). The goal of the NDC is for airlines to create their own product in their own system and provide it directly to consumers. In an airline world where fares are no longer published (open information), the airline would "customize" a price for each consumer who requested a quote. Given the new fare-and-fee strategy that allows the consumer to pay for almost all additional amenities to customize their service experience (meal, more legroom, early boarding, Wi-Fi, and so on), then each quote would indeed be unique AND more difficult to compare (IATA, 2012). As Mr Tyler, Director General of IATA, has noted, price transparency essentially means that almost all cost-reducing efficiencies are handed directly over to consumers in lower fares (FlightGlobal, 2012). While consumers are quite happy with this situation, the airlines are hoping that new technology and the NDC will change this situation, assuming that various governments around the world allow this change.

Labor

The third area of costs targeted for savings by American Airlines CEO Don Carty was labor (Fiorino, 2002). Prior to 9/11, labor was the single largest cost of major US carriers at roughly 40 percent. Experts had suggested that labor costs needed to drop by 20 percent to return the airline industry to profitability. Unfortunately, in the absence of a major crisis there is little probability of gaining union agreement to these reductions. Bankruptcy is just such a crisis. Following September 11, four major US carriers entered bankruptcy: United (2002), US Airways (2002, 2004), Delta and Northwest (2005). American Airlines avoided this round of bankruptcy by signing agreements with its three key unions to lower costs (Nelson and Francolla, 2008). It was not enough to allow American to weather the 2008 GFC and US$147 a barrel oil. So in 2011, American joined the ranks of US airlines who have filed for bankruptcy.

Over the last two decades, some very interesting changes have occurred in the airline labor force. Table 15.3 illustrates one of these trends. It reports the number of mechanics employed by the carriers per aircraft. As you can see, Southwest, true to its LCC beginnings, largely started with an outsourced maintenance operation whereas the traditional legacy carriers started with a mostly in-house maintenance staff which they have shed over the years. The last to maintain their in-house staff was American Airlines and one of the first acts of the bankrupt carrier was to change this dynamic. While none of the legacy carriers has reached the level of Southwest, most have significantly reduced this segment of the unionized workforce. Changes in other areas have allowed the carriers to improve productivity, that is, lower the total number of employees needed per aircraft. Table 15.4 illustrates the reductions in this area that have taken place since 1990. Again, while none of the legacy carriers have reached the level of Southwest, they are shedding employees and reducing the impact of labor on overall operating costs. In short, while US carriers have not quite achieved the 20 percent reduction in labor cost suggested after 9/11, labor now represents only an industry average of 23 percent of operating costs (A4A, 2013).

With reductions in mechanics and other labor, pilots are the biggest single labor group in the airlines and the biggest opportunity for cost reduction. Unions have historically complicated airline mergers and acquisitions at the outset as the pilot talks between groups from Delta and Northwest demonstrated (Weber, 2008). It is not clear how legacy carriers will deal with this group should they try to reduce labor costs further unless they opt to allow more routes to be operated by regional carriers where salaries, even for this group of employees, are much lower.

Table 15.3   Changes in mechanic workforce (mechanics per aircraft)

Year	Alaska	America	Continental	Delta	Northwest	Southwest	United	USAir
1990	13.57	20.95	21.67	15.12	9.77	3.86	17.91	
1991	10.83	21.43	21.62	16.04	14.12	3.88	13.12	
1992	12.6	20.54	22.01	15.11	13.75	4.18	12.43	
1993	11.54	17.91	22.66	14.07	12.47	3.57	11.01	
1994	13.35	16.79	18.12	12.81	12.73	3.65	10.35	
1995	12.39	16.05	8.83	13.15	12.30	3.3	8.4	
1996	12.35	18.03	8.8	11.31	12.53	3.7	3.83	
1997	14.51	19.17	9.2	12.07	13.42		26.38	
1998	14.49	21.48	9.4	13.0	15.15	3.8	27.12	
1999	14.37	22.63	9.27	14.25	14.51	3.67	28.1	13.55
2000	13.93	21.54	9.59	9.83	13.93	3.76	26.5	13.69
2001	14.46	21.58	9.5	9.45	12.6	4.02	24.19	11.18
2002	13.03	20.79	9.56	14.08	10.91	4.06	11.91	12.44
2003	13.22	20.68	9.31	13.69	6.67	4.09	14.64	13.08
2004	13.33	22.56	9.99	13.99	5.87	3.97	10.4	11.89
2005	12.32	20.70	9.84	11.10	3.35	3.7	9.65	7.91
2006	12.42	20.39	10.24	10,02	3.3	3.7	10.52	11.79
2007	11.94	20.83	10.40	11.91	3.24	3.5	10.63	13.6
2008	11.94	21.97	10.66	11.79	3.53	3.3	14.11	9.53
2009	11.89	20.13	10.92	11.91	3.72	3.26	10.04	10.24

Source: Data for employment obtained from the RITA/BTS website http://www.rita.dot.gov/bts/
Data on aircraft in the fleet obtained from Back Aviation database

Looking Ahead

The last decade has been a very difficult one for the global airline industry with 9/11 and the GFC, but two major crises in one decade has for now taught it the wisdom of capacity control and the danger of pursuing market share at all costs. Many questions remain unanswered regarding the issue of airline size, the number of competitors needed for a contestable market, the new distribution system, and the future of airline labor. Whether the great names of airline history will be able to meet the challenges facing them or fall to the younger, smaller, faster competitors rising up before them has yet to be determined. While bankruptcy has allowed the legacy carriers to adjust costs to better compete with LCCs and LCC growth in many regions is slowing, there is still likely to be more airline failures in the foreseeable future. In the absence of government intervention, some carriers may simply not survive the process. As if the problem of profitability were not enough for carriers to face in the new environment, there is another question that is waiting to be asked, namely—what is the future of global aviation liberalization? The

Table 15.4   Changes in total employees, 1990 and 2008

Airline	1990 Total	1990 per aircraft	2008 Total	2008 per aircraft
American	85,680	170	70,924	108
Continental	33,553	104	40,360	111
Delta	64,791	159	47,470	106
Northwest	35,775	107	28,124	79
United	70,179	164	55,160	120
Legacy Total	289,978	145	242,258	106
Southwest	8,267	88	34,680	67

Source: Data for employment obtained from the RITA/BTS website http://www.rita.dot.gov/bts/
Data on aircraft in the fleet obtained from Back Aviation database

industry before 9/11 was on a steady path toward greater freedom to enter, exit, set prices, and establish capacity based on market forces. After a pause, it has lurched ahead finally with the new EU–US Open Skies agreement, but there remain many issues to be resolved. This topic will be the subject of Chapter 16.

Questions

1. What are economies of scale and scope and how do they apply in the airline industry?
2. Discuss the history of financial crisis and the responses taken by airlines.
3. Discuss the key drivers of cost in airlines.
4. What are some of the new responses to crisis and what are their chances of success?
5. Describe a virtual airline. What are the stumbling blocks to such an airline?

References

Airline Leader (2013), "Low-cost airlines, hybridization and the rocky path to profits," retrieved online January 9, 2014 from http://www.airlineleader.com/this-months-highlights/low-cost-airlines-hybridisation-and-the-rocky-path-to-profits.
Airlines for America (A4A) (2013), "A4A Quarterly Cost Index: US passenger airlines," retrieved online March 18, 2014 from http://www.airlines.org/Pages/A4A-Quarterly-Cost-Index-U.S.-Passenger-Airlines.aspx.

Arndt, M. and Woellert, L. (2001), "What kind of rescue: cash won't solve air carriers' long-term woes," *Business Week*, October 1, pp. 36–37.

Ashkenas, R. Ulrich, D., Jick, T. and Kerr, S. (1995), *The Boundaryless Organizations: Breaking the Chains of Organizational Structure*, Jossey-Bass Publishers, San Francisco, CA.

Bartimo, J. (1990), "Wanted: co-pilots for reservation systems," *Business Week*, April 9, p. 79.

Bized (2002), "Economies of scale," retrieved online February 5, 2001 from www.bized.ac.uk.

Caves, R.E. and Porter, M.E. (1976), " Barriers to Exit," in D.P. Qualls and R.T. Masson (eds), *Essays in Industrial Organization in Honor of Joe S. Bain*, Ballinger, Cambridge, MA, pp. 39–69.

Caves, R.E. and Porter, M.E. (1977), "From entry barriers to mobility barriers: conjectural decisions and contrived deterrence to new competition," *Quarterly Journal of Economics*, vol. 91 (3), pp. 241–261.

Compart, A. (2010), "Taking off," *Aviation Week and Space Technology*, November 15, pp. 70–73.

Cook, R.A., Goff, J.L., Yale, L.J. and Wolverton, J.B. (1999), "Fasten Your Seat Belts: Turbulence Ahead for Travel Agencies," in M.L. Taylor (ed.), *Case Set A to Accompany Dess & Lumpkin Strategic Management*, McGraw-Hill/Irwin, Boston, MA, pp. 32–41.

Costa, P.R., Harned, D.S. and Lunquist, J.T. (2002), "Rethinking the aviation industry," *The McKinsey Quarterly*, No. 2: Risk and Resilience.

Davidow, W.H. and Malone, M.S. (1992), *The Virtual Corporation: Structuring and Revitalizing the Corporation for the 21st Century*, HarperCollins Publishing, New York.

Derchin, M. (1995), "What went Wrong?," in P. Cappelli (ed.) *Airline Labor Relations in the Global Era: The New Frontier*, ILR Press, Ithaca, NY, pp. 13-18.

DeWitt, R.L. (1998), "Firm, industry, and strategy influences on choice of downsizing approach," *Strategic Management Journal*, vol. 19 (1), pp. 59–79.

DeWitt, R.L. (1993), "The structural consequences of downsizing," *Organization Science*, vol. 4 (1), pp. 30–40.

Fiorino, F. (2002), "Carty to analysts: AA aims to survive," *Aviation Week and Space Technology*, September 20, pp. 47–48.

FlightGlobal (2012), retrieved online May 19, 2013 from http://www.flightglobal.com/interviews/tony-tyler/the-interview/.

Flottau, J. (2011), "Hybrid hypothesis: Air Berline is trying to be everything to everybody—and may fail." *Aviation Week & Space Technology*, May 30, pp. 48–51.

Flottau, J. (2012), "Desperate state: European airlines opt for outsourcing and cuts in effort to stem losses," *Aviation Week & Space Technology*, May 27, pp. 27–28.

Flottau, J. (2013), "Evolving paradigm," *Aviation Week and Space Technology*, July 8, pp. 36–39.

Flottau, J. and Shannon, D. (2013), "Connecting fight," *Aviation Week and Space Technology*, August 19, pp. 24–27.

Freiberg, K. and Freiberg, J. (1996), *Nuts: Southwest Airlines' Crazy Recipe for Business and Personal Success*, Bard Press, Austin, TX.

Galbraith, J.R. (1995), *Designing Organizations: An Executive Briefing on Strategy, Structure, and Process*, Jossey-Bass Publishers, San Francisco, CA.

Hammer, M. and Champy, J.S. (1993), *Reengineering the Corporation: A Manifesto for Business Revolution*, HarperBusiness, New York.

Harrigan, K.R. (1983), *Strategies for Vertical Integration*, Lexington Books, Lexington, MA.

Harrigan, K.R. (1985), *Strategic Flexibility*, Lexington Books, Lexington, MA.

International Air Transport Association (IATA) (2007), "IATA economic briefing: passenger and freight forecasts 2007–2011," retrieved online January 23, 2008 from http://www.iata.org/economics.

International Air Transport Association (IATA) (2012) "Resolution 787: enhanced airline distribution," retrieved online March 16, 2014 from http://www. businesstravelcoalition.com/press-room/2013/august-14---iatas-ndc-trave. html.

Kasper, D. (2012), "Written testimony by American Airlines expert to the bankruptcy court in the American Airlines Chapter 11 case," retrieved online March 18, 2014 from http://btcnews.co/LGDKbf.

Mahoney, J.T. (1992), "The choice of organizational form and vertical financial ownership versus other methods of vertical integration," *Strategic Management Journal*, vol. 13 (8), pp. 559–584.

McKenney, L., Copeland, D.G. and Mason, R.O. (1967), "American Airlines SABRE system," Harvard Business School Case No. EA-C.

Methner, B.E. and Rospenda, C.J. (2001), "Airline Strategy in a Digital Age: What Does 'e' Mean to Me?," in Gail F. Butler and Martin R. Keller (eds), *Handbook of Airline Strategy*, McGraw-Hill Companies, New York, pp. 389–406.

Michels, J. (2007), "Travelport," *Aviation Daily*, August 22, retrieved online January 6, 2008 from http://www.aviationweek.com/aw/generic/story_channel.jsp.

Nelson, A. and Francolla, G. (2008), "Airlines: a tale of mergers and bankruptcy," CNBC.com, February 21, retrieved online January 6, 2009 from http://www. cnbc.com.

Reuters (2008), "Big US airlines look to shrink to save money," CNBC.com, March 17, retrieved online March 20, 2008 from http://www.cnbc.com.

Reuters (2010), "Less expansion seen for US low-cost airlines," *Airwise*, July 2, 2010.

Reuters (2013), "Delta's refinery turns small profit for first time," retrieved online January 20, 2014 from http://www.reuters.com/article/2013/10/22/delta-refinery-idUSL1N0IC11W20131022.

Rosen, S.D. (1995), "Corporate Restructuring: A Labor Perspective," in P. Cappelli (ed.) *Airline Labor Relations in the Global Era: The New Frontier*, ILR Press, Ithaca, NY, pp. 31-41.

Rosenbush, S., Crockett, R.O., Haddad, C. and Ewing, J. (2002), "The telecom depression: when will it end," *Business Week*, October 7, pp. 66–74.

Saporito, B. (2013), "Cabin pressure," *Time*, September 9, pp. 36–41.

Sparaco, P. (2011) "The crazy recipe," *Aviation Week and Space Technology*, May 30, p. 48.

Sparaco, P. (2012), "OLeary vs McCall," *Aviation Week and Space Technology*, May 7, p. 18.

USA Today (2007), "Southwest Airlines' fuel hedging pushes profits," USA Today Online, retrieved online January 9, 2008 from http://www.usatodat.com/pt/cp t?action=cpt&title=Southwest+Airlines%27.

Weber, H.R. (2008), "Delta pilots say no deal with Northwest," WTOPnews. com, March 18, retrieved online March 24, 2009 from http://www.wtopnews. com/?nid=111&sid=1347940.

Wolf, S.M. (1995), "Where Do We Go from Here: A Management Perspective," in Peter Cappelli (ed.) *Airline Labor Relations in the Global Era: The New Frontier*, ILR Press, Cornell, NY, pp. 18–23.

Zellner, W. (2002), "What's weighing down the big carriers?" *Business Week*, April 29, p. 91.

Website

Business Travel Coalition, http://www.businesstravelcoalition.com/

Chapter 16
Seeking Liberal Markets

Learning Objectives

After reading this chapter, you should have a good understanding of:
- LO1: the evolution of the Open Skies concept.
- LO2: the issues dividing the US and EU on liberalization.
- LO3: the potential winners and losers in liberalization.
- LO4: the prospects for continuing liberalization around the world.

Key Terms, Concepts, and People

ECA	TCAA (CAA)	Right of Establishment
AEA	Winners and losers	
Single Sky	Open Skies	Cabotage

Truly Open Skies

Europeans complained for many years that open skies was an "American term" that did not in fact truly involve open markets, but represented an extension of what bilateral air service agreements have always been about, namely negotiating to achieve maximum national benefit (Lobbenberg, 1994; Sorenson, 1998). In other words, they did not believe the rhetoric of Open Skies; they charged that Open Skies bilaterals were simply another attempt by the US to dominate their aviation systems without allowing them an equal opportunity to compete (Wallerstein, 1991). In the aftermath of World War II, the inequality was largely due to external factors relating to the destruction of commercial aircraft and aviation infrastructure. The inequality after European infrastructure and economic recovery was created by a bilateral system that initially granted US carriers greater access to European markets than European airlines receive into the US, often US carrier had better access than EU carriers into their own markets. This trend continued with the US push for Open Skies since Open Skies included unlimited fifth freedom right. For example, the bilateral system with individual Open Skies EU countries prevented European companies from taking full advantage of the European market, but allowed US carriers to string together the fifth freedom (beyond) rights to fly all over the European market in a more profitable way (ECA, 2000).

Given these perceived disparities in access, it was not surprising that many of the European nations that had been opposed to an open sky in Chicago (1944) began to call for more liberal markets in aviation as the European Single Sky approached. Further, they wanted issues of ownership and domestic market access addressed to eliminate remaining barriers within the aviation market place. When aviation barriers dropped in the EU with the 1997 Single Sky, they proclaimed the US exercise of fifth freedom rights "cabotage" and wanted the same privileges in the US (Sorenson, 1998). The European vision to extend the single aviation market created by the 15-nation EU across the Atlantic was embodied in the so-called Transatlantic Common Aviation Area (TCAA) proposal. At the time that the TCAA was first proposed, the rhetoric of liberalization was certainly in the "best interest" of European carriers. The question was whether it would benefit US and Canadian carriers, individual consumers, and local communities on both sides of the Atlantic. The events of September 11 took this transatlantic fight off of the table for a time, but the stakes were too high to leave it off for long and the US would eventually find a need for its EU allies. It would still be a long road to agreement. The year 2001 marked the signing of the Multilateral Agreement on the Liberalization of International Air Transportation (MALIAT). Negotiations began between the EU and US in 2003 with a final agreement completed in 2007. Even the March 30, 2008 start of the new multilateral EU–US Open Skies agreement was seen by the Europeans as only one step in a process toward an "Open Aviation Area" (EurActiv.com, 2008; EC, 2013). Ironically, the effects of the 2008 GFC have made it very difficult to determine if this agreement, decades in the making, has achieved it purpose, but talks continue with second stage talks beginning in 2010. Still, it is worth following this long journey to understand the issues and concerns in international liberalization.

The Long Road

In a 1995 policy paper on EU external aviation relations, the Association of European Airlines (AEA) put forth a proposal for a new regulatory framework between Europe and the US. The following year the Council of Ministers for the EU issued a mandate to the Commission's work toward establishing a "Common Aviation Area (CAA)." This CAA proposed that air carriers from both sides of the Atlantic be allowed to provide their services within a common commercial framework that ensured competition on a fair and equal basis within an equivalent regulatory regime (AEA, 1999). Under a TCAA, the US and Europe were expected to "harmonize" the following key areas: (1) rules governing market entry, access, and pricing; (2) rules governing airline ownership and the right of establishment; (3) rules governing competitive behavior and policies; and (4) rules governing leased aircraft.

Entry, access, and pricing

The basic objective of a TCAA (or CAA as it is now called) was to insure unrestricted commercial opportunities allowing carriers (and market forces) to determine routes, markets, capacity, and pricing without discrimination anywhere within the countries party to a TCAA agreement. Under the proposal, a distinction would be made between TCAA countries as a group and third parties with whom the traditional bilateral air service agreements would still apply. In other words, the two parties to the bilateral would be the TCAA (as a single unit) and the third party. This was a general principle behind economic integration. One of the problems of a free trade area (FTA) (the first step in economic integration) is that although members of the FTA have eliminated internal barriers to the movement of goods, the external tariff barriers to third-party goods remains in place and may vary in such a way that third parties can benefit by selectively entering the FTA country with the most favorable tariff conditions and then gaining access from there to other member states (Hill, 2001). The AEA suggested a phased approach to establishing this new single aviation area that is similar to the EU liberalization that took place through a series of three packages (Chapter 10). The envisioned approach would have allowed EU countries the flexibility to negotiate with the US subject to achieving some minimum standards set by the overall parties (AEA, 1999).

Ownership and right of establishment

The right of establishment is a legal term relating to the national control of companies. In other words, TCAA proposed granting firms that are: (1) majority owned or controlled by nationals of any of the TCAA parties or their governments or (2) incorporated and have their principle place of business within the territory of a TCAA country equal rights and recognition. With the right of establishment comes the end of "foreign national" restrictions on cross-border mergers, acquisitions, and entry. Under the second definition, airlines from third-party countries could begin operations in a TCAA country and then gain the right to operate throughout TCAA airspace. It would, of course, be possible under option one for a country to apply for membership into the TCAA, thus opening up their aviation system to all TCAA members in the process.

Competition policy

In Chapter 12, the issue of anti-trust or competitiveness policy was discussed as it related to airlines and strategic alliances. From that discussion, it should be clear that although the basic concepts underlying both the US and EU policies are similar, the application of these policies has differed in a number of significant ways. The AEA (1999) suggested that common standards should be developed in the following areas:

a. basic criteria for granting exemptions, and in particular means of reconciling the relevant criteria of the EC competition rules and the US concept of the "public interest;"
b. the definition of the "relevant market;"
c. the concept of "market power" as distinct from "market share;"
d. the notion of "predatory behavior;"
e. the question what "essential facilities" airlines would have to share with each other;
f. the treatment of airline cooperative arrangements;
g. the nature of remedies and sanctions to be applied (AEA, 1999).

The AEA argued in their proposal that strategic alliances whose objective was to create TCAA airlines that were competitive in world markets should be considered by both EU and US standards to contribute to economic progress, the interests of consumers, and the interest of the public at large (AEA, 1999). Further, they believed that codesharing, blocked space, franchising, and other cooperative agreements including activities involving tariff (fare) consultation for interline purposes, should be considered indispensable to the operation of strategic networks.

Leasing aircraft

There are differences between the US and Europe over the question of wet leasing aircraft. The US prevents US airlines from wet leasing non-US registered aircraft from other airlines and requires that non-US leasers have route authority for the operation concerned. EU rules require registration in a member state but permit this to be waived for short-term lease arrangements or other exceptional circumstances. The Association recommended that the US–EU rules be modified to allow any TCAA carrier to lease from or to any other TCAA carrier and that if third-party leasing were permitted, a maximum percentage of fleet standard be set. These rules would be contingent upon all parties complying with established safety standards.

Raising objections

The European Cockpit Association (ECA), which represented over 2,600 pilots from EU countries, endorsed TCAA with several reservations. First, they were concerned that relaxing ownership and leasing rules might create "Flags of Convenience" in aviation similar to those that developed in the maritime industry. In the US, for example, the Jones Act requires that ships carrying cargo from one domestic port to another be built, maintained, and operated (and flagged) in the US, but does not have such a requirement for ships coming from a foreign port. There are a number of countries that allow open registries whereby ships owned by individuals or corporations in other countries may be flagged in their country rather than the country of the ship's owner. Critics have charged that the practice of open registries allowed owners to avoid the fees, taxes, safety requirements, and manning rules of their home country and posed a risk to crews, the marine environment, and the ports into which they enter (Morris, 1996; Ryan, 1996). If TCAA included countries with safety and social standards below EU/US standards, there would be a cost incentive to flag aircraft in that country leading to lowered safety standards for airline operations and the shifting of operations to CAAs offering lower taxes, wages, benefits, and so on. This would obviously affect employment opportunities, local tax bases, and merchants in affected areas. The ECA also expressed concern at that time that liberalized ownership would result in the conversion or merging of alliances into mega-airlines dominated by US carriers with route structures and associated carriers manipulated for cost-cutting purposes (ECA, 2000).

TCAA did not provoke a significant reaction from US aviation groups. Labor delegates at a 1999 aviation summit in the US cautioned against rapid change and any liberalization that failed "to maintain the integrity of companies and to protect jobs" (Ott, 1999: 45). Their reasoning and concerns were very similar to the position stated by the ECA, although they did not even offer a conditional endorsement of TCAA. By and large, US airlines ignored the proposal. The US government was lukewarm to TCAA, although Rodney Slater, then US Secretary of Transportation, committed the US to examining the proposal. This US reaction of "committing to study the issues" was repeated when the President and CEO of Air Canada, Robert Milton, proposed a single aviation market for North America saying that he "urged the two governments to build on the success story of the 1995 Canada–US Open Skies Agreement by progressively removing all restrictions in order to arrive at a fully integrated, common air transport market with the United States" (Melnbardis, 2001: 1). Reacting to the Canadian Proposal, American Airlines and United Airlines indicated that they supported the principle of liberalized air policy, but needed time to study the specifics (Chase and McArthur, 2001).

The whole matter of Atlantic liberalization fell by the wayside with the events of September 11. Not only did the US feel that it had more important issues to consider but security considerations suddenly loomed much larger on everyone's agenda. The fact that US airlines were particularly hard hit by these events did not encourage US airlines or the government that represented them in efforts to open up the US market. The US Congress became increasingly concerned about issues of foreign ownership and control of important US industries and assets. US carriers would struggle back to profitability by 2006 only to be hit with rising fuel prices and the GFC. Still, the idea of a CAA persisted.

Balancing Acts

Before looking at possible effects of a CAA and potential winners and losers in an open aviation market, it might be instructive to examine why it might make sense for the US to consider it (aside from the political pressure of EU allies). First, the TCAA/CAA is the first time that the US has been officially asked (or to consider) trading roughly equivalent domestic markets. A quick look back at Table 9.2 shows that the Open Skies agreements of the past essentially involved countries with significantly smaller domestic markets. Ideology aside, it never made "economic sense" for the US to trade access to its large domestic market for the domestic markets of Singapore, The Netherlands, or even Germany. Given some of the differences between US and EU transportation markets noted in Chapter 10, namely more developed EU intermodal competition and charter market and the higher domestic departures of the US (Sinha, 2001), these markets appear to be roughly similar in size, particularly if we add in the estimated population of Canada (CIA Factbook, 2013). This "equivalent markets" argument raised a question about the proposed single North American market proposed by Air Canada. While the two countries have roughly equal land masses (9,976,140 square kilometers for Canada and 9,629,091 for the US), there is a major difference in the population size (CIA Factbook, 2013). Much of the Canadian land mass is in the far north where the Canadian government has declared many communities in need of essential services, particularly in winter months when air service is a vital link to the outside world. US carriers had little interest in gaining access to these markets and under Open Skies had already gained access to the southern Canadian markets. Air Canada, on the other hand, had a great deal to gain from single markets. The Air Transport Association of Canada, which represents a number of Canadian carriers, supported the idea of "modified sixth-freedom rights" between the US and Canada, but this wording appeared to be only a limited endorsement of the single market concept and probably reflected the view of "other Canadian" carriers not Air Canada. The chairman of WestJet Airlines was on record as opposing the concept of a single market arguing that it would do nothing to lessen the grip of Air Canada on the domestic market and would put Canadian carriers at a disadvantage since they pay much more for fuel than their US counterparts (Chase and McAuthur, 2001). In short, it did not appear that any North American carrier has anything to gain except Air Canada. While the Canadian government considered a single market approach as a way to deflect consumer complaints over the decision to allow Air Canada to become a monopoly, the US government was always likely to receive a great deal of pressure from the US airline industry to oppose a deal. A second issue that argued in favor of CAA was that the safety and security levels of European carriers are equal, if not higher, than their US counterparts. European airports have historically incorporated security designs and policies that limited access in gate areas to ticketed passengers, encouraged bag matching, and other sophisticated screening techniques. In a post-9/11 environment, this was an important consideration and a CAA could facilitate closer cooperation on improving these areas. Finally, the EC was committed to implementing a multilateral aviation approach for the EU to end the current system of bilateral air service agreements. The Commission launched a case in 1998 against eight member states with US Open Skies agreements claiming that these agreements breached single market rules because they disadvantaged other member nations. Further, they charged that the bilateral agreements infringed on the EU external competence in foreign affairs. In January 2002, the European Court of Justice ruled that these countries had broken EU laws in signing such bilateral. The key issue is the nationality requirements (contained in Article 52) and Article 307 of the EC treaty that requires states to make every effort to amend international agreements that violate EC law. In effect, the EU had declared themselves a single market for external purposes and reiterated their belief that extensive fifth freedom rights exercised by US carriers were cabotage. The Commission demanded reciprocal access to the US for their carriers as well as ownership privileges. A 2005 compromise was opposed by the US Congress, throwing the matter back to the respective governments, but the EU was clearly determined to keep the pressure on the US concerning liberalization.

Winners and Losers

Calculations were and continue to be made on both sides of the Atlantic about the costs and benefits of single markets. These calculations included consumer groups, airlines, employee organizations, local communities, and national governments. In this section, the issues relating to these group-specific calculations are discussed. The next section will discuss any evidence of effects on various groups as a result of the EU–US Open Skies.

Consumers

General economic theory suggests that consumers benefit from having more choices of products, services, and firms. Single aviation markets do promise to broaden the choices of consumers. However, the same problems may arise in this next phase of liberalization that occurred in earlier deregulation efforts. First, the heightened competition of earlier periods could be jeopardized by failures to enforce laws on predatory behavior and merger/acquisition leading to high failures rates of "new entrants" and mergers that result in the concentration of the market in a few select carriers. Second, consumers in some markets may lose service as US–EU carriers redeploy their fleets to new, more lucrative markets. Given the cost structure of the entering international carriers, they would likely concentrate on higher yield markets with the all-important business travelers. Markets vacated by these carriers in Europe would be open for LCC entry. In fact, given the changes in Europe caused by the expansion of Ryanair, EU carriers might relish competition in the US. In any event, neither the North Americans nor Europeans are likely to drop their right to insure that essential services are provided to local communities. The difficulty lies in harmonizing the implementation of the rules and policies that define of relevant markets, frequency requirements, carrier types, and so on in the determination of essential services.

Airlines

Sorting out the potential winners and losers among the airlines is in large part a function of two factors—relative costs and relative service levels. The last major study to examine the cost competitiveness of international airlines was conducted by Oum and Yu (1998). They examined the cost of airline inputs (labor, fuel, aircraft, capital, and materials) and the revenue of airlines (outputs) from passengers, freight, and mail to determine the efficiency of carriers and their cost competitiveness. As mentioned briefly in Chapter 9, almost 30 years of deregulation in US markets created carriers with much lower costs and higher levels of productivity and cost competitiveness. In the Oum and Yu (1998) study, only British Airways and KLM were close to achieving a level of cost competitiveness comparable to their US counterparts. Of course, if many of the European carriers began operating in the US they would likely be able to reduce many of these costs, at least in US operations, since fuel prices, the benefits component of labor costs, and many related fees tend to be lower in the US. The Oum and Yu (1998) study did not consider the low-cost European carriers such as Ryanair and EasyJet who may well have cost structures more comparable to Southwest in the US. From a firm point-of-view, single markets increase strategic flexibility by allowing firms to move assets as well as perform work where it makes the most sense to do so from a cost and logistical standpoint. This flexibility is precisely the concern of labor groups, as we will see in a minute. The fact that European airlines recovered more quickly from September 11 and were able to post profits well in advance of their US counterparts probably alleviated the old concern about US carrier dominance in alliances, possible mergers, and so on, but 2008 and the slow recovery in Europe have again given US carriers a slight upper hand in performance.

The second issue is relative service levels between US and European carriers. At least some of the cost differences between US–EU carriers are probably the result of the generally higher levels of service provided by EU carriers. In an environment where carriers are free to operate anywhere within the single market, there are some carriers that may clearly be disadvantaged by high-cost structures and poor quality. At the margin, consumers will decide the issue of price and service level. In general, the trend in the US has been toward viewing air transportation as a basic commodity that is cheap and relatively indistinguishable from one provider to another. Indications are that European markets are beginning to move more in this direction with the success of their own LCCs such as Ryanair. Nationality issues aside, single markets increase the competition on international routes where service level issues are considered more important and would tend to favor the European carriers.

Labor groups

Single markets open up the very real possibility that firms will shift operations from one region to another or utilize labor from one area over another as a means of reducing costs. This shift has occurred in other liberalizing industries and is very likely to occur in aviation. Most at risk may be pilots who account for more labor costs than do mechanics and flight attendants. With or without single markets, however, the losses of recent years will force carriers and labor groups to make some very hard choices in their efforts to bring costs and capacity down to competitive levels. It should be noted that the cost of labor is not the only issue that managers should consider; the productivity of labor can balance this cost in the long run. Oum and Yu (1998) found that while Thai Airways had input costs that were 52.1 percent lower (22.4 percent of which were attributable to labor) than American Airlines, however, in terms of overall efficiency (outputs to inputs), Thai was 42.9 percent less efficient. A higher cost but more efficient labor force can still be cost competitive. In many western countries, productivity gains have been achieved through the adoption of improved information systems, but productivity can also be improved through more flexible work rules, attention to work flows, cross-functional team implementation, and other redesign options. Bankruptcy has allowed most of the major US carriers to reduce their labor (and pension) costs even further. US network carriers removed 13 million seats of capacity just in 2012 and US consolidation has probably created redundancy that directly eliminated jobs (Saporito, 2013).

Local communities

If we define local communities broadly as nations, then there are clearly risks involved in single markets. High-cost, low-productivity, and low-service carriers will probably not survive without government assistance, but the EU has already seen this effect with integration and has been forced to deal with national carriers seeking government subsidies to survive in a more competitive environment. The EU faced this issue over Sabena in Belgium and most recently over flag carriers in Eastern Europe. More narrowly defined, there may be some city and city-pair markets that will see reduced service as carriers adjust their route structure toward higher margin routes. Many of these markets could continue to receive service from LCCs, but the quality and frequency of service is likely to change for some communities.

National governments

There is a saying that "all politics is local." Given the historic attachment of localities to their airlines and the strategic flexibility that single markets give to airlines, there will be pressure on governments to intervene in the process to influence local outcomes. Economists talk about long-run equilibriums and structural adjustments; politicians are concerned about the next election. Predicting the outcome of this political wrangling is far more difficult, particularly when questions of local, national, and supranational jurisdiction, responsibilities, and calculations come into play.

Evidence to Date

In 2013, the Centre for Aviation (CAPA) released a report on the EU–US Open skies market five years after the agreement went into effect. Traffic growth has been modest to flat after a 6.2 percent drop in 2009, although North Atlantic traffic growth was close to world rates for 2008. Load factors and yields have improved since 2009. While CAPA credits any modest improvements to the Open Skies, it argues that the GFC had a dampening effect on expected results. What appears clear it that the mega-alliances now dominate traffic across the North Atlantic, controlling 83 percent of the capacity. The American Enterprise Institute review in 2010 was far harsher in tone, noting that EU consumers could find far cheaper airfare there than consumers in many US markets. The reason for this disparity, according to the report, is the US opposition to cabotage and foreign ownership (Milke, 2010). Now that the US industry has succeeded in consolidating down to three key players, it is even more unlikely that they will embrace new competition from EU carriers. Unfortunately, it is not clear that any of the cited benefits of "truly open-skies" are any different than the claims issued when the EU–US Open Skies was first signed. If there is no clear sign of consumer benefits, there is also little sign of the sometimes dire predictions of labor, small communities, or supporter of the home-country airline (at least none attributable to the Open Skies).

Moving Ahead

After years of negotiations and setbacks, the EU and US finally reached a multilateral agreement to open up the transatlantic in 2008, just in time for the GFC. The agreement did remove restrictions on the number of carriers allowed to fly transatlantic routes and allowed carriers to fly from any EU city to any American city and onward to a third destination. From the US perspective, it achieved one of its major goals in opening up Heathrow airport, but not until the long awaited Terminal 5 was opened. The Europeans did not get the right of cabotage in the US, but the restrictions of the Fly America Act which required all federal government travel to occur on US carriers was lifted in 2007 (US General Services Administration, 2013). Ownership and cabotage remain critical issues for debate between the EU and US in the second stage. While government officials on both sides suggested that the new deal would create 80,000 jobs and generate 12 billion euros in economic benefits, the evidence remains unclear (CAPA, 2013; EurActiv, 2007). Of course, some industry watchers never expected much beyond a few introductory low fares and new flights targeted to the already well-trafficked, high-yield markets (Wilen, 2008). Until the economies on both sides of the Atlantic improve, there may be no way to assess the benefits of this long-awaited agreement.

In short, there was no "Big Bang" approach to transatlantic liberalization or "Big Bang" benefits to move the liberalization forward more rapidly. While the

Europeans would have preferred an agreement that went farther than the current one, most EU groups were satisfied with greater initial access. The US moved reluctantly on the issue given the lukewarm reception in the industry, feeling that they needed to appease the EU somewhat to gain support in other non-aviation areas. It is still too early, of course, to see how the process of harmonizing policies on predatory behavior and merger/acquisition will go or to access any benefits or costs, but it is not unreasonable to assume that there will be many years ahead before the skies clear.

Questions

1. What does Open Skies mean to the US? To the EU?
2. Explain the issue of right of establishment.
3. What was the TCAA proposal? Discuss its history and progress.
4. What role does competition policy play in liberalization?
5. Who stands to gain from open aviation markets? Who is likely to oppose them and why?
6. What evidence is there that the EU–US Open Skies agreement has produced positive benefits?

References

Association of European Airlines (AEA) (1999), "Towards a Transatlantic Common Aviation Area: AEA Policy Statement," September.

Centre for Aviation (CAPA) (2013), "The North Atlantic: the state of the market five years on from EU-US Open Skies," retrieved online January 23, 2014 from http://centreforaviation/analysis/the-north-atlantic-the-state-of -the-market-five-years-on-fromeu-us-open-skies-100315.

Chase, S. and McAuthur, K. (2001), "US warm to proposed increased air competition," *Global Interactive*, December 8.

CIA Factbook (2013), retrieved online January 23, 2014 from www.odci.goc/cia/publications/factbook.

European Cockpit Association (ECA) (2000), *From EASA to TCAA: The Flight Crews View on a New Regulatory Framework in Aviation*, ECA, Brussels.

EurActiv (EU News, Policy Positions) (2008), "EU-US Open Skies Agreement," retrieved online January 23, 2014 from http://www.euractiv.com/en/transport/eu-us-open-skies.

European Commission (EC) (2013), "International aviation: United States," retrieved online January 23, 2014 from http://ec.europa.eu/transport/modes/air/international_aviation/country_index/united_states_en.htm.

Hill, C.W. (2001), *Global Business* (2nd ed.), Irwin-McGrawHill, Boston, MA.

Lobbenberg, A. (1994), "Government relations on the North Atlantic: a case study of five Europe–USA relationships," *Journal of Air Transport Management*, vol. 1 (1), pp. 47–62.

Melnbardis, R. (2001), "Air Canada wants open U.S.–Canada air market," Reuters Newswire, December 6.

Milke, M. (2010), "Economics: regulation outlook," retrieved online January 23, 2014 from http://www.aei.org/article/economics/open-skies/.

Morris, J. (1996), "Flags of convenience give owners a paper refuge," *Houston Chronicle* online edition, retrieved online February 16, 2007 from www.chron.com.

Ott, J. (1999), "Aviation summit yields EU plan for open market," *Aviation Week & Space Technology*, December 13, pp. 43–45.

Oum, T.H. and Yu, C. (1998), *Winning Airlines: Productivity and Cost Competitiveness of the World's Major Airlines*, Kluwer Academic Publishers, Boston, MA.

Ryan, G.J. (1996), "Testimony by George J. Ryan, President-Lake Carriers' Association," Presented before the House Subcommittee on Coast Guard and Maritime Transportation, June 12, Washington, DC.

Saporito, B. (2013), "Cabin pressure," *Time Magazine*, September 9, pp. 36–41.

Sinha, D. (2001), *Deregulation and Liberalization of the Airline Industry: Asia, Europe, North America, and Oceania*, Ashgate Publishing, Aldershot, UK.

Sorenson, F. (1998), "Open Skies in Europe," FAA Commercial Aviation Forecast Conference Proceedings: Overcoming Barriers to World Competition and Growth, March 12–13, Washington, DC, pp. 125–131.

Wallerstein, I. (1991), *Geopolitics and Geoculture: Essays on the Changing World-System*, Cambridge University Press, Cambridge.

Wilen, J. (2008), "Open Skies: more flights, same fares," retrieved online March 29, 2008 from http://biz.yahoo.com/ap/080326/open_skies.html.

US General Services Administration (2013), Fly America Act, retrieved online October 18, 2013 from http://www.gsa.gov/portal/content/103191?utm_source=OGP&utm_medium=print-radio&utm_term=openskies&utm_campaign=shortcuts.

Chapter 17
Spreading the Promise

Learning Objectives

After reading this chapter, you should have a good understanding of:
- LO1: the issues that have hindered aviation development in Africa, Latin America, and other developing regions.
- LO2: how the regional/country issues have been addressed.
- LO3: what the international community might do to help.
- LO4: how these actions would change the historic nature of the international aviation industry.

Key Terms, Concepts, and People

Flight Safety Foundation	Yamoussoukro Declaration	Air Afrique
Asymmetric liberalization	GATS	Open Skies
Waiver of nationality		

Problems and Promises

Aviation and the globalization movement of which it is an integral part promised to transform domestic and global economies by linking distant communities in an ever-shrinking, complex web of interaction. Along these links flow a vast variety of goods, services, and people. As the flow increases, so does the income, standard of living, and general welfare of the people connected to this great web. This is the promise of globalization and aviation, but the reality is that there are a number of countries and regions around the world that have yet to collect on the promise. Two areas in particular have yet to experience the full benefits of this transformation: Africa and Latin America. These areas have not yet been fully linked to the rest of the world, either virtually through the internet or physically through transportation. A third area, the Middle East, has become a hub for traffic between Europe and Asia and is the home to some of the fastest-growing airlines in the world. The purpose of this chapter is to explore the reasons why some areas (and countries) have not yet benefited from civil aviation. It will identify the issues and problems holding back progress. It will also address various means by which the world community and national governments can work to spread the promise.

Africa—Understanding the Problems

Africa is the second largest continent in the world and possesses the population base and the geographically challenging terrain to make it ideal for air transportation. Unfortunately, these advantages are outweighed by a number of factors that have prevented the development of a sustainable civil aviation industry in most African nations. The first factor is the underdeveloped state of the national economies of most of Africa (Graham, 1995; Meredith, 2005; Taneja, 1988). As Table 17.1 demonstrates, the majority of the nations in Africa are poor. In a 2002 report, the World Bank Group noted that over 50 percent of the population in all of the 18 nations for which data was available were living on US$2 or less a day (World Bank Group, 2002). The report estimated that African economies would need to grow at an average of 7 percent a year to halve the poverty level by 2015. According to the 2005 World Bank African Development Indicators report (World Bank, 2005), the average income in Sub-Saharan Africa, excluding South Africa, was US$342. Twenty-four of the 32 countries with the lowest level of human development were also in Africa. There was some good news in this report, namely that net aid had increased 40 percent in 2003 and debt service relief rose to US$43 billion (World Bank, 2005). The World Bank's new twice-yearly publication, *Africa's Pulse* (World Bank, 2012), has reported in 2013 that the average Sub-Saharan growth rate was forecast to be 4.9 percent with a few of the countries in the region growing at almost 6 percent. Private investment, as well as infrastructure projects funded by China, Brazil, and India, have helped increase GDP in a region still relying primarily on raw material exports (World Bank, 2013). This is certainly progress for the region, but there is still a long way to go.

The lack of aviation infrastructure is reflected in a number of ways. First, there is a persisting problem of aviation safety. In 2002, the Flight Safety Foundation reported that Africa had the highest level of accidents per departure of any region in the world at nearly 9.8 accidents per one million departures, compared to a world average of 1.2 accidents per one million departures. This rate of accidents is attributed to poor training for pilots, controllers, and regulatory officials, poor to non-existent radar coverage, high numbers of non-precision approaches, and non-enforced or non-existent legislation (Phillips, 2002). A decade later, IATA (2013) has reported the accident rate at 10.85 accidents per million flight hours, compared to a world average of two. In other words, there is still little or no progress in the safety areas. IATA, working with ICAO, developed the African Strategic Safety Improvement Plan 2012–2015 as well as the IATA Operational Safety Audit System to help improve airline safety (ETN, 2013). It remains to be seen if this and programs by ICAO and other world governments will finally impact the safety numbers in Africa. One problem is the funding mechanism for aviation activity. In many developed nations, revenues generated by aviation activity are placed in designated funds for the upgrade of infrastructure, however, in Africa this is generally not true; aviation revenues go into the general coffers and are spent on other needs (Phillips, 2002).

Table 17.1   Part 1: Information on African countries (A–K)

Country	Area*	Population**	Airports (Paved) ***	GDP $****
Algeria	2,381,741	38,087,812	157 (64)	7,300
Angola	1,246,700	18,565,269	176 (31)	6,100
Benin	112,622	9,877,292	6 (1)	1,600
Botswana	581,730	2,127,825	74 (10)	15,700
Burkina Faso	274,200	17,812,961	23 (2)	1,400
Burundi	27,830	1,060,714	7 (1)	600
Cameroon	475,440	22,534,532	33 (11)	2,300
Cape Verde	4,033	531,046	9 (9)	4,400
Central African Republic	622,984	5,166,510	39 (2)	900
Chad	1,284,000	11,193,452	59 (9)	2,500
Comoros	2,235	752,288	4 (4)	1,300
Congo, Democratic Republic of the	2,344,858	75,507,308	198 (26)	400
Congo, Republic of the	342,000	4,574,099	27 (8)	4,600
Cote d'Ivoire	322,463	22,400,835	27 (7)	1,700
Djibouti	23,200	792,198	13 (3)	2,600
Egypt	1,001,450	85,294,388	83 (72)	6,500
Equatorial Guinea	28,051	704,001	7 (6)	26,500
Eritrea	117,600	6,233,682	13 (4)	700
Ethiopia	1,104,300	93,877,025	57 (17)	1,300
Gabon	267,667	1,640,286	44 (14)	18,100
Gambia, The	11,295	1,883,051	1 (1)	1,900
Ghana	238,533	25,199,609	10 (7)	3,300
Guinea	245,857	11,176,026	16 (4)	1,100
Guinea-Bissau	36,125	1,660,870	8 (2)	1,200
Kenya	580,367	44,037,656	197 (16)	1,800

Second, there is not yet a substantial internal demand for air transportation due to the general level of poverty. Almost all of Africa's airlines remain wholly or partly state-owned. CAPA estimates that the financial subsidies provided to African airlines by their respective governments totals over USD$2.5 billion. The Nigerian government is even planning to relaunch a national airline despite the

Table 17. 2   Information on African countries (L–Z)

Country	Area*	Population**	Airports (Paved)***	GDP $****
Lesotho	30,355	1,936,181	24 (3)	2,100
Liberia	111,369	3,989,703	29 (2)	700
Libya	1,759,540	6,002,347	146 (68)	11,900
Madagascar	587,041	22,599,098	83 (26)	900
Malawi	118,484	16,777,547	32 (7)	800
Mali	1,240,192	15,968,882	25 (8)	1,100
Mauritania	1,030,700	3,437,610	30 (9)	2,100
Mauritius	2,040	1,322,238	5 (2)	15,400
Morocco	446,550	32,649,130	55 (31)	5,200
Mozambique	799,380	24,096,669	98 (21)	1,200
Namibia	824,292	2,182,852	112 (19)	7,800
Niger	1,267,000	16,899,327	30 (10)	800
Nigeria	923,768	174,507,539	54 (40)	2,700
Rwanda	26,338	12,012,589	7 (4)	1,400
Saint Helena, Ascension, and Tristan da Cunha	308	7,754	1 (1)	7,800
Sao Tome and Principe	964	186,817	2 (2)	2,100
Senegal	196,722	13,300,410	20 (9)	2,000
Seychelles	455	90,846	14 (7)	25,000
Sierra Leone	71,740	5,612,685	8 (1)	1,300
Somalia	637,657	10,251,568	61 (6)	600
South Africa	1,219,090	48,601,098	566 (144)	11,300
South Sudan	644,329	11,090,104	85 (3)	1,100
Sudan	1,861,484	34,847,910	74 (16)	2,500
Swaziland	17,364	1,403,362	14 (2)	5,700
Tanzania	947,300	48,261,942	166 (10)	1,600
Togo	56,785	7,154,237	8 (2)	1,100
Tunisia	163,610	10,835,873	29 (15)	9,700
Uganda	241,038	34,758,809	47 (5)	1,400
Western Sahara	266,000	538,811	6 (3)	2,500
Zambia	752,618	14,222,233	88 (8)	1,700
Zimbabwe	390,757	13,182,908	196 (17)	600

Source: CIA Factbook as of February 10, 2014
* Square Km. **Estimated July 2013 figures ***Data from 2013 ****Estimated 2012

presence of several private carriers in the market (CAPA, 2013a). These subsidies support inefficient carriers and act as a barrier to new entrants. Further, traffic patterns in the region have reflected Africa's colonial past running north to south, unfortunately placing African airlines at the wrong end of the route, that is, principal flows originate in the northern, wealthy nations of Europe where passengers tend to fly on European national carriers (Graham, 1995). In order for African carriers to compete effectively with these European carriers they must provide equal or superior service in a number of areas including flight punctuality, in-flight service, superior aircraft, comfortable seats, clean cabins, seats, washrooms, good food, efficient reservation systems, competitive pricing, good check-in, attractive frequent flyer programs, and superior first and business class accommodations. At least seven of these areas are heavily dependent on the quality of the aircraft. Unfortunately, the aircraft of many African airlines are aging and investment for new aircraft is often non-existent. These aging aircraft also do not meet the noise restrictions imposed by many countries and are, therefore, not eligible to land at many international airports. Aircraft leasing is not well developed in Africa, making the acquisition of new aircraft difficult for many carriers who might find this a preferred way to modernize their fleets (Abeyratne, 1998).

Addressing the issues

Given the lack of domestic demand, the need to compete globally with larger, better established carriers, and the limited funding for aviation development, African nations have attempted to join together. In 1961, ten African nations signed the Treaty on Air Transport in Africa, popularly known as the Yaounde Treaty. Under Article 77 and 79 of the Chicago Convention, which provides for joint or international operating organizations, these nations established Air Afrique to operate international service between Contracting States and other nations and to provide domestic service within the territories of Contracting States. The second major event in African aviation was the Yamoussoukro Declaration on a New African Air Transport Policy (1988). The Yamoussoukro Declaration committed African States to achieving the total integration of their airlines through the liberal exchange of air traffic rights, use of an unbiased CRS, and other joint aviation infrastructure developments. The first phase of the Declaration was expected to last two years and result in recommendations for integrating African airlines with the rest of the world. Phase two was to be a three-year effort dedicated to the commercial aspects of aviation including the integration of CRS, joint purchasing of spare parts, maintenance, and overhaul equipment, training of personnel, and so on. In Phase three, African carriers were to be integrated into a consortium of competitive entities that would bring about sustained progress in air transport in Africa (Abeyratne, 1998: 34). Originally, the Declaration was to be implemented in two years, but this was extended to 2006 and has yet to be completely implemented. Progress has been made in a number of areas including the establishment of the Air Tariff Coordination Forum of Africa to assist airlines in adapting to international air tariff policies, the opening up of South Africa to intra-African aviation, increased fifth freedom right, and more cross-border activity, but more challenges remain (Abeyratne, 1998; Kajange, 2009).

Challenging the promise in Africa

Unfortunately, two areas in which Africa has not made significant progress is the integration of airlines and a single aviation sky. Air Afrique, one of the oldest jointly owned airlines, declared bankruptcy in 2002 after years of financial crisis. The company's troubles were blamed on (1) the difficulty of managing an airline owned by 11 states, and (2) Air Afrique mismanagement (BBC News, 2002a). One area of mismanagement cited by critics was the fact that many people with family links to government members and senior officials were allowed to travel free (BBC News 2002b). Other efforts at joint ownership have included East African Airlines, a joint venture between the governments of Kenya, Tanzania, and Uganda, which dissolved in the 1970s, and Alliance Air, jointly owned by South Africa, Uganda, and Tanzania, which ceased operations in 2000 (BBC News, 2002e). A joint service agreement between Air Mali and Cameroon Airlines also ended in 2001 (BBC News, 2002e). These failures should not be attributed solely to the joint nature of the airlines. Like young, small market carriers around the world, African airlines have often struggled. In 2000, Uganda Airlines went into liquidation after South African Airways withdrew its bid (M2 Communications Ltd, 2000). Nigeria Airways announced a cut of 1,000 employees in January 2002 in a "right-sizing exercise" (BBC News, 2002c). Ghana Airways announced in June 2002 that its debt had risen to US$160 million and creditors were threatening to seize assets (BBC News, 2002d). Following 9/11, the collapse of Air Afrique, Sabena, and general reductions in service seemed to create a vacuum in air transport service that appeared to leave room to support new carrier entry (BBC News, 2002b; BBC News, 2002g; BBC News, 2002f). Unfortunately, Africa One, one of the first to get off the ground, suspended operations a year after beginning service to restructure its operations (Wakabi, 2003). There was also a period in the mid-2000s where African governments moved toward privatization with carriers such as Air Tanzania, Kenya Airways, and Air Mali opening up to private investment (BBC News, 2002e; BBC News, 2002g; Godwin, 2002). In 2004, Virgin Nigeria was formed with Nigerian investors holding 51 percent of the equity and UK-based Virgin Atlantic holding the remaining 49 percent. The Virgin Group withdrew from the business in 2008–2010 and the carrier became Nigerian Eagle Airlines, then Air Nigeria. Air Nigeria ceased operations in 2012, leaving Nigeria without a national carrier once again (CAPA, 2013a). The latest new entrant in Africa is fastjet, which is hoping to expand out from bases in Tanzania to Kenya, Uganda, and West Africa, becoming a Pan-African LCC. Unfortunately, while liberalization in bilateral service agreements is taking place and regional Open Skies initiatives exist, these have often not been ratified (Flottau, 2012). In December 2007, Delta Airlines became the first major US carrier to offer direct flights between the US,

Dakar, Accra, Johannesburg, and Lagos (Delta Airlines, 2007). With the end of Singapore Airlines' direct flights to the US, the Atlanta–Johannesburg route became one of the longest nonstop flights in the industry. This first foray into Africa appeared to be the beginning of a new trend that would benefit consumers from both North America and Africa, however, several developments have called this trend into question. CAPA (2013b) recently questioned the economics of many ultra-long-range flights. Further, frequent cancellations and technical problems have caused aviation officials in Liberia and Ghana to issue letters to Delta asking to be allowed to conduct a safety audit on the US carrier (Sesay, 2013).

Prospects for the future

While traffic growth for the world as a whole declined 2.9 percent in 2001, Africa posted a 1.4 percent gain (ICAO, 2002). As of 2013, South African Airways (SAA) and Egyptair continued to be the top carriers in Africa, but SAA has struggled with profitability and a national base that is too far south to become a hub for the European–Asian traffic. Meanwhile, the Arab Spring has affected all of the Northern African carriers, reducing traffic and revenue. The East African market is currently highly competitive with Ethiopian Airlines and Kenya Airways competing aggressively for traffic. Unfortunately, they are often competing against the rapidly growing Middle Eastern carriers (CAPA, 2013a). Boeing's "Current Market Outlook 2013–2032" still places the demand for new aircraft in Africa at the bottom of a world list of regional demand, but estimates traffic growth to be 5.7 percent annually (Boeing, 2012). IATA has reported recent monthly growth rates in African traffic of 9.8 percent for May 2013 (IATA, 2013). Several developments are essential if Africa is to continue taking advantage of the current growth in traffic and increasing liberalization in international markets. First, the continent must make a commitment to improving aviation safety. Second, African nations need to continue the privatization of airlines. This privatization not only has the potential to create viable, competitive airlines, but removes the government incentives to offer preferential treatment to the state's flag carrier. Third, African nations need to continue to sign liberal bilateral agreements within Africa and with the outside world. The newly created carriers of Africa cannot survive if they are not granted access to outside markets.

Latin America and US Challenge

ICAO groups 32 nations into the Latin American region. Table 17.1 provides information on the countries in this group. All of Latin America's domestic markets recorded rapid growth in 2012. The Brazilian market had seen double-digit growth in 2010 and 2011, but slowed to a respectable 7 percent growth in 2012. Meanwhile, the Mexican market posted its first double-digit growth since 2007. The highest growth rates have been recorded on regional international routes. In fact, the intra-Latin American market has been one of the fastest growing in the world and almost all the growth has been captured by the full-service carriers. LCC penetration rates range from 33 and 43 percent depending on the domestic market, but are mainly focused on Brazil, Mexico and Colombia. In fact, the LCCs in these three countries are stimulating new traffic by adding cheap fares that draw consumers away from the bus service that has been the main transportation mode to secondary cities in Latin America. In Colombia, bus trips fell 8 percent while domestic flight rose 17 percent after VivaColombia began flying. In Brazil, 5 percent of the customers in 2011 were first-time flyers. Chile, home to Lan, is the only market not yet touched by LCC competition (CAPA, 2013c; Nicas, 2013).

Compared to Africa, Latin America and the Caribbean are more affluent (Table 17.3), support larger domestic markets, attract more tourists, and possess larger, more modern fleets of aircraft. Like Africa, the transportation network has tended

Table 17.3   Information on South American countries

Country	Area *	Population**	Airports (Paved)***	GDP $****
Argentina	2,780,400	42,610,981	1,138 (161)	17,900
Bolivia	1,098,581	10,461,053	855 (21)	5,000
Brazil	8,514,877	201,009,622	4,093 (698)	11,700
Chile	756,102	17,216,945	481 (90)	18,200
Colombia	1,138,910	45,745,783	836 (121)	10,700
Ecuador	283,561	15,439,429	432 (104)	10,200
El Salvador	21,041	6,108,590	68 (5)	7,300
Falkland Islands (Islas Malvinas)	12,173	3,140	7 (2)	55,400
Guatemala	108,889	14,373,472	291 (16)	5,200
Guyana	214,969	739,903	117 (11)	8,000
Honduras	112,090	8,448,465	103 (13)	4,700
Jamaica	10,991	2,909,714	28 (11)	8,900
Mexico	1,964,375	118,818,228	1,714 (243)	15,400
Nicaragua	130,370	5,788,531	147 (12)	4,400
Panama	75,420	3,559,408	117 (57)	15,400
Paraguay	406,752	6,623,252	799 (15)	6,100
Peru	1,285,216	29,849,303	191 (59)	10,600
Puerto Rico	13,790	3,645,648	29 (17)	16,300
Suriname	163,820	566,846	55 (6)	12,300
Uruguay	176,215	3,324,460	133 (11)	15,900
Venezuela	912,050	28,459,085	444 (127)	13,500

Source: CIA Factbook as of February 10, 2014
* Square Km. **Estimated July 2013 figures ***Data from 2013 ****Estimated 2012

to be dominated by old colonial patterns with international traffic focused primarily on North–South US routes and European links funneled through former imperial capitals (Graham, 1995). Latin America also tends to be far more urbanized than is true for Africa (Taneja, 1988). The most significant trend in recent years has been consolidation, especially cross-border. Table 17.4 shows the top ten airlines groups in Latin America as of March 2013, according to CAPA (2013c). Key merger activity includes LAN and TAM (LATAM Airlines group), Avianca and TACA, Gol and Webjet, Azul and TRIP. Domestically, the two most active countries for consolidation have been Brazil and Mexico. In Brazil, 99 percent of the market is now controlled by four carriers—two LCCs and two full-service carriers. The Mexican market saw six carriers (or carrier groups) cease operations between 2006 and 2010. Currently 95 percent of the market is controlled by Grupo Aeromexico and three LCCs (Interjet, Volaris, and VivaAerobus). The latter LCC is part of a new Viva Group backed by Ryanair founders Irelandia Aviation. The LATAM and Avianca-TACA are examples of cross-border mergers. LATAM now covers seven countries while Avianca-TACA operates in eight (CAPA, 2013c).

Table 17.4   Latin America top ten carriers

Ranking	Carrier	Country
1	Varig-Gol Airlines	Brazil
2	Tam Linhas Aereas	Brazil
3	Lan Airlines	Chile
4	Azul Airlines	Brazil
5	Avianca-TACA	Colombia/El Salvador
6	Aeromexico	Mexico
7	Copa Airlines	Panama
8	Interject	Mexico
9	Volaris	Mexico
10	Aerolineas Argentinas	Argentina

Source: CAPA (2013c) *World Aviation Yearbook 2013: Latin America*

Nuutinen (1993) identified three key problems that had faced Latin American carriers in the era before Open Skies (1992 onward). First, they were competing directly with aggressive US mega-carriers. With their large domestic base, highly sophisticated yield management systems, and lower-cost structures, these US mega-carriers presented their Latin American counterparts with a very difficult challenge. Second, the terms of US bilateral agreements were heavily biased in favor of US interests. The number of Latin American countries signing Open Skies treaties with the US has continued to increase in the first decade of the twenty-first century with Venezuela and Bolivia being notable exceptions (Chapter 9). The experience with liberalized markets was not initially kind to many Latin American carriers. In Chile, the first Latin country to sign an Open Skies agreement in 1997, domestic airlines suffered heavily at the hands of US competitors, American and United Airlines (Graham, 1995). This is far from the case in 2012 where Chile saw the fastest growth in Latin America at 19 percent and LATAM dominated the Chilean market with 76 percent of the domestic and 67 percent of the international market. Strong and sustained economic growth in Chile has combined with solid airline management to overcome the old US competition (CAPA, 2013c). Roughly 14 percent of American Airline's operating revenue came from Latin America during the 1990s and its Latin American route structure was considered by analysts to be the most valuable asset that American would have brought to a possible merger with US Airways. These routes were considered the most profitable in Latin America and it was thought that if US Airways could help American reduce its cost structure, they would be even better positioned (American Airlines, 2001; Yates, 2012). The third key issue noted by Nuutinen (1993) was that less than one-third of Latin America's carriers were state-owned heading into Open Skies. The fact that many Latin American governments rushed into the sale of loss-making carriers as part of the general shift toward market economies in the early 1990s did nothing to help these carriers adjust to the new realities of industry deregulation and liberalized international operations. In fact, this rush to privatize and throw open markets may have done as much or more to destabilize the Latin American carriers as US mega-carrier competition since many carriers started their life as private carriers undercapitalized and poorly managed.

Caribbean nations are a special case in Latin America and have struggled in international aviation. Of the 44 developing nations identified by the Commonwealth Secretariat/World Bank Joint Task Force (2000) as vulnerable small states, that is, with a population below 1.5 million people, 33 are in the Caribbean region. The United Nations Conference on Trade and Development also addressed the problem of small island developing states (SIDS). Both reports cited similar concerns and issues for these nations. According to the UN report, SIDS not only face problems associated with their smallness but are: (1) more susceptible and vulnerable to natural disasters; (2) geographically remote and dispersed; (3) ecologically fragile; and (4) constrained in terms of transportation and communication infrastructure (Abeyratne, 1999; UN General Assembly, 1993). Tourism is a key component in the economy of most of these nations. Given the generally inaccessible nature of SIDS, air transportation has been considered vital in developing tourism. Many of these nations would benefit from direct nonstop service from their major tourist markets; however, these nations tend to lack the fleet or market access to offer these services themselves, forcing their carriers to engage in island hopping (Abeyratne, 1999; Antoniou, 2001). Abeyratne (1999) has suggested that air services in these regions should qualify as natural monopolies and would, therefore, not benefit from the effects of competition, that is, improving efficiency, lowering costs and so on. Caribbean nations could, however, benefit from a greater focus on regional cooperation and/or integration in a number of areas like aviation.

Turbulence in the Middle East

The subheading "Turbulence in the Middle East" was as true for the second edition of this book as for the third. In fact, in some ways the turbulence may be even greater. Carriers outside the Gulf Coast have suffered during the disruptions of the Arab Spring, particularly the smaller state-owned carriers. However, for the 13 countries listed in Table 17.5 there have been some definite changes in the last five years. Aside from the political and social changes, the air carriers in this region have seen significant changes. One of the biggest is the continuing shift in connecting traffic. In just the last five years, three Middle Eastern hubs—Dubai, Doha, and Abu Dhabi—have seen a 60 percent increase in traffic compared to a 5 percent increase for European hubs and a 27 percent increase for Asian hubs. Dubai is now the third largest hub in the world and plans to overtake London Heathrow in the next five years to become the largest hub in the world (CAPA, 2013d). Like Africa, most aviation activities in this region are focused on international travel. In particular, Middle Eastern carriers have focused on long-haul business and premium travel, and given that 80 percent of the world population lies within a ten-hour flight from hubs such as Dubai, there continues to be room to grow. With continued weakness in Europe, there has been less pressure to resist sixth freedom rights for these carriers. For their part, the big three, Emirates, Qatar Airways, and Etihad, have decided to embrace relationships with other carriers, although each in its own way. Emirates has entered a partnership with Qantas that will shift the Australian carrier's European transit hub to Dubai from Singapore. Etihad has entered a partnership with Air France–KLM and continued to purchase equity stakes in a number of foreign carriers (Virgin Australia, Air Seychelles, Aer Lingus, Jet Airways). Qatar Airways has chosen to enter the Oneworld alliance (CAPA, 2013d; Feiler and Goodovitch, 1994).

The LCC sector has finally reached an overall capacity of 10 percent, but a number of bankruptcies have left the region with only four LCCs. One of the strongest and most consistent LCC is Air Arabia based in Sharjah, UAE. Saudi Arabia is a core market for this carrier with 66 weekly frequencies. Other areas of growth include South Asia, North Africa, and Europe. Saudi Arabia possesses a large domestic market, but government policy until recently gave Saudia a virtual monopoly. Two new carriers were approved to operate in Saudi Arabia in 2007, but neither one was able to grow domestic traffic or their share. The Saudi Arabian General Authority of Civil Aviation (GACA) has recently announced that Qatar Airways and Gulf Air will be allowed to launch domestic operations before the end of 2013. Unlike Saudi Arabia, many Middle Eastern carriers have essentially no domestic air services (Taneja, 1988). This would account for the tendency of Gulf Coast carriers to focus on international, connecting traffic.

In 1982, ICAO identified three attributes of the Middle East that affected the demand for air travel. First, there is a relatively large movement of people to, from, and within the area. Second, the population density of the area is comparable to North and Latin America. Third, two-thirds of the area's population lives in

Table 17.5   Information on selected Middle Eastern countries

Country	Area *	Population**	Airports (Paved)***	GDP $****
Bahrain	760	1,281,332	4 (4)	28,700
Iran	1,648,195	79,853,900	319 (140)	13,000
Iraq	438,317	31,858,481	102 (72)	7,000
Israel	20,770	7,707,042	47 (29)	33,900
Jordan	89,342	6,482,081	18 (16)	6,000
Kuwait	17,818	2,695,316	7 (4)	39,900
Lebanon	10,400	4,131,583	8 (5)	15,600
Oman	309,500	3,154,134	132 (13)	28,800
Qatar	11,586	2,042,444	6 (4)	100,900
Saudi Arabia	2,149,690	26,939,583	214 (82)	30,500
Syria	185,180	22,457,336	90 (29)	5,100
UAE	83,600	5,473,972	43 (25)	29,200
Yemen	527,968	25,338,458	57 (17)	2,300

Source: CIA Factbook as of February 10, 2014
* Square Km. **Estimated July 2013 figures ***Data from 2013 ****Estimated 2012

oil-producing nations. In fact, oil and tourism were key factors in the early traffic growth of the Middle East (Graham, 1995; Taneja, 1998). Many Middle Eastern nations invested heavily in infrastructure improvements, particularly airport expansion and fleet renewal. In a virtuous cycle, this investment has helped to foster the big three connector airlines of the region, Emirates, Qatar, and Etihad. As a whole, the Middle East has enjoyed a number of advantages over the other two regions discussed in this chapter. While the wealth is still unevenly distributed in the region, efforts have been made by richer nations to assist their non-oil-producing neighbors. The centrality of the region helped the connecting strategy of the major carriers, particularly those that invested in infrastructure. The single greatest factor limiting the ability of the region to prosper has been political instability and conflict that continue to impede progress (Graham, 1995).

Helping the Developing World

In addition to providing funding and technical advice, developed nations can also contribute to the success of civil aviation in these regions by considering the adoption of a number of recommendations by international agencies and scholars. ICAO addressed these issues in a 1996 report on preferential treatment for member states who are at a competitive disadvantage in international markets. The following is a list of their recommendations for preferential treatment:

1. The asymmetric liberalization of market access in bilaterals with developed countries, including access to more cities and greater fifth freedom rights.
2. More flexibility for air carriers in changing capacity and gauge between routes in bilaterals.
3. Trial periods for carriers of developing nations to operate under liberal arrangements for an agreed period of time.
4. Gradual introduction of more liberal market access over longer periods of time for developing country carriers.
5. Use of liberalized arrangements.
6. Waiver of nationality requirements for ownership.
7. Special allowances for developing nation carriers to use more modern, leased aircraft.
8. Preferential treatment for the purpose of slot allocation.
9. More liberal policies for ground handling, conversion of currency, and employment of foreign personnel (ICAO, 1996).

Several scholars have made some additional recommendations. Abeyratne (1998) has suggested that developed nations consider allowing an air carrier from one country to exercise the air traffic rights on behalf of another carrier in the event that no carrier from that country were able to launch service to that route for economic reasons. Other recommendations by aviation scholars in Findlay, Sein, and Singh's (1997) book on policy reforms in Asian markets include opening freight and charter markets between countries in a region, relaxing codesharing and ownership rules, liberalizing markets before airline privatization, and expanding multilateral agreements with regional neighbors. Longer term, these expanded multilateral agreements could become regional Open Skies and general trade agreements, even inclusion in GATS (these ideas summarize the recommendations of Oum, Forsyth, and Trethaway in Findley, Sein, and Singh, 1997).

Questions

1. What are the problems facing aviation development in Africa and Latin America? How has each region approached them?
2. Can the developing nations afford a national airline? What are the advantages? Disadvantages?
3. What are some actions that national, international, and governmental organizations can take to improve safety?
4. Discuss aviation development in the Middle East. How has it differed from the other two regions?

5. What are some of the actions that developed nations can take to help aviation development? Why have they not been offered or accepted?

References

Abeyratne, R.I.R. (1999), "The environmental impact of tourism and air transport on the sustainable development of small island developing states," *Journal of Transportation World Wide*, vol. 4 (1), pp. 55–66.

Abeyratne, R.I.R. (1998), "The future of African civil aviation," *Journal of Transportation World Wide*, vol 3 (1), pp. 30–48.

American Airlines (2001), "Annual Report-2001," retrieved online June 18, 2002 from www.sec.gov.

Antoniou, A. (2001), "The air transportation policy of small states: meeting the challenges of globalization," *Journal of Transportation World Wide*, vol. 6 (1), pp. 6–92.

BBC News (2002a), "Air Afrique finally goes bust," www.bbc.co.uk, February 7.

BBC News (2002b), "Pan-African airline takes off," www.bbc.co.uk, April 29.

BBC News (2002c), "Nigeria Airways halves workforce," www.bbc.co.uk, January 4.

BBC News (2002d), "Ghana Airways seeks outside help,"www.bbc.co.uk, June 13.

BBC News (2002e), "Air Mali strikes Egyptian alliance," www.bbc.co.uk, May 8.

BBC News (2002f), "New airline for West Africa," www.bbc.co.uk, September 6.

BBC News (2002g), "Air Tanzania sell-off delayed," www.bbc.co.uk, August 5.

Boeing (2012), "Current market outlook 2012–2032," retrieved online June 16, 2013 from http://www.boeing.com/boeing/commercial/cmo/.

Centre for Aviation (CAPA) (2013a), *World Aviation Yearbook 2013: Africa.* retrieved online January 16, 2014 from http://centreforaviation.com/reports/

Centre for Aviation (CAPA) (2013b), "Singapore Airlines upcoming termination of non-stops to US spells end to ultra long-range flights," retrieved online January 16, 2014 from http://centreforaviation.com/reports/.

Centre for Aviation (CAPA) (2013c), *World Aviation Yearbook 2013, Latin America,* retrieved online January 16, 2014 from http://centreforaviation.com/reports/.

Centre for Aviation (CAPA) (2013d), *World Aviation Yearbook 2013, Middle East,* retrieved online January 16, 2014 from http://centreforaviation.com/reports/.

CIA World Factbook (2014), retrieved online February 10, 2014 from https://www.cia.gov/library/publications/the-world-factbook/geos/rp.html.

Commonwealth Secretariat/World Bank (2000), *Small States: Meeting the Challenges in the Global Economy,* A Report of the Commonwealth Secretariat/World Bank Joint Task Force on Small States, London, March.

Delta Airlines (2007), "Delta expands Africa presence with first nonstop flights between Lagos and New York," retrieved online February 4, 2008 from http://news.delta.com/print_doc.cfm?article_id=10917.

eTN Global Travel Industry News (2013), "IATA: high airline accident rate in Africa still a concern," retrieved online February 6, 2014 from http://www. eturbonews.com/35290/iata-high-airline-accident-rate-africa-still-concern.

Feiler, G. and Goodovitch, T. (1994), "Decline and growth, privatization and protectionism in the Middle East airline industry," *Journal of Transport Geography*, vol. 2 (1), pp. 55–64.

Findlay, C., Sein, C.L. and Singh, K. (eds), (1997), *Asian Pacific Air Transport: Challenges and Policy Reform*. Institute of Southeast Asian Studies, Singapore.

Flottau, J. (2012), "Fast forward," *Aviation Week & Space Technology*, December 3, pp. 41–42.

Godwin, N. (2002), "Kenya Airways comes to N. America to 'do Business'," *Boston Ventures Management, Inc.*, June 17.

Graham, B. (1995), *Geography and Air Transport*, John Wiley and Sons, New York.

International Civil Air Organization (ICAO) (1996), *Study on Preferential Measures for Developing Countries*, ICAO Doc AT-WP/1789, August 22.

International Civil Air Organization (ICAO) (2002), "Press release: one year after 11 September events ICAO forecasts world air passenger traffic will exceed 2000 levels in 2003," October 2.

International Air Transport Association (IATA) (2013), "Strong passenger growth trend continues," retrieved online January 6, 2014 from http://www.iata.org/ pressroom/pr/Pages/2013-07-03-01.aspx.

Kajange, D. (2009), "Air transport market liberalization in Africa: The Yamoussoukro decision process," retrieved online February 27, 2014 from http://ec.europa.eu/transport/modes/air/events/doc/eu_africa/session_1_air_ transport_market_liberalisation_in_africa.pdf.

M2 Communications Ltd (2000), "Uganda Airlines Corporation to go into liquidation," retrieved online Match 28, 2008 from www.findarticles.com, March 31.

Meredith, M. (2005), *The Fate of Africa: From the Hopes of Freedom to the Heart of Despair—A History of 50 Years of Independence*, Public Affairs, New York.

Nicas, J. (2013), "Cheap flights woo Latin Americans from buses: discount airlines entice emerging middle class onto planes."

Nuutinen, H. (1993), "Fighting to beat back the US majors," *Avmark Aviation Economist*, vol. 10, pp. 11–18.

Phillips, E.H. (2002), "Africa leads in hull losses: FSF cites challenges to flying," *Aviation Week & Space Technology*, April 22, pp. 44–45.

Sesay, T. (2013), "Liberia President warned against flying Delta Airlines," retrieved online Fabruary 18, 2014 from http://www.africareview.com/Business--- Finance/Liberia-President-warned-against-flying-Delta/-/979184/1663424/-/ w28peu/-/index.html.

Taneja, N.K. (1988), *The International Airline Industry: Trends, Issues, and Challenges*, Lexington Books, Lexington, MA.

United Nations General Assembly (1993), Resolution 47/186, A/RES/47/186, February.

Wakabi, M. (2003), "Africa One suspends flights to 'restructure'," *The East African*, retrieved online February 18, 2014 from http://www.nationaudio.com/News/EastAfrican/17032003/Regional/Regional1703200336.

World Bank Group (2002), "Making Monterrey work for Africa: new study highlights dwindling aid flows, mounting challenges," Press Release no. 2002/273/S.

World Bank (2005), *African Development Indicators*, World Bank, Washington, DC.

World Bank (2012), "Africa's pulse," October 2012, Vol 6, retrieved online March 15, 2014 from http://siteresources.worldbank.org/INTAFRICA/Resources/Africas-Pulse-brochure_Vol6.pdf/.

World Bank (2013), "Africa continues to grow strongly but poverty and inequality remain persistently high," retrieved online March 15, 2014 from http://www.worldbank.org/en/news/press-release/2013/10/07/africa-continues-grow-strongly-poverty-inequality-persistently-high.

Yates, J. (2012), "Latin America routes key to US Airways, American merger, emerging money," retrieved online March 15, 2014 from http://emergingmoney.com/stocks/us-airways-lcc-ba-lfl-cpa/.

Chapter 18

Fighting Mad, Fighting Carbon

Learning Objectives

After reading this chapter, you should have a good understanding of:
- LO1: the issue of carbon emissions and climate change.
- LO2: the role of aviation in emissions.
- LO3: the actions of different segments of the industry to address carbon.
- LO4: the future of carbon policy and the impact on the aviation industry.

Key Terms, Concepts, and People

ETS	ETBE	Greenhouse Gases
ATAG	ACI	Jet A
Biodiesel	Avgas	CDA

In the Spotlight

The December 19, 2006 cover story for *USA Today* proclaimed that, "Concern grows over pollution from jets: Aviation emissions will take off along with worldwide air travel." The article pointed out that each passenger on a commercial jet from New York City to Denver would generate between 840 and 1,600 pounds of carbon dioxide, roughly the same amount of carbon as a Sports Utility Vehicle (SUV) driven over the period of a month (Stoller, 2006). With US air travel projected to climb to one billion passengers per year by 2024, US environmentalists certainly feel they have reason for concern (FAA, 2012). The EC, responding to the concerns of its citizens, has already included emissions from civil aviation into the EU Emissions Trading Scheme (ETS) for all internal EU flights and had planned to include all flights to and from EU airports in 2012, but the ETS has run into a number of problems. First, the price of carbon has been falling. This creates a problem in a carbon trading scheme because "rational" firms will elect to purchase cheap permits to emit carbon rather than invest in means to reduce carbon pollution. In an effort to bolster the price of carbon, the EU has decided to reduce the number of free permits distributed to members (Reuters, 2013). Second, global backlash against the inclusion of international carriers in the ETS, which included threats of legal action and retaliation, have caused the EU to back down on enforcement. The fight in the European Parliament to limit the ETS also proved to be difficult and contentious. To save face, the EU has insisted that it acted because it feared that the ICAO would not be able to act. Now, they seem convinced that it is on the ICAO agenda. In fact, after a May 2013 meeting, the EU announced plans to limit the ETS and the ICAO pledged to work toward an international agreement to reduce emissions by 2016 (Keating, 2013).

The issue of carbon emission and climate change was not on the agenda of the US government under the George W. Bush Administration who barely acknowledged that any issue existed. Under President Obama, climate change seemed set to take center stage until the healthcare debate dragged on and the Democratic party lost seats in the 2010 midterm elections, creating a Republican House of Representatives. Since that time, there has been no legislative action on the issue. The Administration has attempted to take administrative action with limited success and defend earlier efforts to use stimulus money directed to "green" projects in the wake of scandals such as Solyendra (Stephens and Leonnig, 2011). Progress in the UK has not been any smoother than the US as the British Parliament "considered" measures to limit the growth rate of aviation to the rate at which the industry improved its fuel efficiency and local citizens rejected planned increases in aviation activity such as new airport runways or additional flights due to concerns over the environment and global warming (Stoller, 2006). Still, complaints did not stop expansion efforts at Heathrow Airport in London where a fifth terminal was finally added (Michaels, 2008). While groups such as Sustainable Aviation continue to work on plans to insure that aviation becomes part of the solution to the problem of greenhouse gases (GHG), the airline industry has contented itself with a series of biofuel demonstration projects (Sustainable Aviation, 2006).

If political infighting kept carbon off the table, then the spike of fuel to US$147 in 2008 seemed to provide the US and the aviation industry with a reason to consider alternative fuels. According to the US Energy Information Administration (2013), the US consumed roughly 8.74 million barrels of oil a day in 2011, almost 6 percent less than the 2007 peak. Transportation continues to account for almost two-thirds of the total oil consumed with gasoline accounting for 47 percent of all petroleum consumption. Until recently, aviation barely merited an honorable mention in the debate over climate change; the Kyoto Protocol did not include aviation emissions as they were believed to be a minor contributor to climate change when the agreement was first negotiated, but future aviation growth changed the debate (Stoller, 2006). Unfortunately, even the prospect of high fuel prices now seems less threatening with new estimates of US energy supply that suggest that fuel self-sufficiency might be achieved by 2035 given finds of natural gas and non-conventional petroleum (Bruno and Warwick, 2013).

The airline industry that struggled to post a profit after September 11 only to see the GFC of 2008 destroy any brief gains has proven remarkably reluctant to address carbon emissions. It is even less thrilled with the predictions of some geologists and environmentalists such as Colin Campbell, author of *Oil Crisis* and a chief proponent of an early peak for oil production. Campbell has suggested that the "airline business will go into near extinction as fuel costs soar. Very few people actually need to travel by air. Modern communications makes most business travel unnecessary" (2005: 298). Lester R. Brown, president of the Earth Policy Institute, has offered a less dire prediction for the aviation industry, but he still suggests that cheap airfares, fresh fruit transported by aircraft to out-of-season consumers, and citizens willing to "subsidize this high-cost mode of transportation for their more affluent compatriots" will soon be a thing of the past (Brown, 2006: 234). Still, with fuel representing the largest single operating expense at 40 percent (US$47.3 billion in 2012), the issue of petroleum and carbon will drive changes in the aviation industry (Grose, 2013).

Subject to Debate

The debate about the reality of climate change and its causes has largely been settled in much of the world, but it remains a topic of dispute in the US where there is more talk of hoax than change (Kaplan, 2013; Kluger, 2007). The EU put in place a plan to cut energy by 20 percent by 2020 and increase the share of renewable energy to 12 percent by 2010. The US government has no comprehensive plan to address the issue of energy use, carbon emissions, or renewable energy. It is counting on markets to drive change (Brown, 2006; McKinnon and Meckler, 2006). Until recently, it was also counting on the US military to invest for strategic, security reasons and use their massive market power to drive down the costs of alternative fuel for everyone. As noted above, new estimates of self-sufficiency have created political backlash to military projects for alternative fuel that may force a reduction in these programs (Bruno and Warwick, 2013). To the extent that there has been any attention to alternative fuels in the US, it has tended to focus on automobile use, however, ethanol production, mostly from corn, simply raised food prices without making any serious dent in oil consumption (Grunwald, 2008). In aviation, the primary concern has been the cost of petroleum-based jet fuel not carbon and other emissions. While there are technical considerations (discussed later) with the use of alternative fuels in aviation, the primary focus has been on technological improvements and air traffic modernization efforts that reduce fuel use (Pilling and Thompson, 2007).

Growing Impact

The FAA has predicted that the US will continue to see 2 to 3 percent growth over the next 20 years with 1.2 billion passengers flying in 2032 (FAA, 2012). All transport modes are believed to be responsible for 23 percent of the total carbon emissions. Air transport accounts for 12 percent of this total (Ott, 2007). The jet engine is the chief source of carbon emissions. A jet engine emits more carbon dioxide than the actual weight of the fuel that creates combustion within it (Bond, 2007). According to Environmental Defense, burning a gallon of jet fuel will produce 21.1 pounds of carbon dioxide or about half a pound per passenger per domestic mile or one pound per passenger per international mile. The average domestic US fuel efficiency of a jet engine now averages 0.54 aircraft-miles per gallon, a 40 percent increase in efficiency since 2000. For international flights, the average efficiency is only 0.27 aircraft miles per gallon. Multiply this fuel efficiency level by the length of a typical airline flight and the amount of fuel consumed (and carbon emitted) is staggering (Grose, 2013). Further complicating the issue is the fact that these emissions tend to take place at high altitude which may represent a greater problem for global warming than those that occur at sea level (Environmental Defense, 2007; Stoller, 2006). Some sources suggest that non-carbon dioxide GHG emissions may be even more significant. These include nitrogen oxide, sulfur oxide, soot, and water vapor (Stoller, 2006).

The aviation industry can roughly be divided into six segments –airlines, manufacturers, airports, general aviation, airspace, and air cargo. These segments exist to some extent throughout the world, although there are some important structural differences. US airlines and air cargo operators are privately owned. Almost all are publicly traded stock companies and subject to financial as well as operational reporting. Airports in the US, on the other hand, are owned by the city or county in which they are located with the exception of some small general aviation airports and military airfields. All but a small number of airports are open to general aviation traffic. The airspace in the US is tightly regulated with an air traffic system managed by the US FAA. Controllers are public employees who while unionized have limited ability to engage in work actions. For the rest of the world, full or partial government ownership of airlines is common. Airports, on the other hand, are increasingly being privatized or the management of the airport outsourced. General aviation is much less common and many airports are closed to this type of traffic. Airspace is less restricted and in some case such as Africa radar coverage is limited (Rhoades, 2003). These differences may not be the primary factor in driving sector contribution to carbon emissions, but they may affect future support for carbon constraint. Currently, each segment contributes to carbon emissions in a multitude of ways and each is approaching (or not approaching) the issue of emissions at their own pace and in their own way.

Flying Green

US carriers consume roughly 18 billion gallons of jet fuel per year and every penny of increase adds US$180 million in annual cost (ATA, 2013). As for emissions, an aircraft engine emits carbon dioxide and nitrogen oxide on the ground and while in flight. On the ground, fuel may be burned when the aircraft backs from the gate under power, taxis to the runway, or is repositioned on the airport, either to a new gate or a maintenance hangar on airport property. On the ground, fuel burn has tended to raise concerns about local air and noise pollution rather than carbon emission and has been the subject of complaints from citizens surrounding busy commercial airports. It is the in-flight, upper atmosphere emissions and the creation of contrails (condensed water vapor formed in the wake of an aircraft which are believed to contribute to cloud cover) that has raised the most concern from scientists and environmentalists. These concerns are also the most difficult to address (McKinnon and Meckler, 2006).

Greening the Neighborhood

Airports have been a focal point for resident and environmental groups concerned about environmental impacts arising from noise and air pollution. In addition to the activity of the aircraft themselves, airports utilize powered vehicles for baggage transfer, aircraft maintenance, emergency response, terminal-to-terminal transportation, terminal-to-parking transportation, and so on. In the US, most airports are accessed through private automobile which adds to the local pollution levels. Since parking fees represent a substantial source of revenue, airports are often reluctant to tamper with this aspect of the airport. Although airport master planning in the US requires that intermodal transportation issues be addressed through the design of parking facilities, rental cars, and public transportation access, the reality is that only 14 airports in the US are linked to rail systems, one of the least polluting forms of transportation, leaving the rest to rely on other forms of surface transportation (ACI–ATAG, 1998).

Airspace is restricted to a certain extent in all countries due to noise, security, safety, and radar coverage. Examples of restrictions include military facilities, residential neighborhoods, and key public buildings. In the US, airspace is more tightly controlled than in many other regions and is the responsibility of a single entity, the FAA. In regions such as the EU, multiple air traffic control systems increase the inefficiency of the airspace. Another source of global inefficiency are country limitations on the entry of foreign aircraft either by closing entrance to foreign aircraft or charging fees for entry or overflight, thus encouraging aircraft operators to fly around restrictions which add to flight times and fuel consumption. The current system of air traffic management also utilizes step-down approaches that require progressive altitude changes and thrust applications in descent to landing, adding to fuel burn (Hughes, 2007).

Freight Green

World air freight growth is closely linked to the overall growth in world GDP. It recovered slowly after 2001 and was deeply affected by the downturn in the wake of the GFC, however, recent forecasts predict a modest 3 percent annual growth through 2016. Asia, particularly China, is expected to see the highest growth (IATA, 2013). Air freight is carried either as belly cargo on commercial airlines or on dedicated freighter aircraft, some of whom are operated by the airlines themselves. As airlines struggled to return to profitability after 9/11, many increased their reliance on air cargo, particularly on Asia to North America routes. Cargo revenue for the world's airlines has increased from a post-2001 low of US$38 billion in 2002 to US$63 billion in 2008. They dropped precipitously to US$48 billion in 2009 following the GFC, but regained ground in 2010 to post revenues of US$66 billion (IATA, 2013). Many all-cargo operators act as air freight forwarders, handling the air segment of a shipping operation. This includes operators handling oversized cargo such as Volga-Dnepr. Oversized carriers use some of the largest aircraft in the world, C-17 and AN 124, to ship large industrial equipment. These services have been attractive to firms in industries such as oil and gas where the time saved by shipping equipment by air rather than slower modes of transportation may prove an ideal tradeoff to get operations up and running quickly or keep them up and running (Nelms, 2007).

The best known global shippers are the so-called integrated carriers such as UPS, FedEx, and DHL. While air forwarders such as airlines and all-cargo operators are responsible for only the air portion of travel and require shippers to make their own arrangements to get freight to and from the airport, the "integrated" carriers combine all modes of transportation to provide seamless, door-to-door shipping. FedEx started life as an overnight air freight delivery company while UPS began as a ground delivery company that expanded into air freight later in life. This has not stopped either company from amassing an air fleet that would rank them among the largest airlines in the world (Niemann, 2007).

And the Answer is...

The aviation industry is pursuing a number of actions to reduce GHG emissions. The primary hope for significant reduction lies in new technologies. Aircraft engines have continued to increase the efficiency of their fuel burn, doubling fuel efficiency over the past 40 years, and manufacturers are committed to a further improvement of almost 50 percent (Sustainable Aviation, 2006). These technologies would also reduce carbon dioxide emissions, but are estimated to increase nitrogen oxide emissions by about 40 percent over the same period (Dailey, 2010; McKinnon and Meckler, 2006). In terms of engine advances, there are several innovations that could represent game-changing technology. Manufacturers are currently working on open rotor engines. In an open rotor design, the rotors (propellers) normally encased inside the engine housing are mounted outside. Propeller diameter can be increased and the heavy, drag-inducing nacelle removed. Two common configurations are the puller with propeller mounted at the front of the engine and the pusher with propellers mounted behind the turbine (SBAC, 2013). The main drawbacks of the open rotor are increased noise and market acceptance of this unusual design. Pratt & Whitney have announced breakthroughs in engine designs that "add a gear" to the turbofan engine and promise potential fuel reduction of 16 percent, 20 percent reductions in operating costs, lower noise levels, and reduced emissions, however, the new engine has a larger fan and cannot be retrofitted beneath the wings of existing aircraft, limiting its use to new aircraft (Grose, 2013). Even the "design classic" turboprop engine, the PT6 from Pratt & Whitney, has made remarkable improvements in technology with four times more power and 20 percent better fuel efficiency (Norris, 2013).

In addition to new engine designs, there are new design options for the fuselage including the double bubble, a design that merges two fuselages together allowing some of the lift to come from here not just the wings, blended wing designs that fall just short of the flying wing design, a new split winglet, new composite and ceramic designs that reduce weight, various space plane designs, and several new supersonic designs including the ninja that flies like a normal aircraft until it rotates to present a narrower profile (Grose, 2013; NASA, 2012; Warwick, 2013). The latest LCA, the B-787 and A-380, are both billed as more fuel efficient and less costly than earlier models, however, it takes a heavy structure to support a larger plane. These larger planes also carry more fuel, thus reducing gas mileage. It is estimated that an A380 with more than 500 seats will average 65 miles per gallon per seat while the much smaller A320 with 150 seats will average 77 seat-miles (McCartney, 2013).

Aircraft and their engines are long-lived assets. The replacement of existing fleets with newer more fuel efficient aircraft is a slow process given the cost to aircraft operators. Currently, modifications to existing aircraft yield only modest improvements in efficiency (Bond, 2007). Another option for airlines is the use of alternative fuels. The turbine engine of a large commercial jet uses a high octane form of diesel fuel, commonly called Jet A. Jet A must perform under extreme temperature conditions, particularly the cold of high altitude. Smaller general aviation aircraft use what is called Avgas. As the name implies, Avgas is more closely related to gasoline than diesel (US Department of Energy, 2005). A number of airlines have announced biofuel demonstration flights including Virgin Atlantic, China Eastern, Alaska Airlines, and KLM (BiofuelsDigest, 2013; Carey, 2013; United Press International, 2008).

The only "drop in" alternative fuel for Jet A is synthetic jet fuel. It is manufactured through a conversion process from natural gas or coal that produces 1.8 times the carbon dioxide of conventional jet fuel production. Other alternative fuel technologies require engine modification. The use of 100 percent biofuels is not currently viable as they freeze at the normal cruising temperatures of LCA (Daggett, Hendricks, Walther and Corporan, 2007). The Renewable Aviation Fuels Development Center (RAFDC) at Baylor University has run a series of experiments using alternative fuels for aviation. RAFDC tests examined biodiesel blends of 5, 10, 15, 20, and 25 percent. The best results were obtained for the 20 percent blend. Beyond this level of blend, major changes in engine configuration would be required and significant clouding at cold temperatures is likely. The recent biodiesel test run by Virgin Atlantic used a 20 percent blend. Airbus has also conducted a trial run of the A-380 from Filton, UK to Toulouse, France. The A-380 was using Rolls-

Royce Trent 900 engine and a 20 percent blend as well (Next Energy News, 2008; United Press International, 2008). Boeing is currently exploring the use of cryogenic hydrogen and liquid methane (Daggett, Hendricks, Walther and Corporan, 2007).

General aviation includes all non-commercial, non-military aviation. Most of this segment relies on piston-powered, propeller engines. These craft use Avgas rather than Jet A fuel. Avgas is more closely related to ethanol. There are over 320,000 general aviation aircraft including helicopter, single, piston engine craft, and turboprops. In the US, general aviation aircraft fly over 27 million hours annually (GAMA, 2006). RAFDC has tested ethanol and Eythyl Teriary Butyl Ether (ETBE) against Avgas in the piston engines commonly used in general aviation propeller aircraft. While some engine modification is required, tests showed that engine efficiencies were higher for ethanol than Avgas. These improve even more with increased compression. Mileage per gallon of ethanol was lower. Tests indicated that at 80 percent power ethanol consumed 11 percent more fuel than Avgas. Ethanol and ETBE were shown to produce lower emission of carbon monoxide and unburned hydrocarbons, but to increase the emission of carbon dioxide and nitrogen oxide because of lower energy conversion rates, a fact reflected in the level of fuel consumed (Shauck and Zanin, 2001). A modified piston aircraft was flown without significant problems across the Atlantic using ethanol (Shauck and Zanin, 1990). During the transatlantic flight no fuel-related problems were encountered. The overall cost of the ethanol for the crossing was US$160 compared to US$230 for Avgas, even including the reduced mileage (Shauck and Zanin, 2001). Results also indicate that ethanol burns more completely and cleanly than gasoline. The observed reduction in range (mileage) was between 10–15 percent (Johnson, Shauck and Grazia, 2003).

There are a number of technologies that can be implemented to improve airport arrival and departure procedures (see Chapter 21 for more information). The Next Generation Air Transportation System (NGATS) is looking at technologies such as 4D Trajectory Management. This technology would involve runway-to-runway planning with auto negotiation equipment in the aircraft that would allow flight crews to adjust the flight plan as necessary to accommodate weather, aircraft separation, airport delays, and so on. Air Traffic Management (ATM) technologies combined with GPS and Automatic Dependent Surveillance-Broadcast (ADS-B) to implement proper spacing could be used to replace the step-down descents with Continuous Descent Arrivals (CDAs). It is estimated that CDAs could save between 100–300 pounds of fuel (Hughes, 2007). The US ATA, a trade organization representing US airlines, and the FAA support an airspace management initiative called Secure America's Future Energy (SAFE). SAFE would link a satellite-based air traffic system to ground-based technologies in order to reduce delays and shorten travel. SAFE has estimated that implementation of these actions could save 400,000 barrels of oil daily by 2030 and reduce carbon emissions by 57.5 million metric tons per year (ATA, 2007). The European equivalent of this program is the Single European Sky ATM Research Programme (SESAR) and the Advisory Council for Aviation Research in Europe (ACARE).

While there are a number of technological solutions being studied, changing processes can also have an impact on carbon emissions. Airlines are also taking a number of actions that reduce fuel burn and emissions on the ground, primarily out of concern with rising fuel costs. These actions include the elimination of power backing (backing the airplane from the gate using its engines) in favor of small tugs that push the aircraft back from the gate and "supertugs" that can be used to tow aircraft around the airport itself (repositioning it to another gate or a maintenance hanger). Lufthansa is experimenting with a semi-robotic tug, controlled by the pilot that would take the aircraft from the ramp to the runway using 7–15 gallons of fuel rather than the 126 gallons that would be used by the aircraft engines. There are also options for taxiing on electricity with an auxiliary power unit (Warwick, 2013). EU airlines are addressing government and customer concerns by developing explicit plans to manage and report on a range of environmental issues. For example, British Airways has a section on their website that reports on their environmental actions in the area of noise, air quality, waste, and biodiversity. There is also a way to calculate and offset your carbon dioxide emissions. Most of the EU airlines have affirmed their support for the ETS and called for action on an international scheme for emissions trading. Although not stated, a widely adopted international emissions scheme would insure that no airlines are unduly disadvantaged in pursuit of GHG emission deduction (British Airways, 2007). Air France also reports on their actions toward sustainable development including their tracking reports for emissions and efforts to reduce emissions through fleet renewal, alternative fuel ground vehicles, and air–rail link options (Air France, 2007). In contrast to these examples, US airlines generally do not include any information of this nature in their investor reports or on their websites. A few US airlines do mention environmental issues, but usually only to affirm their "commitment" to the environment. Recently, some sites have included information directing concerned customers to outside websites such as GoGreen to explore means of offsetting carbon emissions.

Unlike their airline counterparts, US airports have been more aggressive in their approach to environmental issues. Three examples highlight the types of action that airports are employing. Dallas–Fort Worth Airport (DFW) is the world's third busiest airport with 1,900 flights per day. DFW has taken a very proactive approach to environmental issues and was recently recognized by the US Environmental Protection Agency as part of their National Environmental Performance Tracking program. Over the past five years, DFW has reduced its air emissions by 95 percent and converted 100 percent of its light-to-medium vehicles on-airfield fleet as well as bus and shuttle operations to alternative fuels (DFW News Release, 2007). The Port of Seattle, which includes the Sea-Tac airport as well as the seaport in Seattle, is another example of a committed and proactive local entity. The Port has a staff of 22 individuals responsible for environmental issues and compliance and has converted most of their on-airport vehicles to natural gas. In addition, they have redesigned field operations to reduce the number of tanker trucks needed on the airfield (Port of Seattle, 2006). The Airport

Carbon Management Group (ACMG), based in the UK, was created to explore ways to reduce carbon emissions, primarily through improved energy use. To date, the efforts of this group have reduced carbon emissions by 13,000 tons per year (Sustainable Aviation, 2006). Unlike the US, there are also over 40 airports in Europe with air–rail links and an additional 49 links planned. It has been estimated that the Heathrow Express removes over 3,000 cars a day from London roads (ACI–ATAG, 1998).

The integrated freight carriers are making some of the greatest efforts to address environmental issues, including carbon emissions. DHL has launched its GoGreen program that allows shippers to select low carbon emission modes of shipping. This option was provided to delegates attending the World Economic Forum in Davos as part of the Forum's carbon neutral goal for the 2007 conference. DHL has entered a joint venture with Lufthansa Cargo called AeroLogic. AeroLogic will utilize the more fuel efficient B-777 primarily to Asia. DHL is also exploring the use of biogas, hybrid, and fuel cell vehicles for ground shipping and packaging options that reduce GHG emissions (DHL, 2014; Turney, 2008). FedEx is also exploring alternative fuels for its ground vehicles and has recently launched 18 Optifleet E700 hybrid vehicles to its fleet. On the aviation side, FedEx has retired its remaining B-727 aircraft and hush-kitted older aircraft, both of which reduce the overall fleet emissions and noise levels. Beginning in 2009, FedEx will begin acquiring B-777 freighters which provide 18 percent greater fuel efficiency. The FedEx Oakland, California facility has one of the largest industrial solar operations in the US (FedEx, 2014; Moorman, 2008). UPS was the launch customer in the mid-1990s for the low-emission version of the GE CF6-80C2 engine and is installing ADS-B in all its aircraft. It expects to save a million gallons of jet fuel a year and reduce noise and nitrous oxide emissions (Moorman, 2008). UPS has also taken a number of actions to reduce fuel consumption and emissions from its ground fleet including trailering trucks onto railcars and optimizing driving routes. In addition, they deployed 50 new hybrid vehicles to their fleet in 2006. These hybrids join a fleet of 12,000 low-emission vehicles already in operation (Neimann, 2007). UPS has established Key Performance Indicators (KPI) for environmental performance that includes ground and aviation emissions targets. These are reported on their website (UPS, 2014).

Aviation in Green

With the exception of US airlines, other sectors of the aviation industry are taking important steps to address GHG and climate change. While it would be incorrect to say that the airline industry has taken no actions to reduce energy use, switch to renewable fuels, or reduce emissions, these actions have been driven largely by higher fuel prices rather than other concerns. This segment of the industry has also struggled over time to post a consistent profit and the first decade of the twenty-first century was particularly hard on it with 9/11 and the financial crisis (Loomis and Buffet, 1999). Unfortunately, airlines have tended to react to their external environment rather than taking a proactive stance. If US carriers can continue to control capacity and generate profits with their fare-and-fee strategy, then fuel issue might become the next great frontier in the battle to reduce costs (Saporito, 2013). This would be a good thing for the industry and the world.

Questions

1. How does aviation contribute to carbon pollution?
2. How much carbon is produced by burning a gallon of fuel?
3. What impact might carbon restriction have on the industry?
4. What are the various sectors of the industry doing to address carbon emissions?
5. Discuss the new technologies for reducing carbon and/or fuel burn.

References

Air France (2007), "Sustainable development," retrieved online June 5, 2012 from www.airfrance.us/US/en/local.

Air Transport Association (ATA) (2007), "ATA and 'safe' agree that modernized ATC will significantly reduce fuel consumption and US oil dependence," ATA News Release, retrieved online June 5, 2012 from www.airlines.or/government/issuesbrief/alt+fuels,htm.

Air Transport Association (ATA) (2013), "Airline energy Q&A," retrieved online March 8, 2014 from http://www.airlines.org/Pages/Airline-Energy-QA-.aspx.

Airport Council International (ACI) and Air Transport Action Group (ATAG) (1998), *Air Rail Links: Guide to Best Practice*, Geneva, ACI-ATAG Press.

Biofuels Digest (2013), "China Eastern Airlines to run 100% biofuel flights after successful test run," retrieved online July 18, 2014 from http://www.biofuelsdigest.com/bdigest/2013/04/29/china-eastern-airlines-to-run-100-biofuel-flights-after-successful-test-run/.

Bond, D. (2007), "Green is for go," *Aviation Week & Space Technology*, August 19, pp. 52–55.

British Airways (2007), "The BA way in the environment," retrieved online January 8, 2008 from http://www.britishairways.com/cms/global/pdfs/corporate_responsibility_report_2006/the_BA_way_in_the_environment.pdf.

British Airways (2014), "Environment," retrieved online March 10, 2014 from www.britishairways.com/travel/crenv/public/en_gb.

Brown, L.R. (2006), *Plan B 2.0*, W.W. Norton & Company, London.

Bruno, M. and Warwick, G. (2013), "Energy equation," *Aviation Week & Space Technology*, July 29, pp. 40–41.

Campbell, C.J. (2005), *Oil Crisis*, Multi-Science Publishing Company, Brentwood, UK.

Carey, B. (2013), "KLM begins biofuel flights between New York, Amsterdam," retrieved online January 6, 2014 from http://www.ainonline.com/aviation-news/2013-03-08/klm-begins-biofuel-flights-between-new-york-amsterdam.

Daggett, D.L., Henricks, R.C., Walther, R. and Corporan, E. (2007), *Alternative Fuels for Use in Commercial Aircraft*, Boeing Company, Seattle, WA.

Dailey, B. (2010), *Air Transport and the Environment*, Ashgate Publishing, Aldershot, UK.

Environmental Defense (2007), "How your pollution is calculated," retrieved online January 8, 2008 from http://www.fightglobalwarming.com/content.cfm?contentid=5043.

DFW New Release (2007), "DFW international airport's environmental success lands EPA recognition—earns participation in national environmental performance track program," retrieved online January 10, 2008 from www.dfwairport.com.

DHL (2014), "Green solutions," retrieved online March 5 2014 from http://www.dhttp://www.dhl-usa.com/en/about_us/green_solutions.htmlhl-usa.com/en/about_us/green_solutions.html.

Federal Aviation Administration (FAA) (2012), "FAA aerospace forecast fiscal years 2012–2032," retrieved online February 3, 2013 from http://www.faa.gov/about/office_org/headquarters_offices/apl/aviation_forecasts/aerospace_forecasts/2012-2032/media/2012%20FAA%20Aerospace%20Forecast.pdf.

FedEx (2014), "FedEx and the environment," retrieved online March 5, 2014 from http://www.fedex.com/si/about/sustainability/environment.html.

General Aviation Manufacturers Association (GAMA) (2006), "Industry facts," retrieved online January 8, 2008 from www.gama.aero/aboutGAMA/industryFacts.php.

Grose, T.K. (2013), "Reshaping flight for fuel efficiency: five technologies on the runway," retrieved online February 6, 2014 from http://news.nationalgeographic.com/news/energy/2013/04/130423-reshaping-flight-for-fuel-efficiency/.

Grunwald, M. (2008), "The clean energy scam," *Time*, 7 April, pp. 39–45.

Hughes, D. (2007), "ATM is no silver bullet," *Aviation Week and Space Technology*, August 19, pp. 66–68.

International Air Transport Association (IATA) (2013), "Fact sheet: Industry Statistics," retrieved online March 5, 2014 from http://www.iata.org/pressroom/facts_figures/fact_sheets/Documents/industry-facts.pdf.

Johnson, G., Shauck, M.E. and Zanin, M.G (2003), "Performance and emissions comparison between avgas, ethanol, and ETBE in an aircraft engine," Renewable Aviation Fuel Development Center, Baylor University, retrieved online January 8, 2008 from http://www3.baylor.edu/bias/publications/avgasethanol/etbe.pdf.

Kaplan, J. (2013), "Warming whoops: scientists debate the failing rate of rising temperatures," Fox News, retrieved online February 7, 2014 from http://www.foxnews.com/science/2013/09/17/is-global-warming-actually-far-lower-than-scientists-predicted/.

Keating, D. (2013), "EU offers retreat on aviation emissions," retrieved online February 7, 2014 from http://www.europeanvoice.com/article/imported/eu-offers-retreat-on-aviation-emissions/78094.aspx.

Kluger, J. (2007), "What now?" *Time*, April, pp. 50–60.

Loomis, C. and Buffet, W. (1999), "Mr. Buffet on the stock market," *Fortune*, Special Issue, vol. 140 (10), pp. 212–220.

McCartney, S. (2013), "A Prius with wings vs a guzzler in the clouds," *The Wall Street Journal*, retrieved online February 7, 2014 from http://online.wsj.com/article/sb10001424052748704901104575423261677748380.html.

McKinnon, J.D. and Meckler, L. (2006), "Bush eschews harsh medicine in treating US oil 'addiction'," *The Wall Street Journal*, August 9, pp. A1, A9.

Michaels, D. (2008), "Heathrow makeover to heat up airline wars," *The Wall Street Journal* Online, March 6.

Moorman, R.W. (2008), "Greening the fleet," *Air Cargo World*, January, pp. 21–27.

National Aeronautics and Space Administration (NASA) (2012), "NASA shells out award for ninja star supersonic plan design," retrieved online March 4, 2014 from http://rt.com/news/nasa-grant-supersonic-plane-254/.

Neimann, G. (2007), *Big Brown: The Untold Story of UPS*. John Wiley and Sons, San Francisco, CA.

Nelms, D. (2007), "Oversized ambitions: the outsized air cargo market is growing rapidly," *Air Cargo World*, April, pp. 16–20.

Next Energy News (2008), "Airbus A-380 becomes first commercial jet to use biofuel," retrieved online February 7, 2014 from http://www.nextenergynews.com/news1/next-energy-news2.4d.html.

Norris, G. (2013), "Timeless turbine," *Aviation Week & Space Technology*, July 22, pp. 40–43.

Ott, J. (2007), "Clearing the air," *Aviation Week & Space Technology*, August 19, pp. 54–55.

Pilling, M. and Thompson, J. (2007), "Carbon storm," *Airline Business*, February, pp. 54–56.

Port of Seattle (2006), "Environmental programs," retrieved online January 8, 2008 from www.portseattle.org/community/environment.

Reuters News Agency (2013), "EU ETS wins lifeline after tight EU parliament vote," retrieved online March 7, 2014 from http://www.businessspectator.com.au/news/2013/7/4/carbon-markets/eu-ets-wins-lifeline-after-tight-eu-parliament-vote.

Rhoades, D.L. (2003), *Evolution of International Aviation: Phoenix Rising*, Ashgate Publishing, Aldershot, UK.

Saporito, B. (2013), "Cabin pressure," *Time*, September 9, pp. 37–41.

SBAC (2013), "SBAC Aviation and environment briefing papers: Open rotor engines," retrieved online March 7, 2014 from http://www.sustainableaviation. co.uk/wp-content/uploads/open-rotor-engine-briefing-paper.pdf.

Shauck, M.E. and Zanin, M.G. (1990), "The first transatlantic flight on ethanol fuel," Renewable Aviation Fuel Development Center, Baylor University, retrieved online February, 2007 from www3.baylor.edu/bias/publications/ trasnatlanticflight.pdf.

Shauck, M.E. and Zanin, M.G. (2001), "The present and future potential of biomass fuels in aviation," Renewable Aviation Fuel Development Center, Baylor University, retrieved online February 4, 2007 from www3.baylor.edu/ bias/publications/bomassfuels.pdf.

Stephens, J. and Leonnig, C.D. (2011), "Documents show politics infused Obama 'green' programs," *Washington Post*, retrieved online June 6, 2012 from http:// www.washingtonpost.com/politics/specialreports/solyndra-scandal.

Stoller, G. (2006), "Concern grows over pollution from jets: aviation emissions will take off along with worldwide air travel," *USA Today*, December 19, pp. 1A–2A.

Sustainable Aviation (2006), "Sustainable Aviation Progress Report 2006," retrieved online April 30, 2007 from www.sustainableaviation.co.uk.

Turney, R. (2008), "Virtual air," *Air Cargo World*, March, p. 1314.

United Press International (2008), "Virgin Atlantic to test jet biofuel," retrieved online June 6, 2012 from http://www.upi.com/NewsTrack/Top_ News/2008/02/06/virgin_atlantic.

US Department of Energy (2005), *Biofuels Encyclopedia*, USDOE, Washington, DC.

United Technologies (2007), "Responsibility," retrieved online January 8, 2008 from www.utc.com/responsibility/environment.htm.

UPS (2014), "Corporate responsibility; environment," retrieved online March 5, 2014 from http://www.community.ups.com/Environment.

US Energy Information Administration (2013), "Frequently asked questions," retrieved online March 4, 2014 from http://www.eia.gov/tools/faqs/faq. cfm?id=23&t=10.

Warwick, G. (2013), "Energy-savings technologies to watch," *Aviation Week & Space Technology*, July 29, pp. 44–45.

Chapter 19
Diverging Visions—Changing Times

Learning Objectives

After reading this chapter, you should have a good understanding of:
- LO1: the cases made by Boeing and Airbus for a very large jet.
- LO2: the comparison between the A-380 and the B-787.
- LO3: the aircraft market outlook for Large Commercial Aircraft (LCA).
- LO4: the competitive outlook for aircraft manufacturers.

Key Terms, Concepts, and People

LCA	AVIC	OEM
Aftermarket services	Honda	Mitsubishi
Turboprops	ATR	

Getting From Here to There

A strange thing happened in the closing years of the twentieth century—the vision of the two remaining LCA makers—Boeing and Airbus—began to diverge in ways that seem to suggest that both cannot be right. For its part, Boeing sees a world in which passengers will decide to skip the overcrowded hub with its security lines and airline transfers. Passengers, they believe, will prefer to fly point-to-point to their destination in an airplane with the range to reach distant shores without stopovers. In short, the market of the future involves fragmenting not concentrating passengers. In such a world, the airlines would need an aircraft that can fly internationally to a distance of roughly 8,000 nautical miles at an economical cost. The Boeing solution is the B-787, a mid-sized, twin-engine wide-body aircraft that they believe will use 20 percent less fuel than a comparable sized aircraft. Already, the B-777 has proven to be a very popular aircraft for many international carriers. On the other hand, Airbus sees a world where continuing population growth in major hub cities, time-zone differences, and pressures on airport capacity will necessitate a more intense, efficient use of the hub-and-spoke system. To achieve this efficiency, they believe that airlines will need larger aircraft in order to land more passengers with fewer flights. The Airbus solution is the A-380. The story of how these two giants of the aerospace world came to their visions depends on who is telling the tale. Only time will determine who is right in this high-stakes game of aviation forecasting, however, what neither firm forecast was the GFC or the arrival of US$100 plus for a barrel of oil. Both events may be short-term phenomena, but for highly fuel-sensitive airlines the cost of fuel has already begun to change their calculations on fleet retirement and replacement. It is also changing the discussion about the type of fleet that is most economical. If an airline can use a twin-engine aircraft that offers fewer seats but has a lower cost per available seat mile (kilometer), then do you select the smaller, more efficient aircraft? If the airline industry as a whole is able to control capacity (available seats), then a smaller, more efficient aircraft will also add pricing power. A further complication in the airline and manufacturing calculations is appearing at the lower end of the market where small regional jets had replaced the old turboprop aircraft. When oil was at US$37 a barrel, smaller regional jets took the place of the turboprop aircraft in the short-haul markets of the world. The 50-seat regional jet was first introduced in 1995 and offered a high-speed option for thinner routes up to 1,000 miles (Kownatzki, Hoyland, and Watterson, 2009). As oil prices have climbed and technology has improved, these aircraft are once again surging and moving up from the old 50-seat aircraft to 90-seat options (Perrett, 2013). In short, the future has again confounded its forecasters. The first stop in the chapter, however, is the past and the forecasts and visions that separated the two great competitors in the LCA market.

Downturns and New Visions

The early years of the 1990s were not good for the airlines or the people who supplied them with aircraft. As the economy slowed, airline losses mounted. Airlines engaged in all the usual responses to crisis cited in Chapter 15. It seemed to both aircraft makers as though the answer to the cost pressures on world airlines was a bigger plane with the lower seat mile costs that size would bring. By this time, Airbus had a family of aircraft that could compete with their Boeing rival in every class except the top where the B-747 dominated. Airbus was convinced that it was at this end of the market that Boeing was making its biggest profits. In fact, Aris (2002) put forth the claim that Boeing makes US$30 million per B-747 although Newhouse (2007) disputed this notion and claimed that Boeing's most profitable aircraft was the extended range B-767. Whatever the truth of the matter, Airbus believed these profits allowed Boeing to undersell Airbus on competing models. Further, Airbus felt that they could not achieve their stated goal of 50 percent market share without an aircraft to compete with the B-747. With these considerations in mind, Airbus was determined to enter the market with what they first called the ultra-high-capacity aircraft. They knew that the cost of development would be high and had considered various partnerships, however, it was not until new Boeing CEO Phil Condit mentioned in an interview one month before the Farnborough Air Show that they were exploring "larger aircraft" that Airbus decided to put their planning into high gear and contact Boeing about a possible joint project to study the concept (Aris, 2002).

The results of this joint study would be the subject of much debate while the motives of the two players would result in endless speculation. Both players calculated the cost of development at between US$14.5 and US$15.5 billion, but they did not agree on the market size. Airbus forecast a market for 500 to 600 aircraft over a ten-year period. Boeing saw a much smaller market between 300 and 350. This difference was significant because it determined the all important breakeven number that is a key factor in deciding whether to proceed with an aircraft project. To Boeing, the analysis meant that "for some unknown period of time these airplanes, if built, would be sold for much less than it had cost to develop them because the various factories building them would not yet have come down the learning curve" or not be operating a full capacity (Newhouse, 2007: 149–150). It is difficult to determine at this stage whether the Boeing reluctance to proceed with the project was because they truly did not see a market for the very large aircraft or because the rising costs of the B-777 and the need to modernize the B-737 made the company averse to assuming the risk of this new endeavor. Some inside Boeing even claim that their initial interest was simply a way to trap Airbus in a losing proposition (Newhouse, 2007).

Meanwhile Boeing's behavior during this period seemed to indicate to many observers that the company did not have a strategy for moving forward. Boeing explored a series of new B-747 versions with prospective customers before announcing their intention to proceed with the so-called Sonic Cruiser, an aircraft capable of flying just below Mach 1 over extended ranges. Unfortunately, this aircraft met with even less interest than the slight modifications proposed to the B-747 because trans-sonic flight would save little time and use far too much fuel to do so. Ultimately, Boeing would decide to produce the B-747-800, an aircraft with a new wing and a number of advanced features including lighter construction materials and higher-performance engines that would make it a much bigger leap in design than the earlier proposed derivations, and a totally new aircraft, the B-787. For their part, Airbus would push on alone with the A-3XX as it came to be called. As the 1990s slump turned into a booming new economy, Boeing attempted to ramp up its production and bury Airbus only to be caught in a production nightmare of their own. This disarray and the confusion of its earlier efforts to come up with a strategy certainly helped Airbus in their marketing efforts, their attempt to get launch aid from various European governments, and their reorganization of the Airbus structure itself. The starting gun for the great aircraft order race was fired in April 2000 with the Emirates Airline order of 10 A-3XX aircraft, soon to be given the name A-380 (Aris, 2002)

Comparing Cases, Comparing Planes

The Airbus case for a very large jet was built on several issues. First, the 747 was nearing the natural end of its life. The design had been conceived in the 1950s and developed in the 1960s. The oldest were now approaching 25 years of age. These aging aircraft would have to be replaced by the world's airlines with a craft of equal or larger size that utilized the newest in aviation technology. Second, Airbus looked to the rapidly growing regions of Asia with their large mega-cities and eight of the ten top airports. This area in particular seemed to be an ideal market for the A-380. The vast time differences also meant that an airline catering to passenger preferences for arrival would bunch flights around these preferences making fewer, larger planes a matter of capacity for airports. Third, Airbus reasoned that the operating costs of the A-380 would be 15 to 17 percent better; the plane would have almost 50 percent more space in the cabin but would only require 12 to 15 percent more fuel to lift this weight into the air, thus the cost per seat mile would be less (Aris, 2002). Fourth, Airbus believed that the A-380 would help to protect the A-340 which was not faring well against the B-777. The A-340 was a longer-range mini-jumbo with four engines while the B-777 could fly a similar range with two fewer engines making it more economical to operate. Airbus hoped that fleet commonality would encourage "Airbus customers" to choose the A-340 despite this operating cost issue. Fifth, Airbus countered critics concerned with the size (and potential engineering challenges associated with size) with the argument that the A-380 was really only 35 percent bigger than the B-747 (Newhouse, 2007).

In addition to their concerns about market size resulting from fragmentation of the market itself, Boeing believed that the A-380 with its 550 seats would be too large for many markets, making the B-747-800 with 450-plus seats a better option. Further, they believed the freighter version of this aircraft would prove a better cargo carrier than the A-380 and cost much less. In effect, they believed that the A-380 would be squeezed at the top of the market, further stretching out its time to profitability. Publicly, Boeing remains convinced that they have "guessed right" and that their line-up of the B-747-800, B-777, and the new B-787 will outperform the A-380 (Newhouse, 2007). Table 19.1 shows the vital statistics on the latest entrants into the large commercial market.

Table 19.1   Comparison of B-787 and A-380

	B-787	A-380
Seating	290–330	525–853
Range	7,000 -7,850 nautical miles	8,500 nautical miles
Wing span	170 feet	261.8 feet
Length	186 feet	239.3 feet
Cruising speed	Mach 0.85	Mach 0.89
Maximum takeoff weight	364,000 pounds	1,235,000 pounds
Cargo volume	4,400 cubic feet	650 cubic feet
Fuel savings	20 % < per comparable plane	12 % < per passenger
Orders to date	979	259

Source: Boeing website www.boeing.com. Airbus website www.airbus.com

And the Winner is...

To date, it is clear that Airbus was right about the cost estimate of developing the A-380, but they were well off in the estimate of ten-year sales. The launch customer for the A-380 was Singapore Airlines who made their first flight in October 2007 and so the ten-year mark is upon them. While there is nothing magical about the ten-year forecast of Airbus that led to the development of the A-380, Airbus is clearly behind in their predictions. As of October 2013, Airbus had sold a total of 259 aircraft but had not booked any firm orders in 2013 which would lead to a gap in manufacturing unless they slow production or produce aircraft without a firm order. The Paris Air Show did see Emirates Airlines increase it orders from 90 to 140 which means that a single airline accounts for roughly half of all A-380 orders (Flottau, 2013a). To make matters worse, many of the previously booked orders appear to be in doubt, although only Lufthansa has announced any official cancellations. Whether the GFC with its associated recession and economic slump is to blame or not, the reality is that the shift toward larger aircraft predicted by Airbus has not yet happened. In fact, it appears that the B-777, B-787, and the A-350, highly efficient twin-engine aircraft, appear to be more in demand (Flottau, 2013b). The Aviation Week 2014 Commercial Fleet & MRO forecast expects the world to "be awash in very-long-range twins" by 2020 and questions the long-term future of the four engine aircraft (Mathews, 2013: 12). The 747-800 is not immune to the slowdown affecting the A-380. Boeing still expects the cargo market to double over the next 20 years, but the GFC, high fuel, and the troubles in the Middle East have affected demand here as well (Mecham and Norris, 2013). The four-engine A-340 has delivered only six aircraft since 2010 and has only 377 deliveries since its 1993 introduction (Wikipedia, 2013).

Table 19.2 presents the market outlook issued by these two companies for 2032. The differences reveal the continued divergence in vision as Boeing continues to see a market for smaller aircraft—single aisle or medium- to small-wide-body. Both forecasts agree that the bulk of the market is in single-aisle aircraft. In fact, the major competition for Boeing and Airbus appears to be taking place on two fronts—A-350 vs B-787 and the A-320 vs. B 737. With the troubles over the B-787, the A-350 is now closing on it with 725 orders to the B-787 total-to-date of 979. Even more telling is the fact that Japan Airlines has placed an order for the A-350 after years as a Boeing-only airline (Flottau, 2013b). In the other battle, the A-320 has now passed the 10,000th order mark and is set to begin US production at the new Mobile, Alabama plant. (Sparaco, 2013). Of course, this end of the market is also most vulnerable to potential competition from the number three and four players in commercial aviation, Embraer and Bombardier. Then there is the Asia challenge. To complicate matters, high fuel prices are resulting in renewed interest in the turboprop aircraft that appeared all but dead.

Table 19.2   Boeing/Airbus—aircraft in service 2032

Aircraft Size	Boeing	Airbus
Large wide-body	910	1,711
Medium wide-body	3,610	7,273
Small wide-body	5,410	
Single aisle	29,130	20,242
Regional jet	2,180	
Total	41,240	29,226

Source: Company websites

A Second Life

For Bombardier, the year 2003 was the peak of their deliveries for the Canadian Regional Jet (CRJ) 100/200 (50 seat) and CRJ 700/900 (70–90 seat) aircraft. Between 2003 and 2006, deliveries for the 50-seat CRJs declined an average of 70 percent a year. For Embraer, the 50-seat decline in deliveries has not been as sharp (at 37 percent), but the trend has been clear for both manufacturers; the demand is now for larger jets (Kownatzki, Hoyland, and Watterson, 2009). At Bombardier, it is the new CSeries with a 110-seat configuration that appears to be the future of the company. This new aircraft will have fly-by-wire technology, composite wings, and new turbofan engines (Warwick, 2013). For Embraer, deliveries of their E 170/175/190/195 (70–122 seats) overtook the 50-seat aircraft in 2005 and made up almost all of their deliveries by 2006 (Kownatzki, Hoyland and Watterson, 2009). Even more startling to some observers has been the revival of the turboprop aircraft. Avions de transport régional (ATR) and Bombardier have been joined by the Chinese firm AVIC, Indian firm RTA, and South Korean firm DRA in proposing 90-seat turboprop aircraft. Both ATR and Bombardier are already active in the turboprop market with the ATR 72-seat option straining to meet demand and Bombardier's Q400 selling well. None of the bigger turboprops are scheduled to launch before 2018 and not all will even make it into product. It is also possible that even larger versions may be considered (Perrett, 2013). While oil prices have been driving the revival of the turboprop aircraft, there remains a perception that propeller aircraft are accident-prone and "old technology." This perception is regional and could be subject to change with new technologies on the horizon (*The Economist*, 2012). In other words, there appears to be serious competition on several fronts for single-aisle aircraft and these manufacturers have their sights set on seating in the 90 to 100 plus range, placing them in more direct competition with the big two LCAs.

The Asia Airbus

The question of an Asian competitor in the LCA market has been around for years. While Airbus does its share of outsourcing, typical of aerospace manufacturing, Boeing has relied heavily on Asian companies for manufacturing and, increasingly, design work as well. The Japanese "heavies" helped to design the fuselage for the B-767 in 1978. By the time it came to designing the B-777, Japanese companies were working side-by-side with Boeing engineers for critical component design. The electronic, paperless design of the B-777 saved time and money, but it also facilitated the free flow of design information that in the past would have been unthinkable. To many people in Boeing, the real value-added skill is systems integration, the broad systems understanding of how things work. As long as Boeing retained this position, they believe the competitive risks of information sharing were minimal, however, this close collaboration has periodically raised concerns from others inside Boeing who fear that the company is training a future competitor and losing vital knowledge and skills in its push to outsource more of its operations. Ultimately, many in Boeing believe that the Japanese are too risk-averse to strike out on their own and will be content with the role Boeing allows them to play (Newhouse, 2007). This belief may have been in error as Honda, Mitsubishi, and Toyota have announced plans to enter the market, and Honda and GE have announced a joint effort to produce a jet engine for a new generation of small, low-cost business jets (Woodyard, 2008). Mitsubishi Heavy Industries is not only entering the regional jet market in the 70-90 passenger range but has announced that All Nippon Airways will be the launch customer (Reuters, 2008). Toyota has agreed to invest 10 billion yen in the Mitsubishi project (Watanabe, 2008). It appears that Boeing (and now Airbus) may have underestimated the potential for competition from Japan. Final assembly of the first Mitsubishi Regional Jet (MRJ) aircraft got underway in October 2013 with delivery in 2017 expected. To date, there have been 325 orders for the plane that is expected to be delivered in 2015 (Narabe and Kimura, 2013).

The same cannot be said for the Chinese who have shown themselves capable of moving rapidly into high-tech manufacturing and design. The Chinese are now manufacturing the complete wing for the A-320 as well as landing gear. AVIC International was born out of a restructured China National Aero-Technology Import & Export Corporation (CATIC) in 2008 and has 70,000 employees in more than 180 countries. It is China's largest aerospace company. On the civilian front, the ARJ21 is its first product offering. The ARJ21 with seating capacity of 70–105 is set for delivery of its first aircraft to launch customer Chendu Airlines by the end of 2014 (Toh, 2013). While these aircraft currently compete against the regional jets of Embraer and Bombardier, there is no reason to believe that the Chinese are not interested in expanding their line of aircraft. An Asian Airbus would be well positioned to take market share in one of the most rapidly growing aviation regions of the world and there is only one buyer of aircraft, the Chinese government. As noted throughout this book, the link between aviation, economics, and politics is always close. If China is successful in re-establishing its ancient hegemony over the Asian region, then the aircraft it produces are certain to benefit, directly and indirectly, inside and outside of China.

At the present time, the Asian efforts are targeted at the lower end of the commercial market and not a direct threat to the LCA manufacturers, however, this end of the market appears to be getting very crowded. If the trend toward small aircraft, point-to-point operations continues, then there may be room for all of these new players. On the other hand, two other possibilities are clearly possible. The most immediate threat comes from the prospect that Embraer or Bombardier will be successful in moving up the food chain to produce aircraft to compete with the successor to the B-737/A-320. Given their expertise and existing facilities it would seem to be a less difficult move than for either the new Japanese or Chinese competitors. Further down the road is the potential for competition from the Asia players who, like Airbus before them, may not be content with the lower end of the market. In any event, neither Boeing nor Airbus can afford to underestimate the potential competition as Boeing learned in the case of Airbus. A firm backed by the resources and will of its government is not to be taken lightly.

Real Men Sell Big Engines

There is an old joke in the aviation industry that men sell engines but real men sell big engines (the same, of course, can be said of planes). It is certainly true that the twenty-first century would see the big three LCA engine makers producing engines for big planes. All three have a version for the biggest commercial plane ever produced, the A-380 (Table 19.3), but in some ways the times are changing. The old way of doing business in the aerospace industry was driven by an engineering mentality that said that if you built it to some engineering ideal of performance and standard then they (the airlines) would buy it; real men would sell it in the great game of high-stakes/high-politics aerospace. Increasingly, the engine manufacturers are finding that customer service is the driving factor in sales. For the men selling these engines, this is a profound change. The job no longer centers on dazzling "them" with specifications and performance data; it is all about finding out what the customer wants, listening to their concerns, addressing their needs. In short, customer service not engineering specs win the day. Further, the money is not in the engine sale itself but in the aftermarket services. As an example, GE offers OnPoint Solutions, a comprehensive program to meet operational, financial, and technical needs. The program will collect historical data, establish baselines for use and performance, identify upcoming changes in demand, and forecast future need costs. The program offers "lower, predictable, guaranteed pricing," asset management, leasing, engine swaps, and spare parts control (GE, 2014).

Given the critical nature of the aircraft engine, airlines find that outsourcing the maintenance to the Original Equipment Manufacturer (OEM) only makes sense. The engine makers find that over the life of the engine itself they make far more money in the afterlife service.

Flying Forward

In what Newhouse in a previous book called the sporty game, the future still looks like a high-stakes competition to make really big sales. Each side will announce the total sales after each air show as proof that they are winning, closing the gap, meeting customer needs, and so on. If the past holds true in the future, both Airbus and Boeing will be "surprised" when a new competitor challenges them for a share of the market. The B-787 and A-380, while touted as "changing the experience of flying" will likely end up packing the seats in so that airlines can get the most out of their assets. Presidents and prime ministers will still go out around the world privately pitching "their" aerospace company. However, sometimes things really do change. The industry faces a number of challenges in this new century—carbon emissions limits (Chapter 18), new technology and capacity demands (Chapter 20), rising costs, particularly for fuel (Chapter 15), and liberalizing markets (Chapter 16). If it can keep its eyes on the skies and not on the current sales numbers, then the future may be bright.

Table 19.3   LCA engines

Manufacturer	Engine	In-Service Date	Aircraft Example
Pratt & Whitney	GP7000	2008	A-380
	PW6000	2007	A-318
General Electric	GP7000	2007	A-380
	GEnx	2019	B-787
Rolls-Royce	Trent 900	2007	A-380
	Trent 1000	2014	B-787
	Trent XBW	TBD	A-350

Source: Company websites

Questions

1. Discuss the differing vision of the future airline market that divided Boeing and Airbus.
2. Why might Airbus have felt that they needed s ultra high-capacity aircraft in their "family"?

3. How do the A380 and the B-787 compare? What does the current order book say about airline needs?
4. What is the market outlook for aircraft?
5. Discuss the comeback of the turboprop aircraft and the future of the regional jet.
6. Discuss changing sales concepts at the engine manufacturers.

References

Airbus (2013), "Future journeys: global market forecast 2013–2032," retrieved online January 20, 2014 from http://www.airbus.com/company/market/forecast/?eID=dam_frontend_push&docID=33621.

Aris, S. (2002), *Close to the Sun: How Airbus Challenged America's Domination of the Skies*, Arum Press, London.

Boeing (2013), "Current market outlook 2013–2032," retrieved online January 20, 2014 from http://www.boeing.com/boeing/commercial/cmo/.

Flottau, J. (2013a), "Brave new world," *Aviation Week & Space Technology*, November 25, pp. 28–29.

Flottau, J. (2013b), "Wide opening," *Aviation Week & Space Technology*, October 14, pp. 32–34.

General Electric (GE) Press Release (2003), "GE signs definitive agreement with China for regional jet engines," retrieved online April 23, 2007 from http://www.geae.com/aboutgeae/presscenter/cf34/cf34_20031112.html.

General Electric (GE) (2014), "OnPoint solutions," retrieved online February 23, 2014 from http://www.geaviation.com/services/onpoint-solutions/.

Kownatzki, M., Hoyland, T. and Watterson, A. (2009), *The 50-seat Jet: A Plane with No Future. Think Again!* Oliver Wyman Aviation, Aerospace, and Defense Practice, Oliver Wyman, New York.

Mathews, J. (2013), "Flying over the horizon," *Aviation Week & Space Technology*, November 4, p. 12.

Mecham, M. and Norris, G. (2013), "Bit of a Quandary," *Aviation Week & Space Technology*, December 3, p. 40.

Mitsubishi (2013), "Mitsubishi Regional Jet," retrieved online February 23, 2014 from http://www.mrj-japan.com/.

Narabe, T. and Kimura, H. (2013), "Mitsubishi aircraft delays delivery of 1st passenger jet to 2017," retrieved online February 23, 2014 from http://ajw.asahi.com/article/economy/business/AJ201308230064.

Newhouse, J. (2007), *Boeing versus Airbus: The Inside Story of the Greatest Competition in Business*, Alfred A. Knopf, New York.

Perrett, B. (2013), "Field of five," *Aviation Week & Space Technology*, August 5, pp. 38–40.

Reuters Limited (2008), "ANA weighs buying 30 Mitsubishi regional jets, report says," *USA Today* online edition, retrieved online January 8, 2008 from http:/// www.usatoday.com/pt/cpt?action=cpt&title=ANA+weighs+buying.

Sparaco, P. (2013), "Airbus's big challenge," *Aviation Week & Space Technology*, November 11, p. 23.

The Economist (2012), "Turbo aversion, turbo reversion," retrieved online February 23, 2014 from http://www.economist.com/blogs/gulliver/2012/02/ air-travel-and-turboprop-revival.

Toh, M. (2013), "Comac aims to deliver first ARJ21 by end of 2014," retrieved online February 23, 2014 from http://www.flightglobal.com/news/articles/ comac-aims-to-deliver-first-arj21-by-end-2014-391012/.

Warwick, G. (2013), "Bombardier CSeries conducts second flight," retrieved online February 23, 2014 from http://atwonline.com/airframes/bombardier-cseries-conducts-second-flight.

Watanabe, C. (2008), "Toyota asked to invest in jet project," *USA Today* online edition, retrieved online January 8, 2008 from http:www.usatoday.com/pt/cpt? action=cpt&title=Toyota+asked+...

Wikipedia (2014), "Competition between Airbus and Boeing," retrieved online February 26, 2014 from http://www.ask.com/wiki/Competition_between_ Airbus_and_Boeing?o=2800&qsrc=999&ad=doubleDown&an=apn&ap=ask. com.

Woodyard, C. (2008), "Honda, GE build new jet engine," *USA Today* online edition, retrieved online January 8, 2008 from http:www.usatoday.com/pt/cp t?action=cpt&title=Honda+GE+build+.

Reuters Limited (2008). "ANA averts a big org 30 Mitsubishi regional jets, seeks legal," *USA Today* online edition. Retrieved online, January 8, 2008 from http://www.usatoday.com/blog/factcheck-regs./life-ANA+ wo/just-buying.

Spaceco, T. (2013). Airbus's big challenge, *Aviation Weekly Space Technology*, November 11, p. 23.

The Associated (2013). "Turbo aver-bar, turbo government," retrieved online, February 25, 2014 from http://www.economista.com/blog/gulliver/012007/air-travel-and-turbo-prop-aviation.

Tph Me (2013), "Com air aims to deliver first AKI21 by end of 2013," retrieved online, February 23, 2014 from http://www.flightglobal.com/news/articles/com-air-to-deliver-first-ati21-by-end-2014-391012-2.

Warwick, G. (2013). "Bombardier CSeries conducts second flight," retrieved online, February 25, 2014 from http://www.aviationweek.com/airlines/bombardier-cseries-conducts-second-flight-a.

Watanabe, O. (2008). "Too air asks to refocus in tat project, *USA Today* online edition," retrieved online January 8, 2008 from http://www.usatoday.com/profit-action-cost-due-to-a/art-4-12-g.

Wikipedia (2013). "Competition between Airbus and Boeing," retrieved online, February 26, 2014 from http://www.wikipedia.com/wiki/Competition-between-Airbus-and-Boeing/go/30308.asp?-9994-de-doubleDown.6%20-spice.app.ask.asp.

Woodward, G. (2018). "Honda, GE build new jet engine," *USA Today* online edition. Retrieved online January 8, 2008 from http://www.usatoday.com/ph/description-pix-title-Honda-GE-build-.

Chapter 20
After the Revolution

Learning Objectives

After reading this chapter, you should have a good understanding of:
- LO1: the impact of 9/11 security concerns on the cargo industry.
- LO2: the role of fuel prices in air cargo.
- LO3: the role of 3PL and 4PL in the cargo industry.
- LO4: the growth of the integrated carriers.

Key Terms, Concepts, and People

TSA	FIATA	Integrated carrier
3PL	4PL	Diversification
9/11	Commission	

Trading Time for Money

Like all of the aviation and aerospace industry, the air cargo world was rocked by the events of 9/11. Over a decade after those events, the industry is still facing many unanswered questions, specifically over cargo security requirements and fuel prices. While companies touted the newest and latest technologies for tracking and screening cargo, many industry experts wondered how reliable the new technologies would prove to be, how quickly they could be deployed, and who would pay for them? Then, just as it appeared that things were looking up, the GFC hit and economies around the world faltered and contracted. If the airline industry is cyclical, that is, sensitive to the business cycle, then air cargo is the "canary in the coal mine" that signals when the business cycle is starting to turn down. Unlike the proverbial canary that dies in the presence of toxic gas in the mine, air cargo does not die, but sharp drops in air cargo volumes signal that firms are cutting costs in their supply chain logistics by moving to lower-cost transportation options or closer suppliers. In effect, they are trading longer shipping times for lower costs or moving suppliers closer to reduce shipping costs at the expense of somewhat higher manufacturing or supply costs. The dramatic jump in fuel prices that occurred in 2008 (Table 20.1) led Boeing to talk about the "depressed levels" of air cargo in 2009 in their World Air Cargo Forecast. While air cargo volume rebounded 18.5 percent in 2010, there was a slowdown

Evolution of International Aviation

again in 2011 and 2012. Since 2001, annual air cargo growth has only been 3.7 percent a year. Evidence from freighter conversion orders, particularly for wide-body conversions, would seem to support the fact that air cargo operators continue to see a challenging and uneven landscape ahead for air cargo (Boeing, 2012; McCurry, 2013). In the December issue of *Air Cargo World*, the lead editorial was entitled "How to reflect on a year best to forget." The article laments the troubles at key all-cargo operators such as Air Cargo Germany, CargoLux, the cargo alliance of Air France–KLM, and so on, before ending with the hope that the new year will provide some sign of recovery in air freight (*Air Cargo World*, 2013).

The disadvantage of a tightly linked, time-sensitive system is that it is easily disrupted. Rising prices for transportation (related to the price of oil) and slowing sales have many firms rethinking the need for speed, opting for lower-cost shipping solutions or suppliers closer to home, and building up emergency inventories (or pushing these demands onto suppliers as logistics-leading WalMart has continued to do). Air freight was the only major mode of transportation whose average length of haul rose during the 1990s, but slower modes may supplant it due to cost (Bureau of Transportation Statistics, 2005). If falling transportation costs helped to create the logistics revolution, then the rising cost of fuel and security slow the revolution or redirect it to onshoring (versus offshoring) or insourcing (versus outsourcing). Of course, rising costs could also prompt a classic, economic response—consolidation. Consolidation is one of the ways that industries try to lower their costs by creating economies of scale. As we will see in this chapter, all of these challenges are creating a variety of responses and the jury is out on which "answer" will prevail.

While other industries have been undergoing a revolution in logistics and supply chain that involved more outsourcing and more use of air cargo for time-sensitive delivery, the aviation/aerospace manufacturers have undergone a revolution of their own. In the case of Boeing, the percentages of outsourcing by model are as follows: 30 percent for the B-767, 50 percent for the B-777, and 70 percent for the B-787 (Scott and Kelly, 2013). Of course, at the same time that the major manufacturers are outsourcing more of the aircraft, they are also trying to reduce the overall number of suppliers in an effort to reduce the transaction costs of monitoring. While outsourcing was intended by Boeing to reduce the development time of the B-787 from six to four years, quality and monitoring issues pushed the project back three years and added billions to the budget. Technical problems forced Boeing to send out hundreds of engineers to suppliers and restructure their entire sub-assembly process (Denning, 2013). Thus, as we will see, aviation/aerospace illustrates both the positive and negative sides of the logistics revolution.

Securing the Goods

In the US, the 9/11 Commission made a number of recommendations for securing cargo entering the country, including a requirement for 100 percent physical inspection of all cargo. Of most concern was the cargo carried on passenger aircraft. Only in 2012 did the Transportation Security Administration (TSA) finally set a December 2012 deadline for 100 percent screening for explosives on international inbound passenger carriers (TSA, 2012). However, the 9/11 Commission envisioned the requirement applying to all types and forms of cargo—surface and air. While the concept received wide support when it was first released, it has faced a number of obstacles on the road to implementation. Legislation in the US House of Representatives called for a three-year phase-in to 100 percent screening in 2009, although the Bush White House argued that the technology does not yet exist to handle the level of cargo entering the US without substantially impeding the flow of trade. A debate even developed over the wording between the House and US Senate versions, that is, how does 100 percent inspection differ from 100 percent screening? Screening after all could involve a system for evaluating risk, gathering intelligence, and assessing documentation rather than physically inspecting/scanning cargo. Air cargo operators have argued that they already screen all of their freight shipments in one fashion or another. Further complicating the matter, auditors for the US Congress have suggested that full physical inspection of all cargo on passenger aircraft alone would cost approximately US$3.6 billion over 10 years (Moorman, 2007a). The October 2010 terrorist bomb that involved supposed printer cartridges coming from Yemen to the US was another major blow to the TSA program of 100 percent physical screening. Although the plot was thwarted, it prompted US and EU officials to rethink their policies in many ways, including mandating security controls at the point of origin (Solomon, 2013).

The initial efforts of the TSA to improve cargo security were severely criticized in a report by the US Department of Homeland Security's Office of Inspector General who cited the TSA as having too few cargo inspectors, vague regulations, and an ineffective database for tracking violators (Moorman, 2007b). The TSA proposed the creation of a cargo version of the Known Traveler program, now called the Certified Cargo Screening Program (CCSP). Under the program the TSA certifies cargo screening facilities to screen cargo provided to airlines for shipment on passenger flights. Beyond these achievements in 100 percent screening for passenger flights, the US attempt to create a system of 100 percent physical inspection has given way to the more realistic approach of many foreign trading partners of risk-based assessment. The TSA has signed agreements with a number of trading partners simply acknowledging that they accept the cargo security programs of these nations as commensurate with those of the US. Thus, the US has "found a way" to declare 100 percent screening without the inspection (Hienz, 2012). This outcome should please the IATA and the International Federation of Freight Forwarders (FIATA) whose 2007 Global Air Cargo Security Industry Task Force recommended harmonization of security regimes across countries and expressed concern that some of the national laws being proposed, particularly in the US, were "not proportionate to the threat." John Edwards, then-IATA head of cargo security, suggested that governments avoid comparing security for passengers to air cargo because most air cargo travels on pallets or in containers that have been packed under secure conditions. Like much of the air cargo industry itself, the Task Force argued that the security focus should be shifted to the point of origin rather than the point of departure (airport) and that mandating costly, unproven equipment would be prohibitively expensive and damaging to world trade and economies (Doyle, 2007).

Future of Fuel

The airlines had reported an overall rise of 90 percent in their costs between 2000 and 2008 with fuel costs surpassing labor costs in total operations expenses (26 percent to 23 percent) (Associated Press, 2008). This was before the spike of 2008. Table 20.1 shows the cost of a barrel of oil, the cost in cents per mile for US domestic air travel, and the price of jet fuel from 2000 to 2013. The ATA estimates that every penny paid for jet fuel costs the US airline and air cargo industry US$190 to US$200 million annually (ATA, 2007). As noted in Chapter 15, fuel prices are one of the many costs over which carriers have little leverage. Aside from hedging strategies, fleet renewal, weight reduction, and operational flight changes, there is little that carriers can do to affect fuel costs.

In the first quarter of 2008, the Air Cargo Management Group had forecast a 5–8 percent decline in global air freight traffic on an average monthly jet fuel cost of US$2.769 a gallon, which would force cargo carriers to increase fuel surcharges. These surcharges actually rose from 50 cents in early 2007 to 80–85 cents by January 2008 (*Air Cargo World*, 2008). In 2009, air cargo plummeted from 15.5 billion Freight Ton Kilometers (FTKs) per month to roughly 10 FTKs per month. The cost of air freight was roughly 14 times that of sea transport. Shippers were rethinking their supply chains, restricting air freight to perishable, high-value cargo and even moving some high-value cargos such as LCD and integrated circuits from air to sea (Pearce, 2011). Air freight growth for 2013 continued on a weaker pace than the 3.7 percent that it had averaged since 2001 with the Middle East and Latin America seeing robust growth year-over-year (IATA, 2013). Sadly, all predictions of future cargo volumes have failed to materialize as new exogenous events have arisen to dampen expected growth for this beleaguered industry (Pearce, 2011). CAPA has reported that air cargo growth continues to lag passenger growth with cargo low factors and freighter utilization low (CAPA, 2013).

Third Party Logistics (3PL)

In an era in which cost and time considerations continue to drive logistics and supply chains to new levels of sophistication, it is not surprising to discover that many firms are outsourcing these activities to firms who specialize in these areas, freeing themselves to make or retail the products themselves. These third-party

Table 20.1   Price of fuel and air travel

Year	Crude Oil*	Domestic Travel**	Jet Fuel***
2004	41.51	11.69	115.5
2005	56.64	11.96	166.3
2006	66.05	13.04	196.7
2007	72.34	13.08	210.5
2008	99.67	13.93	306.8
2009	61.95	12.41	189.7
2010	79.48	13.49	224.4
2011	94.87	14.61	286.6
2012	94.05	15.10	295.0
2013	97.98	-	-

* US$ price per barrel; **US$ cents per mile; ***US$ cents per gallon
Source: Airlines for America (A4A) website. Data available at: http://www.airlines.org/Pages/
Annual-Crude-Oil-and-Jet-Fuel-Prices.aspx and http://www.airlines.org/Pages/Annual-Round-
Trip-Fares-and-Fees-Domestic.aspx

logistics providers (3PLs) may specialize in everything from warehousing and inventorying to single or multi-mode transportation. Taking the concept even further are the so-called 4PLs who re-engineer a firm's entire logistics process but frequently do not provide services directly; they contract with other service providers on behalf of their clients and manage the supply chain (Anderson and Leinbach, 2007). The Unisys Global Shippers' Survey (2006) found that most shippers prefer multiple providers as a means of avoiding single-source dependence. Even the largest shippers reported using medium-sized or niche logistics providers who covered only a limited geographic region or provided a limited set of services. Many corporations provided an approved list of transport and logistics providers to regional units who were free to select the ones that best fit their needs. The 2014 Annual Survey of Third-Party Logistics Providers found that 52 percent of companies in their survey met or exceeded revenue projects, but that continued weakness in Europe and the shifting of manufacturing out of China where wages are rising were a factor in the instability of the industry. Still, most companies expected revenue growth in the 5–8 percent range (Penske, 2013).

Hard Times and New Friends

As the new century opened, the venerable USPS announced that it would have a US$300 million loss for the fiscal year. Reasons given for the loss included a decline in first-class cards and letters, increased gasoline prices, and additional labor costs (Robinson, 2000). Although the loss proved to be only US$199 million, the USPS was clearly struggling under the weight of growing competition and changing times. Some of the challenges facing the USPS are well known to older established firms such as growing fixed expenses for pension plans, worker compensation, health benefits, and the interest expense of debt. Further adding to these challenges were concerns that postal volumes would continue to decline due to competition from other express and parcel companies as well as new electronic alternatives. Unfortunately, the USPS has a limited ability to deal with these issues. Even postal rate changes must be approved by the Postal Rate Commission who often hears arguments from "interested parties" for lower rates. The USPS attempted to address these basic problems through a number of classic business tactics: restructuring, layoffs, asset sales, accounting adjustments, and outsourcing (Ho, 2001; Robinson, 2000). It is ironic that one outcome of these struggles was a June 2006 announcement that the USPS had signed a US$100 million deal with UPS to carry US mail on its jets. The three-year contract makes UPS responsible for delivering mail to 96 US cities. After years of battling the USPS for the right to deliver packages across the US, UPS has now made a "pact with the devil" in a sign of the changing world of airmail and small packages (Niemann, 2007). Also in 2006, the Postal Accountability Enhancement Act was passed separating the USPS services into market-dominant and competitive products. Under this legislation, the USPS was able to make and retain profits on competitive product offerings but prohibited from cross-subsidizing between the two categories. The USPS could cut some of its cost in international markets, if it were allowed to include foreign carriers in the bidding process, but at the present time, they are prohibited from doing so unless the services of US carriers are deemed "inadequate." Sadly, 2006 also witnessed the imposition of new rules mandated by the US Congress; these rules required the USPS to make annual payments of US$1.4 billion to a healthcare fund for future retirees. While the USPS reported that operating revenues for the third quarter of 2013 were up 3.6 percent in part due to increased parcel shipping from online purchases, this still equated to a loss of US$740 million for the quarter. Given losses of US$16 billion for the prior year, the USPS has asked to do away with Saturday delivery and the repayment to the healthcare fund, but action by the US Congress appears unlikely (Nawaguna, 2013).

Meanwhile, in sharp contrast to its American cousin (USPS), January 1, 1990 marked the beginning of a new era for a company that traced its roots to a time 500 years ago; new legislation would start the privatization of public postal and telecommunication services and Deutsche Post would seize their opportunities. They would turn around old losses to breakeven by the mid-1990s and go public in 2000. They would acquire Danzas Holding, a Swiss logistics company, Air Express International, and the remaining shares of DHL and Excel. These acquisitions were simply the largest in a series of acquisitions as noted in a 2007 feature in *Aviation Week & Space Technology* entitled "Evolution of the Air Cargo Industry." In the center fold out, the article traces the history of the key players among the integrators, forwarders, and airlines since the 1980s. It visually displays the name, size, and region where each player was acquiring companies and assets. In the middle of all of this activity was a very busy Deutsche Post (CRA International, 2007). Although DHL would withdraw from the US, Deutsche Post DHL would become the world's leading mail and logistics company with a presence in 220 countries (World Economic Forum, 2012). In one of their latest ventures, Deutsche Post DHL has announced that it will begin a German-wide grocery delivery service by 2015 (*Postal News*, 2013). Thus, while the US Congress continues to force a public–private hybrid model on the USPS, Deutsche Post, in the heart of a continent that many US politicians like to think of as socialist, is being very entrepreneurial indeed.

Logistics in Brown

While the deal with the USPS was a sweet one for UPS, they also began a series of acquisitions in 2000 that would strengthen their ground and logistics operations (CRA International, 2007). During the five year period, 2002–2006, UPS completed 11 acquisitions. Some of these acquisitions were designed to strengthen their operations in key regions such as China, Japan, and Europe. Other acquisitions were undertaken to broaden their capabilities in freight-forwarding, heavy freight and less-than-truckload services. The 2001 acquisition of Mail Boxes Etc, at the time the largest franchiser of retail shipping and postal services, would set the stage for The UPS Store. Overall, UPS grew during this period at a compound rate of 4 percent a year. Domestic package delivery accounted for 64 percent of their 2006 revenue with international package delivery accounting for another 19 percent. The remaining 17 percent of their revenue came from their supply chain and freight division (UPS Annual Report, 2006).

In 1999, their logistics/supply chain services became known as UPS Logistics Technologies, and set the stage for UPS Solutions and the ad campaign to rebrand on their love of logistics. As part of this journey, the company's transportation and logistics software, ROADNET, would help firms like Frito-Lay, Costco, and SYSCO optimize routes, plan territories, dispatch vehicles, and track deliveries. UPS would help manufacturing companies with their supply chains, redesigning Ford Motor Company's system for getting cars from the assembly plant to showroom floors, helping Harley-Davidson Motor Company track and inventory inbound parts and accessories, and improving the logistics of the service center of European medical supplier, Royal Philips Electronics (Niemann, 2007). Integration of several acquired units in 2006—the Motor Cargo unit of Overnite and Menlo Worldwide Forwarding—led to some disappointing revenue results for that year but overall revenues for the freight and supply chain unit were up 33 percent from the prior year (UPS Annual Report, 2006). By 2012, total revenue would stand at US\$54.1 billion. Package operations would account for US\$45 billion while supply chain and freight solutions would represent US\$9.1 billion of the total (UPS website, 2013).

Table 20.2 provides an overall snapshot of the operational results for UPS, a company that still defines itself by its primary business of time-definite delivery even as it expands into the broader area of logistics and supply chain. The post-9/11 trends continued upward for UPS driven primarily by international growth. Express package deliveries continue to rise, as does the revenue of the firm overall. The only downward measure was fleet size. Like the passenger carriers, there was a post-9/11 movement to retire older, less fuel-efficient aircraft that reduced capacity, primarily in the domestic market. Fleet number began to climb again in 2005 and 2006. It is too early to determine what impact rising fuel prices might have on fleet size.

Table 20.2   UPS growth 2004–2012

Year	Revenue*	Net Income*	Assets*
2004	36,582	3,333	33,088
2005	42,581	3,870	35,222
2006	47,547	4,202	33,210
2007	49,692	382	39,042
2008	51,486	3,003	31,879
2009	45,297	2,152	31,883
2010	49,545	3,338	33,597
2011	53,105	3,804	34,701
2012	54,127	807	38,863

* US$ in millions
Source: UPS website. Data available at: http://www.investors.ups.com/phoenix.zhtml?c =62900&p=irol-reportsannual

Related Diversifications?

The year 2000 marked a new evolution at Federal Express whose corporate identity changed in 1994 to simply FedEx and which has now established a separate unit called FedEx Express to oversee development in its express-specific service offerings. Ground operations, which began in 1985 with Roadway Package System, a division of Roadway and later Caliber System, became FedEx Ground in 2000 with the acquisition of Caliber. FedEx acquired American Freightways in 2001, adding to earlier acquisitions of Viking Freight (part of Caliber) and Caribbean Transportation Services (1999). In 2006, FedEx acquired Watkins Motor Lines, a ground, freight-forwarding company. These units created FedEx Freight, which became a leading provider of next- and second-day less-than-truckload freight services. By 2013, FedEx would segment itself into four basic units: FedEx Express, FedEx Ground, FedEx Freight, and FedEx Services. Total annual revenues for 2013 topped US$44 billion (FedEx website, 2013).

Table 20.3 shows the growth at FedEx from 2000 to 2013. Like rival UPS, there was a post-9/11 fleet reduction, but the overall trends have remained positive. FedEx has not witnessed the kind of growth in express package volumes that UPS has experienced. In fact, the number of packages has fluctuated over this period and remains relatively static. With the various acquisitions, there has been an overall rise in the number of employees, although FedEx has yet to reach the levels of UPS.

Table 20.3   FedEx growth 2004–2012

Year	Revenue*	Net Income*	Assets*
2004	24,710	838	19,134
2005	29,363	1,449	20,404
2006	32,294	1,806	22,690
2007	35,214	2,016	24,000
2008	37,953	1,125	25,633
2009	35,497	98	24,244
2010	34,734	1,184	24,902
2011	39,304	1,452	27,385
2012	42,680	2,032	29,903

* US$ in millions
Source: FedEx website. Data available at: http://investors.fedex.com/phoenix.zhtml?c =73289&p=irol-reportsannual

Millions of Parts Flying Together

There is probably no better illustration of the complexity possible in a logistics supply chain than the aviation/aerospace industry. An aircraft such as the B-747 has as many as six million parts. Once you add up all of the models or aircraft that a major manufacturer like Boeing makes, then the total number of parts to be procured in any given year will be upward of 750 million (Chamberlin, 2012). At present, the aerospace supply chain consists of four tiers that sit below the Aircraft and Engine Original Equipment Manufacturers, commonly called OEMs. Tier 1 companies supply aircraft systems and major aerostructures. Tier 2 companies are responsible for components and sub-assemblies. Tier 3 companies are machine shops, many make-to-print operations. Finally, Tier 4 represents the materials firms as well as specialty process companies. The latter may include companies engaged in forging or casting of parts. There has recently been a good deal of consolidation in the supply chain, particularly at the Tier 4 level. Several factors are driving the consolidation. First, there is vertical consolidation that allows raw material firms to capture the scrap produced in machining at Tier 3. There are estimates that up to US$8 billion could be lost to scrap in machining and recapturing and reusing can be quite beneficial. A second reason for consolidation is the desire to move up the supply chain since profit margins tend to rise as you move from raw materials to finished products. The same logic of moving up the chain would also apply to Tiers 1–3 (Michaels, 2013). There are concerns with the aerospace supply chain since roughly 70 percent of the chain for all aerospace manufacturers consists of the same companies. So if there are only a few companies making composite material or the fasteners used for airframe construction, then there is concern that surging demand might result in a shortage that raises prices and may slow production. The reverse problem has also plagued the industry, that is, slumps in demand place great financial pressure on these lower-tier firms. A general slump in aircraft demand such as the one the industry experienced after 2008 means that firms must operate below capacity. The farther down the supply chain a firm resides, the more likely it is to be forced to "submit" to cancellations and/or delays in orders that are built into contract. Contracting power normally resides higher in the supply chain, OEM and Tier 1. In any case, these firms dictate terms and conditions to the rest of the supply chain. In fact, many small firms have been forced out-of-business or into consolidation because of stringent requirements to meet rates of production, quality standards, conduct specific testing, bear the cost of tooling or logistics software, and so on (Canaday, 2013). In theory, the number of new models coming out (or planned)—B-787, A-380, A-350, the new CSeries from Bombardier, and the Mitsubishi regional jet, and so on—should be good news for the firms in the aerospace supply chain. Certainly, it should reduce the slack and improve many bottom lines, however, with complexity and demand come other problems as Boeing has discovered.

There are several accounts of what went wrong in the latest Boeing aircraft, the B-787, and there will likely be many more in the coming years, but a brief look at some of the issues reveals the many pitfall and challenges of complex supply chains. Table 20.4 gives a brief overview of the parts breakdown by country and company. Some highlights of the problems encountered include: June 2007, an industry-wide shortage of fasteners as well as the discovery of a misalignment of the cockpit section with the fuselage at the same time, September 2008, an installation of improper fasteners and a union strike, June 2009, discovery of a need for reinforcements in the wing-to-fuselage section, August 2009, discovery of microscopic wrinkles in the fuselage. Boeing has approximately 50 Tier 1 suppliers around the world for the B-787 and while they do have the E20 open applications logistics software that is supposed to help coordinate multi-tier supply chains, it cannot guarantee there are no communication problems with different languages, cultures, or time zones. Further, Boeing mandates that its Tier 1 suppliers coordinate with Tiers 2 and 3 to relieve pressure on themselves and so rely on these suppliers to monitor quality. Their own relationship with the Tier 1 was strained by the Boeing mandate that suppliers had to design and build all tooling for their part of the aircraft without any compensation from Boeing. While outsourcing is not new to Boeing, the level of outsourcing and the fact that the top-tier suppliers were in complete control of the design and lower tier suppliers was new (Collins, 2010; Gates, 2013).

Table 20.4   Boeing 787 parts breakdown

Part	Country	Company
Wingtips	Korea	KAA
Fixed and moveable leading edges (wings)	US	Spirit
Wing	Japan	Mitsubishi
Centre fuselage	Italy	Alenia
Forward fuselage	US Japan	Spirit Kawasaki
Centre wing box	Japan	Fuji
Landing gear structure Forward	France	Messier-Dowty
Lithium-ion batteries	Japan	GS Yuasa
Rear fuselage	US	Boeing
Wing-to-body fairing	US	Boeing
Engine nacelles	US	Goodrich
Engines	US UK	General Electric Rolls-Royce
Horizontal stabilizer	Italy	Alenia
Tail fin	US	Boeing
Passenger entry door	France	Latecoere
Main landing gear	Japan	Kawasaki
Fixed trailing edge (wings)	Japan	Kawasaki
Cargo access doors	Sweden	Saab

Source: Ro, S. (2013) "Boeing's 787 Dreamliner is made of parts from all over the world"

Conclusion

The jury is still out on the direction of the logistics revolution. Like most things in life (and business), it is very possible that the pendulum will swing back toward less outsourcing and more simplified supply chains. In essence, after years of moving key functions out of the company and country, many firms may decide to start reversing these trends. After all, the costs of coordinating and monitoring a highly complex task can be daunting. Thus, just as firms tend to swing back and forth between centralization and decentralization of decision making and operations, there is likely to be swings in this area as well when management perceives that quality, costing, transportation, too tightly linked just-in-time manufacturing, and other considerations are negatively impacting operations. How far the swing will go in the other direction remains to be seen and what impact it will have on air cargo and the aerospace industry is an open question.

Questions

1. How did 9/11 change the cargo industry?
2. What role might technology play in security and logistics?
3. What effect do rising fuel prices have on the air cargo industry?
4. Discuss the changes at the integrated carriers.
5. What is the future of the logistics revolution?

References

Air Cargo World (2008), "Freight's on-off peak," January, p. 4.

Air Cargo World (2013), "How best to reflect on a year best to forget," *Air Cargo World*, December, pp. 6–8.

Air Transport Association (ATA) (2007), "Quarterly cost index: US passenger airlines," retrieved online December 6, 2007 from http://www.airlines.org/economics/finance/Cost+index.htm.

Anderson, W.P. and Leinbach, T.R. (2007), "E-commerce, Logistics, and the Future of Globalized Freight" in Thomas R. Leinbach and Cristina Capineri (eds), *Globalized Freight Transport: Intermodality, E-commerce, Logistics, and Sustainability*, Edward Elgar, Cheltenham, UK.

Associated Press (2008), "Airlines' costs rose in 3Q led by fuel-price jump; soars 91 percent above 2000 levels," retrieved online January 10, 2008 from http://biz.yahoo.com/ap/080129/airleins_costs_index.html.

Boeing Corporation (2012), "World air cargo forecast 2012–13," retrieved online February 16, 2014 from http://www.boeing.com/boeing/commercial/cargo/.

Bureau of Transportation Statistics (2005), "National transportation statistics 2004," retrieved online January 8, 2008 from www.bts.gov.

Canaday, H. (2013), "Volume is not the issue," *Aviation Week & Space Technology*, October 28, pp. 46–48.

The Centre for Aviation (CAPA) (2013), "Air cargo: structural reform urgently needed where capacity exceeds demand by over 100%," retrieved online January 16, 2014 from http://centreforaviation.com/analysis/air-cargo-structural-reform-urgently-needed-where-capacity-exceeds-demand-by-over-100-128013.

Chamberlin, C. (2012), "Trends in aerospace industry, Boeing shared services group supplier management," retrieved March 18, 2013 online from http://washingtonports.org/wp-content/uploads/2013/02/annual12-chamberlinboeing.pdf.

Collins, M. (2010), "The Boeing supply chain model," retrieved online March 18, 2013 from http://www.manufacturing.net/news/2010/07/the-boeing-supply-chain-model.

CRA International (2007), "Evolution of the air cargo industry," *Aviation Week & Space Technology*, May 7–14, pp. 48–53.

Denning, S. (2013), "What went wrong at Boeing?" *Forbes Magazine*, January 21, retrieved online February 3, 2014 from http://www.forbes.com/sites/stevedenning/2013/01/21/what-went-wrong-at-boeing/.

Doyle, J.M. (2007), "Intervention prevention," *Aviation Week & Space Technology*, May 7–14, pp. 63–64.

Gates, D. (2013), "Boeing 787's problems blamed on outsourcing, lack of oversight," *The Seattle Times*, February 2, retrieved online February 3, 2014 from http://seattletimes.com/html/businesstechnology/2020275838_boeingoutsourcingxml.html.

Hienz, J. (2012), "100 percent air cargo screening exists without fanfare," retrieved online March 9, 2014 from http://www.defensemedianetwork.com/stories/100-percent-air-cargo-screening-exits-without-fanfare/.

Ho, D. (2001), "Post office may stop Saturday mail delivery," Associated Press, April 3, retrieved online February 18, 2007 from www.apwu73.com/bulletin/Post%20may%20stop%20Saturday%.

International Air Transport Association (IATA) (2013), "Air freight volumes show signs of life in June," retrieved online March 26, 2014 from http://www.iata.org/pressroom/pr/pages/2013-07-30-01.aspx.

McCurry, J.W. (2013), "Narrow-bodies pace conversion market," *Air Cargo World*, August, pp. 24–27.

Michaels, K. (2013), "Revolution from below," *Aviation Week & Space Technology*, September 9, p. 18.

Moorman, R. (2007a), "Drawing new security lines," *Air Cargo World*, March, pp. 20–24.

Moorman, R. (2007b), "Secure funding" *Air Cargo World*, October, pp. 10–11.

Nawaguna, E. (2013), "US Postal Service loss narrows on cost cutting," retrieved online January 16, 2014 from http://www.reuters.com/article/2013/08/09/us-usa-postal-idUSBRE9780VC20130809.

Niemann, G. (2007), *Big Brown: The Untold Story of UPS*, Jossey-Bass, San Francisco, CA.

Page, P. (2006), "Cargo's trading places," *Air Cargo World*, August, pp. 27–32.

Pearce, B. (2011), "Understanding air cargo markets and their importance," retrieved online January 7, 2008 from http://www.aci.aero/aci/aci/file/2011%20Events/WAGA2011/presentations/Brian_Pearce_IATA.pdf.

Penske (2013), "Penske Logistics: Survey finds 3PL CEOs project growth," retrieved online March 26, 2014 from http://www.penskelogistics.com/newsroom/2013_10_21_pl_3pl_study_projects_growth.html.

Postal News (2013), "Deutsche Post to launch online groceries service," retrieved online March 25, 2014 from http://postalnews.com/postalnewsblog/2013/08/07/deutsche-post-to-launch-online-groceries-service/.

Ro, S. (2013), "Boeing's 787 Dreamliner is made of parts from all over the world," *Business Insider*, retrieved online February 14, 2012 from http://www.businessinsider.com/boeing-787-dreamliner-structure-suppliers-2013-10.

Robinson, A.M. (2000), "USPS finances: are we on the road from universal to invisible?" retrieved online October 13, 2002 from http://www.aircargoworld.com/features/0208_1.htm.

Scott, A. and Kelly, T. (2013), "Analysis: Boeing's JAL loss may bring work back to the US," retrieved online March 25, 2014 from http://www.reuters.com/article/2013/10/11/us-boeing-suppliers-analysis-idUSBRE99A0Y420131011.

Seemuth, M. (2008), "Cargo's truck factor," retrieved online January 9, 2008 from http://www.postcom.org/public/articles/2000articles/101000a.htm.

Solomon, A. (2013), "A new day for global air cargo security," *Air Cargo World*, retrieved online March 26, 2014 from http://www.aircargoworld.com/Air-Cargo-News/2013/03/a-new-day-for-global-air-cargo-security/0812813.

Transportation Security Administration (TSA) (2012), "TSA sets cargo screening deadline for international inbound passenger aircraft," retrieved online March 26, 2014 from http://www.tsa.gov/press/releases/2012/05/16/tsa-sets-cargo-screening-deadline-international-inbound-passenger-aircraft.

World Economic Forum (2012), "Seutsche Post DHL," retrieved online March 25, 2014 from http://www.weforum.org/strategic-partners/deutsche-post-dhl.

Unisys (2006), Unisys Global Shippers' Survey 2006, *Fastforward Q3*.

UPS Annual Report (2006), retrieved online January 6, 2008 from http://www.ups.com.

Websites

Deutsche Post DH: http://www.dp-dhl.de
FedEx: http://www.fedex.com
UPS: http://www.ups.com

Chapter 21

A Twenty-First Century Air Space

Learning Objectives

After reading this chapter, you should have a good understanding of:

- LO1: the projected growth in air travel.
- LO2: the advantages of using technology to expand airspace over infrastructure expansion.
- LO3: the key elements of NextGen/SESAR systems.
- LO4: the stumbling blocks to NextGen deployment.

Key Terms, Concepts, and People

NextGen	SESAR	ADS-B
SWIM	DataComm	User fee
FMS	ERAM	NATCA

Crowded Skies

After witnessing a 2009 decline in revenue passenger and freight tonnes per kilometers in the wake of the GFC, IATA reported that international passenger traffic grew between 6.0 and 8.5 percent annually through 2013. Passenger growth and revenues during this period were weakest in Europe and Africa with Asia continuing to experience the strongest growth (IATA, 2013). In their Vision 2050 report, IATA predicts that there will be continued growth in passenger traffic with 16 billion passengers by 2050. While much of this growth is predicted for the developing world, the air traffic systems of many developed nations are already straining to meet their more limited growth rates (IATA, 2011). For example, monthly traffic in the US has been between 50–70 million since May 2008 (Bureau of Transportation Statistics, 2013). Given the size of the existing base, even a small annual increase adds up quickly. The FAA is now predicting that traffic levels will reach one billion passengers per year by 2024 (FAA, 2012). In Europe, there were 9.6 million flights per year. By 2030, Eurocontrol expects this total to rise to 16.9 million (SESAR, 2012b).

Accommodating these levels of air traffic will require the nations of the world to make some very significant investments in aviation infrastructure otherwise the current capacity shortfall will grow to critical levels, threatening growth and the safety of the system. In developing nations, the current emphasis is on building the basic infrastructure of an aviation system—airports (runways, terminals), radar stations, and supporting infrastructure (access roads, warehouses, intermodal links, maintenance facilities). These regions will also have to address the need for trained personnel to man the system. Some of these nations are making rapid strides in their efforts while others are struggling, usually for the lack of money. Specific regional issues have already been covered in earlier chapters. Here it is important to note that the nations that can and are investing now have the opportunity to take advantage of technological advances in air space management without facing the difficult and sometimes wrenching transitions that more developed regions are facing. In some ways the situation is similar to the industrial rebuilding that took place in Europe and Asia after World War II. A new steel mill would incorporate the new closed hearth rather than the less efficient open hearth technology. In a similar way, developing nations can leapfrog to a satellite-based system rather than the old ground-based radar of the post-World War II era.

For the early pioneers in aviation (mostly those in the US and Europe), the problems are different—maintaining an aging infrastructure while transitioning to a new system of organization. James C. May of the ATA has noted that Charles Lindbergh, who made history in 1927 with his solo transatlantic flight, would be surprised to discover that 80 years later "we still rely on old technology that forces aircraft to fly inefficient, less direct routes, with unnecessarily inefficient separation requirements" (May, 2006). In fact, the ground radar, voice communication system in use today dates from the period just after World War II. The system has been modernized over the decades, but is essentially based on the same general technology and framework. These nations must make the transition to a new system in the face of rising traffic, active environmental movements, vocal consumer rights groups, and traditional carriers under pressure from new international and low cost competition. Key indicators that the aviation systems of North America and Europe are struggling with capacity issues include slot controls at airports, flight delays, and flight cancellations. Although North America has the space to construct more basic infrastructure, that is, airports and runways, doing so raises environmental concerns as well as the more general not-in-my-backyard (NIMBY) reaction. The closing of a number of US military bases had raised the hope that some of these facilities could be converted to civilian use, but in many cases local opposition halted these plans (FAA, 2008).

In this chapter, we will explore the technologies that are expected to shape the air space and aviation system of the twenty-first century in the context of the developed systems of North America and Europe. While some of the conditions and constraints vary, both regions are facing the difficult task of changing the tires on a rapidly moving vehicle. Further, each region is dealing with a set of political and economic problems that threaten to derail deployment.

Creating the Future

In the US, the Next Generation Air Transportation System (NGATS), commonly referred to as NextGen, is the air transportation solution for the twenty-first century. In Europe, the roughly equivalent concepts fall under the Single European Sky ATM Research (SESAR) program, although European efforts are also an attempt to integrate the air space in the EU in accordance with the Single Sky concept. The definition phase (2005–2008) of SESAR was jointly funded by EUROCONTROL and the EC. It was tasked with delivering a European ATM Master Plan based on future aviation requirements as defined by key stakeholders in the system. This plan was adopted in October 2012. SESAR and NextGen envision a totally new architecture that will allow information integration, combining new technologies on the ground and in the sky to create a more efficient system. They are expected to "create" new capacity by allowing air traffic to more efficiently utilize the existing airspace. The proposed new systems will also help to address many of the economic and environmental concerns facing the industry and the public. More efficient, direct continuous descents and ascents use less fuel, thus contributing less carbon and other GHGs to the environment and reducing the national dependence on petroleum. Improved utilization of existing airspace relieves some of the need for more airport construction with the environmental impacts that such construction almost always entails. Both US and European efforts began at roughly the same time and are planned for full implementation sometime around 2020–2025.

As with all things aviation, the discussion is filled with acronyms. To avoid confusion, the technological discussion that follows will try to broadly identify the systems and concepts. The NextGen system requires the development and implementation of eight capabilities: network-enabled information access, performance-based services, aircraft trajectory-based operations, weather assimilation into decision loops, broad-area precision navigation, equivalent visual operations, super density operations, and layered adaptive security (FAA, 2007b). There are at least three key technologies:

Automatic Dependent Surveillance-Broadcast (ADS-B) is a satellite-based system that allows aircraft to broadcast their position to others. ADS-B *out* will replace many ground radars with ground-based transceivers. ADS-B *in* would allow aircraft to receive signals from the ground-based transceivers as well as from ADS-B equipment onboard other aircraft.

System-wide Information Management (SWIM) is a new system architecture that would allow airspace users to access a wide array of data on the National Air Space (NAS) and weather. SWIM is a net-centric link between air traffic management, customers, and the departments of Homeland Security and Defense which would provide full automation and data convergence/synchronization across all authorized users on a common display format.

DataComm is the data communication system that will link airport towers, airline operations centers, and aircraft. It is the satellite, internet-based communication platform of the twenty-first century that will replace much of the old voice communication system.

While it was originally intended simply as a replacement for an earlier air traffic control system and predates NextGen, the En Route Automation Modernization (ERAM) system has come to be viewed as a critical foundation for NextGen capabilities such as DataComm and SWIM. ERAM is the high-altitude traffic platform to be used to control en route aircraft in the US. After some delay in deployment of the en route center which caused delays in the DataComm contract and the SWIM program, ERAM is set to be operational at all 20 en route air traffic centers in 2014, assuming that sequestration does not create further problems. Still, the General Accounting Office is concerned that some of the delays in the NextGen system might extend for years (FAA, 2013a; Perera, 2012). Further, there is now an issue of synchronizing ERAM with other systems used on board aircraft and in the airport area in order to provide the common situational awareness that is viewed as critical to proper, optimized airspace management (Schofield, 2013). For example, since ERAM was designed to manage high-altitude, en route traffic, it does not have the detailed airport information (runway configurations, arrival fixes, and so on) that are contained in modern on board Flight Management Systems (FMS).

In short, the old system of ground-based radar and positive voice control is to be replaced with an "intelligent" aircraft capable of using satellite technology to finds its own position, calculate its best flight path, communicate and coordinate its position with other craft in the airspace and with ground traffic control, and integrate multiple streams of information. Working within this overall system, specific tools such as broad-area precision navigation will allow for continuous descent approaches (CDA) while 4D trajectory flight management will allow for time-based arrival/departure planning; the aircraft will arrive at the airport just in time to join the line of landing aircraft and avoid the need to vector around in the airport area until a landing slot is available. The system would create the kind of precision necessary to allow for reduced aircraft separation and the simultaneous use of closely spaced parallel runways. In addition, new groundside technologies will detect runway and intruder incursions, improve taxiway and ramp management, and permit improved all-weather operations (FAA, 2007b). These new Surface Management Systems will generate moving maps of the airport surface, provide data-linked taxi instructions, and allow flight planning feedback and negotiation.

The US and NextGen

In the US, the last major airport constructed was Denver International Airport (DIA) which opened in 1995. While DIA is the largest piece of real estate dedicated to commercial aviation in the world, it cannot make up for capacity shortfalls at other key airports (Dempsey, Goetz, and Szyliowicz, 1995). The FAA

(2007a) report "Capacity Needs in the National Airspace System, 2007–2025" reviewed 291 commercial service airports in the US, including the 35 large hubs. The first report (FACT 1) was published in 2004 and identified capacity constraints at many of the hub airports reviewed. Since FACT 1, six new runways have been opened and runway improvements and extensions were planned at other key airports. The FACT 2 (2007) report found that two of these airports— Atlanta and Philadelphia—had seen improvements in capacity, however, it is projected that by 2015 the following airports will need additional capacity even after already planned improvements: Charlotte Douglas International, Fort Lauderdale–Hollywood International, George Bush Intercontinental, John F. Kennedy International, John Wayne–Orange County, LaGuardia, Long Beach–Daugherty Field, McCarran International, Metropolitan Oakland International, Midway Airport, Newark Liberty International, O'Hare International, Palm Beach International, Philadelphia International, Phoenix Sky Harbor International, T.F. Green, Tuscon International, and William P. Hobby.

Although new airport construction will help the situation, it alone will not solve the current (and predicted) capacity crunch. Another area requiring major investment is the air traffic management system and related ground-based systems on airports. In the highly complex New York/New Jersey area which hosts three large, international airports, John F. Kennedy (JFK), Newark, and La Guardia, the FAA had capped flights into JFK to reduce delays at peak times (Schofield, 2008). Further, the Port Authority of New York and New Jersey assumed operation of Stewart International Airport, 55 miles north of New York City, to use it and some redesign of the airspace to reduce delays, however, it should be noted that the FAA still places airports in this area into the needed capacity list for 2015 (FAA, 2007b). Again, the FAA believes that the long-term solution is to increase the efficiency of the existing air space, that is, to implement NextGen. The NextGen Implementation Plan (FAA, 2013a) estimates that by the end of 2020, NextGen improvements will reduce delays by 41 percent and result in fuel savings of US$38 billion.

In 2003, the US Congress passed Vision 100—Century of Aviation Reauthorization Act, This act created the Joint Planning and Development Organization (JPDO) to manage work related to the creation of the NGATS. JPDO is also responsible for coordinating with partner agencies—Department of Transportation (DOT), Department of Commerce (DOC), Department of Defense (DOD), Department of Homeland Security (DHS), Federal Aviation Administration (FAA), the National Aeronautics and Space Administration (NASA), the White House Office of Science and Technology Policy (OSTP), and the Office of Management and Budget (OMB). JPDO is a planning and coordinating body with no authority over the human and financial resources necessary to create and deploy the system. However, the FAA's overall NextGen effort has been restructured several times including an effort to force internal buy in at the FAA itself. With the final confirmation of Michael P. Heurta, former chief NextGen official, as the new head of the FAA it is possible that the program will continue the momentum that it has built up in recent years. This assumes that funding hurdles do not intervene to throw the program into disarray (Bruno and Schofield, 2013).

Funding NextGen

There has been almost universal agreement that the "FAA's funding structure is obsolete and unpredictable." In fact, special commissions such as the so-called Mineta Commission have called for reform for over 20 years (May, 2006; Oster and Strong, 2006). However, beyond this recognition, there is no agreement on a new means of funding the FAA or NextGen. While some FAA funding comes from the General Fund, most of their funding comes from the Airports and Airways Trust Fund whose revenues are generated through excise taxes. Roughly 70 percent of the 2004 revenues came from the passenger ticket tax, flight segment tax, rural airport tax, and frequent flyer tax (Oster and Strong, 2006). Given the other obligations of the US government and the current deficit, and the escalating battles in the US Congress over budgetary issues, it is likely that General Fund contributions will decrease in the future. Further, the trend in the US has been for LCCs to drive down average fares and LCCs are predicted to increase their share of the domestic market over the next few years (Cordle and Poole, 2005). The 2004 uncommitted balance in the Trust Fund was US$7.3 billion. By 2006, the uncommitted balance had dropped to US$1.2 billion (May, 2006). With sequestration in the US, Congress has allowed a transfer of revenue from the Trust Fund to cover controller salaries and prevent tower closures. As of 2013, the Trust Fund provided 71.5 percent of the funding for the FAA, up from 66.6 percent in 2010 (FAA, 2013b).

The actual cost of NextGen has also been a subject of debate. The FAA had originally "estimated that its ATC modernization efforts would cost $12 billion and could be completed over 10 years. Two decades and $35 billion later, the FAA estimated another $16 billion would be needed through 2007 to complete key projects, for a total of $51 billion" (GAO, 2004). In a 2012 General Accounting office (GAO) report, 15 of 30 programs faced delays that averaged four years and the total project was once again over budget by some USUS$4.2 billion. The FAA 2007 Reauthorization bill proposed moving from the current system of excise taxes to a cost-based user fee system in which the aircraft operator would pay for the air traffic services they used. The Reauthorization legislation ran into early trouble over contract talks with the air traffic controllers union (National Air Traffic Controllers Association—NATCA). NATCA, angered over the FAA-imposed contract in 2006, also charged that the FAA had neglected facilities maintenance, creating unsafe conditions, and wasted money in the Air Traffic Organization (ATO) reorganization and modernization efforts (NATCA, 2008a; 2008b; 2008c). Further opposition to Reauthorization came from the general aviation community because the proposed charge would be levied whether the aircraft carried two or 200 people. The general aviation community argued that many general aviation flights operate in uncongested airspace under visual flight rules and hence do not use significant air traffic services, however, several studies have estimated the general aviation share of ATC costs at between 10 and 25 percent, well above their 3 percent contribution to the Trust Fund (Oster and Strong, 2006). Unfortunately, the FAA has historically been unable or unwilling to deal with the issue of cost of service. The FAA can account for its inputs—labor, facilities, equipment, and supplies—and it can provide a broad list of outputs from its activities—aircraft movements, departures—but it has not clearly connected the cost of inputs to the cost of specific outputs. The FAA's (1996) report, "A Cost Allocation Study of FAA's 1995 Costs," assigned costs to various services, but these appear to be based more on the ability to pay than on the actual cost of the services provided. This inability to clearly identify the usage and cost of service hampered the FAA's ability to make an argument for user fee charges.

Broadly speaking, the FAA has six key services that it provides to external customers—air traffic control, regulation and certification, civil aviation security, airport development, and commercial space. Air traffic control accounts for almost two-thirds of the total FAA budget while airport development is roughly 18 percent (FAA, 1996). In 2005, the FAA outsourced the Automated Flight Service Station (AFSS), formerly a part of their air traffic services program, to Lockheed-Martin. The AFSS provides weather briefings, flight plan filing services, and other assistance to private pilots. This contract was expected to save the FAA US$2.2 billion over the next 10 years (Cordle and Poole, 2005). The Oster Report (2006) suggested that there were really only two options for advancing the NextGen vision: (1) leave air traffic services with FAA under a user fee structure (essentially the approach of the 2008 FAA Reauthorization bill) or (2) remove the system from the FAA and establish an autonomous agency similar to NAV CANADA and National Air Traffic Services (NATS). The 2008 FAA Authorization with its user fee system failed and now the FAA is facing new challenges under the sequestration budget battles in the US Congress. The FAA had announced the closing of 149 small contract towers and a plan to limit 72 others to daytime operation. There were also planned eliminations/furloughs of some controllers and control shifts (Lowy, 2013). These were stopped with the Trust Fund transfer discussed above, but new budget battles loom. The 2014 FAA reauthorization bill is set to reintroduce the user fee once again. The proposal this time would call for a US$100 per flight surcharge for the use of federal air traffic service. The Experimental Aircraft Association and the General Aviation Caucus with includes the General Aviation Manufacturers Association (GAMA) are again expected to oppose the user fee (Aero News Network, 2013). These latest budget battles will further jeopardize the timeline for NextGen deployment.

Deploying NextGen

The air traffic control function was reorganized in 2004 into the ATO with a newly appointed chief operating officer. The ATO was billed as a "performance-based organization" that breaks the existing "stovepipes" within the FAA, bringing the key units responsible for management and modernization together. While this reorganization changed the reporting lines of Air Traffic Service (ATS)-related branches within FAA, the ATO remained an agency within the FAA subject to the annual budget appropriations process of Congress. In 2005, the ATO was reorganized from nine to three service areas and staff support services for En Route, Terminal, and Technical Operations were placed in shared service centers in the three service areas. Both this reorganization and the original one were contrary to the recommendations of the FAA-hired consultant Booz Allen Hamilton which called for ATO headquarter consolidation into five service and two staff units and greater cuts in managerial staff (NATCA, 2008b).

In addition to the structural issues that complicated deployment, the FAA has contended with its own poor performance record on previous projects. Specifically, they have been cited for "(1) promising more capability than they ultimately deliver, (2) being completed later than promised, and (3) costing far more by the time they are completed than the initial cost estimates" (Oster and Strong, 2006). A 2005 report by the USDOT inspector general noted "that cost growth, schedule delays, and performance shortfalls with major acquisitions continue to stall air traffic modernization." Eleven of the 16 projects cited in the 2005 report were experiencing total cost growth while over half were experiencing schedule slips from two to 12 years. One of the examples noted was the development and implementation of the Wide Area Augmentation System (WAAS). WAAS was projected in 1994 to cost US$509 million. In 2004, the Inspector General testified to Congress that the projected cost of the yet-to-be implemented program was over US$2.9 billion. This represents a 227 percent increase in the cost of a program whose implementation has been extended by 13 years (NATCA, 2008c). The 2012 GAO report has noted that delays in ERAM deployment will cause additional delays in the DataComm and SWIM programs which could extend for years (Perera, 2012). Still, the FAA NextGen Implementation Plan notes that ADS-B will be deployed at about 700 ground stations by 2014 and equipage incentives will speed the way to a critical mass needed to demonstrate system benefits (FAA, 2013a).

Europe and SESAR

In Europe, physical expansion of infrastructure—new airports and new runways—is expected to be very difficult because of space, environmental, and social constraints. As in the US, the European answer is to unlock the latent capacity in the system through the application of new technologies to air and groundside operation. In other words, Europe too must create and deploy their answer to a twenty-first century airspace system. The key elements of SESAR are traffic synchronization, airport integration and throughput, 4D Trajectory Management, network collaboration and capacity balancing, and conflict management and automation. The SESAR program has set a series of performance goals for 2020: (1) a 27 percent increase in Europe's airspace; (2) a 40 percent reduction in accident risk per flight; (3) a 2.8 percent reduction per flight in environmental impact; and (4) a 6 percent reduction in cost per flight. They expect the new technologies to shorten flights by nine minutes and result in 50 percent fewer cancellations and delays (SESAR, 2012a). As noted above, the SESAR concept embodies not only the European answer to the aviation system of the future but the first ever European effort to involve all of the aviation stakeholders (civil and military, legislators, industry, operators, users, ground and airborne) in the process of defining, committing to, and implementing a pan-European program consistent with the Single European Sky legislation. In 2011, SESAR launched a Release program which involves validating R&D projects in operational environments. In 2012, Release 2 involved 30 exercises conducted over 18 EU destinations (SESAR, 2012a).

Funding SESAR

In order to develop the system, a legal entity was created under EC law, the SESAR Joint Undertaking. The SESAR JU will: (1) secure the appropriate funding and concentrate the necessary research and development resources into SESAR; (2) define and update the work program, including allocating tasks and organizing calls for tender; (3) ensure technical progress; and (4) report on the development phase. The first phase of tender contracts is set to close on February 29, 2008 (EUROCONTROL, 2008). It is estimated that funding for all three steps in the Master Plan will be between 23 and 32 billion euros over the period 2014–2030 (SESAR, 2012b). However, this estimate assumes that SESAR, unlike NextGen, can stay on target with its implementation program. Like the US, SESAR is already lagging behind in meeting some of its performance targets. In fact, EUROCONTROL noted in May 2011 that ATM performance was actually getting worse in some areas such as delays and en route extensions that increased miles flown. There are also serious issues of funding for planned projects as well as questions about the best way to encourage early equipage (CAPA, 2011). It remains to be seen if the current economic weakness in Europe will have further impacts on the SESAR initiative. As in the US, efforts to change the air traffic control system have received backlash from controllers who believe that it is a direct assault on working conditions and a threat to aviation safety. Strikes and threatened strikes by controller unions continue to plague the EU and slow further the program for a European Single Sky and SESAR (Keating, 2013).

"Final Answer"

There is very little disagreement over the general shape and technologies needed for the twenty-first century aviation system. All parties also agree that the current system cannot meet the traffic demands of the future and must be replaced and/or improved as soon as possible. Unfortunately, this is as far as the general agreement goes and understanding the general shape does not help in achieving agreement over the fine details. In fact, there are a great many devils in these details. In the US, the disagreement over technical detail is matched by fundamental disagreements over questions of structure and funding. While these issues remain unresolved, NextGen work on the technologies proceeds in a haphazard, stop-and-start way because of funding uncertainty (NATCA, 2008d). Meanwhile, industry vendors tout their twenty-first century solutions to government and other key stakeholders who marvel at its possibilities and baulk at paying the bill. The existing system continues to age and deteriorate while the FAA, scrambling to meet current operational and maintenance budgets, reduces the number of facilities set for modernization and extends the deployment dates of planned new technology for the remaining sites. It is far too early to assess the success of development and deployment in NextGen. Decades of efforts at European integration might work in favor of a smoother process for Europe, but this is far from certain. The EU could also benefit from prior work in the US on various components of the system, but past experience would tend to suggest that harmonizing systems, rules, and standards between the US and Europe will be difficult at best. National/regional self-interest can easily hide under the cloak of technical specification on system performance. Still, if the Europeans can indeed bring SESAR online for 30 billion euros they will be well ahead of NextGen which the US GAO has predicted could cost upward of US$160 billion under worst case scenarios (CAPA, 2011). This is certainly a far cry from the original estimate of US$12 billion over ten years.

In the US, there are three key, closely-linked recommendations that must be undertaken if NextGen has any hope of deployment in this century. First, an effort should be undertaken to develop a clear set of cost-of-service parameters. This effort can NOT be led by the FAA. They have shown neither the willingness nor the ability to undertake such an effort. Further, poor planning, cost overruns, and mismanagement have eroded what little credibility the Agency had with its stakeholders. Second, a concerted, sustained effort must be made to involve all of the key stakeholders in the process of shaping and deploying NextGen. This recommendation is not new. The GAO (2004) cited this lack of input as one of the factors contributing to cost overruns and implementation delays. NATCA, representatives of the primary users of any air traffic system, have complained that their input is rarely sought and often only after serious problems arise. Recent collaborative efforts between the FAA and controllers on the Domestic Reduced Vertical Separation Minimum (DVRSM), the Airport Surface Detection Equipment—Model X (ASDE-X), and Advanced Technologies and Oceanic Procedures (ATOP) have proven that cooperation is possible and productive (NATCA, 2008c). Of course, these projects were relatively narrow in scope. For NATCA, a more fundamental issue relates to working conditions and employee attrition. Air traffic controllers are leaving in numbers not seen since the PATCO strike of 1981. There are several reasons for these departures: normal baby boomer attrition, general working conditions, and the newly imposed work rules and pay cuts of the September 2006 contract. The attrition in 2007 was 33 percent higher than FAA projections (NATCA, 2007). The US reached a 15-year low in fully certified controllers in 2006 (Hall, 2007). This staffing crisis can be added to projected shortages in airline pilots. Like air traffic controllers, the baby boomer generation of pilots is retiring. Instability in US airlines and attractive wages from expanding international carriers are driving many pre-retirement pilots out of the US market (Darby, 2008). Given the direct impact that NextGen systems have on the job of this group, they also deserve a voice in the way forward.

Other groups that need a seat at the table for these discussions include GAMA and the National Business Aviation Association (NBAA). Both groups represent the general aviation community in the US. The primary concern of the general aviation community is, of course, the question of funding and its impact on private and business flyers. The goal is to keep their contribution as low as possible, however, if capacity is not increased in the system, then they may find themselves increasingly shut out of airports that are struggling to accommodate commercial traffic. The large commercial airlines, individually and through the ATA and the IATA, have exercised their political voice in these matters. Their concern is that they not be singled out as a source of funding over the general aviation community because they are perceived to have a greater "ability to pay." Airports have a stake in the system as well. The failure to implement NextGen seriously impairs their ability to grow capacity and meet the service quality levels demanded by customers. The New York–New Jersey airports are a case in point.

The third recommendation is to settle, possibly as part of the stakeholder process in recommendation two, on a structure as soon as politically possible. In 2006, an extensive report on ten major international air navigation service providers (Australia, Canada, France, Germany, Ireland, Netherlands, New Zealand, South Africa, Switzerland, and the UK) found that there was an increasing movement toward corporatizing or privatizing Air Navigation Systems (ANS) due to considerations of cost, efficiency, procurement, capacity constraints, and the desire to access private capital markets. Most of the ANS providers reviewed utilized user fees and were expected to be self-sufficient. Some were allowed to make a profit directly, although most could establish for-profit subsidiaries. All ANS providers reviewed could issue bonds securing the debt with revenue streams. Only a few could issue government-guaranteed debt (Dempsey, Janda, Nyampong, Saba, and Wilson, 2006). The two examples most often cited as models for the US are Canada and the UK. NAV CANADA was the first private sector company to use a non-share capital structure to commercialize a government function and is governed by a stakeholder cooperative with Transport Canada, a government entity, assuming safety oversight. In the UK, NATS is a public–private partnership in which the government owns 49 percent while the remaining ownership is split between an airline consortium (42 percent), NATS employees (5 percent), and BAA, plc (4 percent). The current FAA ATO is not a self-supporting Air Navigation Service Provider (ANSP) nor is it apparently intended to be. It seems contradictory to many observers outside of the US that a nation that has devoted much of its recent efforts to promoting free market ideas and policies should so strongly resist privatizing or corporatizing any aspects of the aviation system, but this debate has already been long, hard, and bloody. Robert Poole of the Reason Foundation has pointed out that any ATO change that tries to combine customer-supported revenue with partially tax-supported revenue may well create another USPS disaster, a disaster that we have already discussed in Chapter 20 (Poole, 2013). Unfortunately, the political climate in the US makes any progress on this third recommendation even more unlikely in 2014 than it was in 2008.

Conclusion

As both the US and EU have discovered, it is one thing to have a notional idea of the capabilities that you need to reshape the air traffic system, but actually developing, testing, and integrating the various technologies while still operating the existing system is an entirely different proposition. Add in budget constraints and a free market system that mandates only the final date for equipage for operators whose incentive may be to wait as long as possible before making the investment and the future of the twenty-first century airspace can seem very cloudy. The issue of incentives has been very thorny. In effect, if an operator does not invest in equipment while others do, then they could gain some benefit without the cost, but the true benefits of NextGen and SESAR do not begin to truly materialize until a critical mass of operators participate. Without this critical mass, the argument for others to equip become weaker, the benefits are smaller, and the costs rise. In the end, the success of both projects requires political will and public support to implement these systems *before* the twenty-second century arrives or before it becomes what US Rep Rick Larsen calls LastGen (Bruno and Schofield, 2013). A solution would seem to be in the best interest of all parties, but in the highly contentious aviation industry it is often difficult to get "agreement" on issues even when the parties do agree.

Questions

1. What is NextGen and what does it hope to accomplish?
2. What are the key components of the NextGen system?
3. How is air traffic service funded in the US?
4. Debate air traffic management privatization.
5. Debate airspace automation.

References

Aero News Network (2013), "EAA opposes user fees proposed in President's budget," retrieved online January 20, 2014 from http://www.aero-news.net/index.cfm?do=main.textpost&id=d154f01e-031d-42df-9664-49434a6f06f8.

Bruno, M. and Schofield, A. (2013), "Dark skies," *Aviation Week & Space Technology*, July 29, pp. 16–17.

Bureau of Transportation Statistics (2013), "Passenger and freight," retrieved online from February 3, 2014 https://www.rita.dot.gov/bts/data_and_statistics/by_mode/airline_and_airports/airlines_and_airports_passengers_and_freight.

Center for Aviation (CAPA) (2011), "Europe faces up to question of funding for Single European Sky," retrieved online February 6, 2014 from http://centreforaviation.com/analysis/europe-faces-up-to-question-of-funding-for-single-european-sky-54971.

Cordle, V. and Poole, R.C. (2005), *Resolving the Crisis in Air Traffic Control Funding*, Reason Foundation, Washington, DC, retrieved online March 21, 2007 from www.rppi.org/ps332.pdf.

Darby, K. (2008), "How will growth in pilot demand be met in the future?" TRB 87th Conference, Washington, DC.

Dempsey, P.S., Goetz, A.R. and Szyliowicz, J.S. (1995), *Denver International Airport: Lessons Learned*, McGraw-Hill Publishers, New York.

Dempsey, P.S., Janda, R., Nyampong, N., Saba, J. and Wilson, J. (2006), "The McGill Report on Governance of Commercialized Air Navigation Services," *Annual of Air and Space Law*, Vol. XXXI, pp. 214–349.

Federal Aviation Administration (FAA) (1996), "A cost allocation study of FAA's 1995 costs," US Department of Transportation, Washington, DC.

Federal Aviation Administration (FAA) (2007a), "Capacity needs in the National Airspace System," retrieved online January 15, 2008 from http://www.faa.gov/airports/resources/publications/reports/media/fact_2.pdf.

Federal Aviation Administration (FAA) (2007b), "National plan of integrated aAirport systems," retrieved online January 15, 2008 from http://www.docstoc.com/docs/840312/National-Plan-of-Integrated-Airport-Systems-(NPIAS)-March-2007.

EUROCONTROL (2008), retrieved online January 18, 2008 from http://www.eurocontrol.int/sesar/public/subsite_homepage/homepage.html.

Federal Aviation Administration (FAA) (2008), "Capacity: annual service volume," retrieved online February 8, 2008 from www.faa.gov/about/plans_reports/portfolio_2008/media/annaul%20service%20volume.pdf.

Federal Aviation Administration (FAA) (2012), "FAA aerospace forecast fiscal years 2012–2032," retrieved online March 3, 2013 from http://www.faa.gov/about/office_org/headquarters_offices/apl/aviation_forecasts/aerospace_forecasts/2012-2032/media/2012%20FAA%20Aerospace%20Forecast.pdf

Federal Aviation Administration (FAA) (2013a), "NextGen implementation plan," retrieved online f January 23, 2014 rom http://www.faa.gov/nextgen.

Federal Aviation Administration (FAA) (2013b), "Airport and Airway Trust Fund," retrieved online January 23, 2014 from http://www.faa.gov/about/office_org/headquarters_offices/apl/aatf/media/AATF_Fact_Sheet.pdf.

General Accounting Office (GAO) (2004), "Air Traffic Control, FAA's Modernization Efforts—Past, Present, and Future, Statement of Gerald L. Dillingham, Director, Physical Infrastructure Issues," GAO-04-227T.

Hall, J. (2007), "Despite advances, more must be done," *Tennessean*, retrieved online from July 17, 2007 www.tennessean.com/apps/pbcs.dll/article?AID-/2007/1030/OPINION1/71/1030034.

International Airline Transport Association (IATA) (2011), "Vision 2050—shaping aviation's future," retrieved online April 23, 2012 from http://www.iata.org/pressroom/facts_figures/Pages/vision-2050.aspx.

International Airline Transport Association (IATA) (2013), "Fact sheet: industry statistics," retrieved online February 19, 2014 from http://www.iata.org/pressroom/facts_figures/fact_sheets/Documents/industry-facts.pdf.

Keating, D. (2013), "Air traffic strike set for 10 October," retrieved online December 6, 2013 from http://www.europeanvoice.com/article/2013/september/air-traffic-strike-set-for-10-october/78091.aspx.

Lowy, J. (2013), "FAA to staff 72 airport control towers at night," retrieved online January 14, 2014 from http://bigstory.ap.org/article/faa-staff-72-airport-control-towers-night.

May, J.C. (2006), "Speech by James C. May: smart—and fair—skies: blueprint for the future," International Aviation Club, Washington, DC, retrieved online January 16, 2008 from www.airlines.org/news/speeches/speech_4-18-06.htm.

National Air Traffic Controllers Association (NACTA) (2007), "Controller staffing crisis: fact sheet," retrieved online January 26, 2008 from www.natca.org.

National Air Traffic Controllers Association (NACTA) (2008a), "NATCA opposes the nomination of Bobby Sturgell for FAA administrator," Press release, retrieved online January 26, 2008 from www.natca.org/mediacenter/press-release-detail.aspx?id=460.

National Air Traffic Controllers Association (NACTA) (2008b), "ATO service area restructuring: when change may not guarantee progress," retrieved online January 26, 2008 from www.natca.org/legislationcenter/ATOService.msp.

National Air Traffic Controllers Association (NACTA) (2008c), "Modernization: still doing today's work with yesterday's tools," retrieved online January 26, 2008 from www.natca.org/legislationcenter/Modernization.msp.

National Air Traffic Controllers Association (NACTA) (2008d), "Modernization cutbacks: program descriptions," retrieved online January 26, 2008 from www.natca.net/safetytechnology/modernizationcutbacksdetails.msp.

Oster, C.V. and Strong, J.S. (2006), *Reforming the Federal Aviation Administration: Lessons from Canada and the United Kingdom*, IBM Center for the Business of Government, Virginia.

Perera, D. (2012), "ERAM lateness having secondary NextGen effects, says, GAO," retrieved online December 6, 2012 from http://www.fiercegovernmentit.com/story/eram-lateness-having-secondary-nextgen-effects-says-gao/2012-02-20.

Poole, R. (2013), "Backlash over politicized air traffic control funding, user taxes vs user fees—a big difference," retrieved online September 16, 2013 from http://reason.org/news/printer/air-traffic-control-newsletter-102.

Schofield, A. (2008), "Debate over JFK delays sparks talk of congestion pricing," *Aviation Daily*.

Schofield, A. (2013), "Gaining ground," *Aviation Week & Space Technology*, July 29, pp. 17–19.

SESAR (2012a), "Annual report 2012," retrieved online April 6, 2013 from http://www.sesarju.eu/news-press/documents/2012-annual-report.

SESAR (2012b), "European ATM master plan: the roadmap for sustainable air traffic management—executive summary—air navigation service providers," retrieved online April 6, 2013 from https://www.atmmasterplan.eu/.

Federal Aviation Administration, Report Number AV-2005-061, date issued: May 26, 2005.

Chapter 22
Selling Space

Learning Objectives

After reading this chapter, you should have a good understanding of:
- LO1: the current issues surrounding the space programs of the US and Russia.
- LO2: the direction of the EU, India, and China in space exploration.
- LO3: the issues driving the commercialization of space.
- LO4: the new players, ships, technologies, and spaceports participating in the commercial space race.

Key Terms,Concepts, and People

Mars Direct	Spaceport	Dragon X
SpaceX	Blue Origin	Bigelow Aerospace
XCOR	Sierra Nevada	Virgin Galactic

The Next Step to Where

We left the great spacefaring nations of the US and Russia in Chapter 7 apparently in two very different places. President Putin of Russia had announced an increase in the budget for Roscosmos to "catch up to NASA" and was pouring money into an over-budget new spaceport at Vostochny to replace Baikonur in Kazahstan (Steadman, 2013; Zak, 2013). Of course, catching up to NASA should be easy in budgetary terms since the current NASA budget is less than one half of 1 percent of the US budget (Wikipedia, 2013). Budgetary issues aside, the accepted long-term goal of space exploration has been to send humans to Mars. Unfortunately, there is no clear, accepted path from here to there. Aside from conceptual drawing of bases on the Moon and/or Mars or largely conceptual work on launch systems and crew capsules, little actual actions and no long-term budgetary commitment can be cited to support these missions. Meanwhile, China appears to be on course to recreate the accomplishments of bygone days with their own space station and manned launches to support it. Where does all of this leave the space aspirations of mankind? Are we destined to watch science fiction but never participate in space fact? Have governments and their citizens lost their appetite for space spending? What is the future of space exploration?

In the first part of this chapter we will explore the halting, uncertain steps taken by the US and Russian programs. This journey to nowhere is more visible in the US where it has played out in Congressional hearings, Presidential speeches, and editorial pleas, but the apparent lack of Russian missions beyond Low Earth Orbit (LEO) suggests a similar struggle. Next, we will examine the space programs of the Europeans and more recently, India and China. These nations have joined the space club and have a key role to play in the future of mankind in space.

The new element in the space race—commercial space operators—will be the subject of the remainder of the chapter. Communication companies have been involved in space before (Chapter 7) to build satellites and fund their launch, but now a host of new companies are emerging with a wide range of goals for space involvement. This new development is partly the result of US policy. In May 2012, the US Congress passed the Commercial Space Launch Activities Act. The purpose of the act was to align government and private space activities. Specifically, it requires private entities to receive approval for launch and re-entry and insurance in the event of death, injury, or property loss. It also opened the door for NASA to contract with these entities to supply the ISS (US Congress, 2012). Many of these new operators are truly private firms seeking to find profit in space, entrepreneurs like Richard Branson whose Virgin Galactic is aiming for the space tourist in all of us or SpaceX who provided the first cargo delivery to the ISS by a private firm. Other ventures are public–private partnerships attempting to spread the costs and risks of space activity. To explore this new frontier in space, this chapter will look at the space companies, space vehicles, and spaceports that hope to participate in the new commercial space frontier.

Getting from Here to There

If "we" all agree that Mars is the goal of manned exploration for the coming century, then why has it been so difficult to agree on what it takes to get there and what interim steps need to be established? This was one of many questions asked by the US House Science, Space, and Technology Committee in a May 21, 2013 meeting (Morring, 2013a). A report by the National Research Council (NRC), commissioned by NASA at the behest of Congress, concluded that the space agency was under increasing stress from more expensive missions, an aging infrastructure, and a lack of national consensus over a long-term vision for human spaceflight. While the report concluded that the problems NASA faced are not primarily their fault, it did suggest that their response (and strategic plan) could have included a clearer set of priorities and more transparent budget. In fact, NASA's 2011 strategic plan and accompanying vision and mission was called "generic," vague on details, and of little value in helping them to set a clear direction (NRC, 2012). The fault, as Shakespeare would say, is in ourselves.

In 1990, Robert Zubrin and others had proposed The Mars Direct plan, arguing that the US had the capability even then to pursue manned missions to Mars. This plan would first launch an Earth Return Vehicle (ERV) to Mars. This unmanned unit would land on Mars and begin making the fuel necessary for a return trip to Earth, eliminating the need for manned missions to transport their own return fuel, thus reducing the launch weight. While the ERV made the necessary fuel, robotic units would explore the area. Once the ERV had produced the necessary fuel, a manned mission would be launched to land near the ERV sight with their habitat. As we know, this vision did not occur. President George H.W. Bush had already proclaimed on July 20, 1989 that the ten-year plan for US space exploration was to be a space station (ISS), then a return to the Moon, with the "journey of tomorrow," a manned mission to Mars. The path was laid out. It pleased the contractors already working on the ISS who wanted to get the money for their first step on the journey, but left Zubrin unimpressed and had little for those interested in the science of space. In response to the call, NASA produced "The 90-Day Report" that set out a 30-year plan for space infrastructure build up (Zubrin and Wagner, 1996). Once this train left the station, there would be no Mars Direct. The immediate focus of US space efforts would remain the ISS and the Space Shuttle that would serve it.

As former astronaut, Vance Brand, pointed out in a 2012 editorial in *Aviation Week & Space Technology*, it has been 40 years since the Apollo 17 mission to the Moon. The capabilities in manned exploration that were built up since the 1950s are on the verge of withering and dying (Brand, 2012). Again, much of the fault is not with NASA. A Mars mission would require a ten-year program with some assurances of funding. Instead, NASA has struggled as they did with the Space Shuttle (Chapter 7) to cobble together constituencies (with influence on funding) to get the necessary resources while watching their path shift as one US President kills the approach of the last (Constellation for the Space Launch System and a Moon orbit in 2017 for an asteroid capture by 2025). According to the NRC, NASA personnel themselves are divided on direction. Currently, the debate is on the value of the asteroid capture plan. This plan would capture an asteroid and place it in lunar orbit. Proponents have argued that it provides a testing ground for the systems needed for a return to planetary exploration. Opponents see it as a waste of resources, an asteroid to nowhere. The fact that NASA has now linked the asteroid capture to efforts to identify Near Earth Objects (NEOs) that might impact Earth smacks of the old Space Shuttle efforts to be all-things-to-all-people. In other words, design a mission and systems that truly serves no one's needs or wants (Morring, 2013b). In essence, the options under consideration are: (1) flight around the Moon with eventual landing; (2) a space station at a Lagrange point near the Moon; (3) asteroid landing and/or capture with possible placement near the Moon; and (4) manned orbital mission to Mars with eventual landing (Brand, 2012; Wilson, 2013). Of course, if this menu of options looks simple, then consider that there remains no agreement about whether they (or some combination of them) are necessary stepping stones to Mars. Brand, like Zubrin before him, argues that space stations, Moon landing, and so on are not necessary steps to Mars, certainly not the shortest path. Brand even argues that mission dissimilarity make these goals inconsistent (Brand, 2012). The NRC (2012) report did not weigh into details of vision and steps, but did lay out four options to avoid the cost overruns that have plagued NASA and keep the projects in their existing portfolio of operations on track: (1) restructure the agency; (2) commit more to cost-sharing partnerships with the private sector and other countries; (3) grow NASA's budget; or (4) reduce the size and scope of its mission portfolio (NRC, 2012). It is possible that the House Science, Space and Technology Committee debate will help the citizens of the US to clarify their goals for space. If not, then we are all riding Wilson's "rocket to nowhere" (Wilson, 2013).

Meanwhile, in Russia, they seem to be having a NASA moment as well with a host of proposed projects, insufficient funding, and little agreement on the way forward. The most recent plan of Roscomsos, the Russian Space Agency, outlines a series of goals through 2030, most of which Anatoly Zak of Russianspaceweb. com calls "practically impossible to fulfill." These include the completion of the new cosmodrome Vostochny in 2015, a launch complex for a new family of Russia rockets (Rus-M) by 2020, a new crew spacecraft to replace the Soyuz, a new space station, and robotic missions to Mars, Jupiter, and Saturn. Zak has criticized the plan as "vague wording and hefty proclamations" (Zak, 2013). Like NASA, Roscosmos has suffered its share of defeats including a series of failed Mars probes and an unusual number of launch failures in recent years (http://www. spacepolicyonline.com/news/russia-outlines-human-and-robotic-spaceflight-plans-to-2030). If good competitors make you better, then the old Space Racers need a few good competitors to get back on track.

A European Vision

As the website for the European Space Agency (ESA) notes, the idea of a European space organization first surfaced in the early 1960s, but ESA did not come into being until 1980. Despite the late entry into space exploration and research, ESA has some impressive accomplishments as Table 22.1 makes clear. Of particular note is the Huygens probe landing on Titan, the first ever landing of a human craft in the outer solar system. While ESA does not have a specific manned vision beyond the ISS, their Cosmic Vision 2015–2025 includes Gaia (2013) to count and track stars in the Milky Way, participation in the James Webb Space Telescope, the Solar Orbiter, Euclid to explore dark matter, and Juice to explore the moons of Jupiter (http://www.esa.int/ESA). Perhaps because of the nature of its multination creation, ESA has been an active and successful voice for collaboration with other nations. Sadly, the identity and budget crisis of NASA has not always made it a good partner as the recent decision to pull out of cooperation with ESA on two Mars probes proves (http://www.spacepolicyonline.com/civil).

Table 22.1   European (ESA) space accomplishments

Year	Accomplishment
1980	Arianespace formed to produce, operate, and market the Ariane 5 rocket
1983	First ESA astronaut to fly on the Space Shuttle
1986	Giotto: First deep-space mission to study comets
1990s	Cooperation with NASA on Ulysses and Hubble Telescopes and Cassini-Huygen
2003	Mars Express orbiter
2005	Huygens probe lands on Titan, Saturn's largest moon
2008	Columbus Laboratory for ISS
2009	ESA astronauts to the ISS
2010	Node-3 and Cupola installed on ISS to study ice cover
2013	ESA astronaut to the ISS

Source: http://www.esa.int/ESA

The Latest Entrants

If ESA has sought collaboration more than competition, then perhaps the competition that once spurred the Great Space Race will come from two new entrants—China and India. China has announced plans that include its own orbiting space station and continuation of the Chang probe series; the near-term goal is a lunar probe landing (http://www.space.com/8017-china-targets-space-program-firsts.html). China launched their first satellite in 1970, but the manned space program did not begin until 2003. The pace of their activity has increased dramatically since 2010, but it remains unclear what their goals are beyond the space station and a lunar probe.

The Indian space program also began in the 1970s with a satellite program, however, they are now working on their own launch vehicle, the GSLV MK III, as well as reusable launch technology. The first interplanetary effort by the Indian space program is the 2013 Mars Orbiter. There are plans for an Indo–Russian probe to land on the Moon. Currently, the Human Spaceflight Programme is exploring a mission to send a crew of two into LEO. The Indian Space Research Organization (ISRO) sums up the reasons why a developing nation would invest in space as demonstrating that they are "second-to-none in the application of advanced technologies to the real problems of man and society" (http://www.isro.org/scripts/futureprogramme.aspx#Human). In short, like the original spacefaring nations, nations reach for space not simply to generate new technologies but to demonstrate to themselves and the world their ability to participate in the challenge and excitement of space exploration.

Opportunities in Space

While governments struggle to find their way in space, the new pioneers are looking for money in space. This section will explore the space companies, vehicles, and spaceports searching for their place in the new frontier.

Companies and vehicles

Table 22.2 provides a list of some of the companies looking to space. Some of the names are familiar to anyone interested in aviation or aerospace. The first company on the list, Astrium, a wholly-owned company of EADS, is the leading European company in the space industry. It is probably most noted for its Ariane 5 launch program which has notched 48 successful launches to date, but it has also contributed to the ISS with the Automated Transfer Vehicle and Columbus Laboratory. Astrium's Eurostar telecommunication satellites provide TV, telephone, and internet service while the SMOS and CryoSat satellites collect scientific information. In interplanetary exploration, the BepiColombo Mercury probe will be the newest project for the company that was the prime contractor for the Rosetta comet mission as well as the Herschel space telescope (http://www.astrium.eads.net/en/).

Other well-known names include Boeing and Pratt & Whitney, two large US companies involved in aviation/aerospace. Boeing is currently developing the CST-100 seven-person commercial crew vehicle that would be powered by four P&W Rocketdyne Bantam abort engines (Morring, 2011). The CTS-100 is undergoing wind tunnel tests and is set to complete all of its milestones in mid-2014. The launch vehicle would be the standard Atlas V. Boeing is one of two companies vying for crew delivery to the ISS and the Bigelow Aerospace Orbital Complex. Boeing has announced plans to allow Space Adventures (discussed below) sell any unused seats on future CST-100 flights to adventurous tourists (www.space.com/19367-boeing-cst-100.html).

Table 22.2   Space companies

Name/Location	Ownership	Mission	Technologies
Astrium	EADS	Space transportation, satellite systems and service	Ariane, satellite design
Astra Rocket Co., TX	Public–Private	Development of plasma rocket launch propulsion	VASIMIR, propulsion technology
Blue Origin, WA	Private	Reliable, cost-effective human access to space	Suborbital and orbital craft
Boeing, MI	Private	Commercial launch provider	Heavy lift rockets Satellites CST-100
China Aerospace International Holdings	Private	Launch vehicle manufacturer	Spacecraft, carrier rockets, satellites
China Aerospace Science & Technology Corp.	Public	Development of space technologies and products	Rockets
Dubai Aerospace Enterprise, UAE	Public		
National Aerospace Laboratories, India	Private	Aerospace Laboratory	Trainer and transport aircraft
Orbital Science	Private	LEO launch	Antares Launch
Pratt & Whitney Space Propulsion	Private	Design and manufacture liquid propellant rockets	Rocket engines
Space Explorations Technologies (SpaceX)	Private	Develop rocket systems and provide Launch	Falcon, dragon, and Grasshopper

Source: Various company websites

Three less familiar names are Space Exploration Technologies or SpaceX, Orbital Science, and Blue Origin. SpaceX was the first private company to return a spacecraft from LEO and the first to deliver cargo to the ISS. SpaceX has a contract with NASA to fly at least 11 cargo missions to the ISS and is working to modify its

Dragon system to deliver crew as well. A potentially game-changing technology is the SpaceX Grasshopper, a vertical takeoff and landing vehicle (www.spacex. com). Orbital Sciences Corp. is set to begin fulfilling its resupply contract with the ISS in December 2013 using the Cygnus resupply capsule (Carreau, 2013). The Blue Origin New Sheppard system is being designed as a reuseable vertical launch system. Their systems are currently in testing (www.blueorigin.com).

In fact, many of the new companies are associated with the development of their own systems as Tables 22.3 shows. As this table illustrates, there are currently three broad areas of focus for these private companies: cargo operations (currently to the ISS, but possibly expanding in the future), space tourism, and launch operations, mostly of satellites. The cargo delivery area has already been discussed and has posted its first success with the SpaceX delivery. The Russians pioneered space tourism, but may have to give way to the new entrepreneurs of space. Richard Branson and his Virgin group—Virgin Galactic—are already booking flights on SpaceShipTwo. With over 500 prospective astronauts, Branson is hoping to make the Galactic name a reality (www.virongalactic.com).

Bigelow Aerospace is currently the only company in the private space habitats/ facilities area. Billed as the "next generation space station," the patented, inflatable design is based on work by NASA which was licensed to Bigelow in 1999 (Vastag, 2013). In 2015, Bigelow is set to launch (SpaceX) a new module for the ISS. The goal is to test the use of inflatable modules as laboratories and living space. Two prototypes were launched in 2006–2007 and considered a successful preliminary test of the system (www.bigelowaerospace.com). Robert Bigelow envisions not only a series of research facilities in space, but a space hotel for the up-and-coming space tourist industry (McGarry and Miller, 2013). Some of these companies could also participate in microgravity activity that requires limited weightless flight for crystal growth, pharmaceutical development, and so on. While China and Russia are already talking about space stations to replace the ISS once it reaches the end-of-life, the US is counting on private entities for space station development and research (Morring, 2013c).

Spaceports

Of course, all of this space activity requires a port to launch and return and there are a growing number of facilities hoping to fill this bill. The first question to answer is what does a facility need to be a spaceport, aside from governmental recognition. To answer this question, it is first necessary to understand the different types of orbits possible. There are essentially three types: geostationary, polar, and molniya. A geostationary orbit is a circular orbit at 22,236 miles (35,786 kilometers) above the Earth. An object in this type of an orbit has an orbital period equal to the Earth, thus it maintains a fixed position in the sky. This type of orbit is ideal for most communications and weather satellites. A polar orbit is one in which an object passes above both poles each revolution. Earth-mapping, observation, and reconnaissance satellites most often utilize this type of orbit. A molniya orbit

Table 22.3   Space vehicles

Vehicle	Company	Technology	Mission
Armadillo's Vertical Tourship	Space Adventures	Vertical launch	Suborbital flight
Cygnus/Taurus 2	Orbital Sciences	Antares Launch vehicle with two stages powered by Aerojet AJ26-62	Cargo delivery to ISS
Dragon/Falcon 9	SpaceX	Falcon 9 launch vehicle with 6 Merlin engines-first stage and one Merlin engine-second stage	Cargo delivery to ISS
Dream Chaser	Sierra Nevada Corp	Atlas V launch vehicle with conventional landing	Cargo delivery to ISS
Lynx	XCOR	Horizontal takeoff and landing powered by four kerosene/liquid oxygen XR-5K18 rocket engines	Suborbital vehicle
New Shepard	Blue Origin	Reusable Propulsion Module	Suborbital launch
Silver Dart	PlanetSpace	Under development	Suborbital rapid point-to-point delivery of cargo/ passengers
Space Ride	Excaliber Almaz Ltd	4 Reusable Reentry Vehicles and Salyut-class spacecraft	Refurbish/reuse Russian spacecraft
SpaceShip/ WhiteKnight Two	Virgin Galactic and Scaled Composites	Launch vehicle to LEO	LEO Space tourism; micro-gravity
Sundancer	Bigelow Aerospace	Inflatable space habitats	

Source: Space.com, http://www.space.com/2-top-10-fantasy-spaceships-headed-reality.html

is highly elliptical with an inclination of 63.4 degrees north and will spend most of its time over the northern hemisphere. Rockets launched at or near the equator in an easterly direction can utilize the Earth's rotational speed to more easily attain orbit. This type of launch profile is best for achieving a geostationary orbit. More northerly launches can be utilized for the other types of launches. Other important features for a spaceport would include: distance from population centers and/or launch over water, launch facilities (runways for horizontal launch vehicles and launch pads for vertical launch), and facilities for mission control.

Table 22.4 shows the US spaceports while Table 22.5 highlights the international options. Spaceport America houses the first purpose-designed launch facility for space tourism and is the base for Virgin Galactic. The spaceport is adjacent to the White Sands Missile range and has already hosted vertical launches using the nearby restricted airspace. Compare this to the first spaceport in the Table, Cecil Field, which officially became the eight designated spaceport in the US in August 2012 (www.cecilfieldspaceport.com). Cecil Field started life in 1941 as a Naval Air Station. It was closed in the 1993 Base Realignment and Closure (BRAC) decision. This former home of the Atlantic Fleet is now a joint civil–military airport and spaceport authorized for horizontal operations. Of special note in this list is Sea Launch which is headquartered in Bern, Switzerland. Sea Launch has two specialized sea vessels—Odyssey and Sea Launch Commander—based on Long Beach, California that transport the contracted payload to a platform located on the equator. While the January 2013 launch of Intelsat 27 failed, Sea Launch can claim a number of successes (http://www.sea-launch.com/about.aspx). It should be noted that Kennedy Space Center in Florida may be the site of another

Table 22.4   US spaceports

Name/Location	Ownership	Facilities	Operations
Cecil Field, FL	Jacksonville Aviation Authority	4 paved runways	
Clinton–Sherman, OK	OK Space industry Development Authority	2 paved runways	
Corn Ranch, TX	Jeff Bezos		Commercial tourist
Kodiak Launch Complex, AS	Alaska Aerospace Corporation	2 launch pads with mission control	Suborbital operations
Mid-Atlantic Regional, VA	Virginia Commercial Space Flight Authority	2 active launch pads	
Mojave Air and Space port, CA	Public Airport, CA		Horizontal launches of reusable craft
Sea Launch, CA	Sea Launch AG	Homeport, Launch platform	
Spaceport America, NM	State of New Mexico	1 paved runway	Suborbital operations

spaceport if Space Florida is successful in the environmental study for a 150-acre site that is located in the Merritt Island National Wildlife Refuge (Pallone, 2013).

Table 22.5 starts with the original Russian spaceport or cosmodrome (Baikonur) and ends with the planned replacement for this cosmosdrome (Vostochny). In between, we have Jiuquan, current site of the Chinese manned program, Satish Dhawan, the primary satellite launch site of India, and Guiana Space Centre, the ESA site for launches of the Ariane 5.

Table 22.5   International spaceports

Name/Location	Ownership	Facilities	Operations
Baikonur, Kazakhstan	Public	1 launch pad	Manned launches
Guiana Space Centre, Guiana	Public		Satellite launch; equatorial launch
Jiuquan Launch Center, China	Public	Launch pads, control and command center	Satellites
Plesetsk, Russia	Public	Launch pads	Unmanned LEO; polar orbit; satellites
Ras Al Khaimah, UAE	Prodea and Space Adventures	Under construction	Suborbital tourism
Satish Dhawan, India	Indian Space Research Agency	3 launch pads	Satellite launch
Spaceport Curacao, Netherland Antilles	Public		Suborbital operations
Vostochny, Russia	Government	7 launch pads	

Questions with No Answers

There are a number of questions raised by the last 40 years of space exploration. The first question is whether the US and Russia can recapture their dedication to space and map out a path forward that will receive the funding and national support necessary to succeed. The second question concerns the US approach to privatizing space. In Chapter 4, we discussed the different international approaches to supporting the development of the air transport system. The Europeans and many others opted for a direct governmental approach that involved governments assuming all or partial ownership as well as direct, governmental action to forge consolidation in the industry. The US used an indirect approach, choosing instead to "support" the airlines through payments for the carriage of airmail. In a sense, this is the same approach that they are trying now. They have contracted with private companies to deliver supplies and people to the ISS and are hoping that private space stations will fill the void once the ISS is no more. Will this approach work? Is it enough? Remember that the Postmaster General also resorted to illegal means to force consolidation of airlines as a prerequisite for airmail contracts. If the ISS comes to rely on private firms for delivery to the ISS, then financial troubles could destabilize some firms and might "force" some governmental intervention. It is too early to tell if a viable private space industry can be fostered with the current approach, but it will be an interesting exercise to watch. The private sector has a great deal that it could bring to the table, but it all comes down to profit. Is there money to be made in space? Once someone demonstrates a viable business case for some space proposition, then there will be others willing to take the risks. Of course, this leads to the last set of questions. Can a private company own a piece of the Moon? Can it then mine it for minerals? Can it buy its own asteroid? Can a private developer establish their own gated community on Mars? These are not trivial questions. If you remember the discussion on early days of aviation, then you remember the debates about "freedom of the skies." A similar debate took place over the "freedom of the seas." As we know, many nations raced to declare ownership and control of the air above their nation. Similarly, nations declared ownership and control of the sea adjacent to their country—three, ten, 200 miles. This still left the open ocean (and air) to be "regulated" and fought over. The open seas debate is particularly applicable since many of the arguments centered on questions over the "riches of the sea"—who owned them and who could harvest them. A similar situation can certainly arise regarding space. The United Nations 1967 Outer Space Treaty opened by declaring outer space as the "province of all mankind" and forbidding any state from making territorial claims of sovereignty (United Nations, 2002). Non-governmental entities require authorization and supervision by the State Party to the Treaty, however, treaties are only good as long as the parties to it agree to abide by them and/or the other members are prepared to enforce them. Dr David Livingston, a respected commercial space consultant, has raised the notion of a "Code of Ethics for Off-Earth Commerce." This code of ethics would provide a framework for a modified free-market economy within outer space. It could also help to facilitate private company involvement by clearly defining the requirements, obligations, and responsibilities of private parties (Livingston, 2002). Of course, this code is no different than a treaty in that it is only as good as the enforcement behind it. How far can privatization extend? This is a final question to be answered. Currently NASA is seeking to raise interest in a private commercial lunar probe (Morring, 2013d). If private companies begin to take on more of the risks of space, then they are likely to demand more of the rewards and shape space activity to suit their profit motive.

What Next?

This decade should provide key clues to the future of space exploration. If national governments are not willing or are unable to increase funding for space efforts, then it is likely that plans for manned exploration and colonization will be deferred to the latter half of the century if they occur at all. The US House of Representatives has already cut the proposed NASA funding for 2014 citing "debilitating insolvency" in federal spending (Bruno, 2013). So space appears to be something that the US cannot afford, according to some. A similar fight in Russia could leave the way clear for the Chinese. On the other hand, governmental withdrawal from space funding could encourage more private sector involvement. In this case, the key issue might well be a global debate on who owns space and who has the right to profit from it.

Questions

1. Discuss the issues and challenges facing the US and Russian space programs. What can be done to overcome them?
2. What are the goals of the newest entrants into space? Why have they chosen to participate in space activity?
3. What is driving the commercialization of space?
4. What are the key segments in the commercial space industry? Who are the key players in each segment?
5. Analyze the developing commercial space industry and discuss the possible winners and losers.

References

Brand, V. (2012), "US human space exploration in peril," *Aviation Week & Space Technology*, October 8, p. 58.

Bruno, M. (2013), "No-comity committee," *Aviation Week & Space Technology*, July 15, p. 19.

Carreau, M. (2013), "Special delivery: Orbital Sciences' Cygnus berths at the ISS to complete COTS demo," *Aviation Week & Space Technology*, October 7, p. 27

Livingston, D.M. (2002), *A Code of Ethics for Off-earth Commerce*. Manuscript submitted for publication, American Institute of Aeronautics and Astronautics, Inc.

McGarry, B. and Miller, K. (2013), "NASA goes IKEA to test inflatable annex for state station," retrieved online July 17, 2013 from http://www.bloomberg.com/news/2013-01-16/nasa-goes-ikea-to-test-inflatable-annex-for-space-station.html.

Morring, F. (2011), "Tunnel tests," *Aviation Week & Space Technology*, October 24, p. 26.

Morring, F. (2013a), "Stepping stones," *Aviation Week & Space Technology*, June 3, p. 22.

Morring, F. (2013b), "Sweetening the pot," *Aviation Week & Space Technology*, June 24, p. 39.

Morring, F. (2013c), "What's next: after ISS, a mix of human outposts," *Aviation Week & Space Technology*, September 30, p. 24.

Morring, F. (2013d), "Getting down," *Aviation Week & Space Technology*, July 15, p. 18.

National Research Council (NRC) (2012), "NASA's strategic direction and the need for national consensus," retrieved online October 10, 2013 from The National Academies Press at http://www.nap.edu/openbook.php?record_id=18248&page=2.

Pallone, G. (2013), "Possible expansion planned for Kennedy Space Center," retrieved online July 17, 2013 from http://www.cfnews13.com/content/news/cfnews13/news/article.html/content/news/articles/cfn/2013/7/16/possible_expansion_f.html.

Steadman, I. (2013). "Vladimir Putin announces big new budget for Russian space agency," retrieved online June 16, 2013 from http://www.wired.co.uk/news/archive/2013-04/12/russian-space-budget.

United Nations Office for Outer Space Affairs (2002), "United Nations treaties and principles on outer space (ST/SPACE/11 No. E.02.I.20)," retrieved online January 18, 2013 from http://www.unoosa.org/pdf/publications/STSPACE11E.pdf.

US Congress (2012), "Commercial space launch activities (51 USC Chapter 509)," retrieved online January 18, 2013 from http://uscode.house.gov/download/pls/51C509.txt.

Vastag, B. (2013), "International space stations to receive inflatable module," *The Washington Post*, retrieved July 16, 2013 from http://www.washingtonpost.com/national/health-science/international-space-station-to-receive-inflatable-module/2013/01/16/8a102712-5ffc-11e2-9940-6fc488f3fecd_story.html.

Wikipedia (2013), "Budget of NASA," retrieved online January 19, 2013 from http://www.ask.com/wiki/Budget_of_NASA?o=2800&qsrc=999&ad=doubleDown&an=apn&ap=ask.com.

Wilson, P. (2013), "NASA's rocket to nowhere," *Aviation Week & Space Technology*, April 1, p. 66.

Zak, A. (2013), "Vostochny (formerly Svobodny) cosmodrome," retrieved April 10, 2013 from http://www.russianspaceweb.com/svobodny.html.

Zubrin, R. and Wagner, R. (1996), *The Case for Mars: The Plan to Settle the Red Planet and Why We Must*, Touchstone, New York, NY.

Chapter 23
Wave of the Future

Learning Objectives

After reading this chapter, you should have a good understanding of:
* LO1: the continuing consolidation in the airline industry.
* LO2: the carrier-within-a-carrier concept to LCC competition.
* LO3: other options to industry stability.

Key Terms, Concepts, and People

Consolidation	Merger	LCC
PSOD	Ryanair	Re-regulation
Single Sky	GFC	

Waves of Change

In *The Third Wave*, Alvin Toffler (1980), noted futurist, talks about wave-front analysis or the examination of history as a succession of waves of change that represent the discontinuities or breakpoints in the pattern. The goal of the futurist or forecaster is, of course, to identify the wave-front, the leading edge of the approaching wave; the goal of the firm is to position itself to ride the "wave of the future." Unfortunately, the present sometimes resides between two waves of change or, worse still, the trailing wave has begun to overtake the earlier wave creating a clash of currents that makes it difficult to see the wave-front, much less to catch it. In the 1960s, an observant watcher of aviation might have detected the rolling motion that would eventually become the breaking wave of change as the bottom began to shallow. On this wave, among other things, rode the principle of deregulation. Even as this wave washed back from the shore in the early 1990s, another wave was gathering momentum that carried with it another change to the way we see aviation, international liberalization. The international airline industry was already swimming hard to catch the trailing wave of liberalization before 9/11, trying to prepare its national carriers for global competition. For a moment, September 11 seemed to freeze this scene, but after catching a long, slow breath the wave began moving again. The US finally came to the table with the EU over a multilateral treaty that recognized the Single Sky, but has yet to consider extending that sky to North America (or any variation that involves foreign carriers flying between two points within the US). Other regions have also grappled with liberalization and its meaning for national carriers. Two new trends promise to bring great change to the airline industry in the coming years–fuel price uncertainty and climate change.

Before the ink was dry on the first edition of this book, United Air Lines became the second US carrier to file for bankruptcy in the wake of 9/11. Before the post-9/11 bankruptcy wave was over, US Airways would file twice, emerge from bankruptcy and then merge with America West in 2005. Delta and Northwest would enter bankruptcy in 2006 and emerge in 2007 (Nelson and Francolla, 2008). US Airways would pursue a merger with Delta, but be strongly rebuffed by that carrier whose employees could be seen wearing buttons saying "Keep Delta My Delta" (Steffy, 2007). By April 2008, Delta and Northwest would work out the details on a merger plan that would (temporarily) create the world's largest carrier (Grantham and Tharpe, 2008). As the ink was drying on the second edition, the GFC was beginning to emerge, but was not yet clearly understood. Certainly, few knew the range, scope, or depth of the looming crisis. It is almost inevitable that sometime between the submission of this manuscript and the time the first copy hits the bookshelves something will happen to change the face of the aviation industry. In fact a week after the draft was sent to the publisher, MH-370 disappeared and was not found before the final editions were complete. Whether the shock of this event will have long lasting effects on the industry is unknown, but it does illustrate two facts. First, the global aviation industry is subject to many outside shocks that can have long range implications. Second, it remains a high profile industry which attracts attention both good and bad on a regular basis. This seems to be the nature of the industry itself. This is what makes it such an exciting and risky business. Forecasting is also a risky (and thankless) business, however, the purpose of this final chapter is to summarize what "we think we know" about what is happening in the aviation industry and where "we think it is going." There are no certainties and miraculous turnarounds do occasionally happen, but the odds-makers in Las Vegas and the practitioners of hindsight in industry and academia will have to deal with these issues when the future becomes the past and "prediction" becomes easy.

Not Dead Yet!

It certainly appeared that the legacy mega-carrier concept in North America was dead (or at least dying) when the first issue of this book went to press in 2003. The mega-carrier concept, as articulated by Taneja (1988) and pursued by the large US carriers, demanded the creation of large domestic and international route networks linked at key hubs to a low-cost feeder system of regional airlines that many of the majors would eventually acquire. The system was managed by a system of mainframe legacy computers with some add-on "new" hardware. Software (often designed in-house using the extensive historical data of these carriers) sought to maximize revenues (yields), manage capacity, match aircraft to routes, and aircraft to flight crew according to "established work rules," and recover the schedule as quickly as possible when disruptions occurred. Carriers consolidated their hold on their strategic hubs, utilizing large aircraft that waited at the gates for banks of smaller feeder aircraft to arrive with passengers to fill the available seats. These large aircraft allowed carriers to spread their higher-cost worker salaries over more passengers, giving them a somewhat better productivity per worker. On the other hand, these crews waited at the gates, often for extended periods, for the arriving bank of passengers. The revenue system which "managed" these passengers often had as many as ten different fare classes with attached rules and restrictions. The system was run frequently to determine if the pre-assigned number of seats in each class were filling up to expectations. If not, adjustments were made in fares to achieve maximum yield. These two factors created conflicting demands on the mega-carrier. First, the pressure of low-cost price competition necessitated cuts in airline spending, many in the visible areas of service quality, fare restrictions, meal quality, and so on. Second, the revenue system placed consumers in the same cabin who were receiving the same service but at very different fare levels. This gave rise to the ultimate airline shopper, the individual whose mission in life was to shop until they had achieved the lowest fare possible and "beaten the system." They were usually sitting next to you so that they could tell you all about their great deal just to make sure you knew that your shopping skills were subpar. In the past, these "shoppers" were primarily leisure travelers who could, and did, arrange their travel around deals. Business passengers had continued to pay higher fares in exchange for the ability to book with little notice and travel at certain times of the day or week.

The events of 9/11 did not create the problems that the industry faced post-9/11, but it did accelerate many of the trends; two trailing waves seemed to endanger the mega-carrier concept. The first change was the growth of LCCs who had increased their expansion rates in North America and Europe. In fact, post-9/11 these carriers were the only ones expanding. As major carriers around the world pulled out of marginal markets in an effort to improve profitability, LCCs moved in to fill the gaps. These carriers offered simplified fare structures, few restrictions, and, in many cases, reliable, consistent basic service. In Europe, "doing a Ryanair" became a catchphrase for buying a cheap ticket to some out-of-the-way location for a weekend jaunt (Creaton, 2005). Communities across the US that had lost service in the early years of deregulation or struggled along with high fares from one or two legacy carriers intent on flying them miles out of their way to the closest hub before putting them on a bigger plane to their final destination actively courted the LCCs with some success (Grossman, 2007). The second change was the flight of the traditional business traveler away from the high fare–high restriction traditional carriers and toward either less travel overall, LCCs, or one of the new boutique international carriers offering single, business class cabins and better service. Domestically, the per-seat-on-demand (PSOD), air taxi concept of firms like DayJet tried to lure the domestic business passenger away with promises of more convenience and less hassle. These business travelers had subsidized the cost-minded, post-deregulation leisure traveler for years and accumulated more frequent flyer miles than they could ever use. They had sat in lounges around the world drinking little bottles of wine while reading the financial publications of a dozen nations. They did not need any more gifts from the frequent flyer magazine or little salt-and-pepper shakers with their meals. If the business traveler of bygone days was truly gone in sizeable numbers, then high-cost legacy carriers sensed that they were in serious trouble.

It now appears that the death of the mega-carrier was greatly exaggerated as the new merger wave in the mid-2000s showed. Following the GFC, this merger wave continued, creating even larger carriers. Some carriers disappeared, falling victim to more efficient, LCCs or to their own mistakes—overexpansion of routes, industry high labor costs, uncompetitive route structures, and so on. It can be argued that some carriers fell victim to "bad timing," that is, starting up in a capital-intensive business just as fuel prices rose. Fuel prices were the primary reason cited for four US bankruptcies in 2008—Aloha Airlines, ATA, Skybus, and Frontier (Associated Press, 2008). Even more damning for the airlines may be the harsh realities of the industry itself. Robert Crandall, former CEO of American Airlines, has said that "[i]f some of the steps that have been proposed to restore the industry's health are implemented, such as reducing labor costs and rationalizing fleets, US carriers would stop hemorrhaging cash. But that's different from saying [the industry] can be economically and financially successful—which is to say, earn its cost of capital" ("Crandall's Rx for Airlines," 2002). Robert Crandall's own American Airlines had resisted bankruptcy and maintenance outsourcing through ruthless cost control until finally the pressure became too great. Now it has joined the mega-merger list with US Airways (Flottau, Ray and Shannon, 2013). Whether the airline industry has finally found a long-term way to earn the cost of its own capital remains unclear. Bankruptcy has allowed the legacy carriers to reduce labor costs, rationalize fleets, and re-capitalize. Following the latest crisis in 2008, the industry has also shown an unusual ability to resist adding capacity. This (and consolidation) have given them a pricing power that has helped keep most out of the red. If high fuel costs have made the small regional jets less profitable, then reduced schedules have allowed carriers to fill larger aircraft. New attention to service for business travelers has returned many to their legacy home. What remains to be seen is whether consolidation is over (for a time at least) and carriers can gain enough control over their distribution systems to end what they see as price transparency gone wild.

Dire times give rise to dire measures and the airline industry has tried many things over the years of crisis. American Airlines (and others) experimented with a new "rolling hub" system that spreads flights out during the day to increase the utilization of planes and flight crews and fare structures at the legacy carriers simplified following 2001 as LCCs were gaining market share (Arndt and Zellner, 2002). The system of rigid work rules began to change and raise productivity (Velocci, 2002a, 2002b). The "carrier-within-a-carrier" concept was revisited as Delta Air Lines launched Song and United announced the formation of TED

(Haddad and Zellner, 2002). Both are now gone as the organizational strain of balancing these divergent strategies proved too much. Aside from the very real difference in mindset inherent in a cost-focus strategy, there are two other significant problems. First, in order to be successful the low-cost unit needs low-cost labor. Differences in wage scales tend to create dissension among employees of "one company." Any reasonable thinking employee of the low-cost unit has to at least consider strategies for moving up in the company world. Second, if the two units are set up to run independently, then competition is likely to arise between the two units as both attempt to appeal to the same customer groups to "grow their market share." Again, any "right-minded" low-cost unit of "one company" would have to be considering how best to lure the dissatisfied business traveler to their operation. While it would be nice to think that they were luring these passengers away from the competition, some will inevitably come from their higher-cost, traditional operations.

Few if any carriers have able to match the success of the Southwest (Ryanair) low-cost, no-frills strategy even when they started out with the concept. Yet, both carriers seem to have reached a stage where growth is no longer the driving force of their strategy; improving no-frills service seems to be the order of the day (CAPA, 2013). Certainly in the US, domestic service has increasingly been seen as a commodity and price as the driver of consumer choice. The efforts to change the distribution system (discussed in Chapter 15) could change this dynamic, if regulators allow it. In the name of customizing consumer options, airlines could succeed in obfuscating costs enough to make comparison shopping more difficult and time consuming. The US domestic battleground is likely to be the few high-density, high-yield routes, although Robert Crandall once suggested that less than 500 of the roughly 6,000 routes in the US would qualify for nonstop service ("Crandall's Rx for Airlines", 2002). With consolidation, the battleground has shrunk again. With fewer players and less transparency in pricing, it would seem that fares will continue to rise until profits give impetus to new carrier start-up.

If the "carrier-within-a-carrier" concept did not work, then another questionable concept was the repositioning of legacy airlines to compete with the low-cost competitor threat. Two bankruptcies did allow Continental Airlines to achieve lower input costs (primarily labor costs) than their major traditional competitors, but this was not the same as repositioning to achieve the cost structure of a Southwest (Oum and Yu, 1998). Delta, in fact, suggested that Song did not die but transformed Delta itself. There is no evidence to suggest that this is true, but it makes a good story. Under former Delta CEO Ron Allen, Delta had a "Leadership 7.5" program designed to get their available seat mile costs down to Southwest Airline levels. His successor, Leo Mullin, blamed this program for declining morale, customer service, and falling financial performance, instituting his own program. In a stinging indictment of all of these efforts, Nolan (2005) suggested that the end result of all the savings claimed by Allen, Mullin, and Grinstein (Mullin's successor) "has been thousands of people without a job, tens of thousands of people with their pensions at serious risk and a company in bankruptcy—and wealthy retired CEOs" (182). While consolidation should allow carriers to reduce some redundancy (and some costs), it is more likely that it will help the industry maintain some pricing power (raising revenues). In fact, it is no longer about chasing market share. The new mantra is maximizing revenue and ancilliary fees (combined with capacity controls) which seems to be working for now (Saporito, 2013).

Riding the Waves

In a report to the US Congress, the GAO called the airline industry inherently unstable because of the structure of the industry and its economics (GAO, 2005). While the airlines have been the most visible victims of change over the last few decades, they have not been alone; air cargo operators, manufacturers, and related suppliers have also felt the tension and experienced many a sleepless night. However, it seems inconceivable that the overall industry can thrive without a more stable airline industry. As we noted in the introduction to this book, the conventional wisdom that air travel is directly linked to growth in GDP may no longer be such a wise bet. This has not been true for the US over the last decade and Europe is beginning to show the same trend. It is true that there is still room for growth in the developing and emerging world, but even these markets cannot grow fast enough to keep air travel trends on an upward trajectory (Michaels, 2013). What is the future for the airline industry?

Airline deregulation has been praised for the dramatic lowering of fares and damned for creating the destructive price competition that has been a part of the financial crisis experienced by the industry in each of the last three decades. International liberalization has faced similar charges. The truth is that the industry is still subject to a number of regulations; it is not regulation-free. The question becomes not whether you have regulation or not, but what you choose to regulate. The airline industry will never achieve the ideal of perfect competition extolled by economists, but how many competitors are necessary to insure "workable" or "contestable" markets. Should governments intervene to save failing carriers? Should the government act to change bankruptcy laws to allow the market to adjust overcapacity more quickly or will investors and lenders self-adjust to the realities of a failing market? What should government do regarding questions of consolidation and foreign ownership? There are as many answers to these questions as there are "experts" in aviation and economics. Let's consider the following possibilities:

No action at all

In almost any situation, one possible response is to "do nothing." Sometimes doing nothing turns out to be better than "doing something wrong." The problem has been that governments generally want to be seen as "doing something." In the case of troubled national airlines or aerospace manufacturers, there is tremendous pressure from citizens groups and other stakeholders to act. This pressure can be seen in the noise over the Air France–KLM and Alitalia deal (now SkyTeam and Alitalia). The Northrop–EADS tanker contract and the BAE–EADS proposed merger are other examples (Flottau, Butler, Svitak, and Morris, 2012; Reuters, 2008; Tessler, 2008). If governments choose to act, there is a range of actions that they can pursue.

Consolidation

The first type of government action is to allow further consolidation in domestic markets. This option has a long history in aviation. Weaker carriers are either acquired outright or, as in the case of TWA, Eastern or Pan Am, another carrier may acquire the assets (not the liabilities) of the failing company. This action has the potential to save some jobs, airports/local communities, and so on. It could reduce some of the overcapacity (or prevent more capacity from entering) in domestic markets while saving, hopefully, the valuable assets of the failing companies. Mergers between very similar competitors generally result in greater competitive losses than mergers between complementary carriers. The effect of mergers between carriers with very similar routes structures has the potential to severely reduce capacity (and competition) in certain markets, resulting in higher prices, fewer choices, and lower capacity. In almost any conceivable merger or consolidation, there is likely to be some loss of jobs, cutbacks on redundant service or unprofitable routes, and closure of redundant facilities. This is simply the nature of transactions whose aims are lowering costs through economies of scale, elimination of redundancy, or synergistic sharing between the units of the "new company." Consolidation, of course, does not guarantee that any of these things will occur. Unfortunately, only one of the 20 major airline merger/acquisitions since the 1978 deregulation has been judged by experts a "success." The majority have fallen "victim to runaway costs, dissatisfied passengers and labor disputes" (The Holmes Report, 2009). It remains to be seen if the latest mega-mergers—Delta–Northwest, United–Continental, and American–US Airways—are eventually judged a success by the many experts.

The recently approved American/US Airways merger highlights many of the issues facing governments, airlines, and passengers in this area. The US DOJ had initially stopped the merger saying that it was necessary to examine more than the impact of merger activity on nonstop (Origin & Destination) routes; it was now important to look at the effects on connecting flight and airports that might be left with a single, very dominant carrier. Some scholars of regulation even suggested that a three-firm oligopoly, whatever the specific route or connection numbers showed, would undermine all competitive dynamics in the industry by allowing the kind of tacit collusion that comes when industry incentives align. In this case, the industry incentive is to restrict capacity to maintain pricing power and insure the ability of airlines to reap the major benefits of any cost-cutting efficiencies rather than pass them on to consumers. While the merger has been allowed to move forward with some conditions, including the surrender of landing slots at certain airports, it is not clear that better analysis of competitive dynamics is responsible for the change. It is certainly not clear that consumers will benefit from the change. Proponents have argued that consumers have benefited tremendously in recent years from lower prices, but this may be a function of the very price transparency that airlines would like to eliminate and not the result of consolidation. Few experts see the American–US Airways merger as the last. While the three-legged stool is relatively stable, this does not tend to work for competition in the long run. As anyone who has ever sat on a three-legged stool knows, it is a difficult and uncomfortable experience when one of the legs is not the same length as the other two. In the absence of the kind of rigid regulation employed in China to maintain balance between the national carriers, it is likely that the three-firm oligopoly US stool will wobble considerably. Further, there is likely to be consolidation pressure at the LCC end of the industry as well (Flottau and Shannon, 2013. It is noteworthy that the first thing that the new Delta did after completing their integration was work on service enhancements such as those made to the Business Elite cabins (Freed, 2010). It may be true that Song is gone but not forgotten, however, the new Delta is not a no-frills LCC; it is an airline intent on bringing back the business traveler and upping its game on the still more profitable international routes.

Government loans, guarantees, and so on

While governments intervened in great and small ways in the post-9/11industry, in the post- GFC world this option looks untenable unless you are in Eastern Europe and even here the doors have been closing thanks to the EU Commission (Flottau, 2011). Of course, this has not stopped the Italian government from attempting to rescue its national carrier. What remains to be seen is what action the EU Commission will take given its rulings on state aid to national carriers (*The Economist*, 2013). The last major effort by the US government involved United and it (and taxpayers) did play a significant role in saving United after 9/11, including the US government assumption of pension plan obligations through the Pension Benefits Guaranty Corporation. The obligation for United and US Airways alone totaled US$9.6 billion (GAO, 2005), but almost any intervention in the current US political climate seems unlikely. Given US action, we will never know if the sudden and rapid fall of a carrier responsible for roughly 20 percent of the domestic flights in the US would have proved too disruptive to endure. There was enough capacity in the US system to adjust to the loss of United, but this factor did not count for much in this very political decision. If significant government assistance is unlikely for most airlines in the current economic and political climate, then governments will have to intervene in ways that do not involve opening the public purse.

Re-regulation

The crisis following 9/11 did cause some governments to re-examine the question of deregulation itself. Joseph Stiglitz, the 2001 Nobel Prize winner in economics, has pointed out that deregulation episodes tend to give rise to a bubble-and-bust cycle, a description that certainly seems to fit the airline industry (Stiglitz, 2002). This also explains the GFC, but in the near term this option appears to be off-the-table in the US at least. The two main US political parties would appear to have diametrically opposed positions in this regard. If you are not directly affiliated with one of these parties, then where you stand on the issue of re-regulation depends on where you sit, as the saying goes. Even those who might favor some form of re-regulation will not necessarily agree on what form that regulation should take. Does the government set service level standards? Does it control entry into the industry, establishing a maximum number of carriers or market share limits? Does it intervene to establish minimum/maximum prices? Does it intervene in labor issues, financial practices, alliance arrangements? The list of possible interventions is legion and the pros and cons of each action can, and will, be debated. Whatever the outcome in various countries, an ultimate judgment must be made on whether air transportation is an essential service that can be provided in a safe, economical way by a free market. A radical, minority view of the industry has suggested that it suffers from an "empty core" and is inherently unable to make a long-term profit. The solution would be to "suspend" anti-trust rules when the times are tough and allow carriers to "collude over fares and routes in order to maintain service levels without bleeding each other to death" (Jenkins, 2008). In other words, they would be allowed to fix prices and divide up markets. This may be the actual result of new consolidation whether it is intended or not and this view is probably no more farfetched than the idea that most of the new mergers will result in profitable, efficient carriers.

The other key markets to watch in the coming years are China and India. While India has made efforts to deregulate and allow foreign ownership, the Chinese domestic market remains firmly in the control of a government that carefully limits capacity and access to maintain the kind of stately competition that US airlines saw in the 1950s. This stability hides a wealth of inefficiency and highlights the lack of LCC penetration. Even most critics of deregulation would not suggest returning to the Chinese model and it is not clear how long the Chinese will be able to maintain it as wages rise, the middle class develops, and consumers want to experience the commonplace norm of frequent air travel.

What about the Rest?

While this book (and chapter) have focused heavily on the airline industry, this is not the only segment of the aviation/aerospace industry. The fact that it has been one of the most unstable has affected the rest of the industry, but at present it is hard to image a future for the rest of the industry without some kind of airline industry. The air cargo industry is even more sensitive to business cycles than the airline industry and will not make a recovery until there is a more general global economic recovery. It is also not clear whether economic recovery will reverse some of the trends in outsourcing and offshoring that have been a boom for air cargo. As wages rise in China and manufacturing starts to look for lower-cost labor, where will it go? Will predictions of new oil lead to lower-cost fuel taking transportation costs out of the logistics decision or will climate change alter decision-making options?

For now, it appears that airlines are voting with their orders and voting for the smaller, twin-engine aircraft (A-350, B-777, B-787) over the A-380. Outside of the Middle East, the plane is judged too big and fuel consuming. Still, the A-350 is making headway against a B-787 that is struggling with the usual new plane glitches and a logistics/supply chain that has added to the troubles. Most of the commercial manufacturers have diversified into other areas—space, military, and so on—however, even US military spending is likely to decline in the coming years. If the airline industry has been a rollercoaster ride where the thrills are a function of economic ups and downs rather than the excitement of the early industry, then perhaps the next frontier for those seeking the thrill of new discovery and new innovation is the commercial space industry. This edition of the book included chapters on this area for the first time. Space may be the next frontier for the entrepreneur and the consumer.

A Buffet Ending?

It is difficult to imagine a future without some form of commercial air transportation. Air transportation has been vital to the growth and prosperity of the world economy. This is the good news for those who have loved this industry for so long. The bad news is that aviation growth is slowing as the industry truly matures around the world. Mature industries do not innovate and create; they try to control, cut costs, and limit competition. Mature industries do not excite. In fact, they are hardly noticed until something happens to disrupt the service we take for granted. Of course, while the airlines are trying to disprove Warren Buffet's observation that they are doomed to make zero long-term profit, perhaps the commercial space industry could bring back the excitement of flying in ways that we cannot yet predict. In the same way that the telegraph was a primitive form of Victorian internet, linking people around the world in a network of communication, the airline industry might be the quaint travel mode of the twentieth century. It is also possible that Delta, United, Boeing, and Airbus will be the Western Unions of the twenty-second century. In 1880, Western Union controlled 80 percent of the telegraph traffic in the US and, while there were at the time 30,000 of those new telephones, it was certainly not clear that the one of the most profitable businesses of its day was in danger. While Western Union still helps the world move money, it is in a very different place 160 years after its founding (Standage, 1998). In the twenty-second century, SpaceX or Blue Origin may be the household names and the dominant forces in transportation. It is even possible that one of the dinosaurs of the twentieth century will reinvent itself and survive to surprise a new generation of business students unfamiliar with its beginnings. Shaping this new world of transport is a challenge worthy of the next generation. It is my hope that the students of today will take up this challenge, not forgetting the past but not bound to its old ways and conventional wisdom.

Questions

1. Discuss the issues involved in industry consolidation.
2. What are the possible options for re-regulation?
3. Analyze the issues involved in government support of the industry.
4. What do you see as the major challenges facing the aviation/aerospace industry for the remainder of the twenty-first century?

References

Arndt, M. and Zellner, W. (2002), "How to keep United flying," *Business Week*, December 23, pp. 34–35.

Associate Press (2008), "Frontier Airlines files for bankruptcy," 11 April, retrieved online January 13, 2008 from http://www.cnbs.com/id/24060605.

Centre for Aviation (CAPA) (2013), "Ryanair: what's going on? Profit warnings, low growth and customer service are not what we expect." retrieved online March 16, 2014 from http://centreforaviation.com/analysis/ryanair-whats-going-on-profit-warnings-low-growth-and-customer-service-are-not-what-we-expect-137354.

"Crandall's Rx for Airlines" (2002), *Aviation Week & Space Technology*, November 18, p. 54.

Creaton, S. (2005), *Ryanair: How a Small Irish Airline Conquered Europe*, Arum Press, London.

Flottau, J. and Shannon, D. (2013), "Connecting fight," *Aviation Week & Space Technology*, August 19, pp. 24–27.

Flottau, J., Ray, S. and Shannon, D. (2013), "Scale tale," *Aviation Week & Space Technology*, November 25, pp. 35–36.

Flottau, J., Butler, A., Svitak, A. and Morris, J. (2012), "Mating dance," *Aviation Week & Space Technology*, September 17, pp. 28–31.

Flottau, J. (2011), "Stalled progress," *Aviation Week & Space Technology*, September 12, p. 21.

Freed, J. (2010), "Delta plans 747 seating upgrade," AP, retrieved online May 9, 2012 from http://travel.usatoday.com/flights/2010-09-02-delta-747-upgrade_N.htm.

General Accounting Office (GAO) (2005), "Structural Costs Continue to Challenge Legacy Airlines Financial Performance" GAO-05-834T, Washington, DC.

Grantham, R. and Tharpe, J. (2008), "NWA merger agreement keeps Delta in Atlanta," *The Atlanta Journal-Constitution*, retrieved online March 29, 2008 from http://www.ajc.com/pt/cpt?action=cpt&title=NWA+merger+agreement.

Grossman, D. (2007), "Bringing a low-cost airline to town," USAToday. com, retrieved online March 7, 2008 from www.usatoday.com/pt/cpt?action=cpt&title=Bringing.

Haddad, C. and Zellner, W. (2002), "Getting down and dirty with discounters," *Business Week*, October 28, pp. 77–78.

Jenkins, H.W. (2008), "Plane wreck," *The Wall Street Journal*, 16 April, pp. A18.

Michaels, K. (2013), "The great stagnation," *Aviation Week & Space Technology*, October 14, p. 20.

Nolan, H.L., Jr. (2005), *Airline Without a Pilot: Lessons in Leadership*, Targetmark Books, New York.

Nelson, A. and Francolla, G. (2008), "Airlines: tale of merger and bankruptcy," CNBC.com, 21 February. retrieved online February 16, 2008 from www.cnbc. com/id/23260075.

Oum, T.H. and Yu, C. (1998), *Winning Airlines: Productivity and Cost Competitiveness of the World's Major Airlines*, Kluwer Academic Publishers, Boston, MA.

Reuters (2008), "Delta, Northwest merger faces another hurdle," CNBS.com, retrieved online March 29, 2008 from www.cnbc.com/id/23289650.

Saporito, B. (2013), "Cabin pressure," *Time*, September 9, pp. 36–41.

Standage, T. (1998), *The Victorian Internet: The Remarkable Story of the Telegraph and the Nineteenth Century's On-line Pioneers*, Berkley Books, New York.

Steffy, L. (2007), "Airline mergers usually don't fly," *Houston Chronicle*, retrieved online November 6, 2007 from http://www.chron.com/disp/story.mpl/business/steffy/5309876.html.

Stiglitz, J. (2002), "The roaring nineties," *Atlantic Monthly*, October, pp. 76–89.

Taneja, N.K. (1988), *The International Airline Industry: Trends, Issues & Challenges*, Lexington Books, Lexington, MA.

Tessler, J. (2008), "Northrop, EADS win $35B Air Force deal," ABCNews, retrieved online March 10, 2008 from http://abcnews.go.com/print?id=4367303.

The Economist (2013), "How not to rescue an airline," retrieved online February 5, 2014 from http://www.economist.com/news/europe/21588109-italian-government-pumping-even-more-cash-its-ailing-carrier-how-not-rescu e?zid=303&ah=27090cf03414b8c5065d64ed0dad813d.

The Holmes Report (2009), "The campaign to keep Delta My Delta," retrieved online June 6, 2014 from http://www.holmesreport.com/casestudy-info/8168/The-Campaign-to-Keep-Delta-My-Delta.aspx.

Toffler, A. (1980), *The Third Wave*, William Morrow and Company Inc. New York.

Velocci, A.L. (2002a), "Can majors shift focus fast enough to survive?" *Aviation Week & Space Technology*, November 18, pp. 52–54.

Velocci, A.L. (2002b), "No silver bullet seen for airlines' dilemma," *Aviation Week & Space Technology*, November 18, pp. 52–54.

Index